THE AUTHORITY

TRANSFER OF POWER

THE AUTHORITY

TRANSFER OF POWER

"Brave New World"

Mark Millar
Writer

Frank Quitely (Part One)
Arthur Adams (Parts Two & Three)
Gary Erskine (Part Four)
Pencillers

Trevor Scott (Part One)   Tim Townsend (Part Two)
Tim Townsend with Trevor Scott (Part Three)
Gary Erskine (Part Four)
Inkers

David Baron
Colorist

Ryan Cline (Part One)   Bill O'Neil (Parts Two & Three)
Tom Long and Sergio Garcia (Part Four)
Letterers

"Transfer of Power"

Tom Peyer
Writer

Dustin Nguyen
Penciller

Richard Friend and Jason Martin (Parts One & Two)
Richard Friend (Part Three) Richard Friend, Jason Martin,
Derek Fridolfs, and Dustin Nguyen (Part Four)
Inkers

David Baron
Colorist

Ryan Cline (Part One)
Bill O'Neil (Parts Two, Three, & Four)
Letterers

The Authority created by Warren Ellis and Bryan Hitch

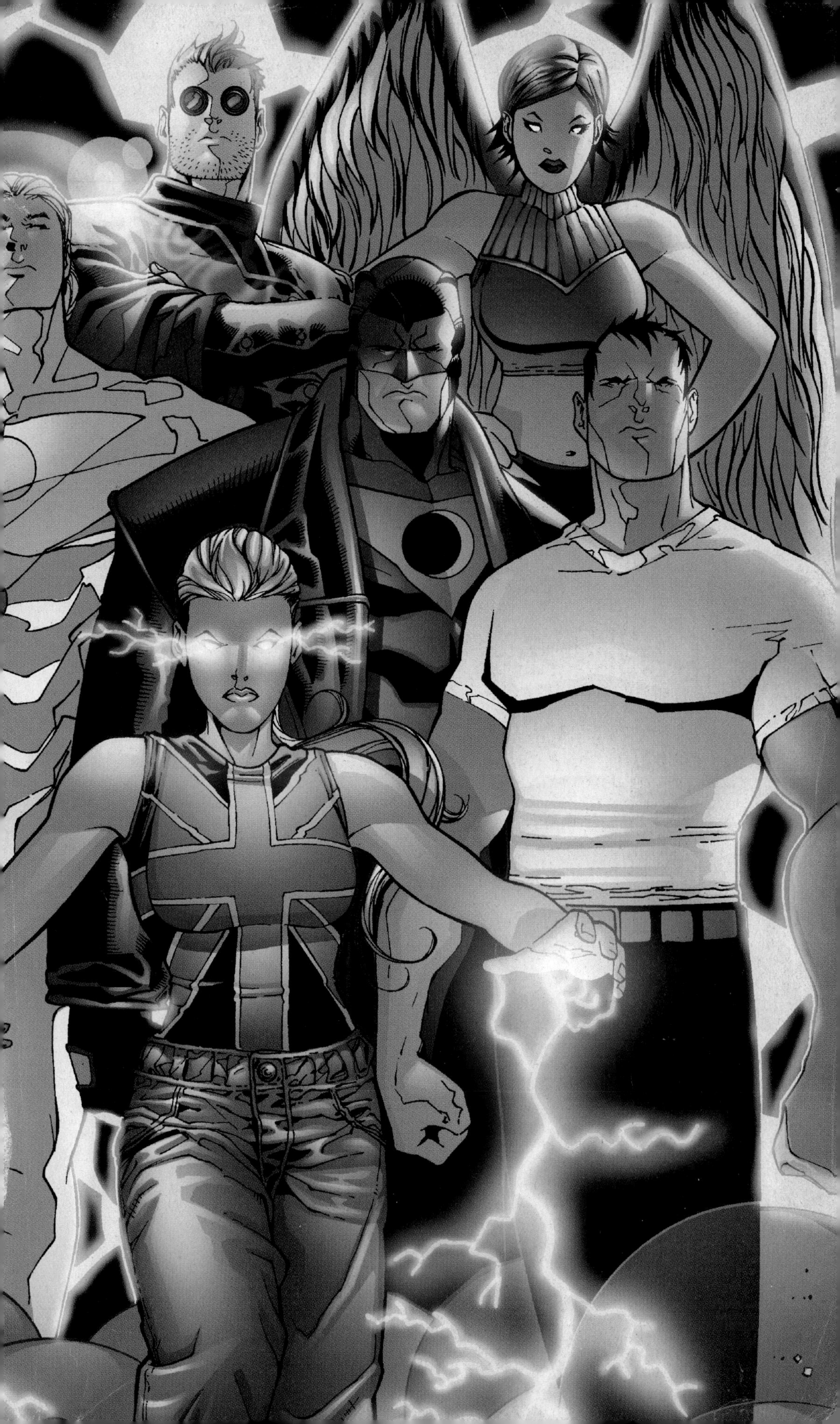

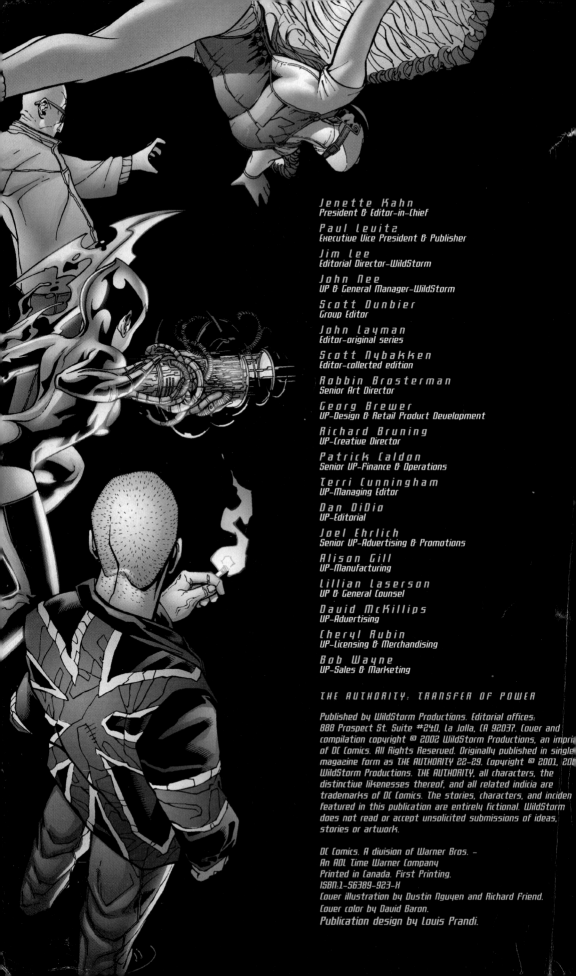

Jenette Kahn
President & Editor-in-Chief

Paul Levitz
Executive Vice President & Publisher

Jim Lee
Editorial Director-WildStorm

John Nee
VP & General Manager-WildStorm

Scott Dunbier
Group Editor

John Layman
Editor-original series

Scott Nybakken
Editor-collected edition

Robbin Brosterman
Senior Art Director

Georg Brewer
VP-Design & Retail Product Development

Richard Bruning
VP-Creative Director

Patrick Caldon
Senior VP-Finance & Operations

Terri Cunningham
VP-Managing Editor

Dan DiDio
VP-Editorial

Joel Ehrlich
Senior VP-Advertising & Promotions

Alison Gill
VP-Manufacturing

Lillian Laserson
VP & General Counsel

David McKillips
VP-Advertising

Cheryl Rubin
VP-Licensing & Merchandising

Bob Wayne
VP-Sales & Marketing

THE AUTHORITY: TRANSFER OF POWER

Published by WildStorm Productions. Editorial offices:
888 Prospect St. Suite #240, La Jolla, CA 92037. Cover and
compilation copyright © 2002 WildStorm Productions, an impri
of DC Comics. All Rights Reserved. Originally published in single
magazine form as THE AUTHORITY 22-29. Copyright © 2001, 20
WildStorm Productions. THE AUTHORITY, all characters, the
distinctive likenesses thereof, and all related indicia are
trademarks of DC Comics. The stories, characters, and inciden
featured in this publication are entirely fictional. WildStorm
does not read or accept unsolicited submissions of ideas,
stories or artwork.

DC Comics. A division of Warner Bros. —
An AOL Time Warner Company
Printed in Canada. First Printing.
ISBN:1-56389-923-X
Cover illustration by Dustin Nguyen and Richard Friend.
Cover color by David Baron.
Publication design by Louis Prandi.

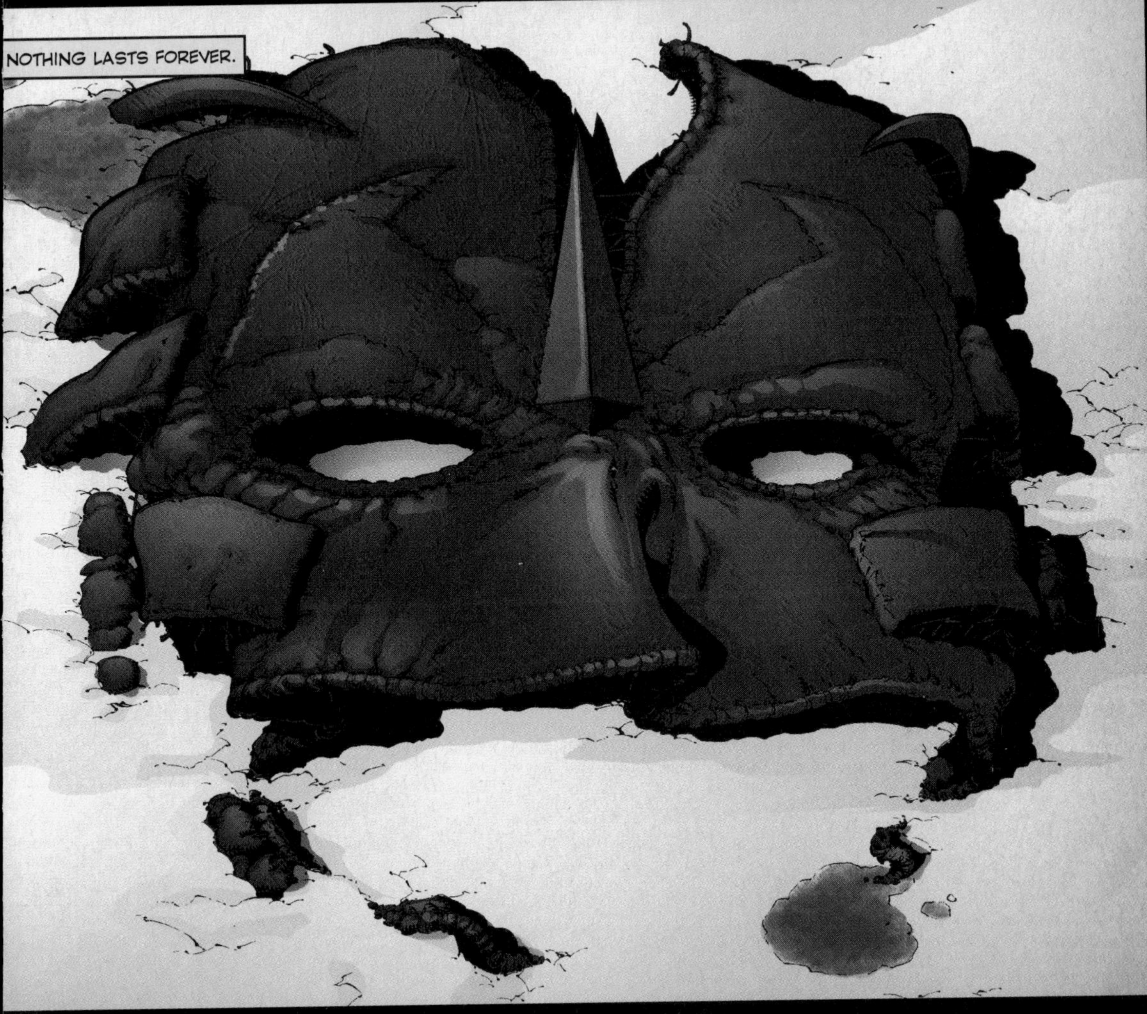
NOTHING LASTS FOREVER.

BRAVE NEW WORLD

One of Four

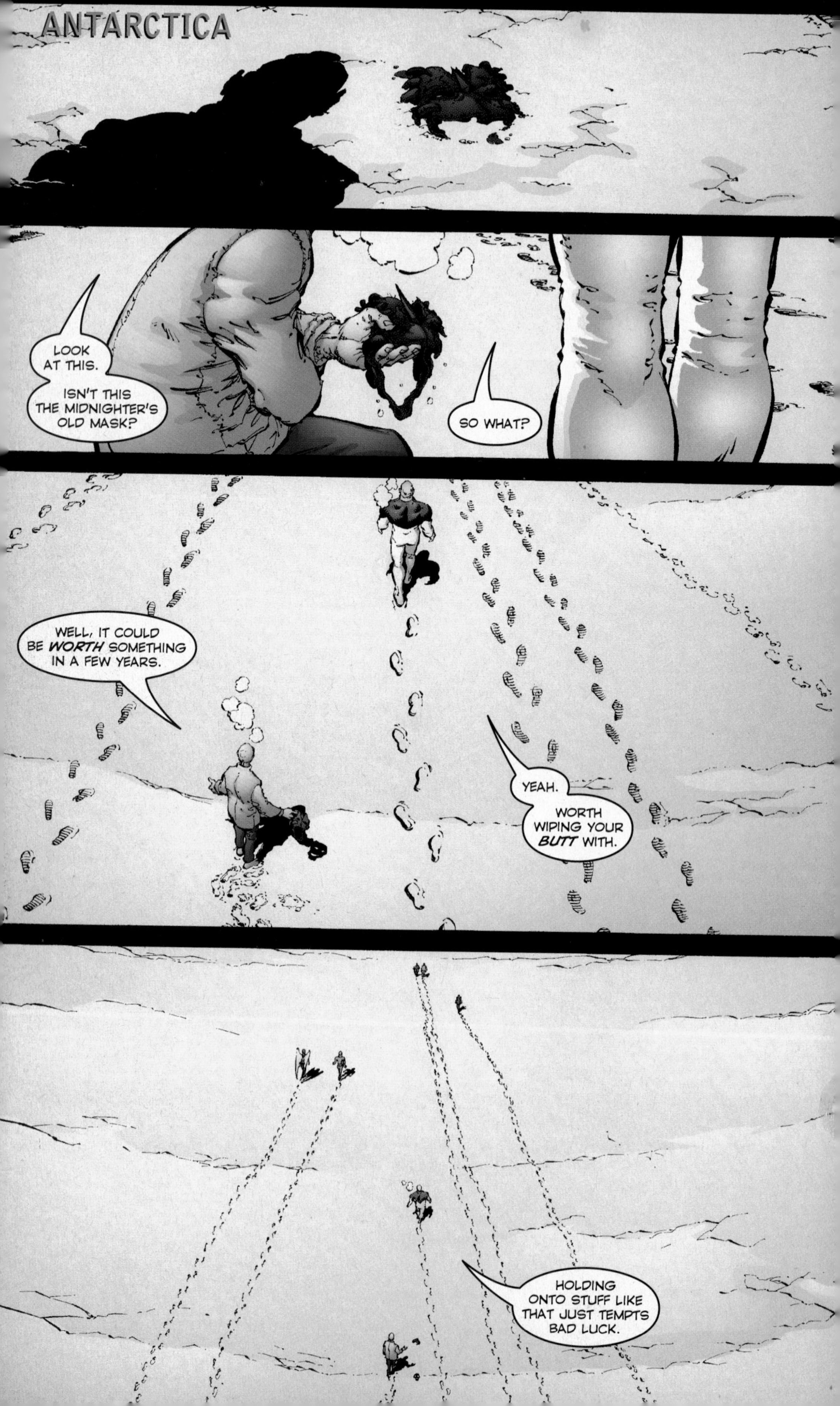
ANTARCTICA
LOOK AT THIS.
ISN'T THIS THE MIDNIGHTER'S OLD MASK?
SO WHAT?
WELL, IT COULD BE *WORTH* SOMETHING IN A FEW YEARS.
YEAH.
WORTH WIPING YOUR *BUTT* WITH.
HOLDING ONTO STUFF LIKE THAT JUST TEMPTS BAD LUCK.

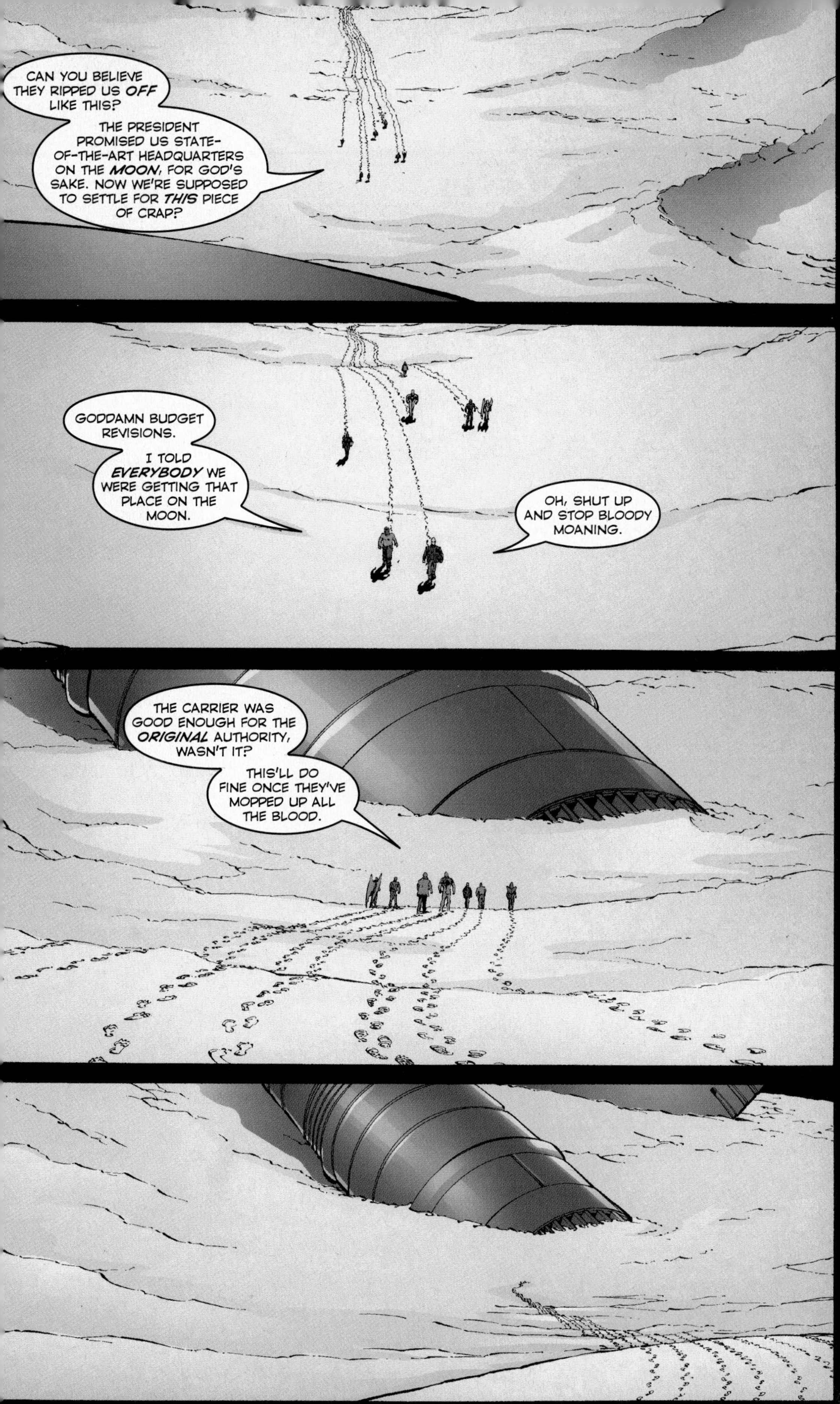
CAN YOU BELIEVE THEY RIPPED US *OFF* LIKE THIS?
THE PRESIDENT PROMISED US STATE-OF-THE-ART HEADQUARTERS ON THE *MOON*, FOR GOD'S SAKE. NOW WE'RE SUPPOSED TO SETTLE FOR *THIS* PIECE OF CRAP?
GODDAMN BUDGET REVISIONS.
I TOLD *EVERYBODY* WE WERE GETTING THAT PLACE ON THE MOON.
OH, SHUT UP AND STOP BLOODY MOANING.
THE CARRIER WAS GOOD ENOUGH FOR THE *ORIGINAL* AUTHORITY, WASN'T IT?
THIS'LL DO FINE ONCE THEY'VE MOPPED UP ALL THE BLOOD.

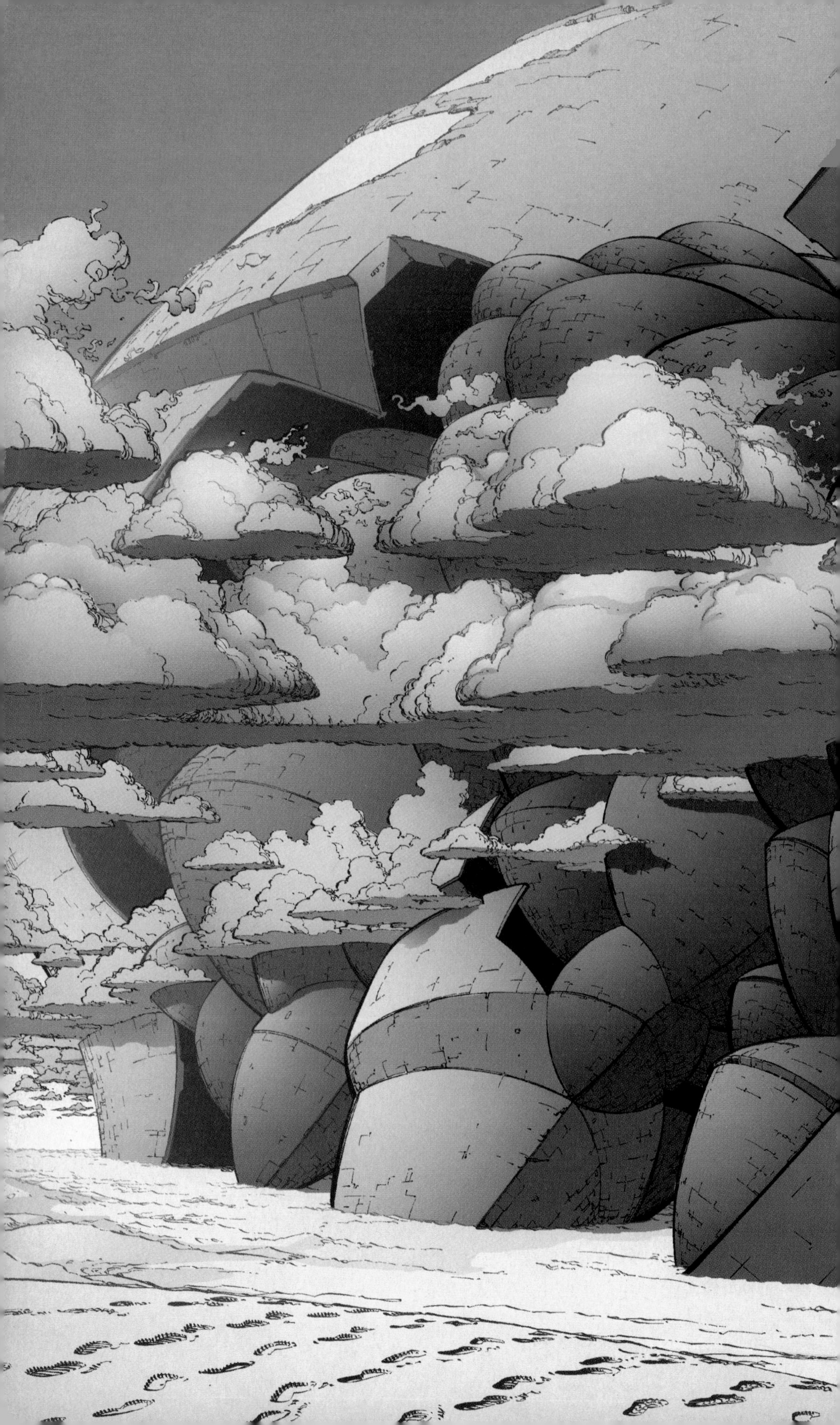

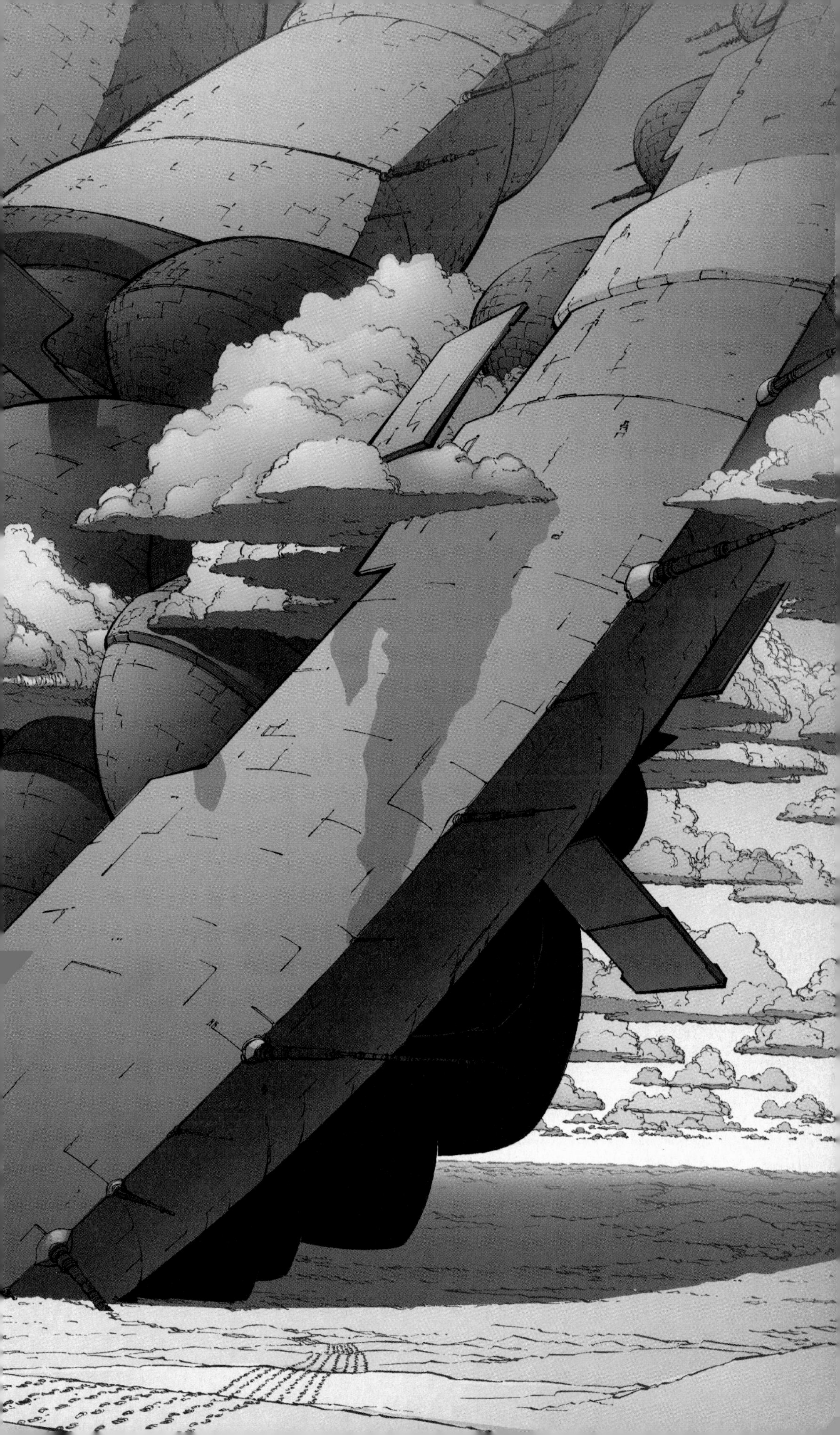

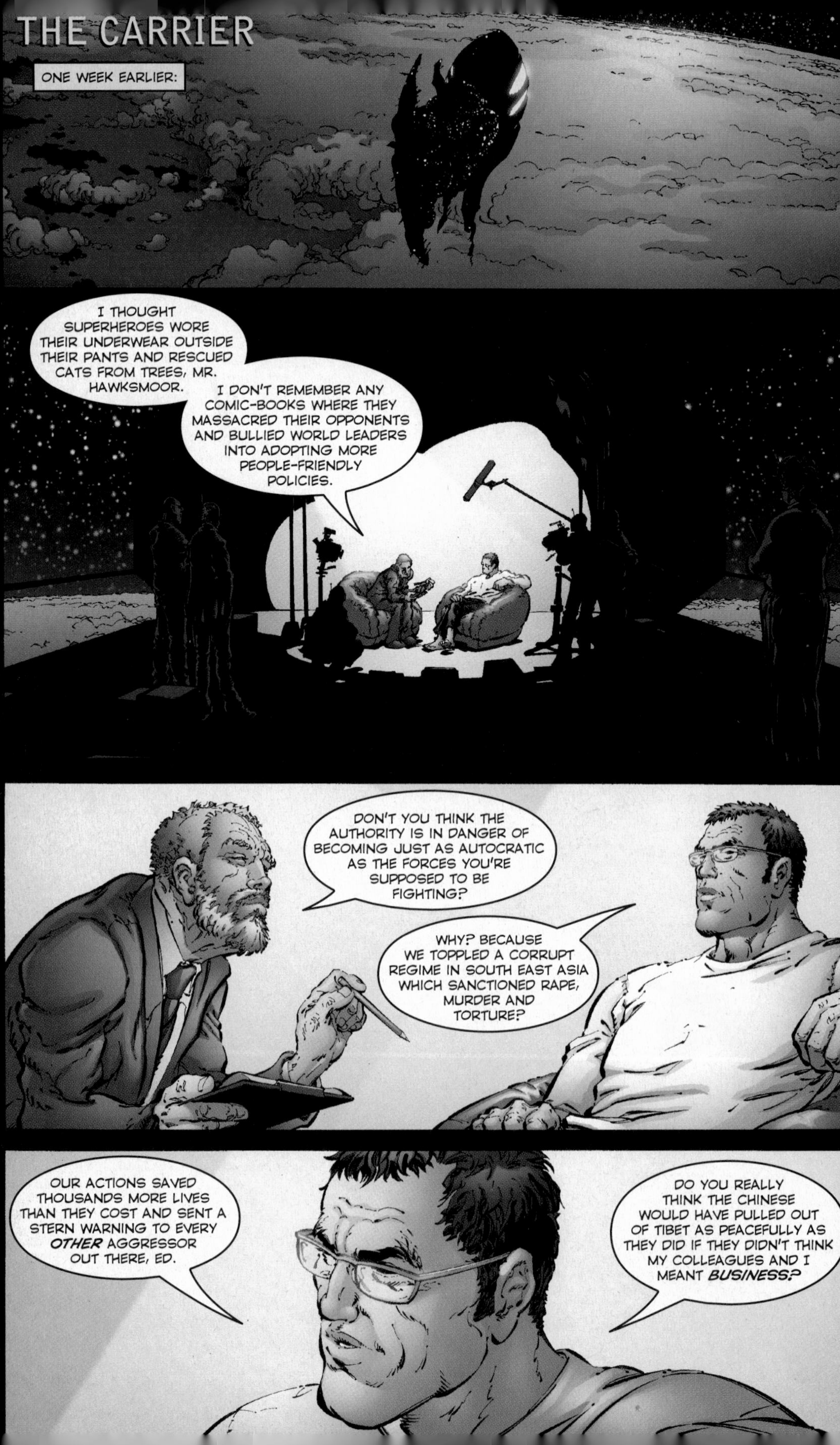
THE CARRIER
ONE WEEK EARLIER:
I THOUGHT SUPERHEROES WORE THEIR UNDERWEAR OUTSIDE THEIR PANTS AND RESCUED CATS FROM TREES, MR. HAWKSMOOR.
I DON'T REMEMBER ANY COMIC-BOOKS WHERE THEY MASSACRED THEIR OPPONENTS AND BULLIED WORLD LEADERS INTO ADOPTING MORE PEOPLE-FRIENDLY POLICIES.
DON'T YOU THINK THE AUTHORITY IS IN DANGER OF BECOMING JUST AS AUTOCRATIC AS THE FORCES YOU'RE SUPPOSED TO BE FIGHTING?
WHY? BECAUSE WE TOPPLED A CORRUPT REGIME IN SOUTH EAST ASIA WHICH SANCTIONED RAPE, MURDER AND TORTURE?
OUR ACTIONS SAVED THOUSANDS MORE LIVES THAN THEY COST AND SENT A STERN WARNING TO EVERY *OTHER* AGGRESSOR OUT THERE, ED.
DO YOU REALLY THINK THE CHINESE WOULD HAVE PULLED OUT OF TIBET AS PEACEFULLY AS THEY DID IF THEY DIDN'T THINK MY COLLEAGUES AND I MEANT *BUSINESS?*

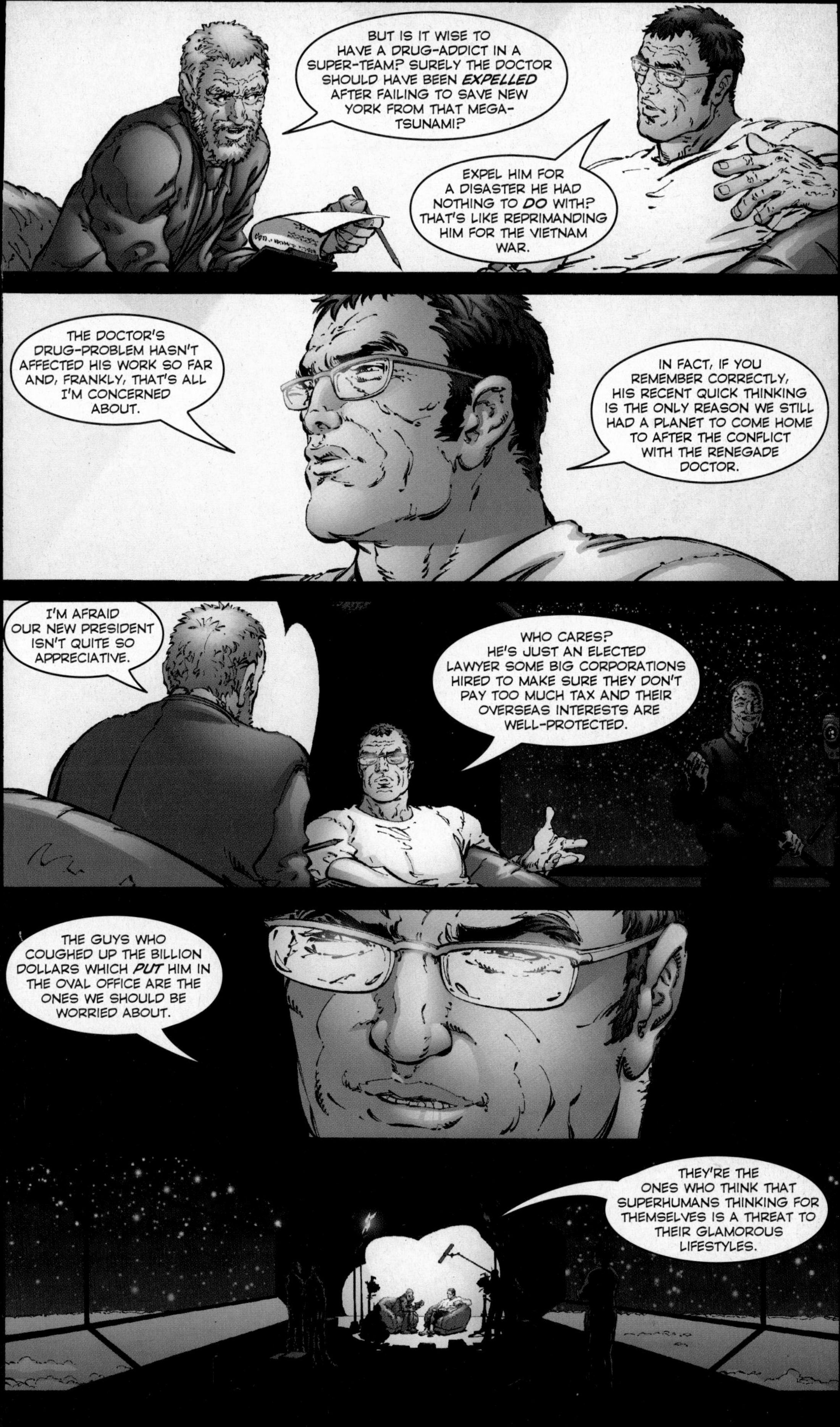
BUT IS IT WISE TO HAVE A DRUG-ADDICT IN A SUPER-TEAM? SURELY THE DOCTOR SHOULD HAVE BEEN *EXPELLED* AFTER FAILING TO SAVE NEW YORK FROM THAT MEGA-TSUNAMI?
EXPEL HIM FOR A DISASTER HE HAD NOTHING TO *DO* WITH? THAT'S LIKE REPRIMANDING HIM FOR THE VIETNAM WAR.
THE DOCTOR'S DRUG-PROBLEM HASN'T AFFECTED HIS WORK SO FAR AND, FRANKLY, THAT'S ALL I'M CONCERNED ABOUT.
IN FACT, IF YOU REMEMBER CORRECTLY, HIS RECENT QUICK THINKING IS THE ONLY REASON WE STILL HAD A PLANET TO COME HOME TO AFTER THE CONFLICT WITH THE RENEGADE DOCTOR.
I'M AFRAID OUR NEW PRESIDENT ISN'T QUITE SO APPRECIATIVE.
WHO CARES? HE'S JUST AN ELECTED LAWYER SOME BIG CORPORATIONS HIRED TO MAKE SURE THEY DON'T PAY TOO MUCH TAX AND THEIR OVERSEAS INTERESTS ARE WELL-PROTECTED.
THE GUYS WHO COUGHED UP THE BILLION DOLLARS WHICH *PUT* HIM IN THE OVAL OFFICE ARE THE ONES WE SHOULD BE WORRIED ABOUT.
THEY'RE THE ONES WHO THINK THAT SUPERHUMANS THINKING FOR THEMSELVES IS A THREAT TO THEIR GLAMOROUS LIFESTYLES.

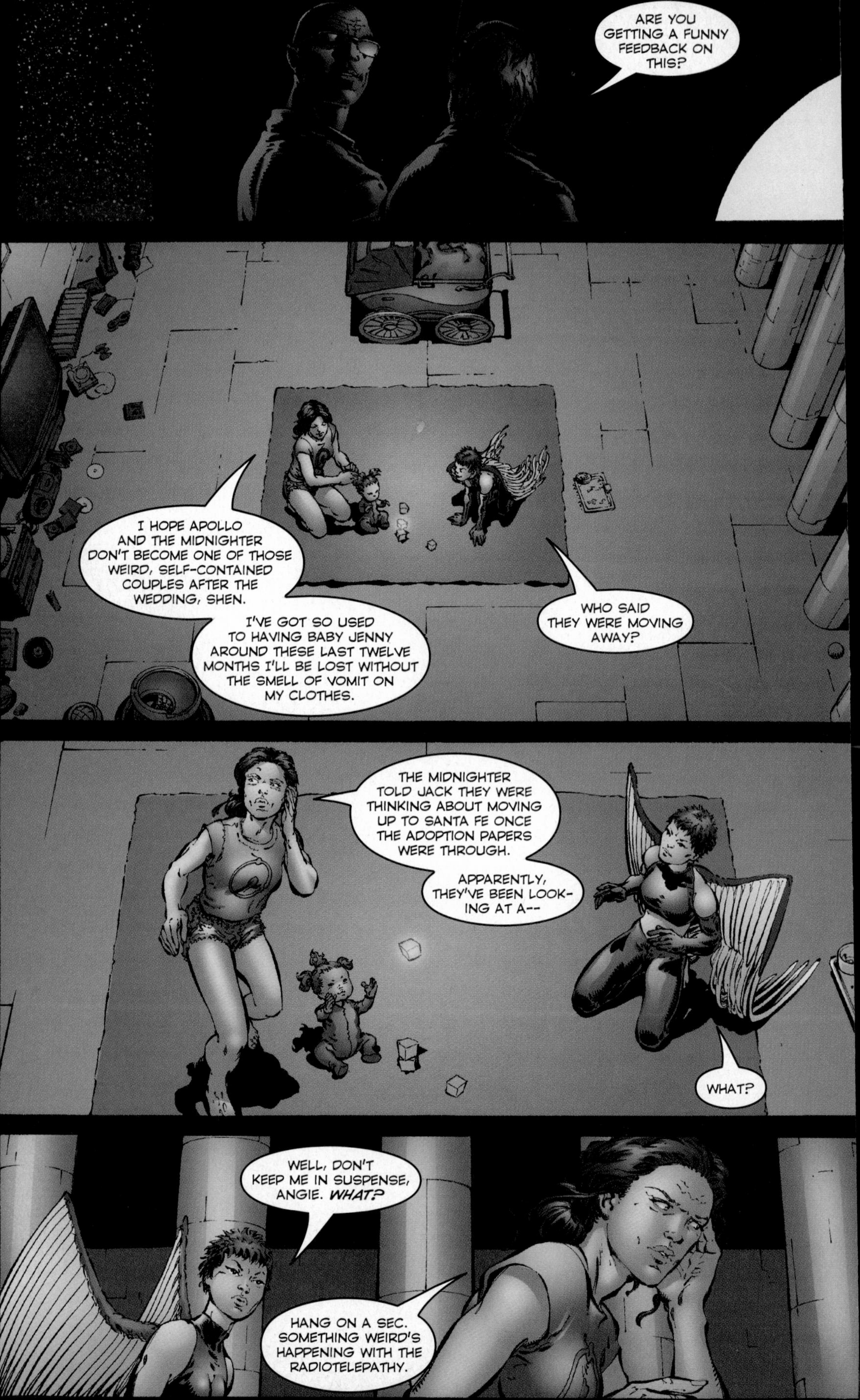
ARE YOU GETTING A FUNNY FEEDBACK ON THIS?
I HOPE APOLLO AND THE MIDNIGHTER DON'T BECOME ONE OF THOSE WEIRD, SELF-CONTAINED COUPLES AFTER THE WEDDING, SHEN.
I'VE GOT SO USED TO HAVING BABY JENNY AROUND THESE LAST TWELVE MONTHS I'LL BE LOST WITHOUT THE SMELL OF VOMIT ON MY CLOTHES.
WHO SAID THEY WERE MOVING AWAY?
THE MIDNIGHTER TOLD JACK THEY WERE THINKING ABOUT MOVING UP TO SANTA FE ONCE THE ADOPTION PAPERS WERE THROUGH.
APPARENTLY, THEY'VE BEEN LOOKING AT A--
WHAT?
WELL, DON'T KEEP ME IN SUSPENSE, ANGIE. *WHAT?*
HANG ON A SEC. SOMETHING WEIRD'S HAPPENING WITH THE RADIOTELEPATHY.

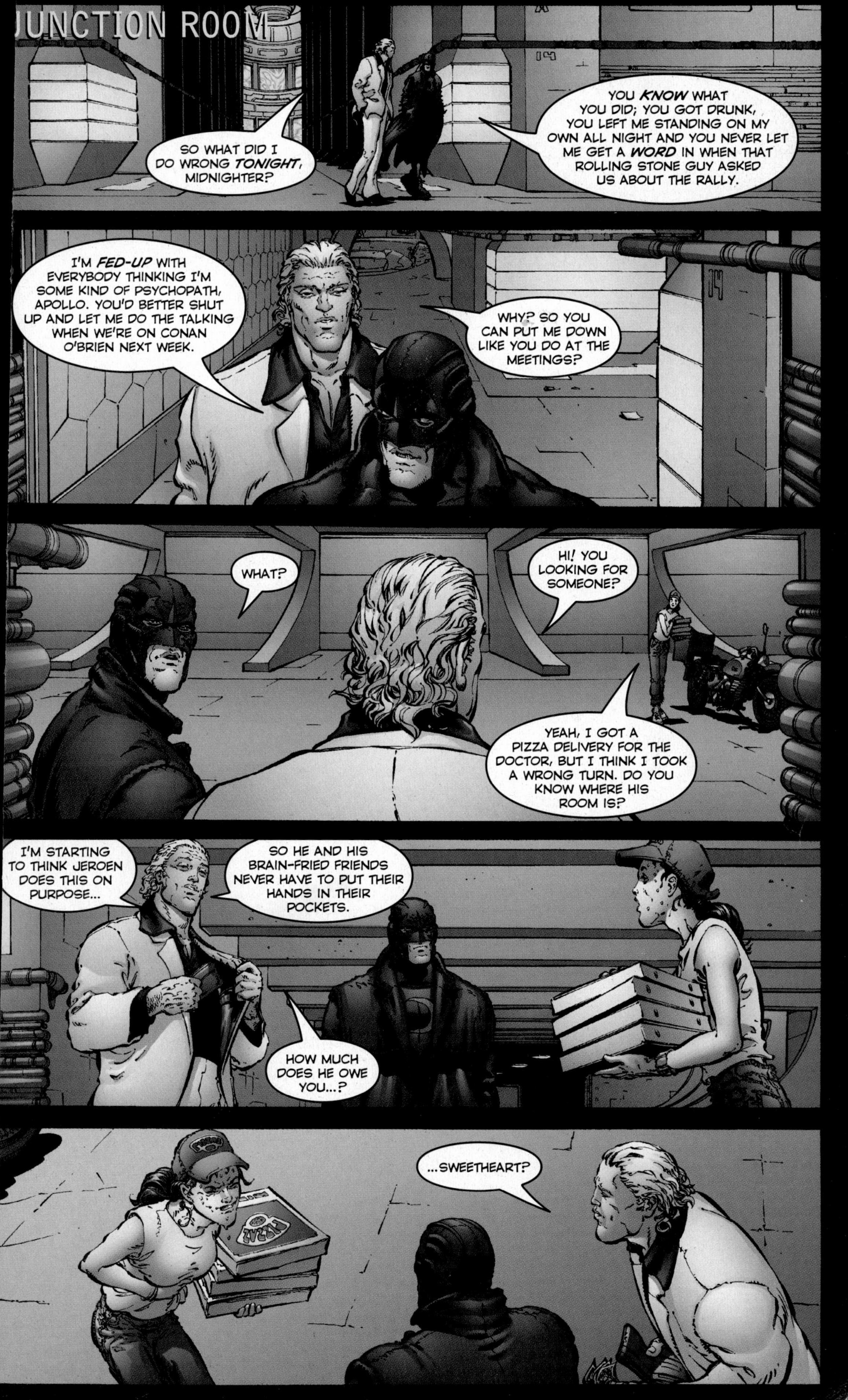
JUNCTION ROOM
SO WHAT DID I DO WRONG TONIGHT, MIDNIGHTER?
YOU KNOW WHAT YOU DID; YOU GOT DRUNK, YOU LEFT ME STANDING ON MY OWN ALL NIGHT AND YOU NEVER LET ME GET A WORD IN WHEN THAT ROLLING STONE GUY ASKED US ABOUT THE RALLY.
I'M FED-UP WITH EVERYBODY THINKING I'M SOME KIND OF PSYCHOPATH, APOLLO. YOU'D BETTER SHUT UP AND LET ME DO THE TALKING WHEN WE'RE ON CONAN O'BRIEN NEXT WEEK.
WHY? SO YOU CAN PUT ME DOWN LIKE YOU DO AT THE MEETINGS?
WHAT?
HI! YOU LOOKING FOR SOMEONE?
YEAH, I GOT A PIZZA DELIVERY FOR THE DOCTOR, BUT I THINK I TOOK A WRONG TURN. DO YOU KNOW WHERE HIS ROOM IS?
I'M STARTING TO THINK JEROEN DOES THIS ON PURPOSE...
SO HE AND HIS BRAIN-FRIED FRIENDS NEVER HAVE TO PUT THEIR HANDS IN THEIR POCKETS.
HOW MUCH DOES HE OWE YOU...?
...SWEETHEART?

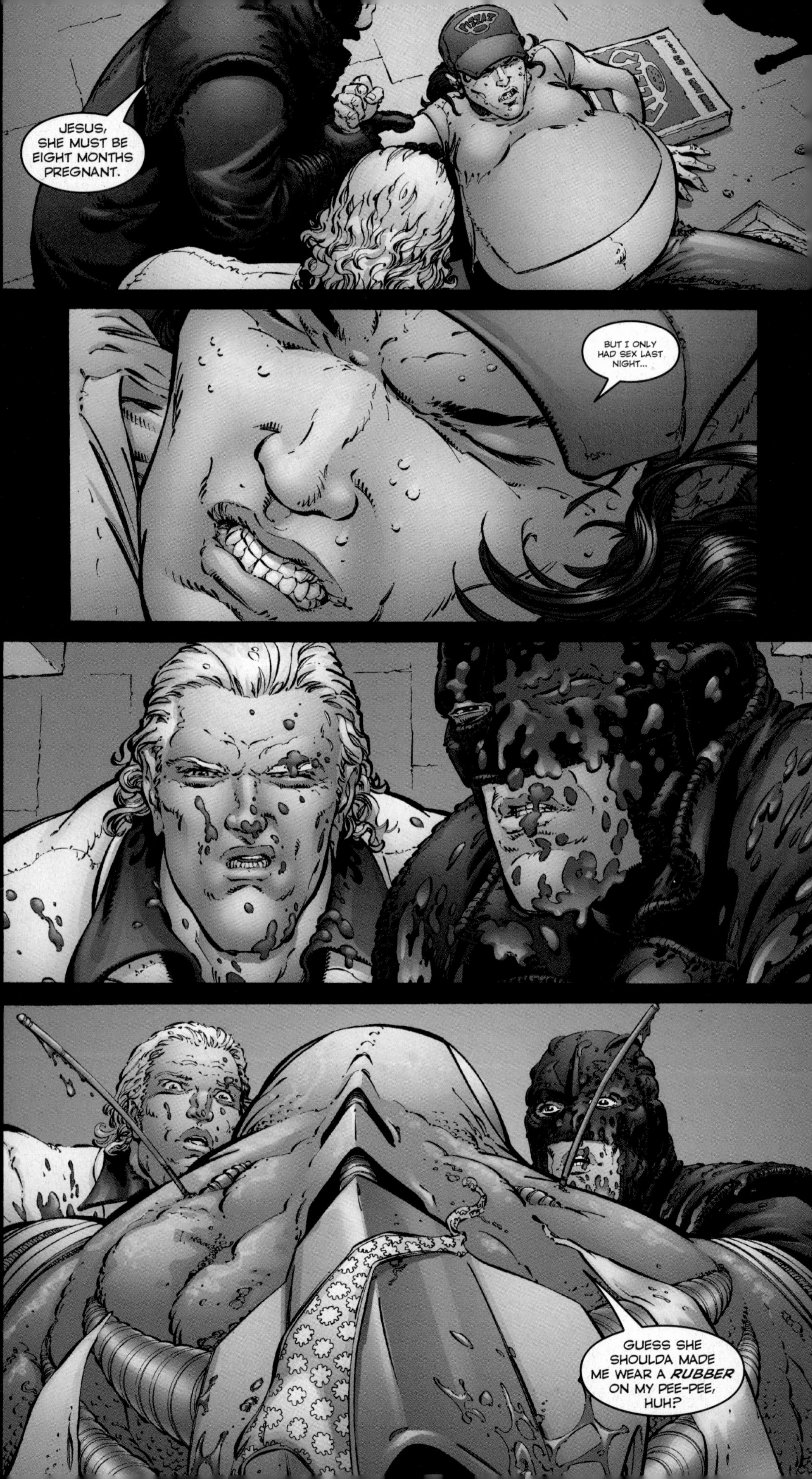
JESUS, SHE MUST BE EIGHT MONTHS PREGNANT.
BUT I ONLY HAD SEX LAST NIGHT...
GUESS SHE SHOULDA MADE ME WEAR A *RUBBER* ON MY PEE-PEE, HUH?

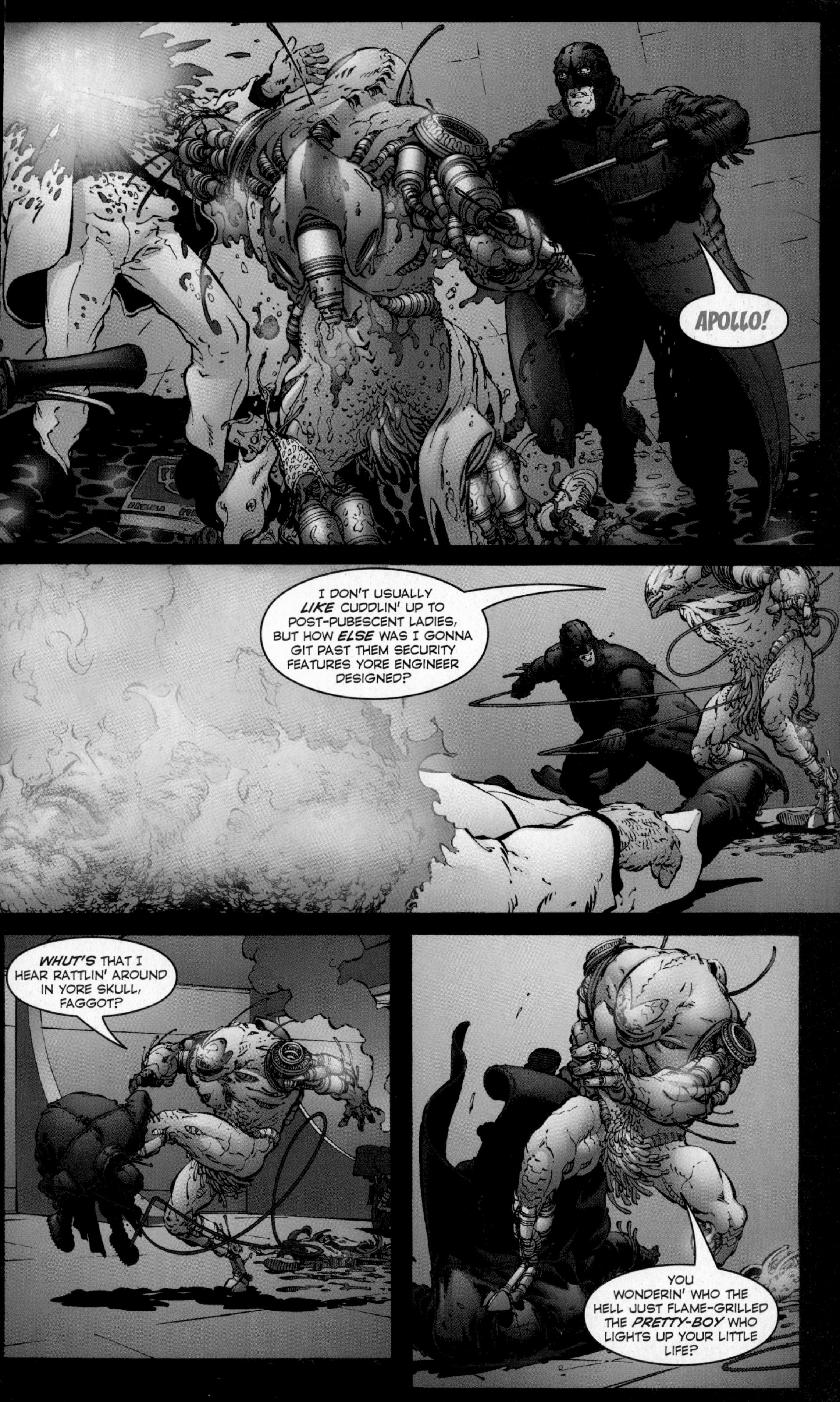
APOLLO!
I DON'T USUALLY LIKE CUDDLIN' UP TO POST-PUBESCENT LADIES, BUT HOW ELSE WAS I GONNA GIT PAST THEM SECURITY FEATURES YORE ENGINEER DESIGNED?
WHUT'S THAT I HEAR RATTLIN' AROUND IN YORE SKULL, FAGGOT?
YOU WONDERIN' WHO THE HELL JUST FLAME-GRILLED THE PRETTY-BOY WHO LIGHTS UP YOUR LITTLE LIFE?

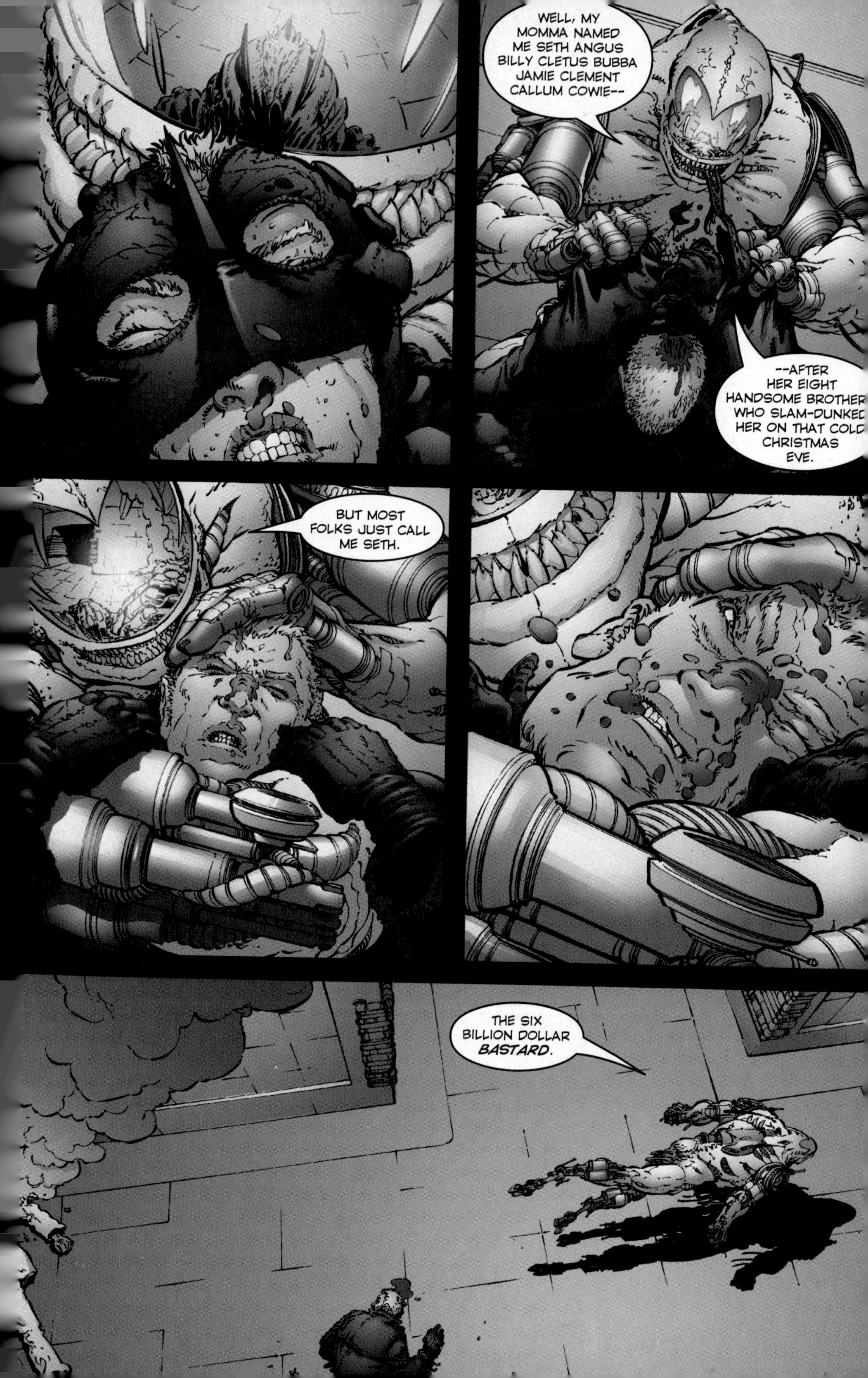
WELL, MY MOMMA NAMED ME SETH ANGUS BILLY CLETUS BUBBA JAMIE CLEMENT CALLUM COWIE--
--AFTER HER EIGHT HANDSOME BROTHER WHO SLAM-DUNKED HER ON THAT COLD CHRISTMAS EVE.
BUT MOST FOLKS JUST CALL ME SETH.
THE SIX BILLION DOLLAR *BASTARD*.

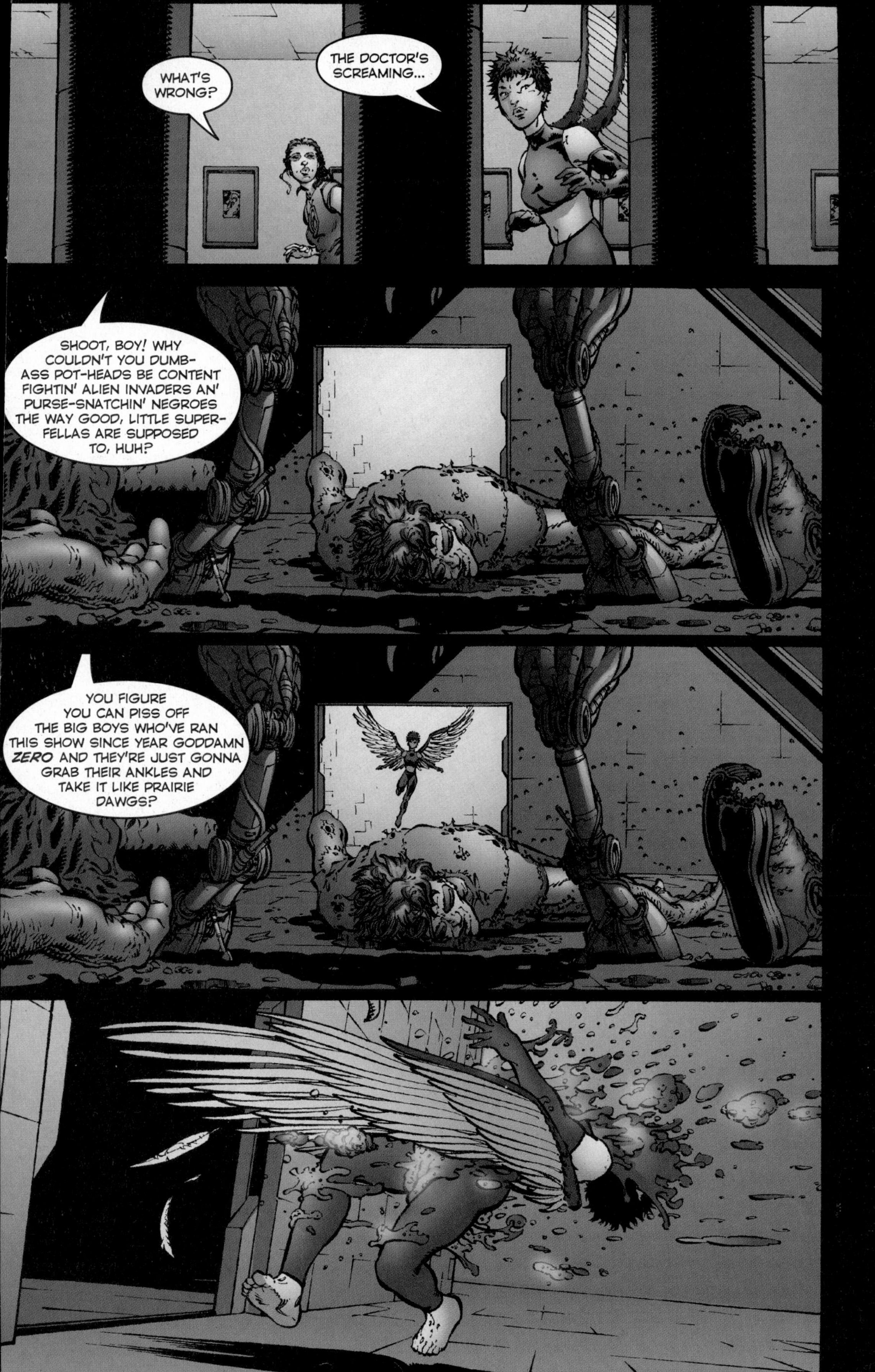
WHAT'S WRONG?
THE DOCTOR'S SCREAMING...
SHOOT, BOY! WHY COULDN'T YOU DUMB-ASS POT-HEADS BE CONTENT FIGHTIN' ALIEN INVADERS AN' PURSE-SNATCHIN' NEGROES THE WAY GOOD, LITTLE SUPER-FELLAS ARE SUPPOSED TO, HUH?
YOU FIGURE YOU CAN PISS OFF THE BIG BOYS WHO'VE RAN THIS SHOW SINCE YEAR GODDAMN *ZERO* AND THEY'RE JUST GONNA GRAB THEIR ANKLES AND TAKE IT LIKE PRAIRIE DAWGS?

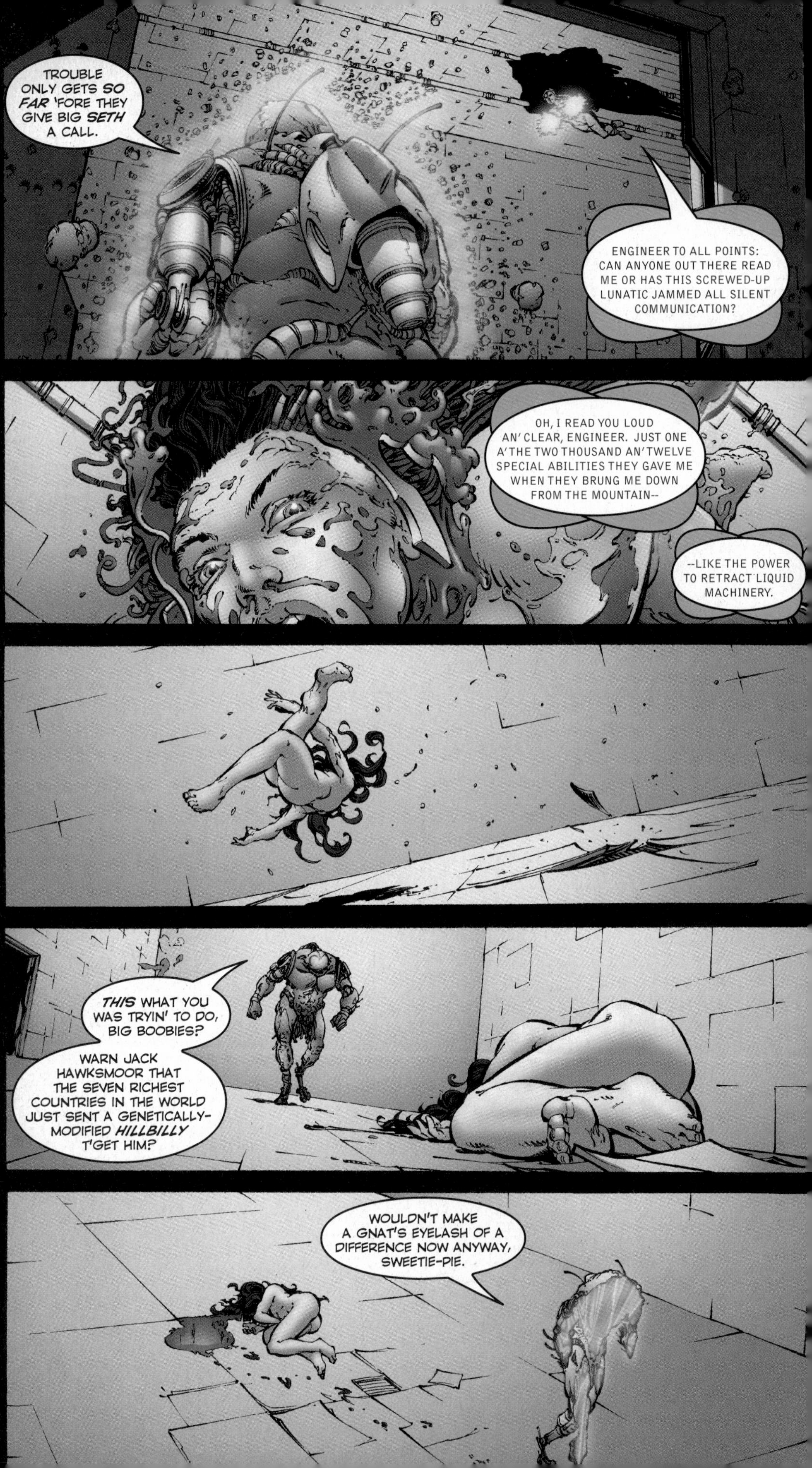

TROUBLE ONLY GETS SO FAR 'FORE THEY GIVE BIG SETH A CALL.
ENGINEER TO ALL POINTS: CAN ANYONE OUT THERE READ ME OR HAS THIS SCREWED-UP LUNATIC JAMMED ALL SILENT COMMUNICATION?
OH, I READ YOU LOUD AN' CLEAR, ENGINEER. JUST ONE A'THE TWO THOUSAND AN'TWELVE SPECIAL ABILITIES THEY GAVE ME WHEN THEY BRUNG ME DOWN FROM THE MOUNTAIN--
--LIKE THE POWER TO RETRACT LIQUID MACHINERY.
THIS WHAT YOU WAS TRYIN' TO DO, BIG BOOBIES?
WARN JACK HAWKSMOOR THAT THE SEVEN RICHEST COUNTRIES IN THE WORLD JUST SENT A GENETICALLY-MODIFIED HILLBILLY T'GET HIM?
WOULDN'T MAKE A GNAT'S EYELASH OF A DIFFERENCE NOW ANYWAY, SWEETIE-PIE.

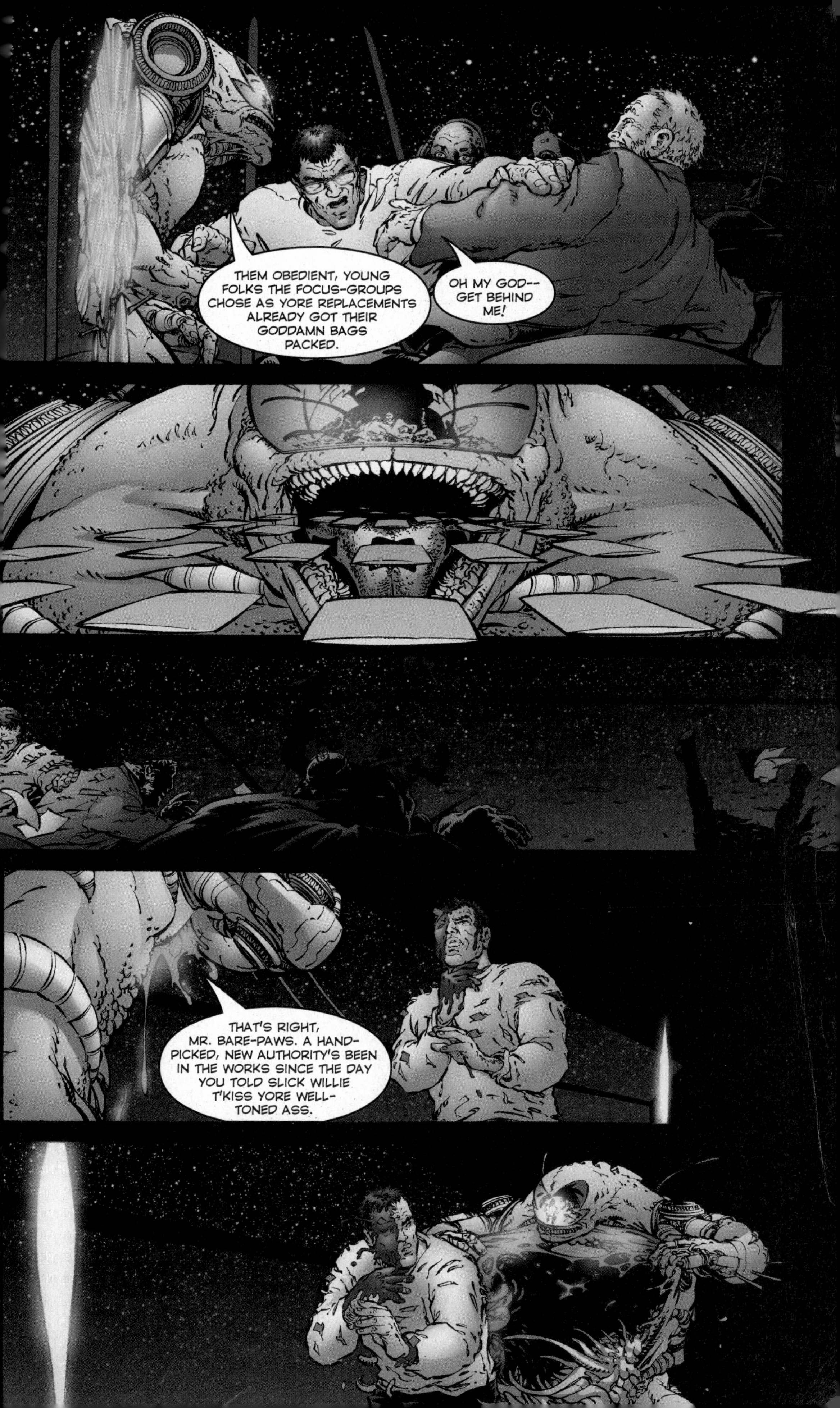
THEM OBEDIENT, YOUNG FOLKS THE FOCUS-GROUPS CHOSE AS YORE REPLACEMENTS ALREADY GOT THEIR GODDAMN BAGS PACKED.
OH MY GOD-- GET BEHIND ME!
THAT'S RIGHT, MR. BARE-PAWS. A HAND-PICKED, NEW AUTHORITY'S BEEN IN THE WORKS SINCE THE DAY YOU TOLD SLICK WILLIE T'KISS YORE WELL-TONED ASS.

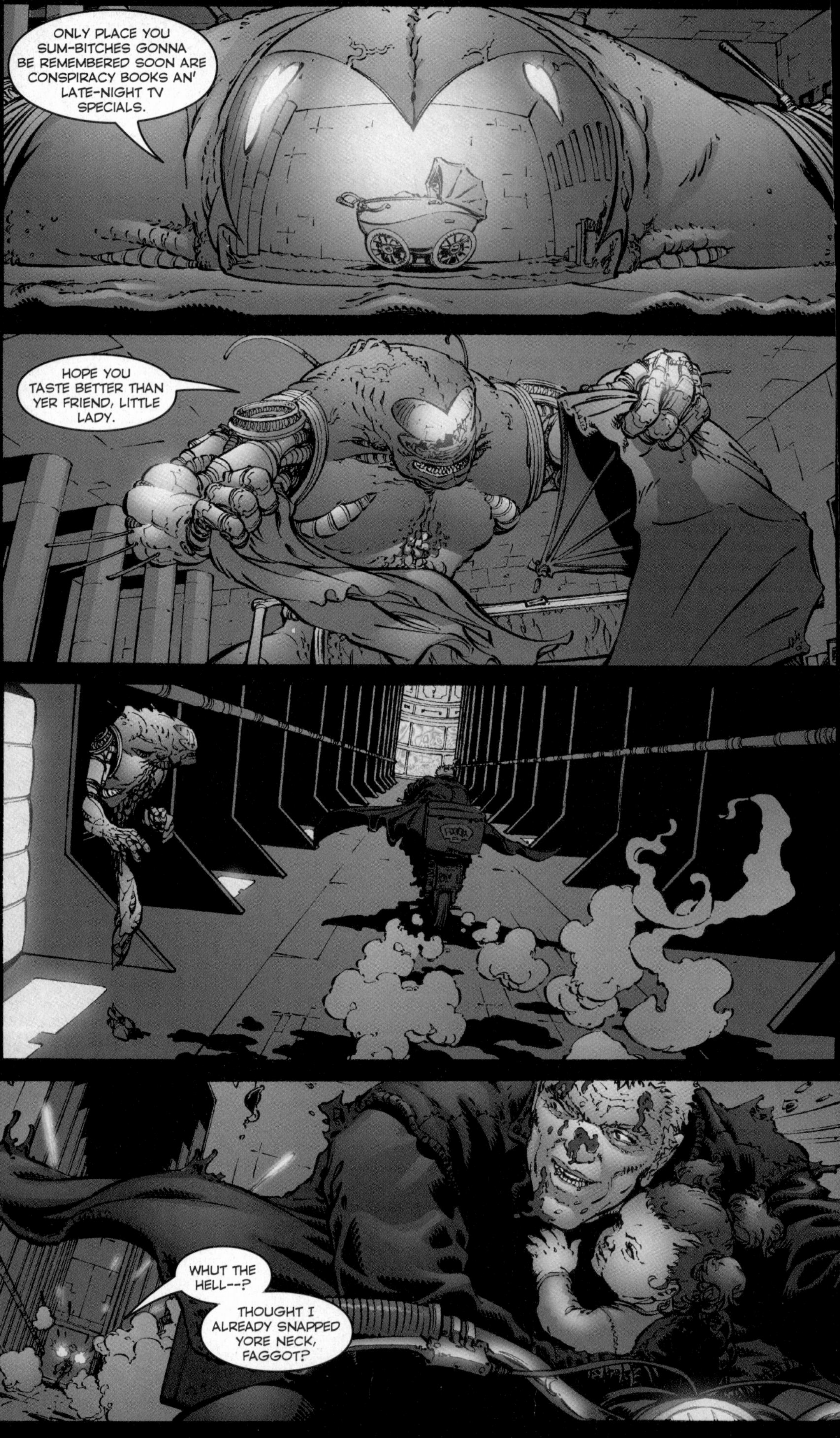
ONLY PLACE YOU SUM-BITCHES GONNA BE REMEMBERED SOON ARE CONSPIRACY BOOKS AN' LATE-NIGHT TV SPECIALS.
HOPE YOU TASTE BETTER THAN YER FRIEND, LITTLE LADY.
WHUT THE HELL--?
THOUGHT I ALREADY SNAPPED YORE NECK, FAGGOT?

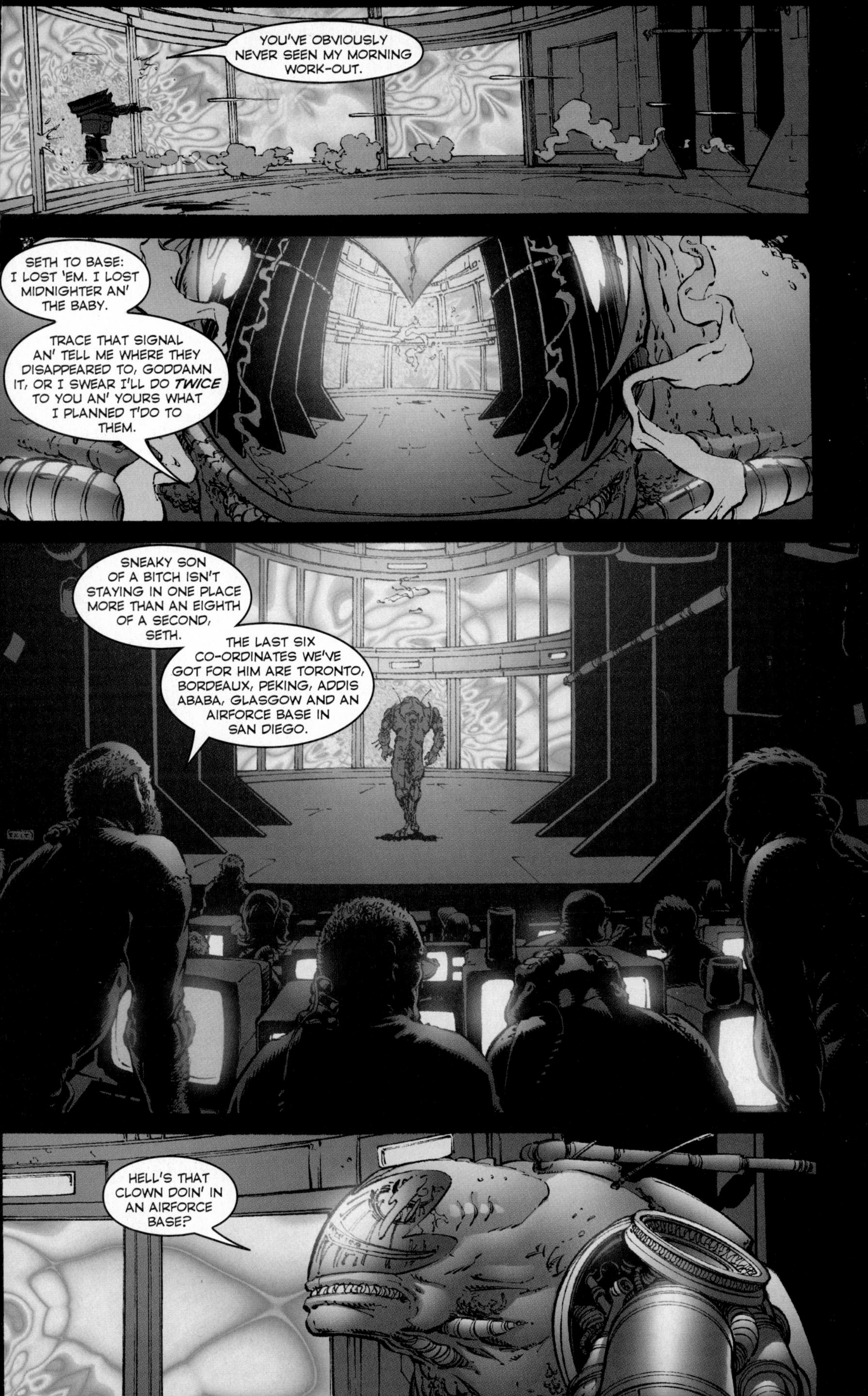
YOU'VE OBVIOUSLY NEVER SEEN MY MORNING WORK-OUT.
SETH TO BASE: I LOST 'EM. I LOST MIDNIGHTER AN' THE BABY.
TRACE THAT SIGNAL AN' TELL ME WHERE THEY DISAPPEARED TO, GODDAMN IT, OR I SWEAR I'LL DO *TWICE* TO YOU AN' YOURS WHAT I PLANNED T'DO TO THEM.
SNEAKY SON OF A BITCH ISN'T STAYING IN ONE PLACE MORE THAN AN EIGHTH OF A SECOND, SETH.
THE LAST SIX CO-ORDINATES WE'VE GOT FOR HIM ARE TORONTO, BORDEAUX, PEKING, ADDIS ABABA, GLASGOW AND AN AIRFORCE BASE IN SAN DIEGO.
HELL'S THAT CLOWN DOIN' IN AN AIRFORCE BASE?

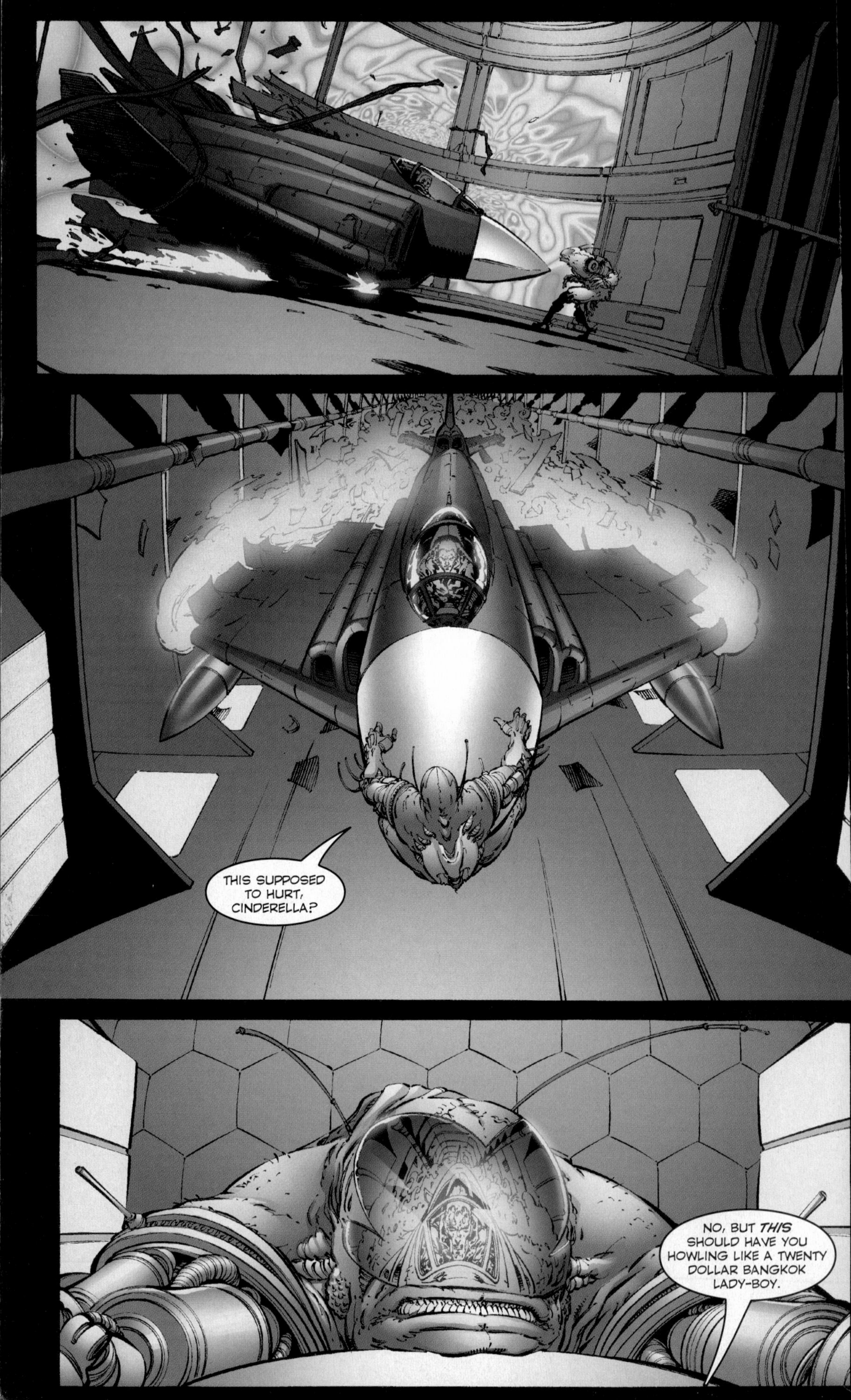
THIS SUPPOSED TO HURT, CINDERELLA?
NO, BUT *THIS* SHOULD HAVE YOU HOWLING LIKE A TWENTY DOLLAR BANGKOK LADY-BOY.

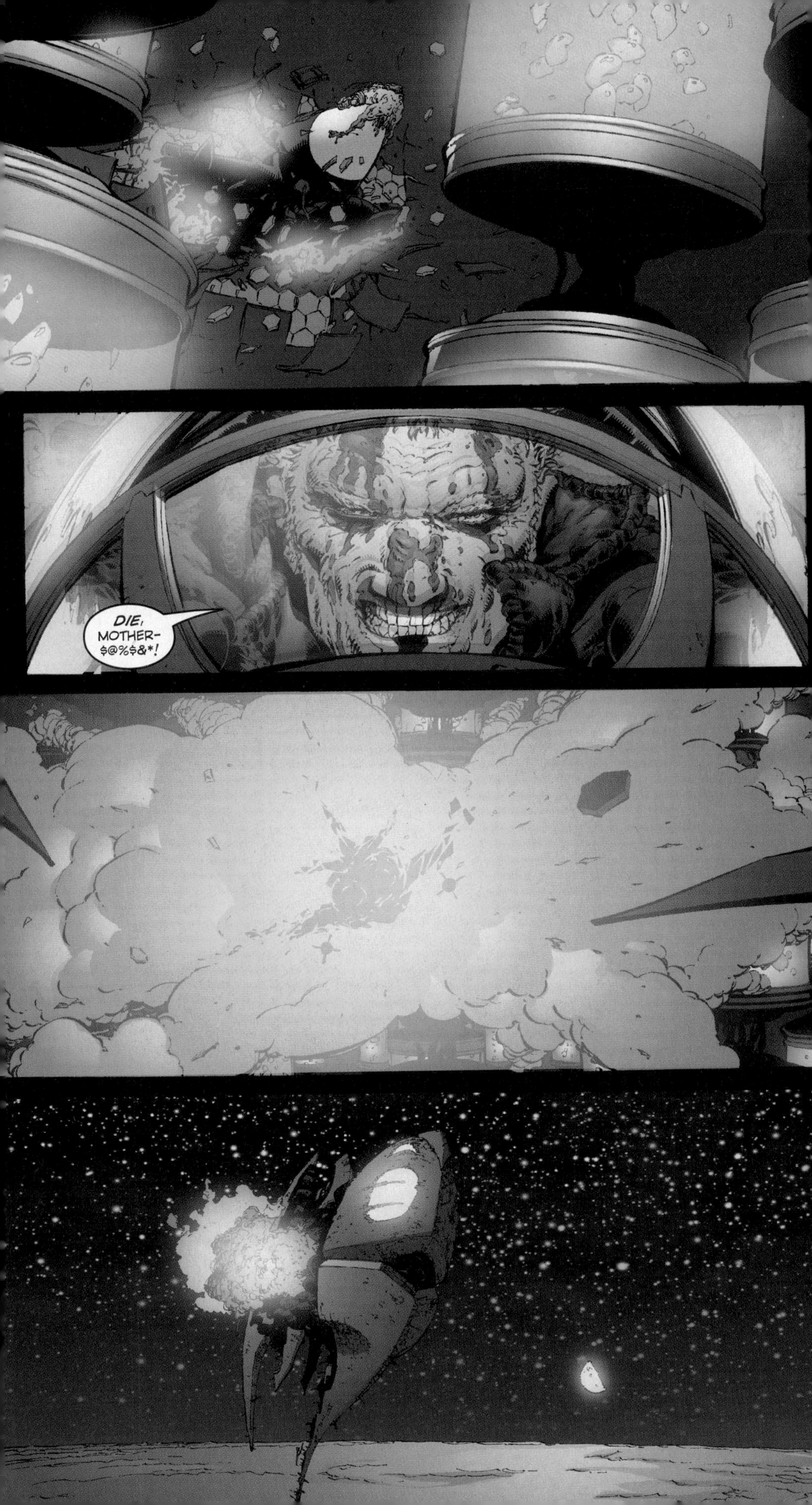
DIE, MOTHER-$@%$&*!

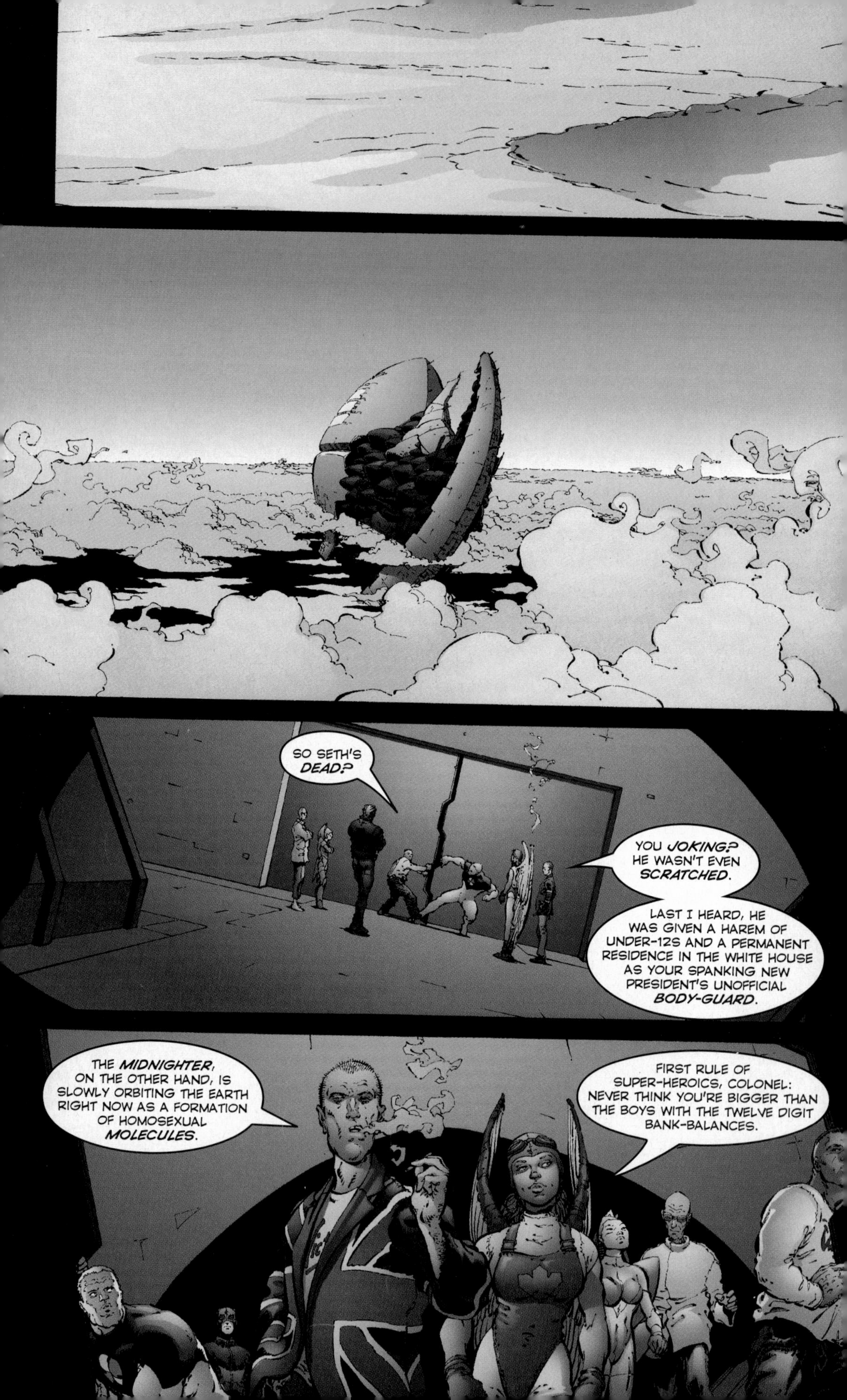
SO SETH'S DEAD?
YOU JOKING? HE WASN'T EVEN SCRATCHED.
LAST I HEARD, HE WAS GIVEN A HAREM OF UNDER-12S AND A PERMANENT RESIDENCE IN THE WHITE HOUSE AS YOUR SPANKING NEW PRESIDENT'S UNOFFICIAL BODY-GUARD.
THE MIDNIGHTER, ON THE OTHER HAND, IS SLOWLY ORBITING THE EARTH RIGHT NOW AS A FORMATION OF HOMOSEXUAL MOLECULES.
FIRST RULE OF SUPER-HEROICS, COLONEL: NEVER THINK YOU'RE BIGGER THAN THE BOYS WITH THE TWELVE DIGIT BANK-BALANCES.

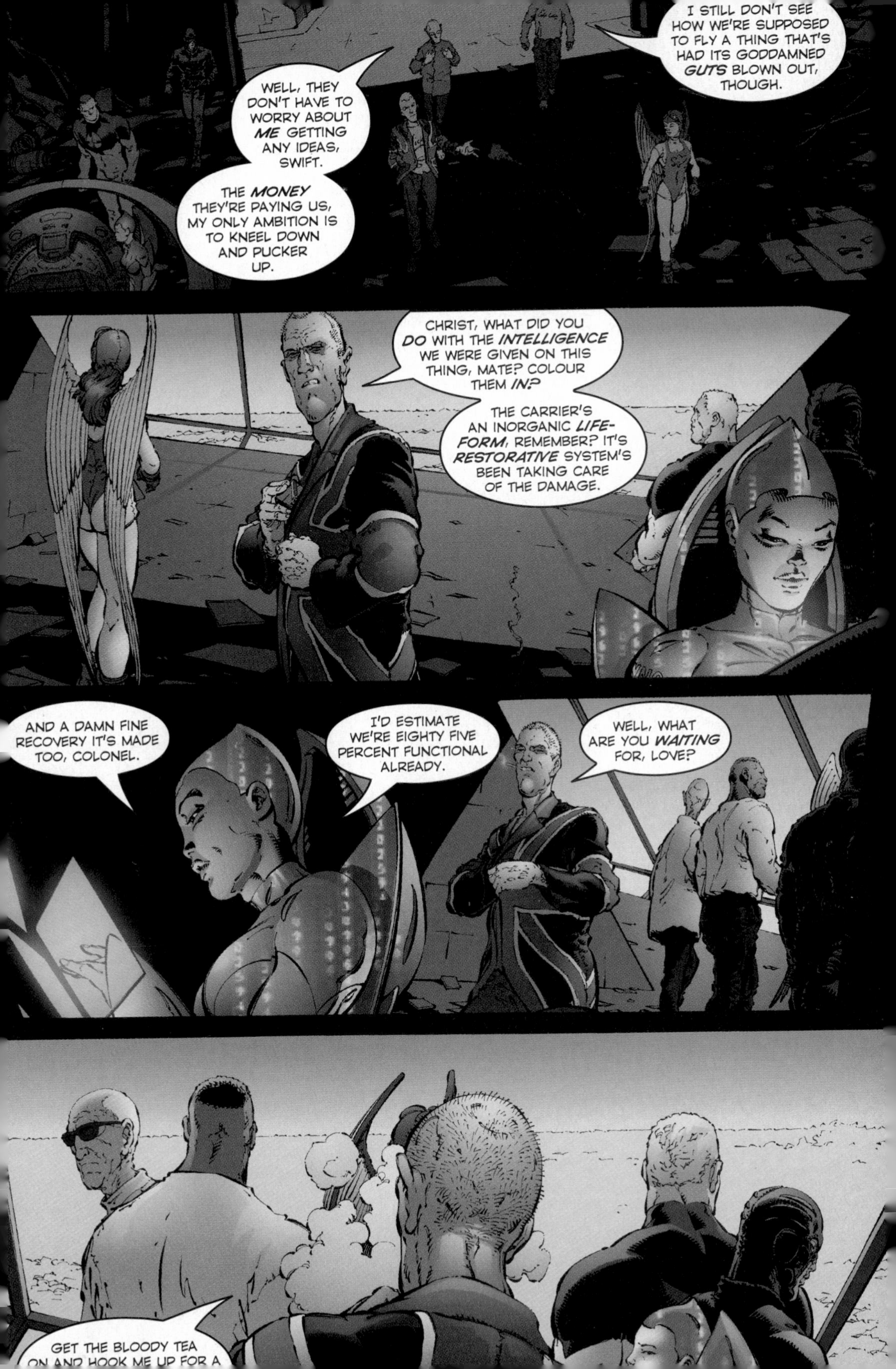
WELL, THEY DON'T HAVE TO WORRY ABOUT *ME* GETTING ANY IDEAS, SWIFT.
THE *MONEY* THEY'RE PAYING US, MY ONLY AMBITION IS TO KNEEL DOWN AND PUCKER UP.
I STILL DON'T SEE HOW WE'RE SUPPOSED TO FLY A THING THAT'S HAD ITS GODDAMNED *GUTS* BLOWN OUT, THOUGH.
CHRIST, WHAT DID YOU *DO* WITH THE *INTELLIGENCE* WE WERE GIVEN ON THIS THING, MATE? COLOUR THEM *IN?*
THE CARRIER'S AN INORGANIC *LIFE-FORM*, REMEMBER? IT'S *RESTORATIVE* SYSTEM'S BEEN TAKING CARE OF THE DAMAGE.
AND A DAMN FINE RECOVERY IT'S MADE TOO, COLONEL.
I'D ESTIMATE WE'RE EIGHTY FIVE PERCENT FUNCTIONAL ALREADY.
WELL, WHAT ARE YOU *WAITING* FOR, LOVE?
GET THE BLOODY TEA
ON AND HOOK ME UP FOR A

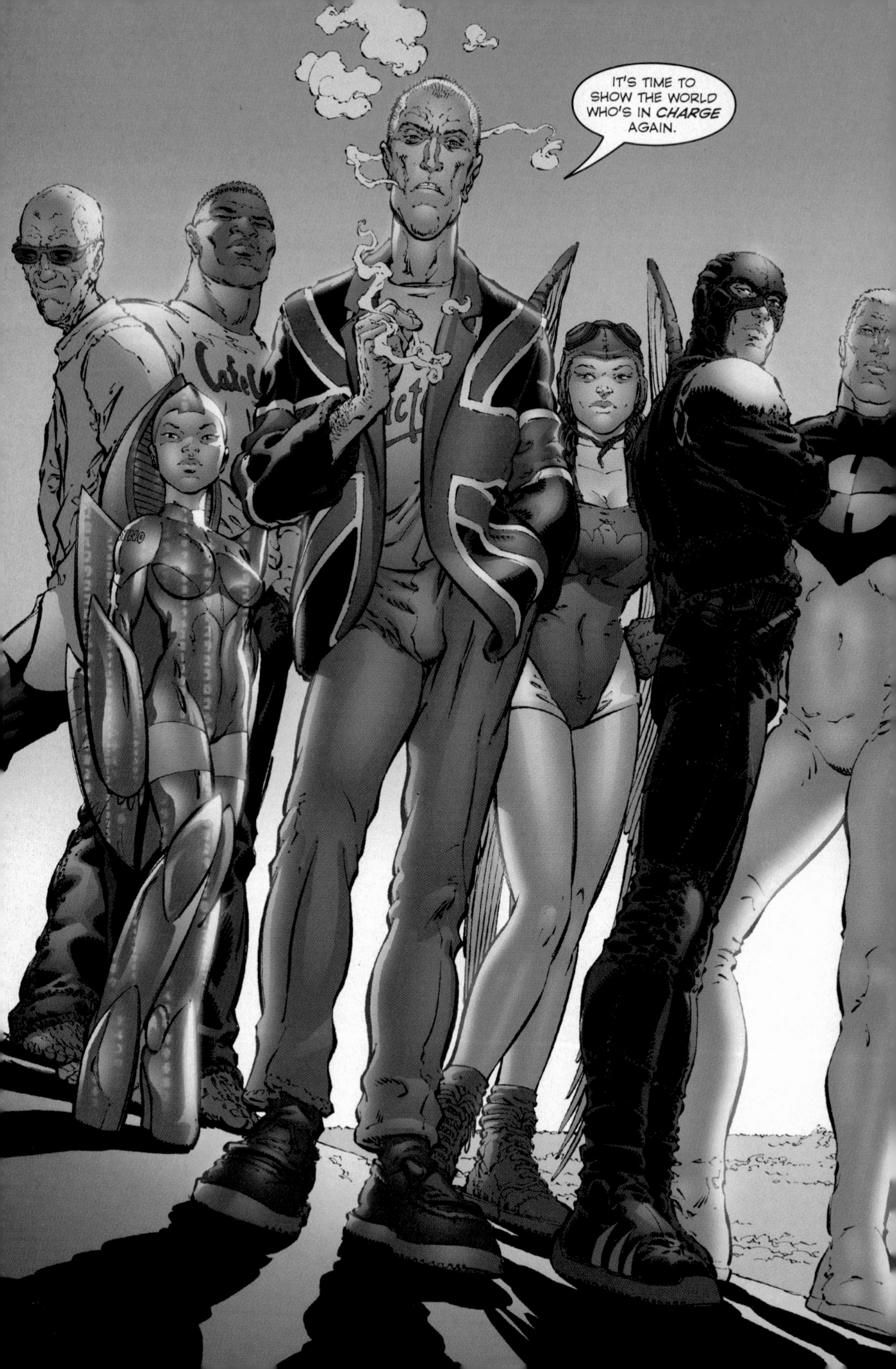
IT'S TIME TO SHOW THE WORLD WHO'S IN *CHARGE* AGAIN.

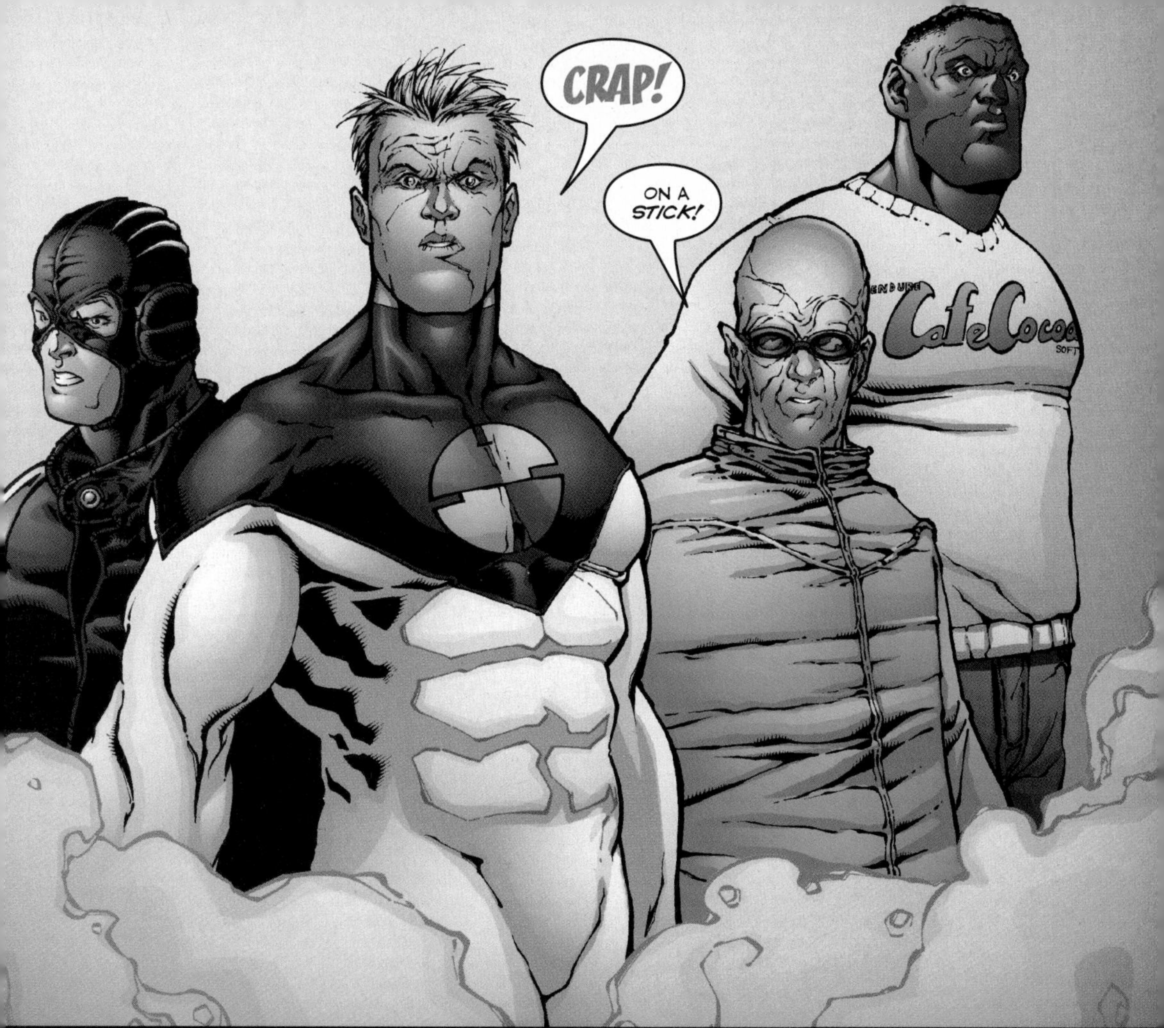
CRAP!
ON A STICK!
ENDURE Cafe Cocoa SOFT

TRANSFER OF POWER

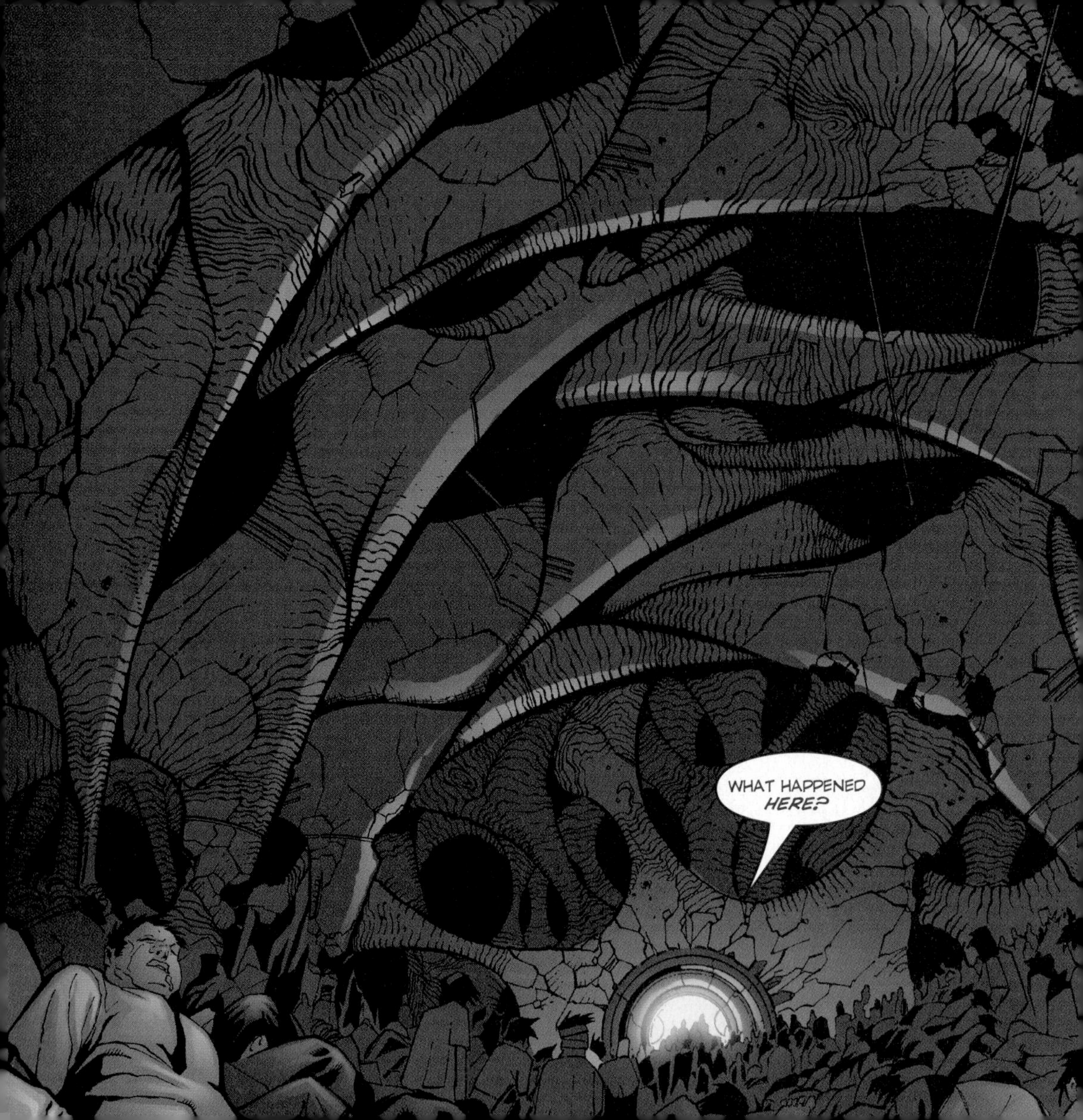
WHAT HAPPENED HERE?

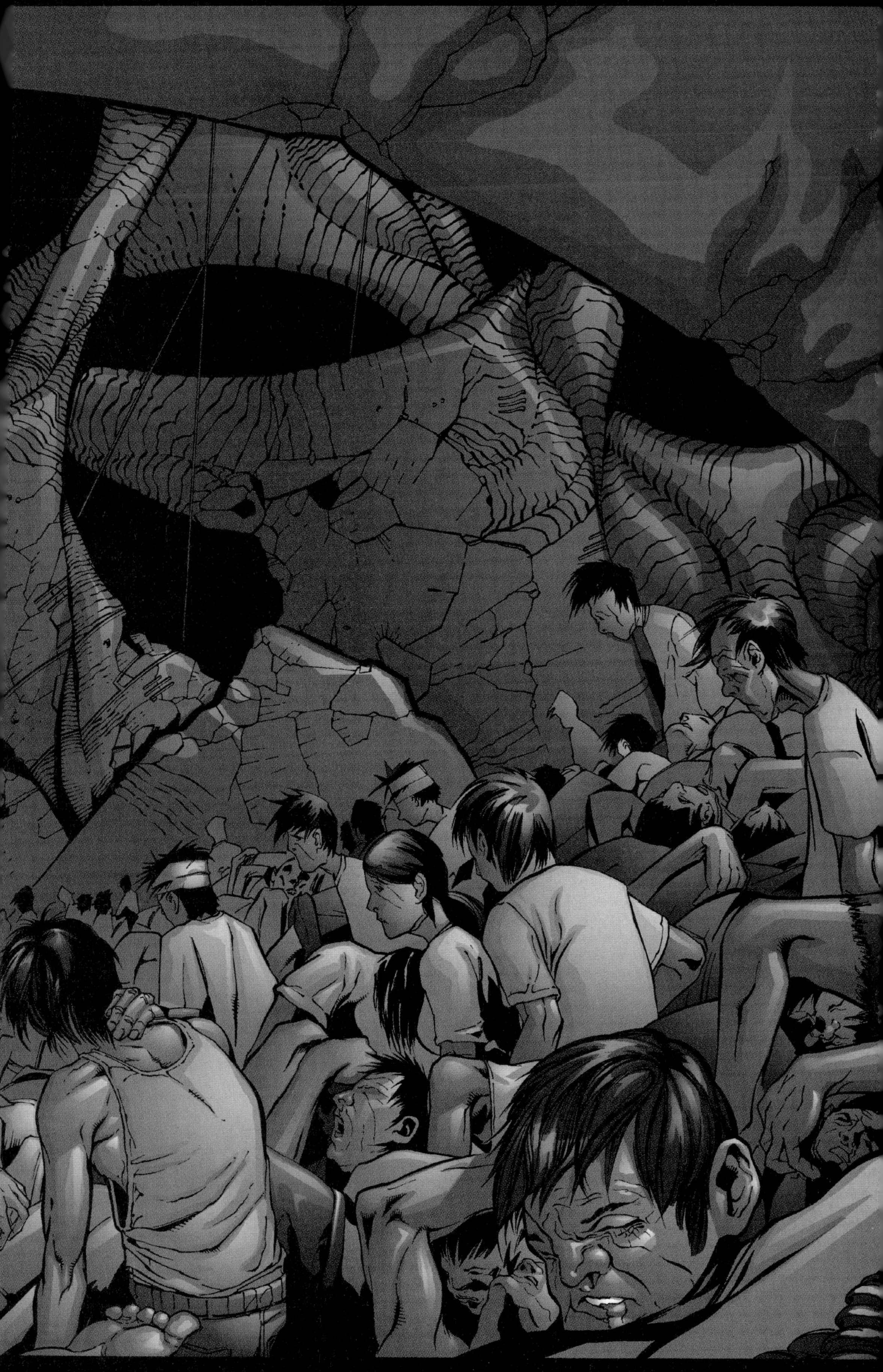

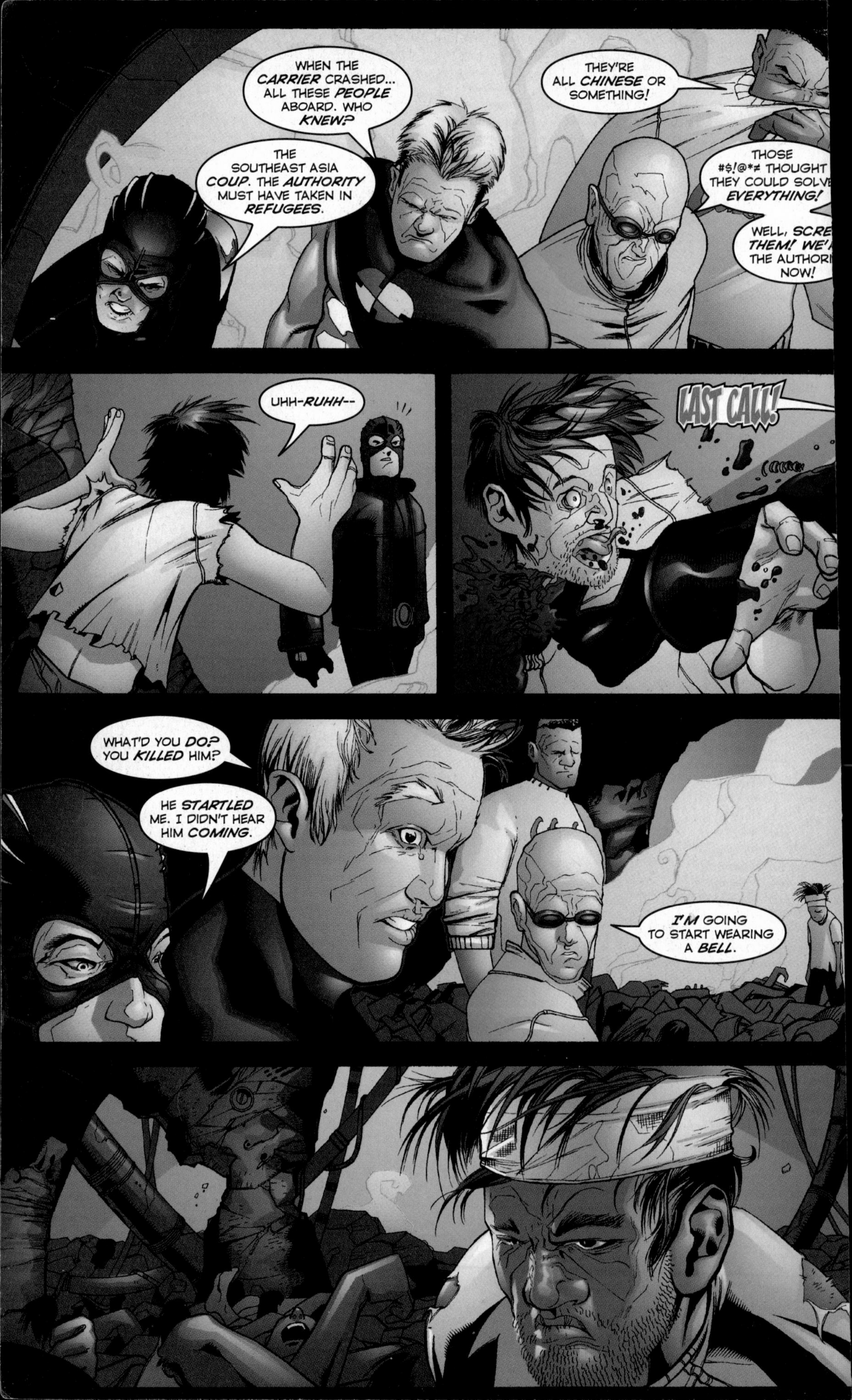
WHEN THE CARRIER CRASHED... ALL THESE PEOPLE ABOARD. WHO KNEW?
THEY'RE ALL CHINESE OR SOMETHING!
THE SOUTHEAST ASIA COUP. THE AUTHORITY MUST HAVE TAKEN IN REFUGEES.
THOSE #$!@*≠ THOUGHT THEY COULD SOLVE EVERYTHING!
WELL, SCRE THEM! WE' THE AUTHOR NOW!
UHH-RUHH--
LAST CALL!
WHAT'D YOU DO? YOU KILLED HIM?
HE STARTLED ME. I DIDN'T HEAR HIM COMING.
I'M GOING TO START WEARING A BELL.

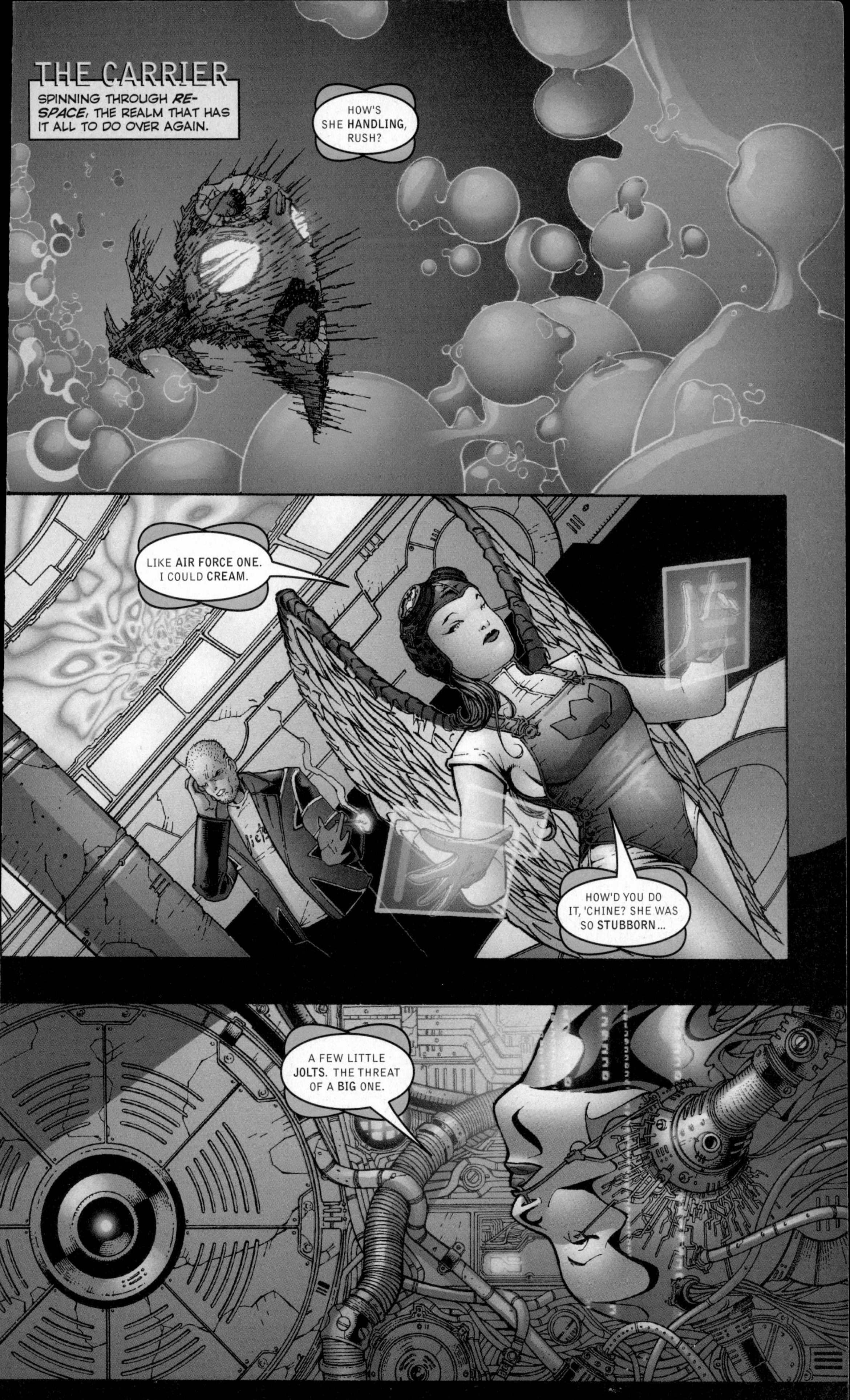
THE CARRIER
SPINNING THROUGH RE-SPACE, THE REALM THAT HAS IT ALL TO DO OVER AGAIN.
HOW'S SHE HANDLING, RUSH?
LIKE AIR FORCE ONE. I COULD CREAM.
HOW'D YOU DO IT, 'CHINE? SHE WAS SO STUBBORN...
A FEW LITTLE JOLTS. THE THREAT OF A BIG ONE.

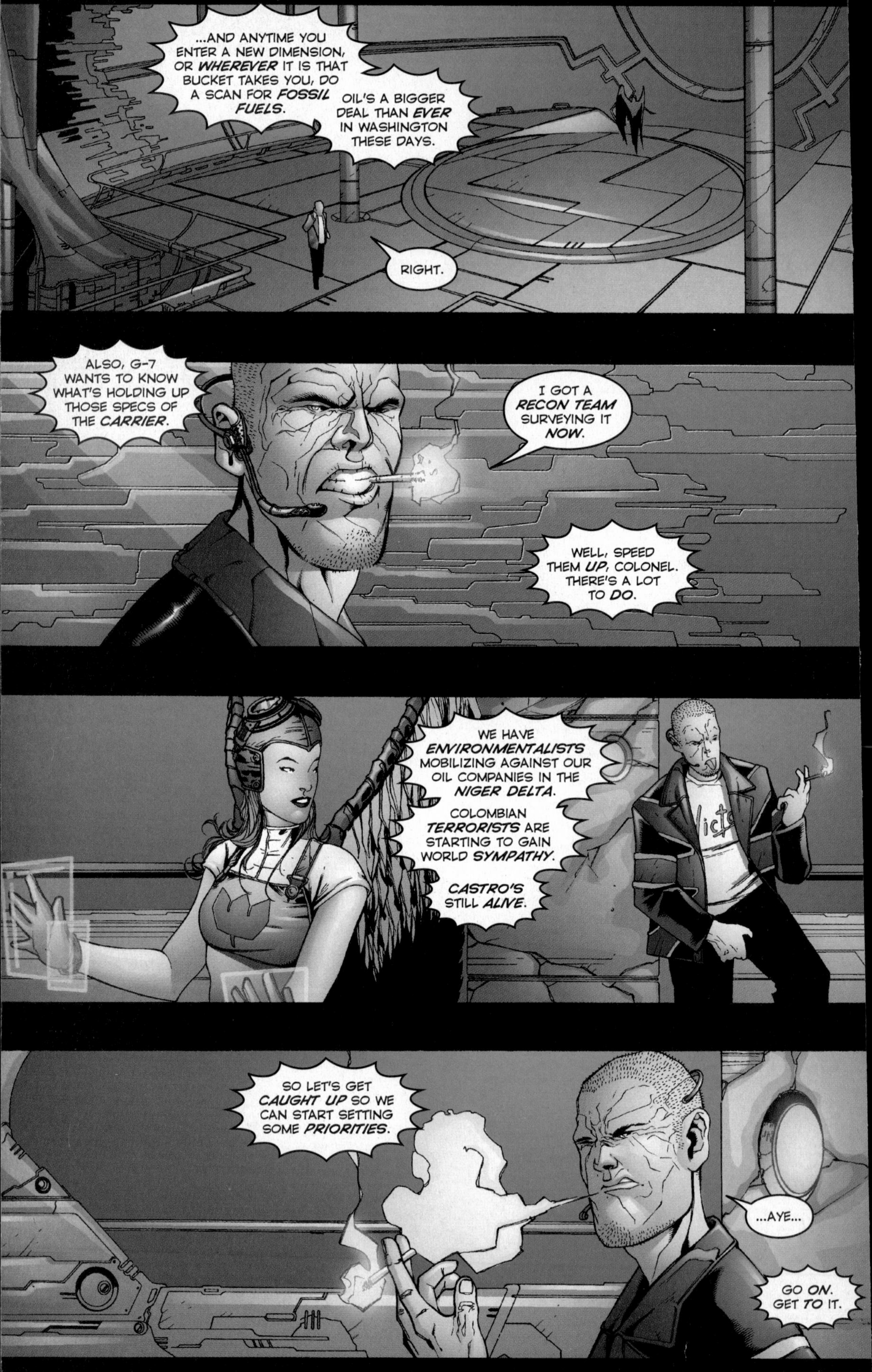
...AND ANYTIME YOU ENTER A NEW DIMENSION, OR WHEREVER IT IS THAT BUCKET TAKES YOU, DO A SCAN FOR FOSSIL FUELS.
OIL'S A BIGGER DEAL THAN EVER IN WASHINGTON THESE DAYS.
RIGHT.
ALSO, G-7 WANTS TO KNOW WHAT'S HOLDING UP THOSE SPECS OF THE CARRIER.
I GOT A RECON TEAM SURVEYING IT NOW.
WELL, SPEED THEM UP, COLONEL. THERE'S A LOT TO DO.
WE HAVE ENVIRONMENTALISTS MOBILIZING AGAINST OUR OIL COMPANIES IN THE NIGER DELTA.
COLOMBIAN TERRORISTS ARE STARTING TO GAIN WORLD SYMPATHY.
CASTRO'S STILL ALIVE.
SO LET'S GET CAUGHT UP SO WE CAN START SETTING SOME PRIORITIES.
...AYE...
GO ON. GET TO IT.

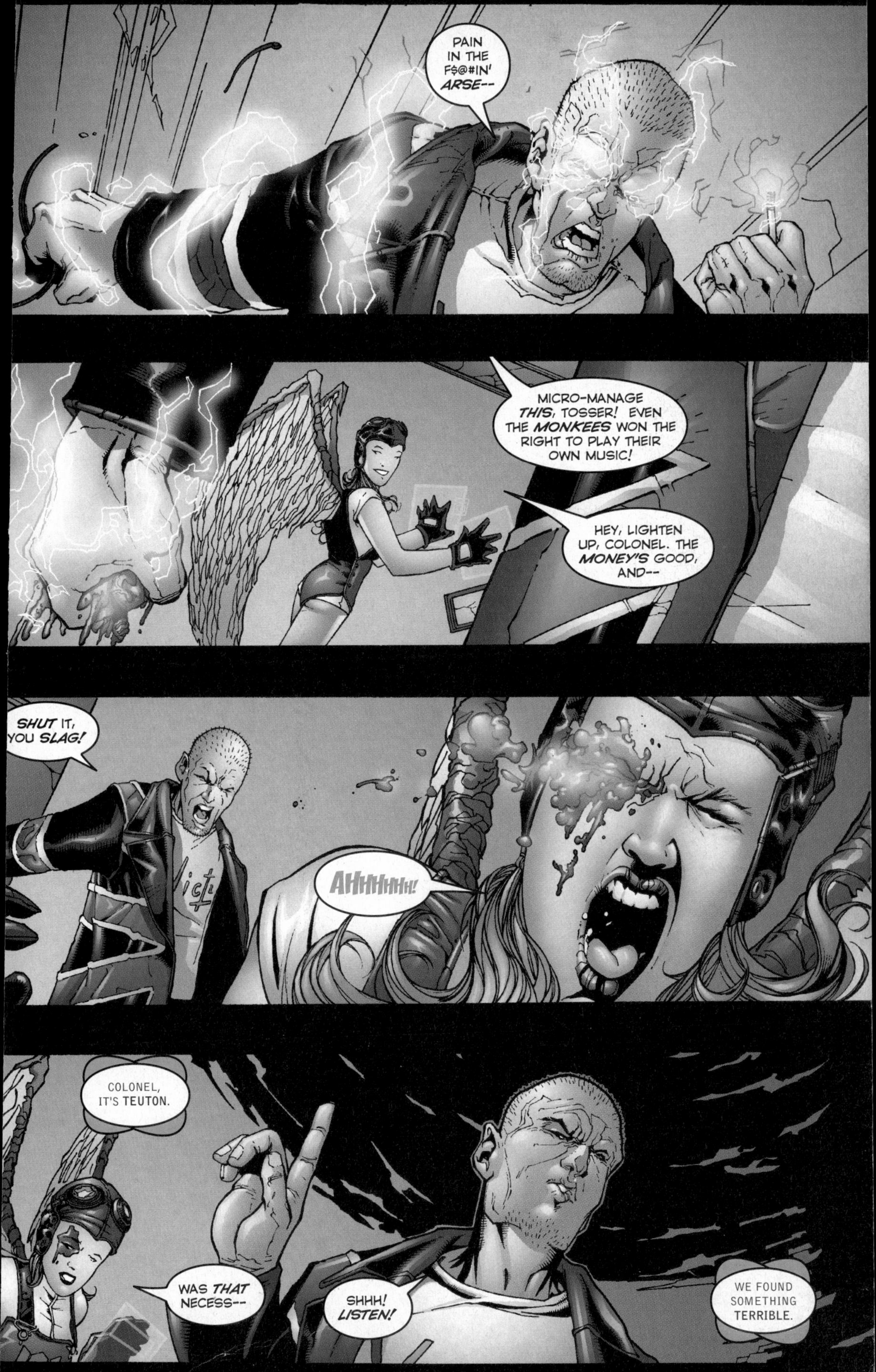
PAIN IN THE F$@#IN' ARSE--
MICRO-MANAGE THIS, TOSSER! EVEN THE MONKEES WON THE RIGHT TO PLAY THEIR OWN MUSIC!
HEY, LIGHTEN UP, COLONEL. THE MONEY'S GOOD, AND--
SHUT IT, YOU SLAG!
AHHHHHH!
COLONEL, IT'S TEUTON.
WAS THAT NECESS--
SHHH! LISTEN!
WE FOUND SOMETHING TERRIBLE.

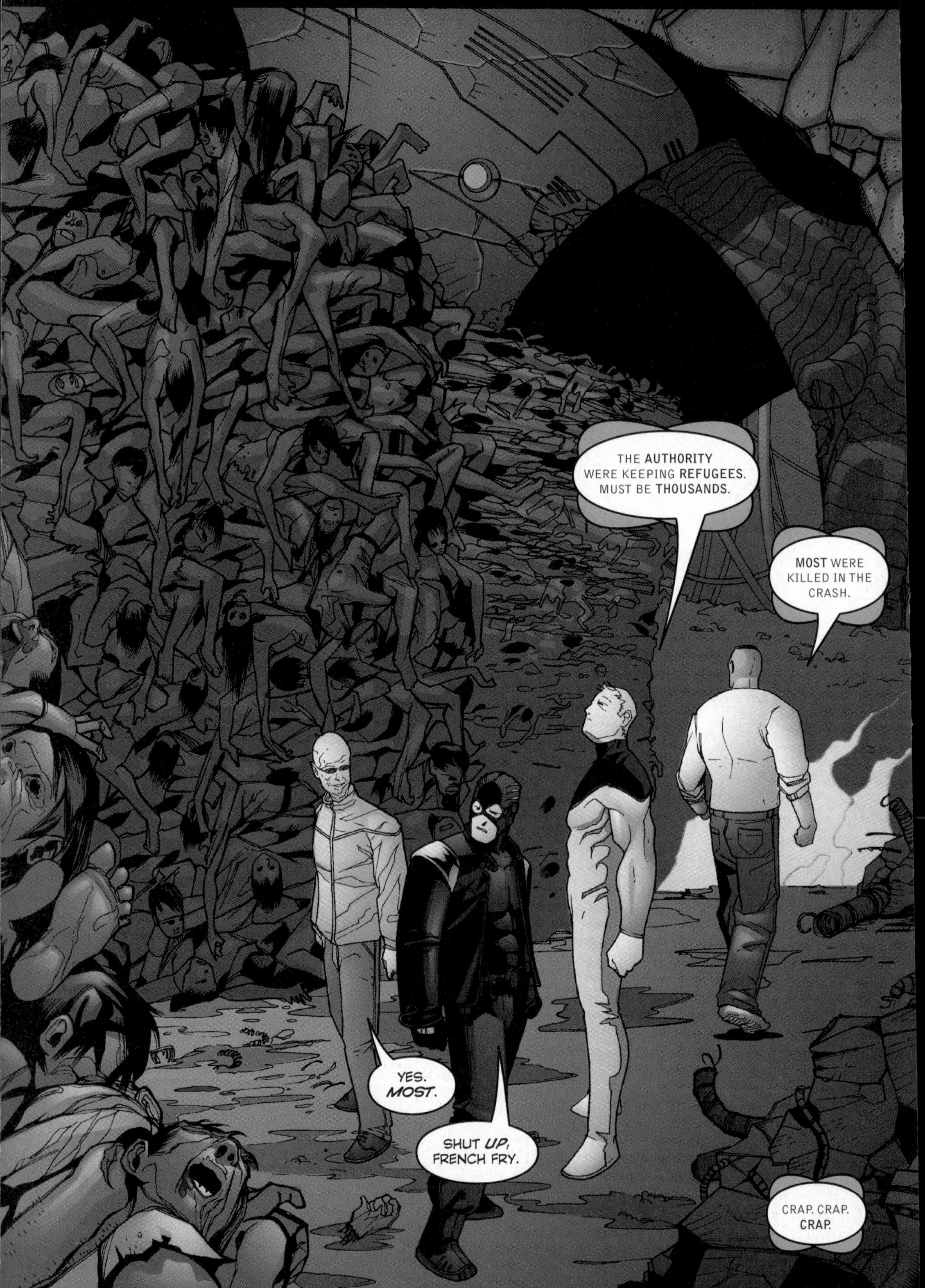
THE AUTHORITY WERE KEEPING REFUGEES. MUST BE THOUSANDS.
MOST WERE KILLED IN THE CRASH.
YES. MOST.
SHUT UP, FRENCH FRY.
CRAP. CRAP. CRAP.
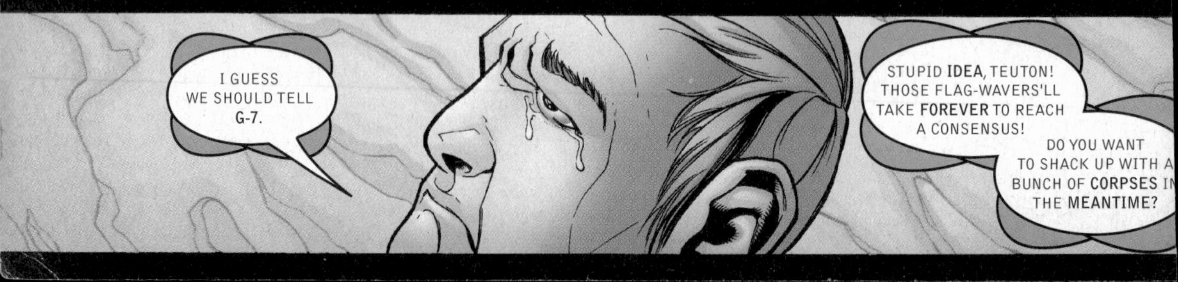
I GUESS WE SHOULD TELL G-7.
STUPID IDEA, TEUTON! THOSE FLAG-WAVERS'LL TAKE FOREVER TO REACH A CONSENSUS!
DO YOU WANT TO SHACK UP WITH A BUNCH OF CORPSES IN THE MEANTIME?

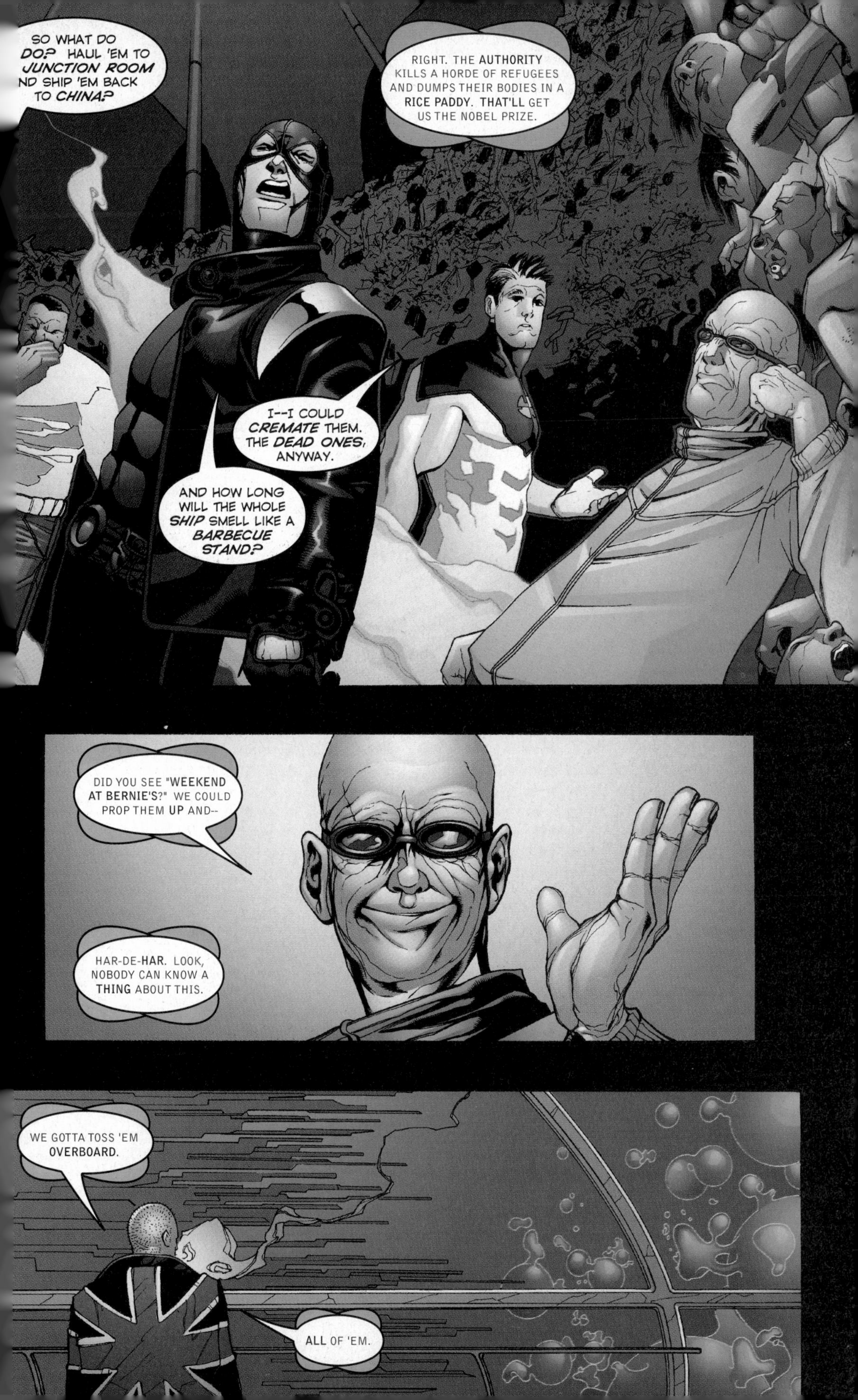
SO WHAT DO DO? HAUL 'EM TO JUNCTION ROOM ND SHIP 'EM BACK TO CHINA?
RIGHT. THE AUTHORITY KILLS A HORDE OF REFUGEES AND DUMPS THEIR BODIES IN A RICE PADDY. THAT'LL GET US THE NOBEL PRIZE.
I--I COULD CREMATE THEM. THE DEAD ONES, ANYWAY.
AND HOW LONG WILL THE WHOLE SHIP SMELL LIKE A BARBECUE STAND?
DID YOU SEE "WEEKEND AT BERNIE'S?" WE COULD PROP THEM UP AND--
HAR-DE-HAR. LOOK, NOBODY CAN KNOW A THING ABOUT THIS.
WE GOTTA TOSS 'EM OVERBOARD.
ALL OF 'EM.

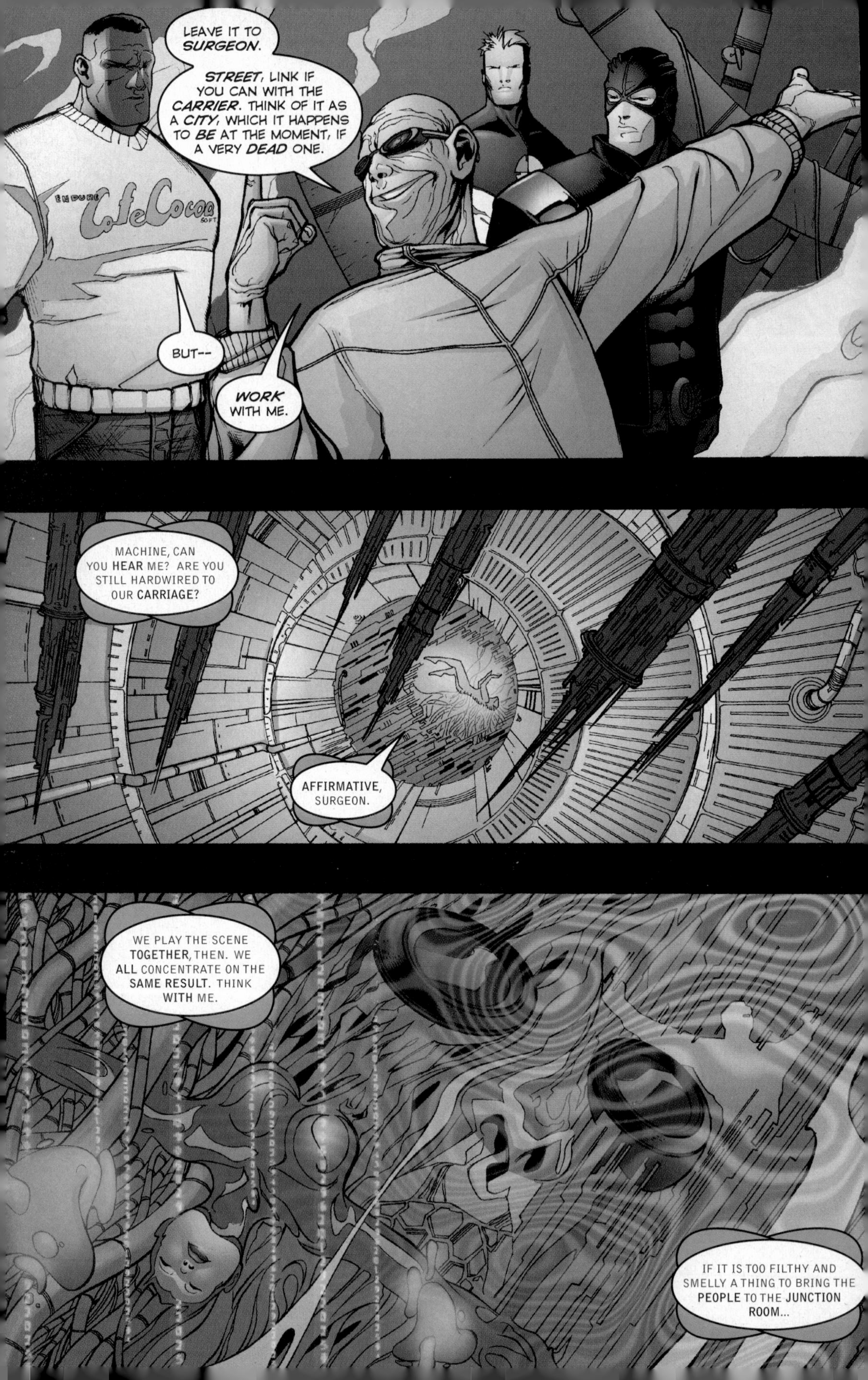
LEAVE IT TO SURGEON.
STREET, LINK IF YOU CAN WITH THE CARRIER. THINK OF IT AS A CITY, WHICH IT HAPPENS TO BE AT THE MOMENT, IF A VERY DEAD ONE.
BUT--
WORK WITH ME.
MACHINE, CAN YOU HEAR ME? ARE YOU STILL HARDWIRED TO OUR CARRIAGE?
AFFIRMATIVE, SURGEON.
WE PLAY THE SCENE TOGETHER, THEN. WE ALL CONCENTRATE ON THE SAME RESULT. THINK WITH ME.
IF IT IS TOO FILTHY AND SMELLY A THING TO BRING THE PEOPLE TO THE JUNCTION ROOM...

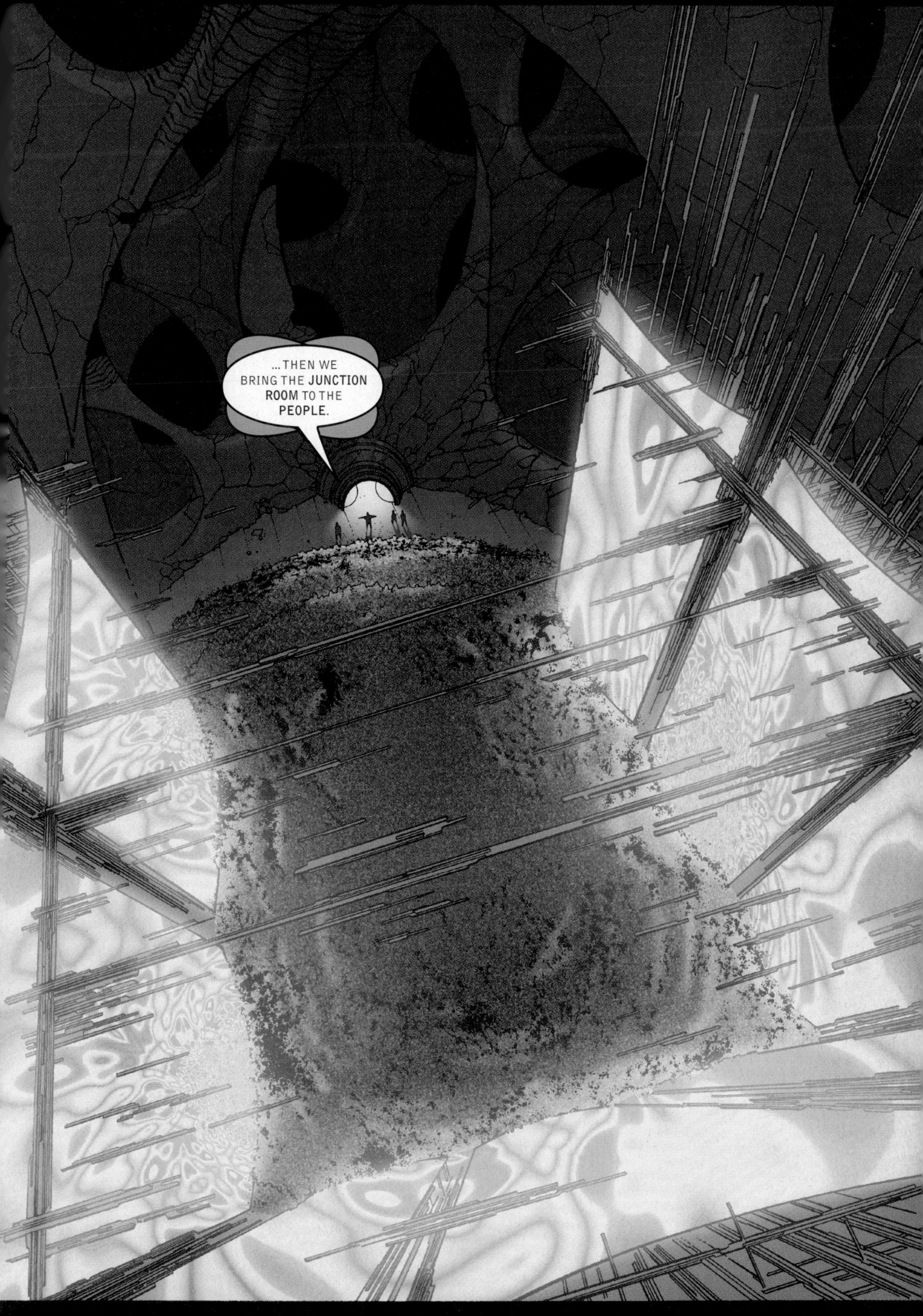
...THEN WE BRING THE JUNCTION ROOM TO THE PEOPLE.

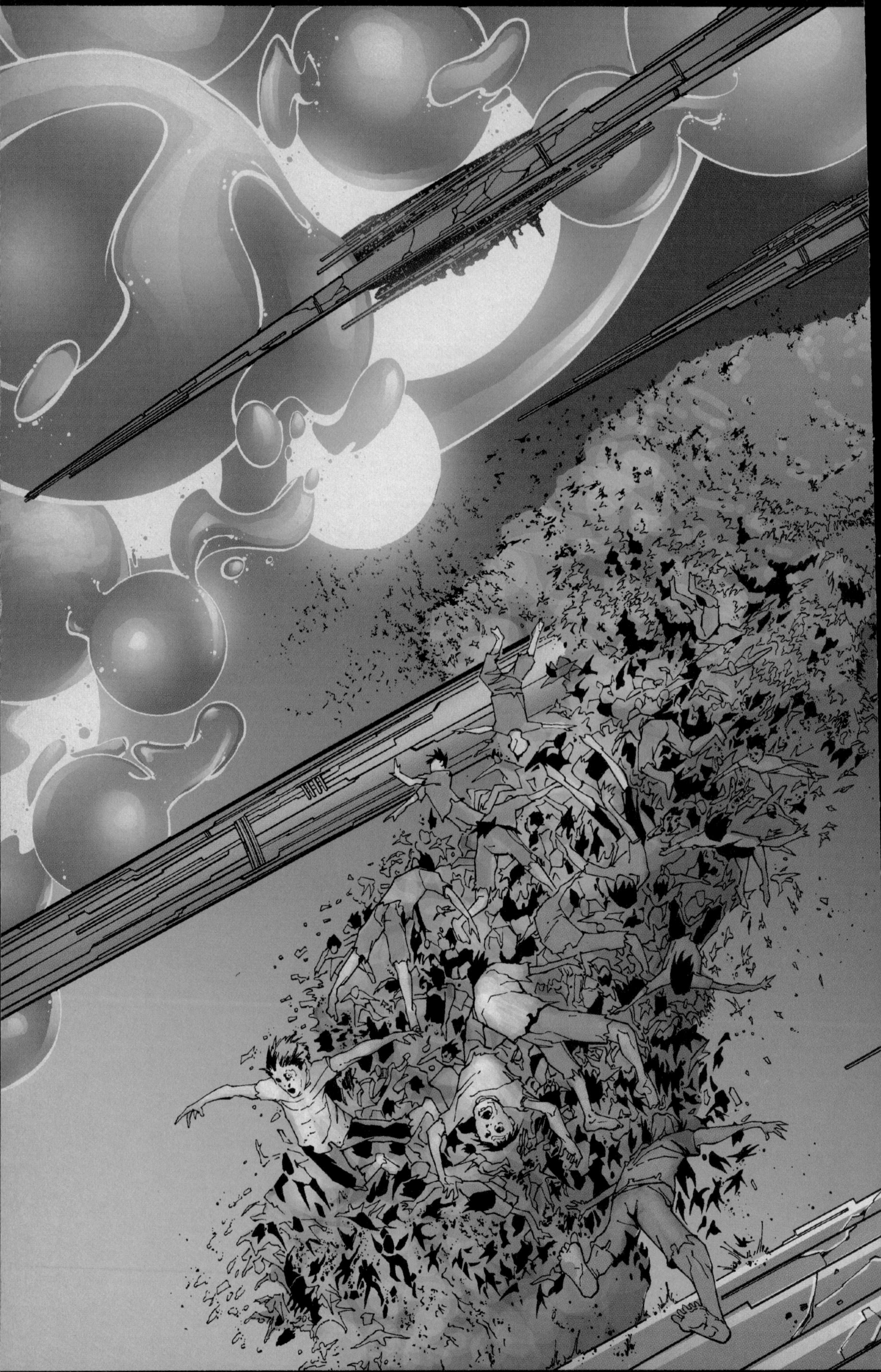

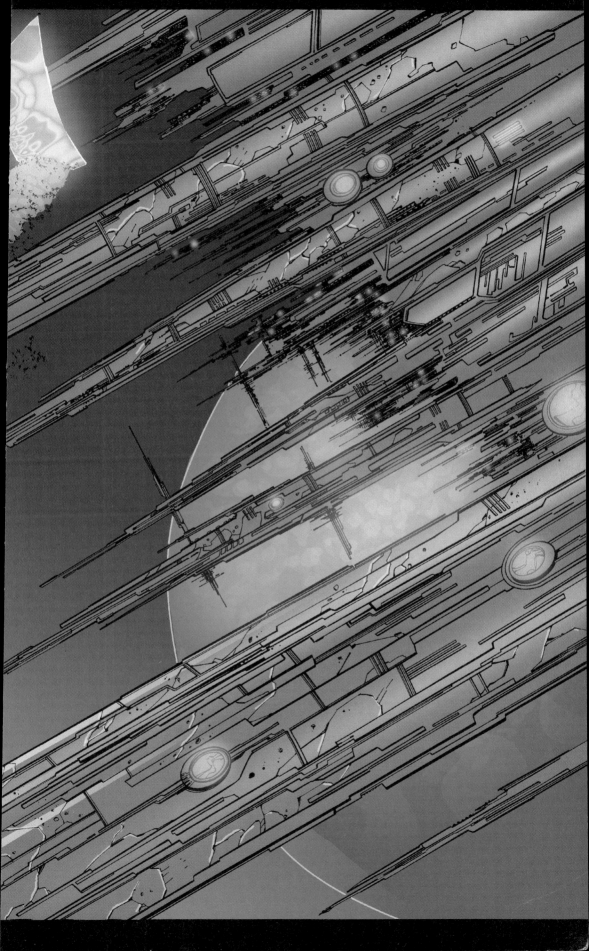

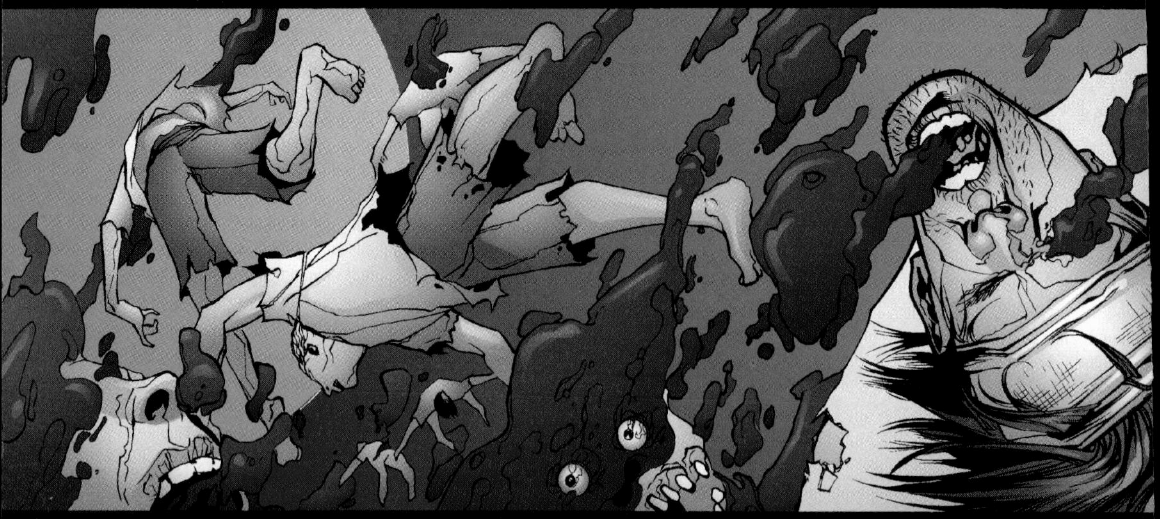
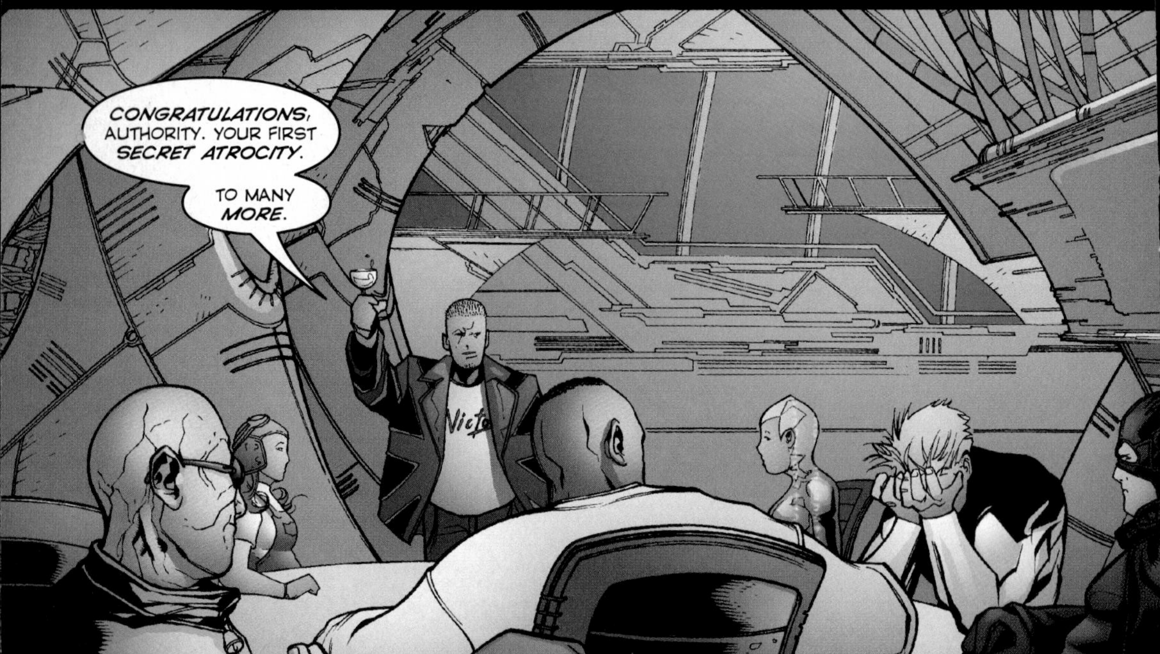
CONGRATULATIONS, AUTHORITY. YOUR FIRST SECRET ATROCITY.
TO MANY MORE.
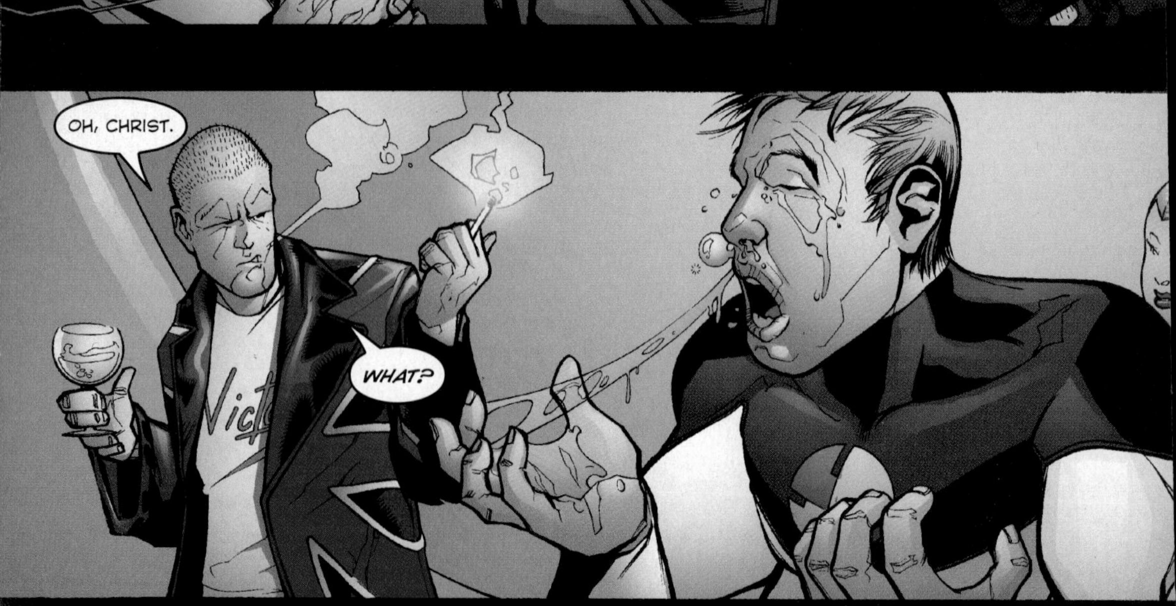
OH, CHRIST.
WHAT?

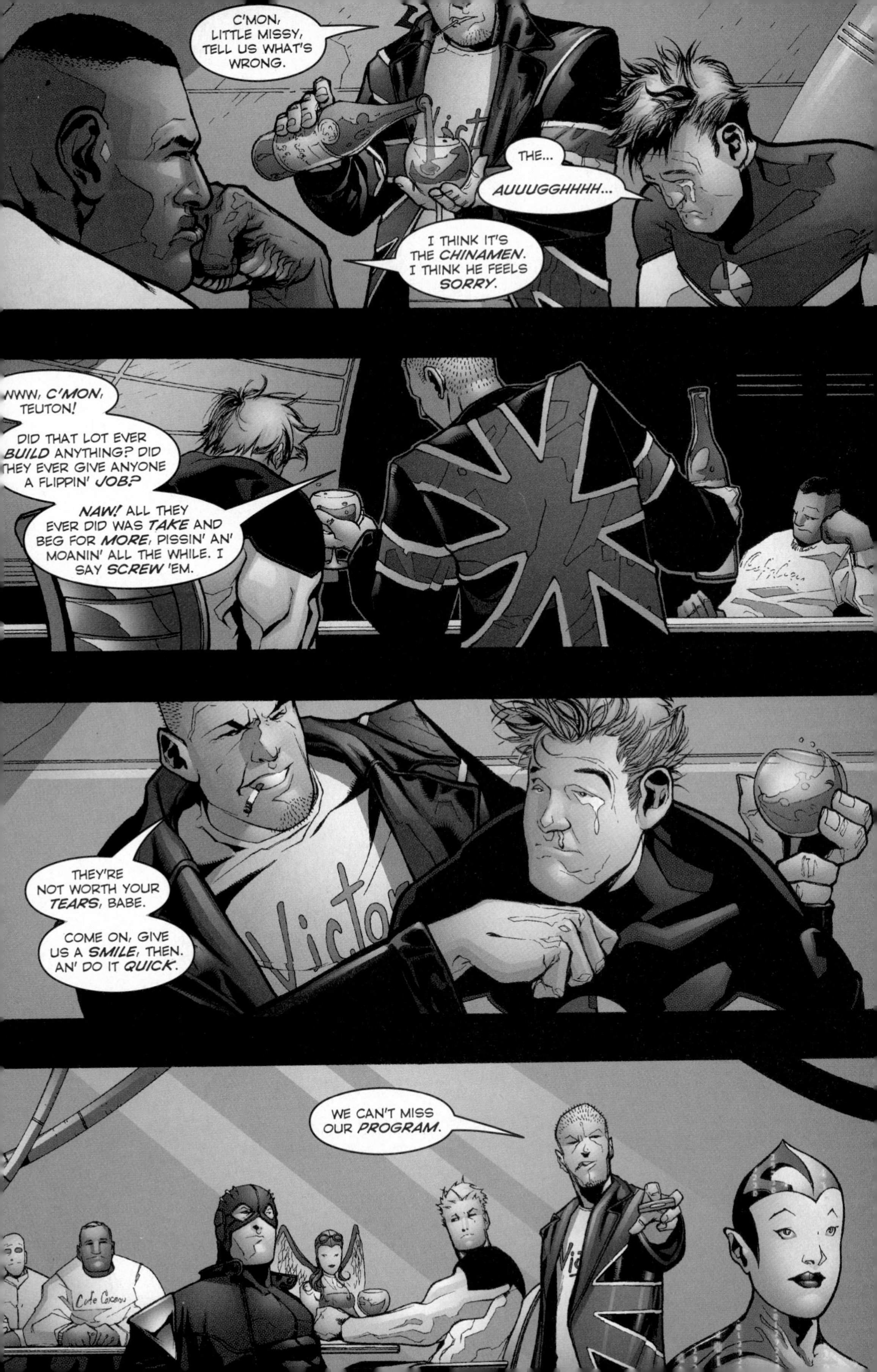
C'MON, LITTLE MISSY, TELL US WHAT'S WRONG.
THE...
AUUUGGHHHH...
I THINK IT'S THE CHINAMEN. I THINK HE FEELS SORRY.
NWW, C'MON, TEUTON!
DID THAT LOT EVER BUILD ANYTHING? DID THEY EVER GIVE ANYONE A FLIPPIN' JOB?
NAW! ALL THEY EVER DID WAS TAKE AND BEG FOR MORE, PISSIN' AN' MOANIN' ALL THE WHILE. I SAY SCREW 'EM.
THEY'RE NOT WORTH YOUR TEARS, BABE.
COME ON, GIVE US A SMILE, THEN. AN' DO IT QUICK.
WE CAN'T MISS OUR PROGRAM.

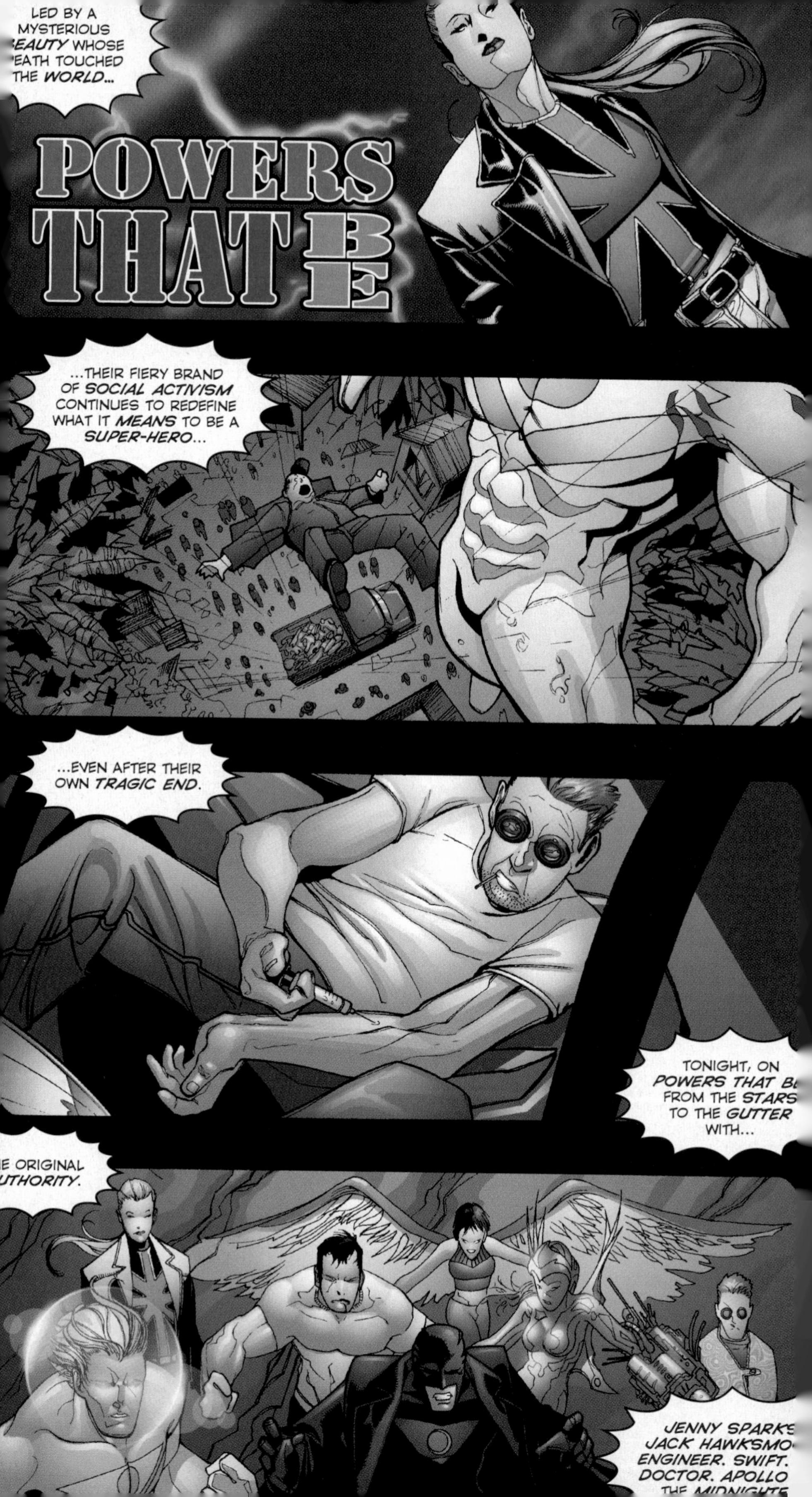
LED BY A MYSTERIOUS EAUTY WHOSE EATH TOUCHED THE WORLD...
POWERS THAT BE
...THEIR FIERY BRAND OF SOCIAL ACTIVISM CONTINUES TO REDEFINE WHAT IT MEANS TO BE A SUPER-HERO...
...EVEN AFTER THEIR OWN TRAGIC END.
TONIGHT, ON POWERS THAT B FROM THE STARS TO THE GUTTER WITH...
E ORIGINAL UTHORITY.
JENNY SPARKS JACK HAWKSMO ENGINEER. SWIFT. DOCTOR. APOLLO

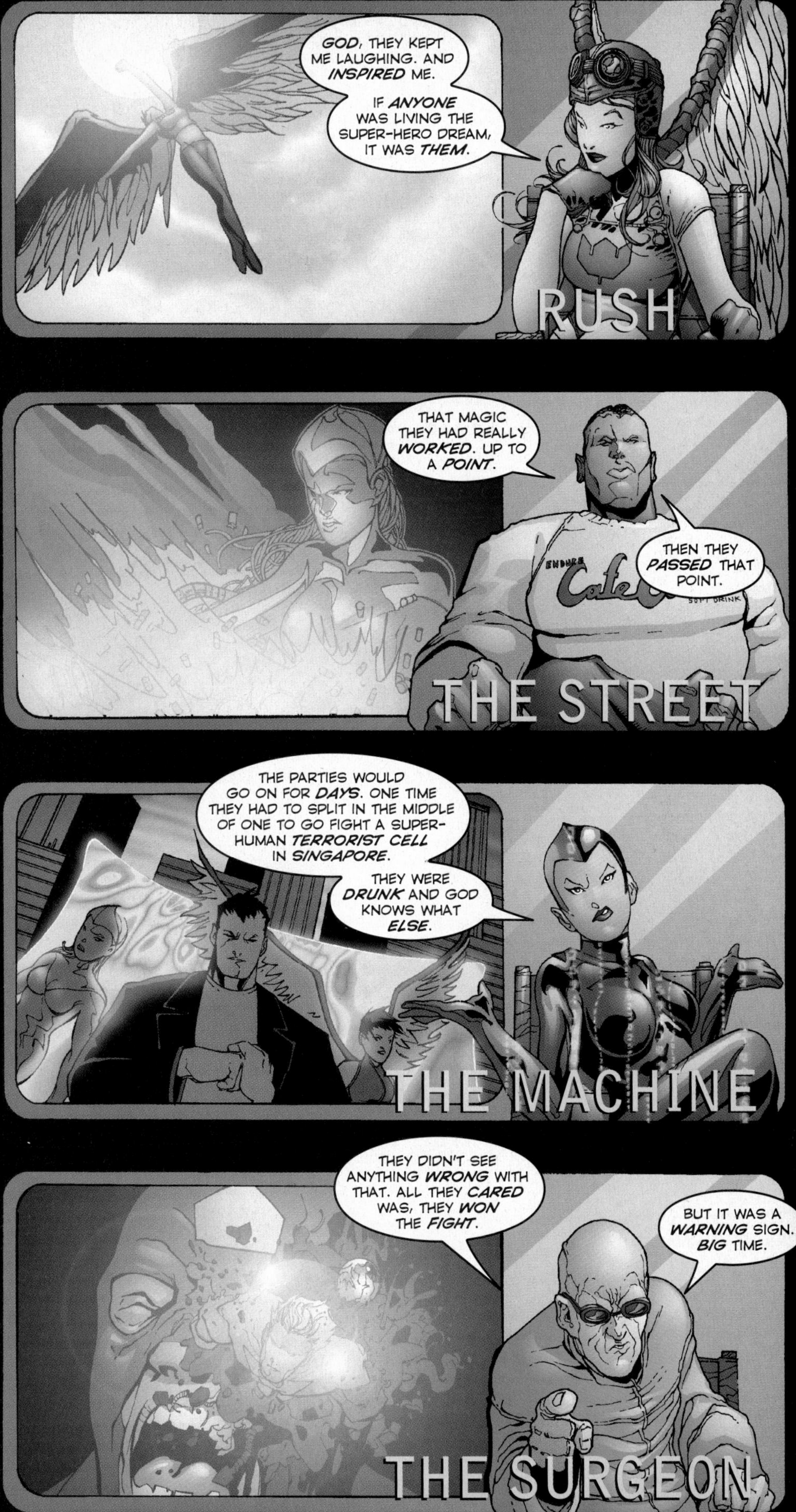
GOD, THEY KEPT ME LAUGHING. AND INSPIRED ME.
IF ANYONE WAS LIVING THE SUPER-HERO DREAM, IT WAS THEM.
RUSH
THAT MAGIC THEY HAD REALLY WORKED. UP TO A POINT.
THEN THEY PASSED THAT POINT.
THE STREET
THE PARTIES WOULD GO ON FOR DAYS. ONE TIME THEY HAD TO SPLIT IN THE MIDDLE OF ONE TO GO FIGHT A SUPER-HUMAN TERRORIST CELL IN SINGAPORE.
THEY WERE DRUNK AND GOD KNOWS WHAT ELSE.
THE MACHINE
THEY DIDN'T SEE ANYTHING WRONG WITH THAT. ALL THEY CARED WAS, THEY WON THE FIGHT.
BUT IT WAS A WARNING SIGN. BIG TIME.
THE SURGEON

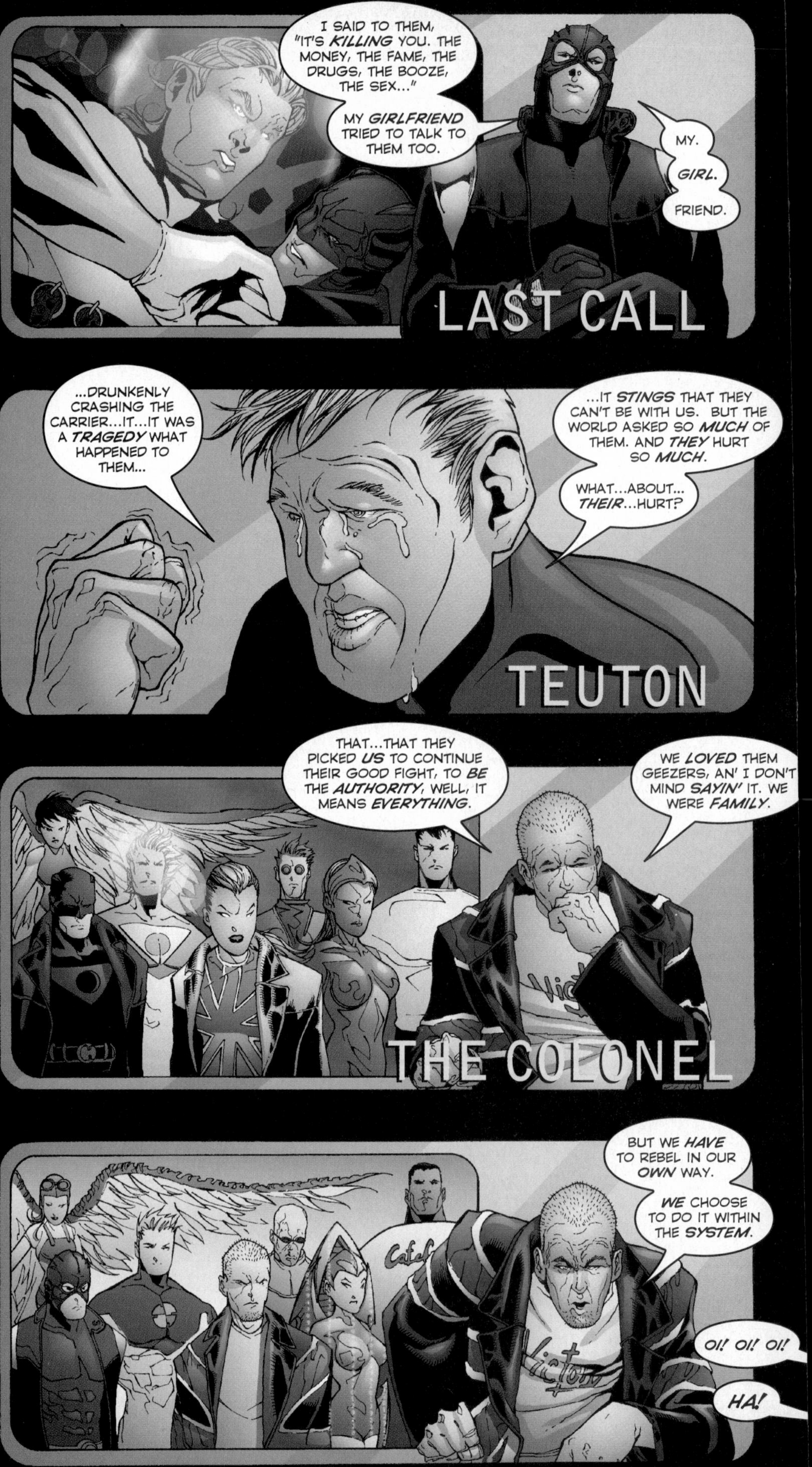
I SAID TO THEM, "IT'S KILLING YOU. THE MONEY, THE FAME, THE DRUGS, THE BOOZE, THE SEX..."
MY GIRLFRIEND TRIED TO TALK TO THEM TOO.
MY.
GIRL.
FRIEND.
LAST CALL
...DRUNKENLY CRASHING THE CARRIER...IT...IT WAS A TRAGEDY WHAT HAPPENED TO THEM...
...IT STINGS THAT THEY CAN'T BE WITH US. BUT THE WORLD ASKED SO MUCH OF THEM. AND THEY HURT SO MUCH.
WHAT...ABOUT... THEIR...HURT?
TEUTON
THAT...THAT THEY PICKED US TO CONTINUE THEIR GOOD FIGHT, TO BE THE AUTHORITY, WELL, IT MEANS EVERYTHING.
WE LOVED THEM GEEZERS, AN' I DON'T MIND SAYIN' IT. WE WERE FAMILY.
THE COLONEL
BUT WE HAVE TO REBEL IN OUR OWN WAY.
WE CHOOSE TO DO IT WITHIN THE SYSTEM.
OI! OI! OI!
HA!

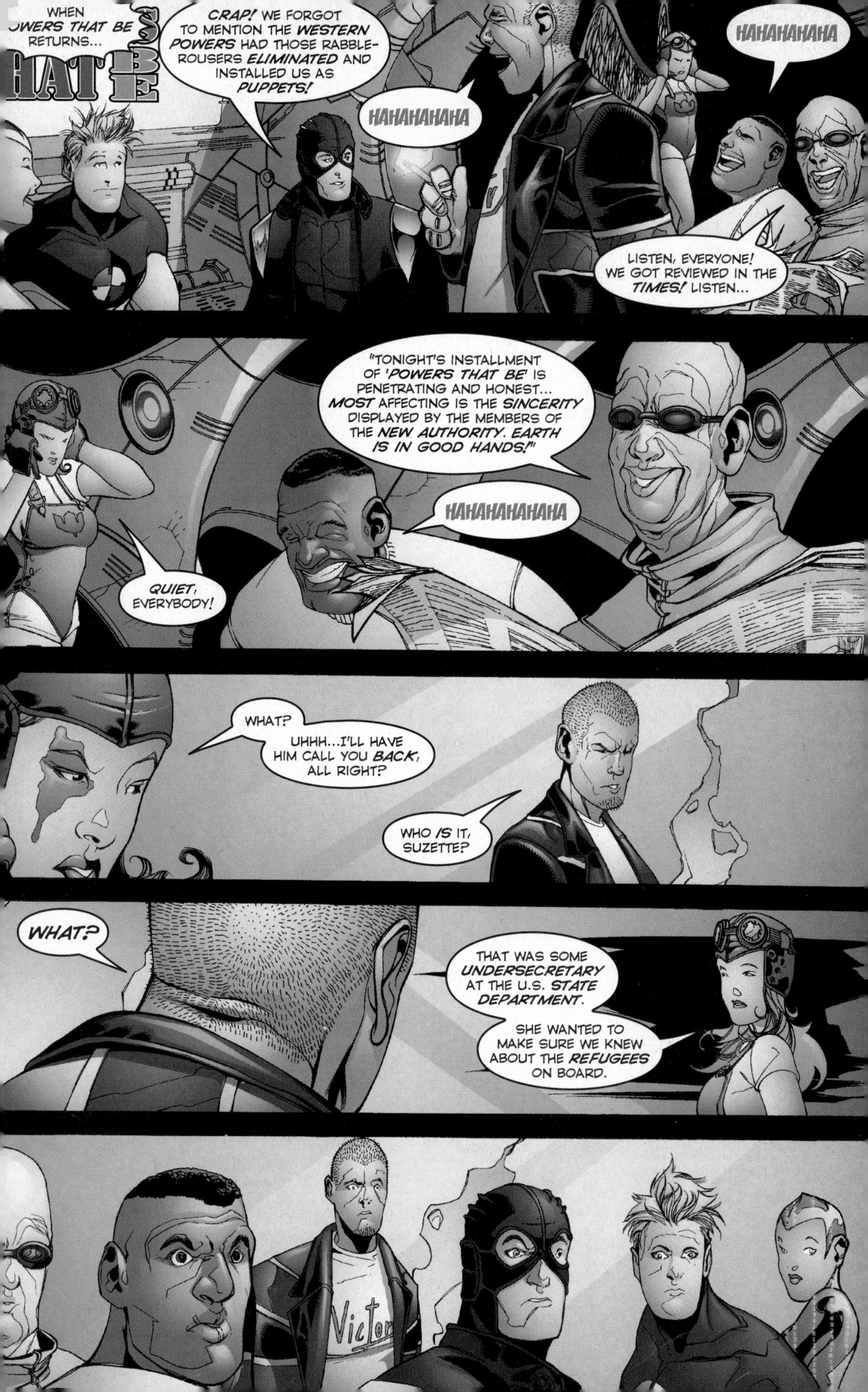
WHEN POWERS THAT BE RETURNS...
THAT BE
CRAP! WE FORGOT TO MENTION THE WESTERN POWERS HAD THOSE RABBLE-ROUSERS ELIMINATED AND INSTALLED US AS PUPPETS!
HAHAHAHAHA
HAHAHAHAHA
LISTEN, EVERYONE! WE GOT REVIEWED IN THE TIMES! LISTEN...
"TONIGHT'S INSTALLMENT OF 'POWERS THAT BE' IS PENETRATING AND HONEST... MOST AFFECTING IS THE SINCERITY DISPLAYED BY THE MEMBERS OF THE NEW AUTHORITY. EARTH IS IN GOOD HANDS!"
HAHAHAHAHAHA
QUIET, EVERYBODY!
WHAT?
UHHH...I'LL HAVE HIM CALL YOU BACK, ALL RIGHT?
WHO IS IT, SUZETTE?
WHAT?
THAT WAS SOME UNDERSECRETARY AT THE U.S. STATE DEPARTMENT.
SHE WANTED TO MAKE SURE WE KNEW ABOUT THE REFUGEES ON BOARD.
Victor

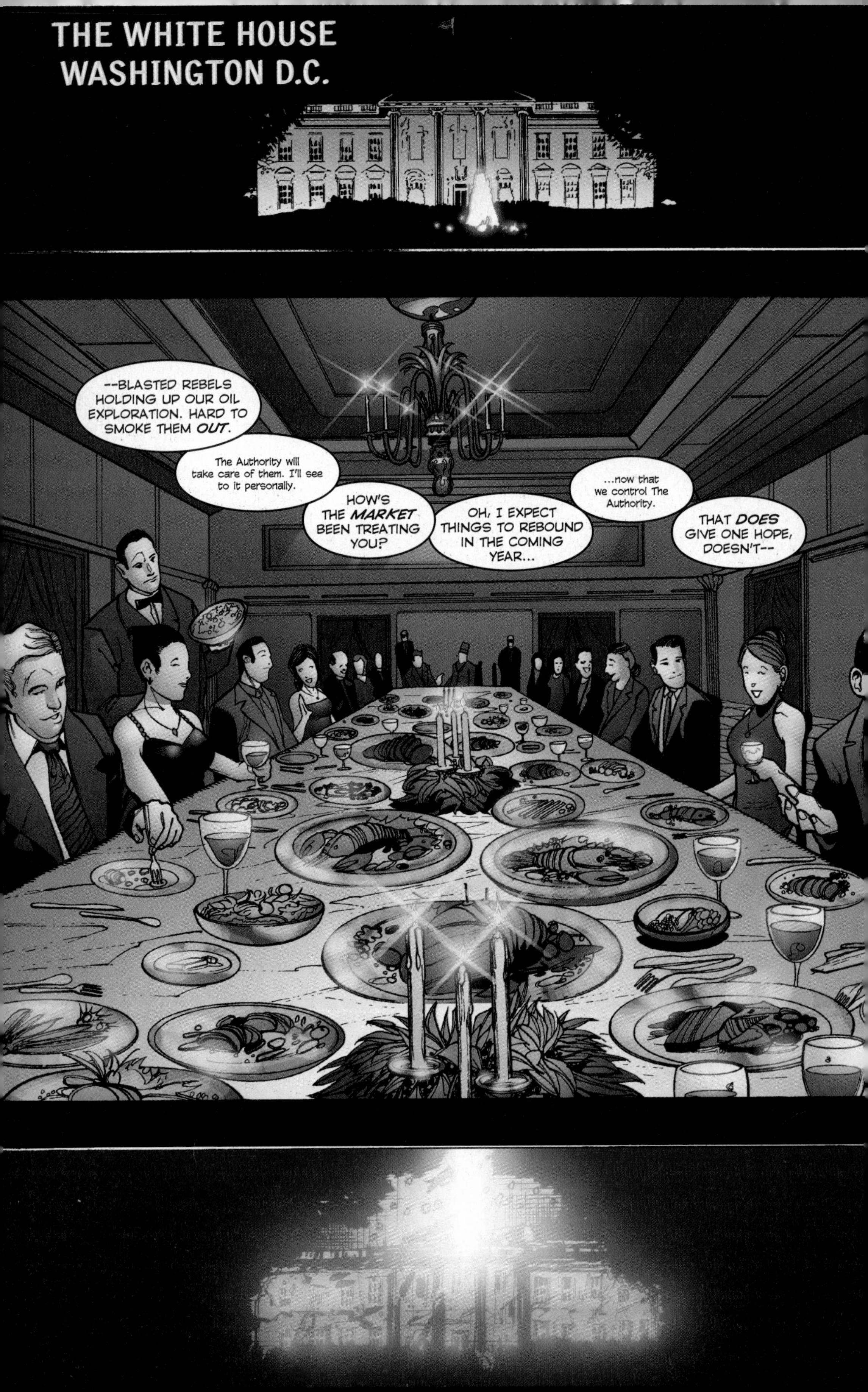
THE WHITE HOUSE
WASHINGTON D.C.
--BLASTED REBELS HOLDING UP OUR OIL EXPLORATION. HARD TO SMOKE THEM OUT.
The Authority will take care of them. I'll see to it personally.
HOW'S THE MARKET BEEN TREATING YOU?
OH, I EXPECT THINGS TO REBOUND IN THE COMING YEAR...
...now that we control The Authority.
THAT DOES GIVE ONE HOPE, DOESN'T--

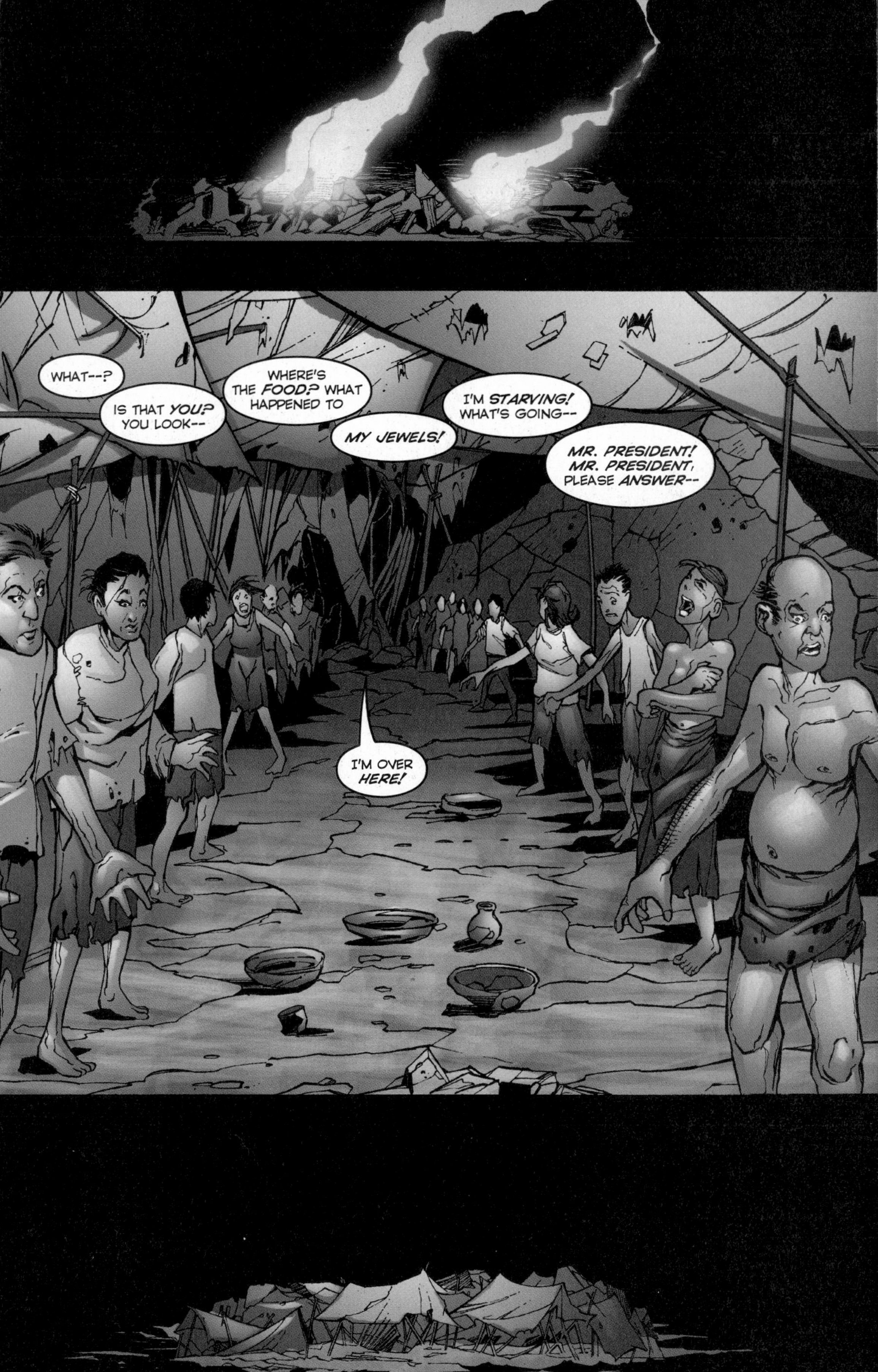

WHAT--?
IS THAT YOU? YOU LOOK--
WHERE'S THE FOOD? WHAT HAPPENED TO
MY JEWELS!
I'M STARVING! WHAT'S GOING--
MR. PRESIDENT! MR. PRESIDENT! PLEASE ANSWER--
I'M OVER HERE!

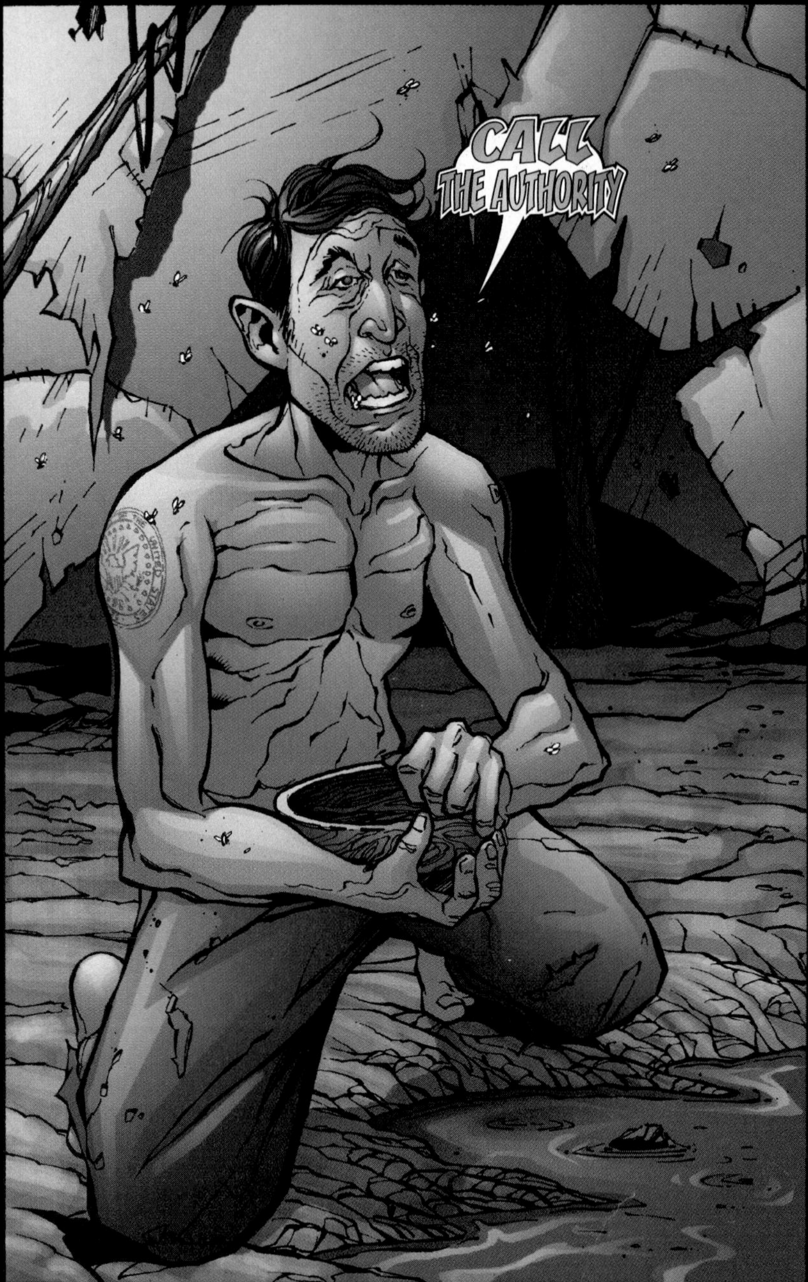
CALL THE AUTHORITY

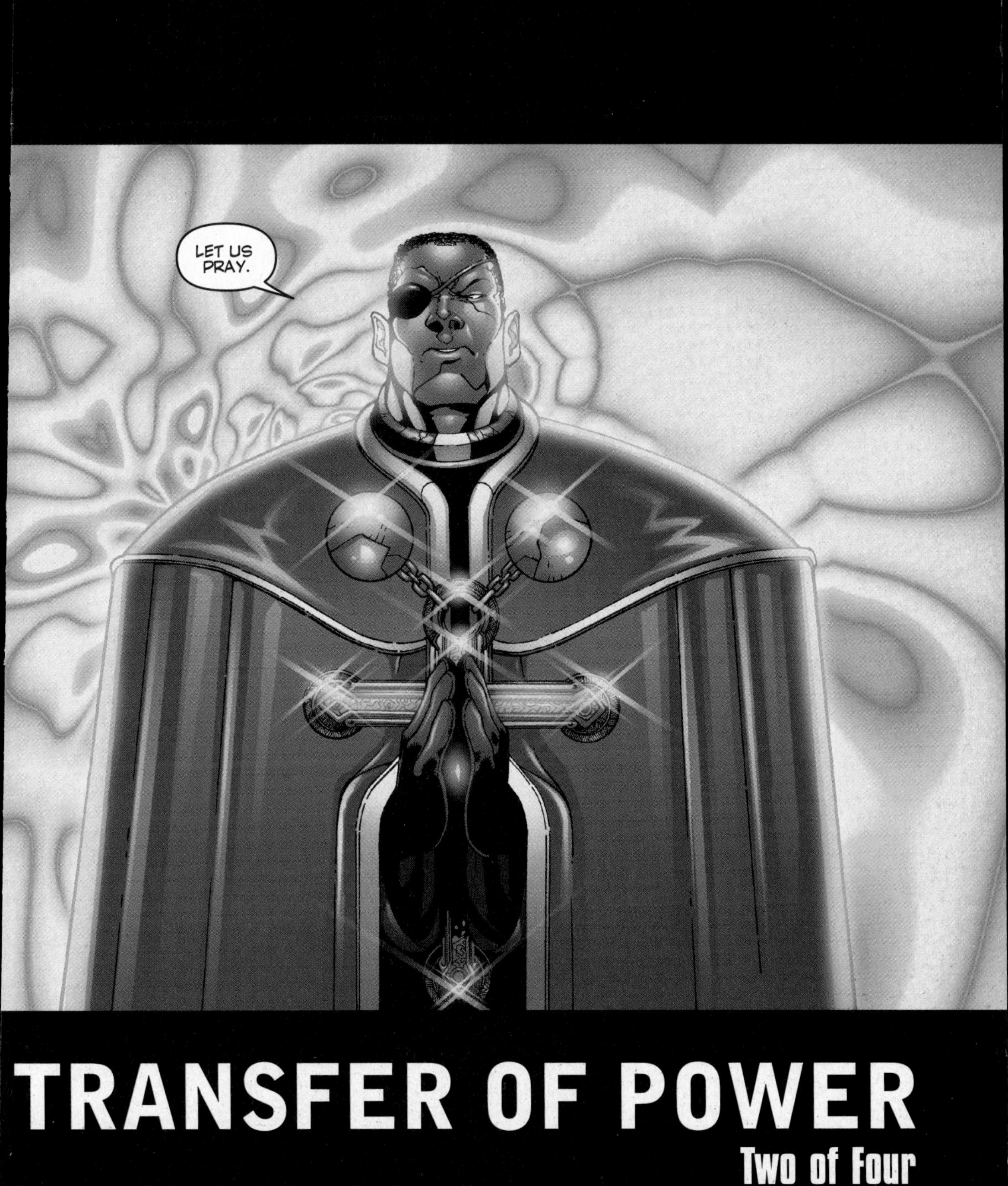
LET US PRAY.

TRANSFER OF POWER

Two of Four

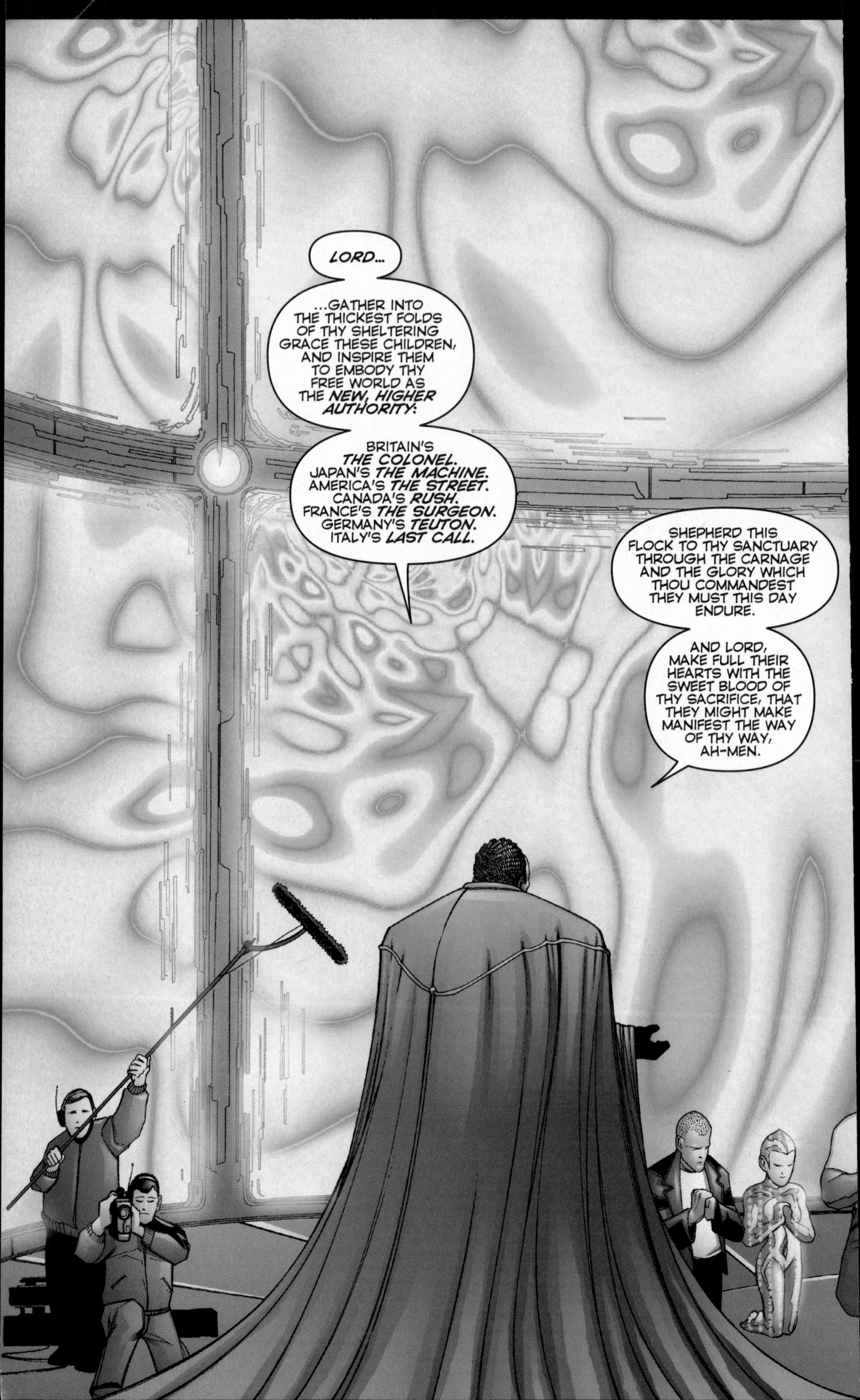
LORD...
...GATHER INTO THE THICKEST FOLDS OF THY SHELTERING GRACE THESE CHILDREN, AND INSPIRE THEM TO EMBODY THY FREE WORLD AS THE *NEW, HIGHER AUTHORITY*:
BRITAIN'S *THE COLONEL*. JAPAN'S *THE MACHINE*. AMERICA'S *THE STREET*. CANADA'S *RUSH*. FRANCE'S *THE SURGEON*. GERMANY'S *TEUTON*. ITALY'S *LAST CALL*.
SHEPHERD THIS FLOCK TO THY SANCTUARY THROUGH THE CARNAGE AND THE GLORY WHICH THOU COMMANDEST THEY MUST THIS DAY ENDURE.
AND LORD, MAKE FULL THEIR HEARTS WITH THE SWEET BLOOD OF THY SACRIFICE, THAT THEY MIGHT MAKE MANIFEST THE WAY OF THY WAY, AH-MEN.

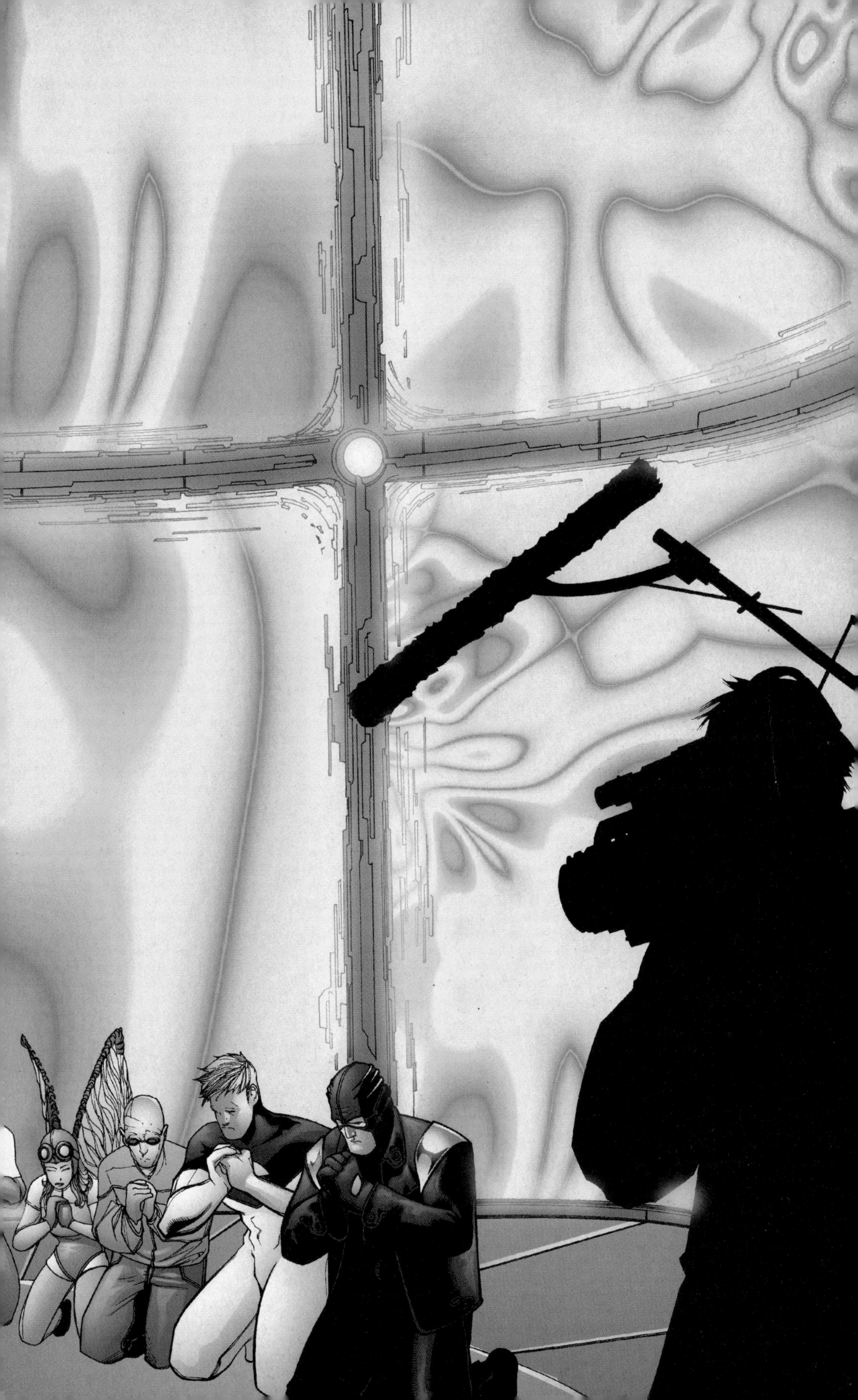

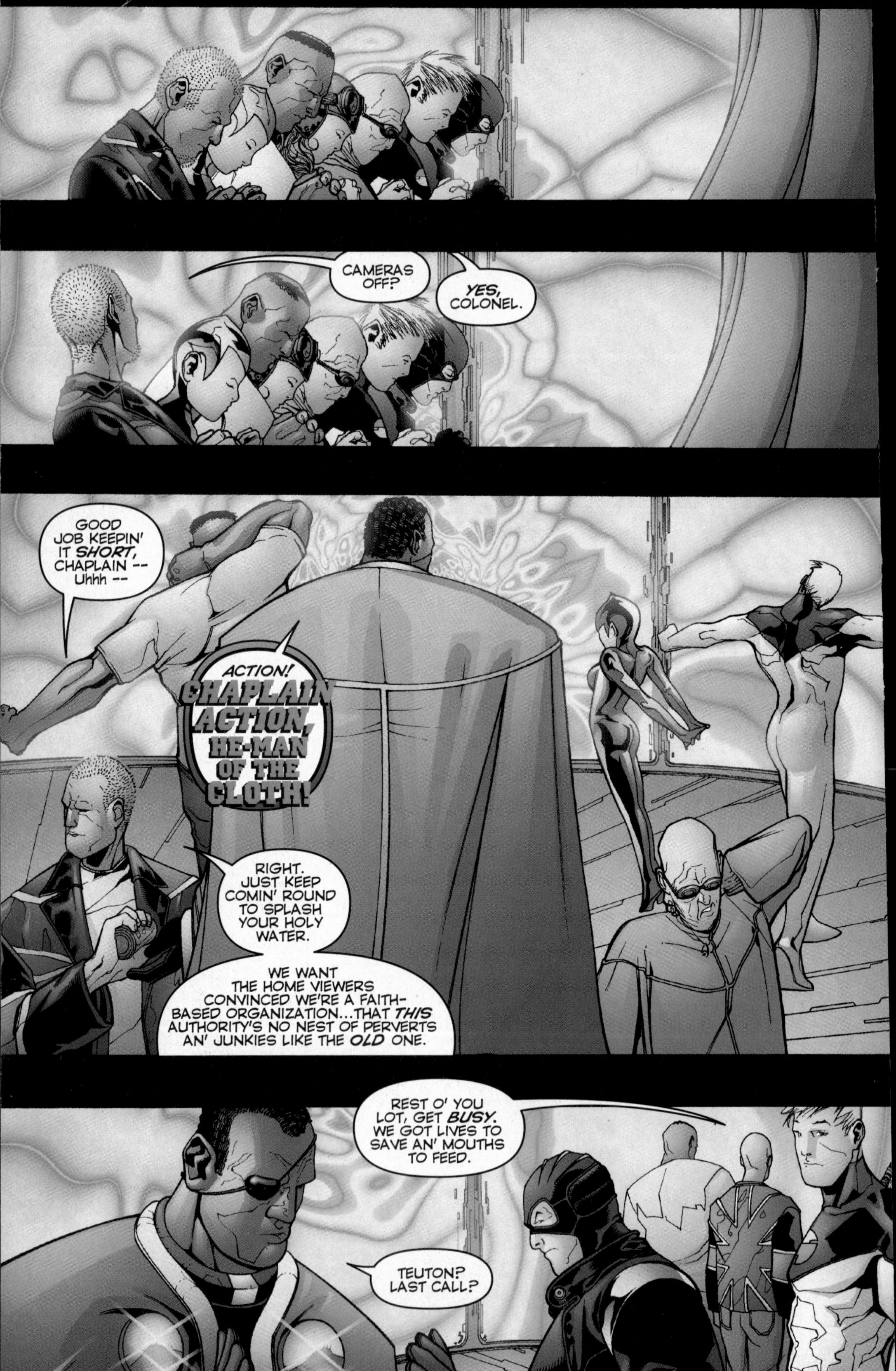
CAMERAS OFF?
YES, COLONEL.
GOOD JOB KEEPIN' IT SHORT, CHAPLAIN -- Uhhh --
ACTION! CHAPLAIN ACTION, HE-MAN OF THE CLOTH!
RIGHT. JUST KEEP COMIN' ROUND TO SPLASH YOUR HOLY WATER.
WE WANT THE HOME VIEWERS CONVINCED WE'RE A FAITH-BASED ORGANIZATION...THAT THIS AUTHORITY'S NO NEST OF PERVERTS AN' JUNKIES LIKE THE OLD ONE.
REST O' YOU LOT, GET BUSY. WE GOT LIVES TO SAVE AN' MOUTHS TO FEED.
TEUTON? LAST CALL?

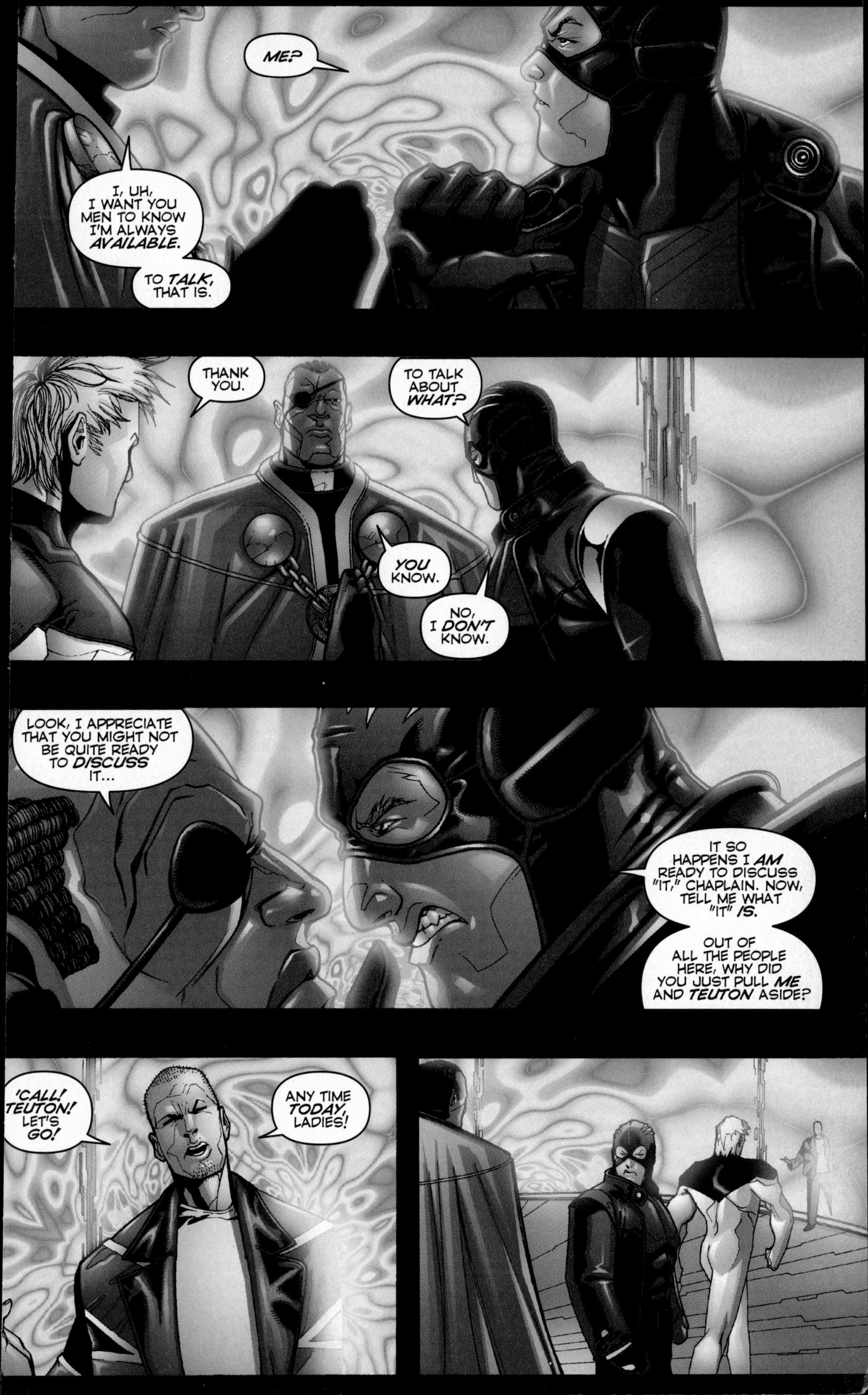
ME?
I, UH, I WANT YOU MEN TO KNOW I'M ALWAYS *AVAILABLE*.
TO *TALK*, THAT IS.
THANK YOU.
TO TALK ABOUT *WHAT?*
YOU KNOW.
NO, I *DON'T* KNOW.
LOOK, I APPRECIATE THAT YOU MIGHT NOT BE QUITE READY TO *DISCUSS* IT...
IT SO HAPPENS I *AM* READY TO DISCUSS "IT," CHAPLAIN. NOW, TELL ME WHAT "IT" *IS*.
OUT OF ALL THE PEOPLE HERE, WHY DID YOU JUST PULL *ME* AND *TEUTON* ASIDE?
'CALL! TEUTON! LET'S *GO!*
ANY TIME *TODAY*, LADIES!

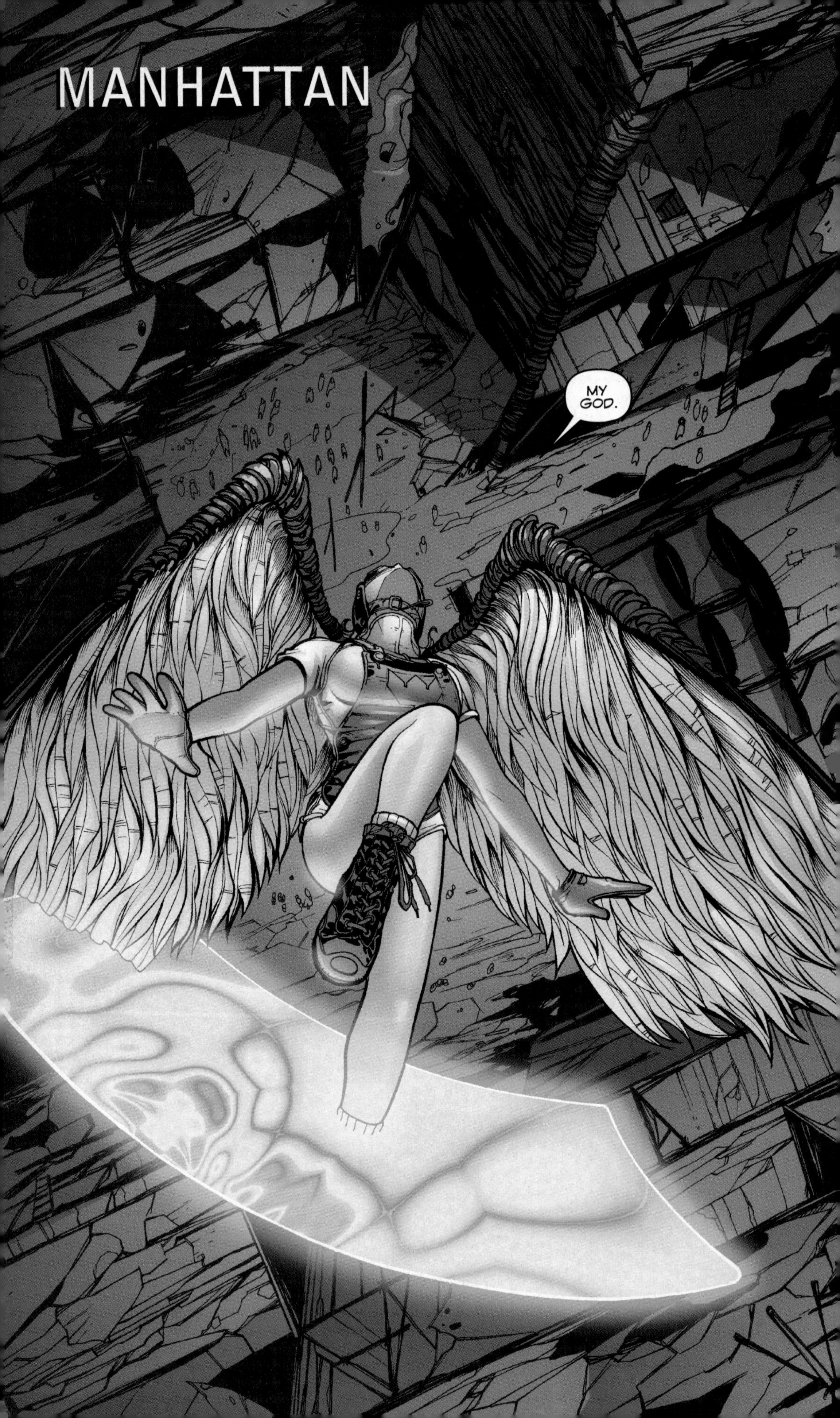
MANHATTAN
MY GOD.

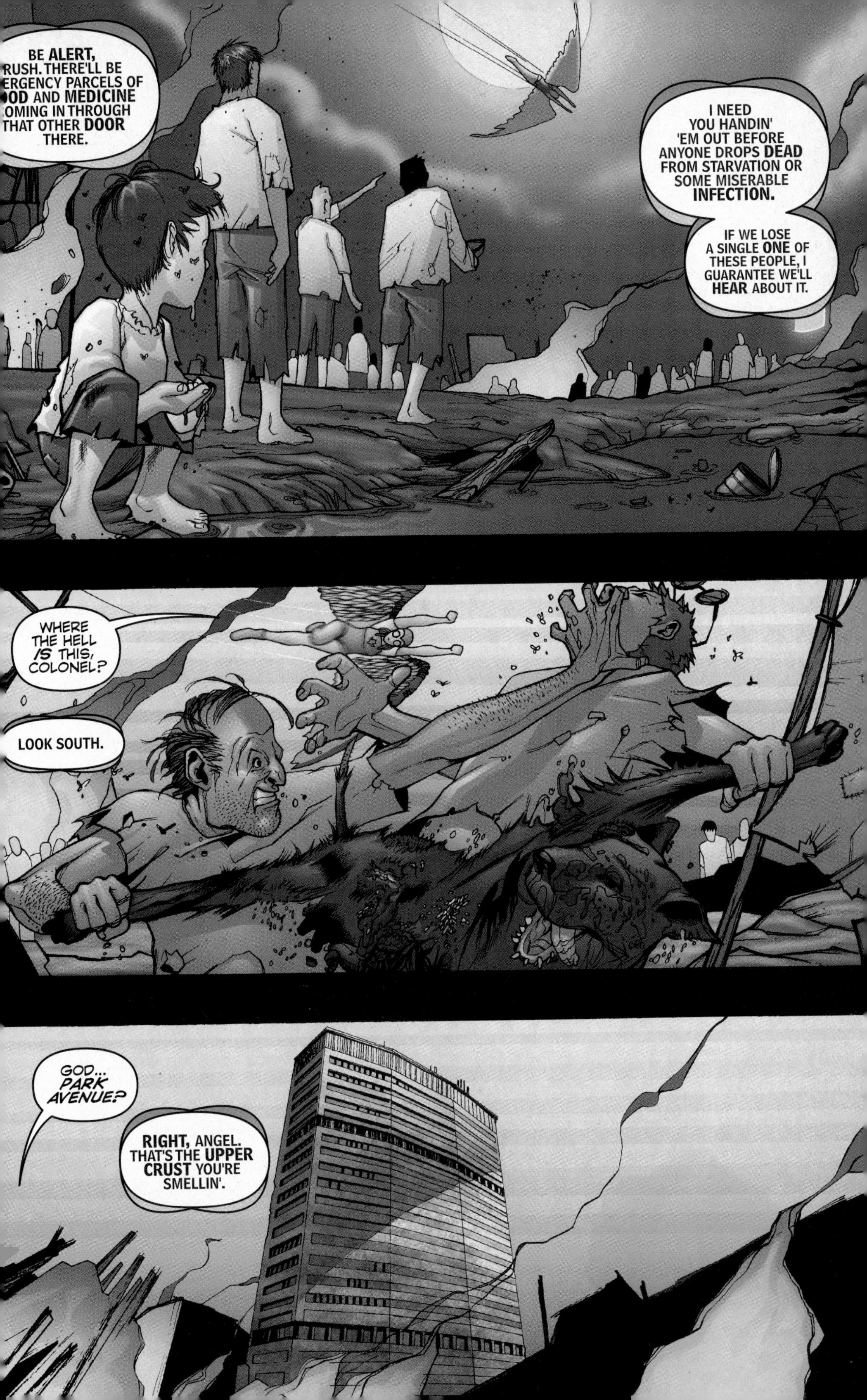

BE ALERT, RUSH. THERE'LL BE ERGENCY PARCELS OF OOD AND MEDICINE OMING IN THROUGH THAT OTHER DOOR THERE.
I NEED YOU HANDIN' 'EM OUT BEFORE ANYONE DROPS DEAD FROM STARVATION OR SOME MISERABLE INFECTION.
IF WE LOSE A SINGLE ONE OF THESE PEOPLE, I GUARANTEE WE'LL HEAR ABOUT IT.
WHERE THE HELL IS THIS, COLONEL?
LOOK SOUTH.
GOD... PARK AVENUE?
RIGHT, ANGEL. THAT'S THE UPPER CRUST YOU'RE SMELLIN'.

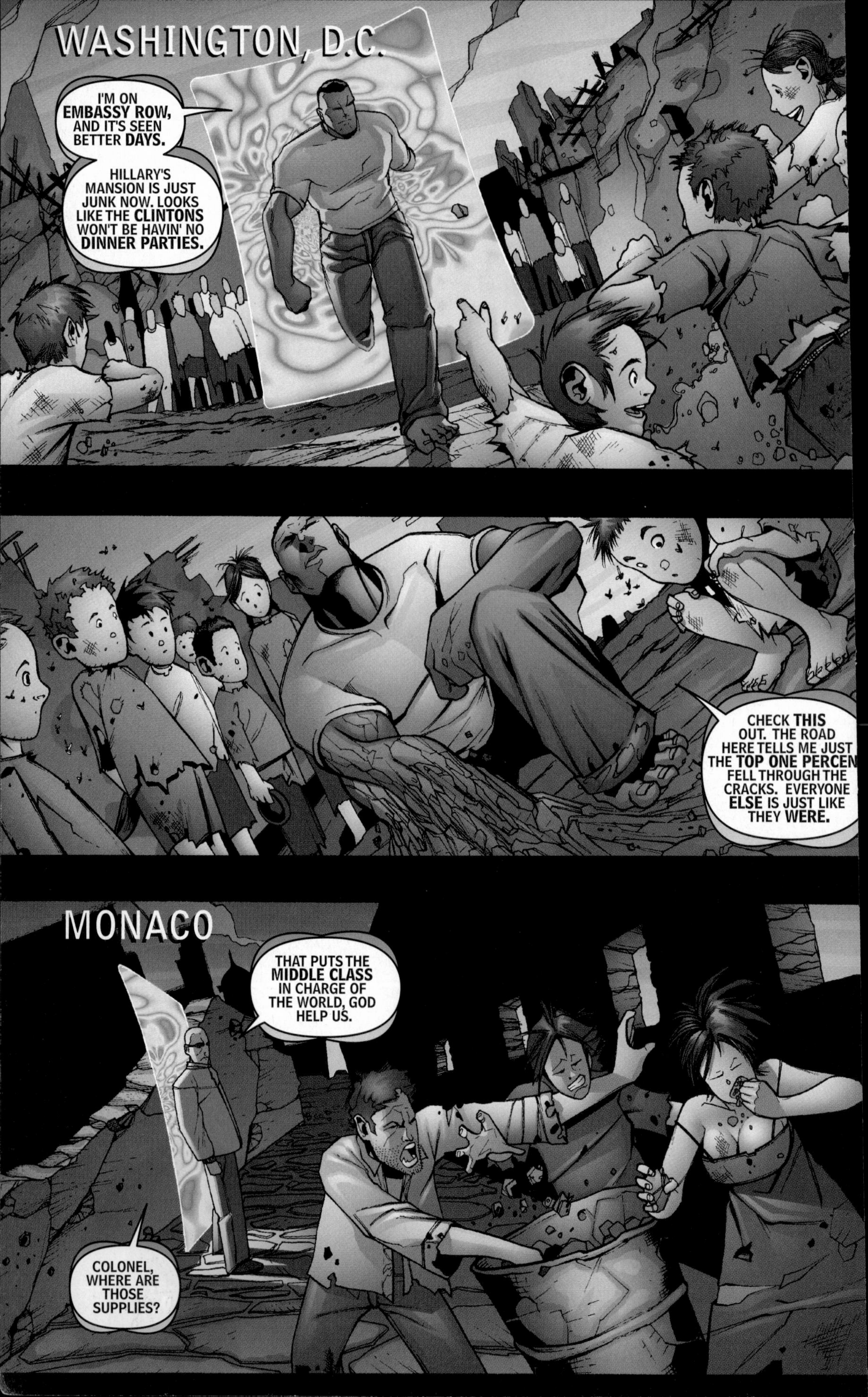
WASHINGTON, D.C.
I'M ON EMBASSY ROW, AND IT'S SEEN BETTER DAYS.
HILLARY'S MANSION IS JUST JUNK NOW. LOOKS LIKE THE CLINTONS WON'T BE HAVIN' NO DINNER PARTIES.
CHECK THIS OUT. THE ROAD HERE TELLS ME JUST THE TOP ONE PERCEN FELL THROUGH THE CRACKS. EVERYONE ELSE IS JUST LIKE THEY WERE.
MONACO
THAT PUTS THE MIDDLE CLASS IN CHARGE OF THE WORLD, GOD HELP US.
COLONEL, WHERE ARE THOSE SUPPLIES?

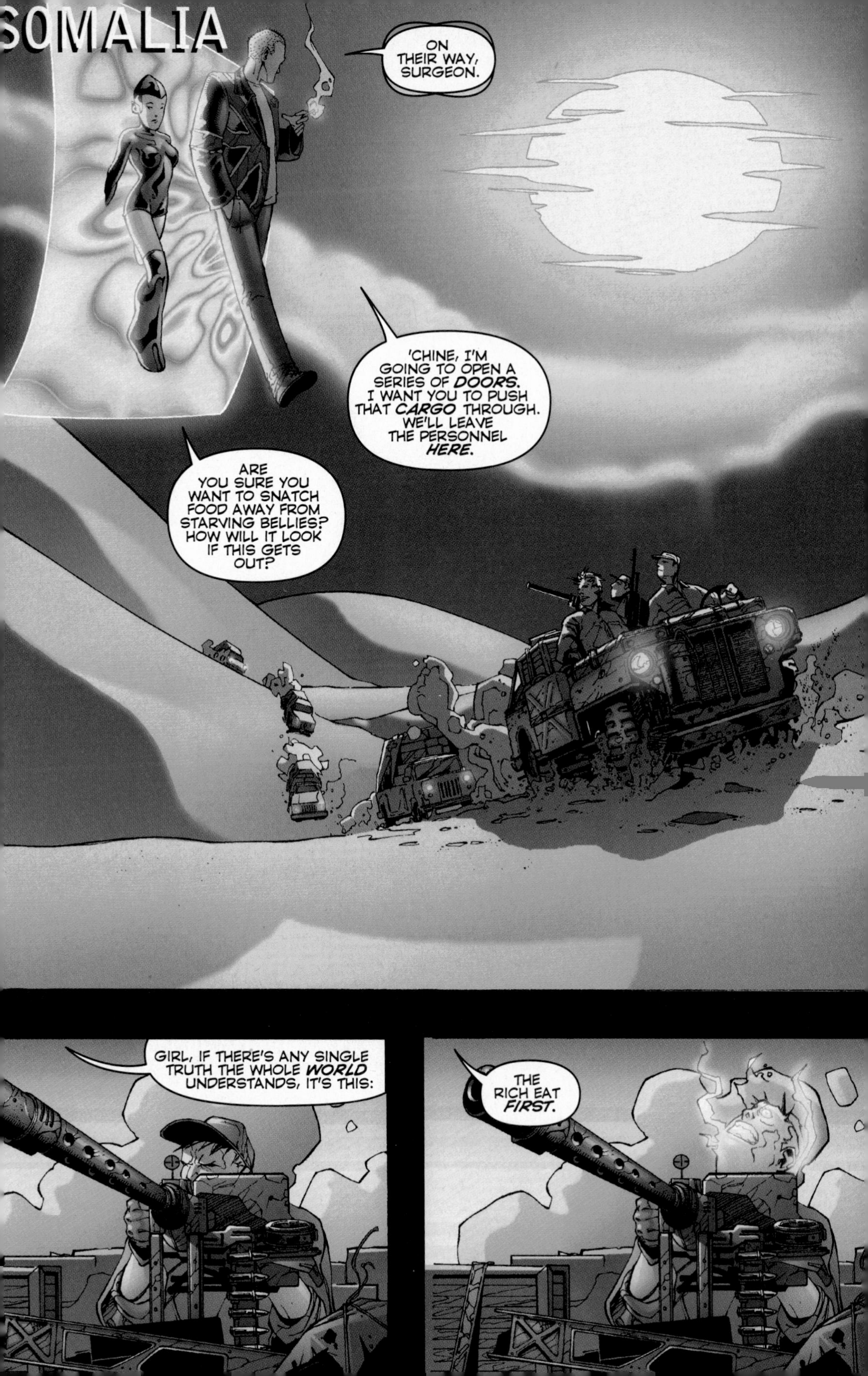
SOMALIA
ON THEIR WAY, SURGEON.
'CHINE, I'M GOING TO OPEN A SERIES OF DOORS. I WANT YOU TO PUSH THAT CARGO THROUGH. WE'LL LEAVE THE PERSONNEL HERE.
ARE YOU SURE YOU WANT TO SNATCH FOOD AWAY FROM STARVING BELLIES? HOW WILL IT LOOK IF THIS GETS OUT?
GIRL, IF THERE'S ANY SINGLE TRUTH THE WHOLE WORLD UNDERSTANDS, IT'S THIS:
THE RICH EAT FIRST.

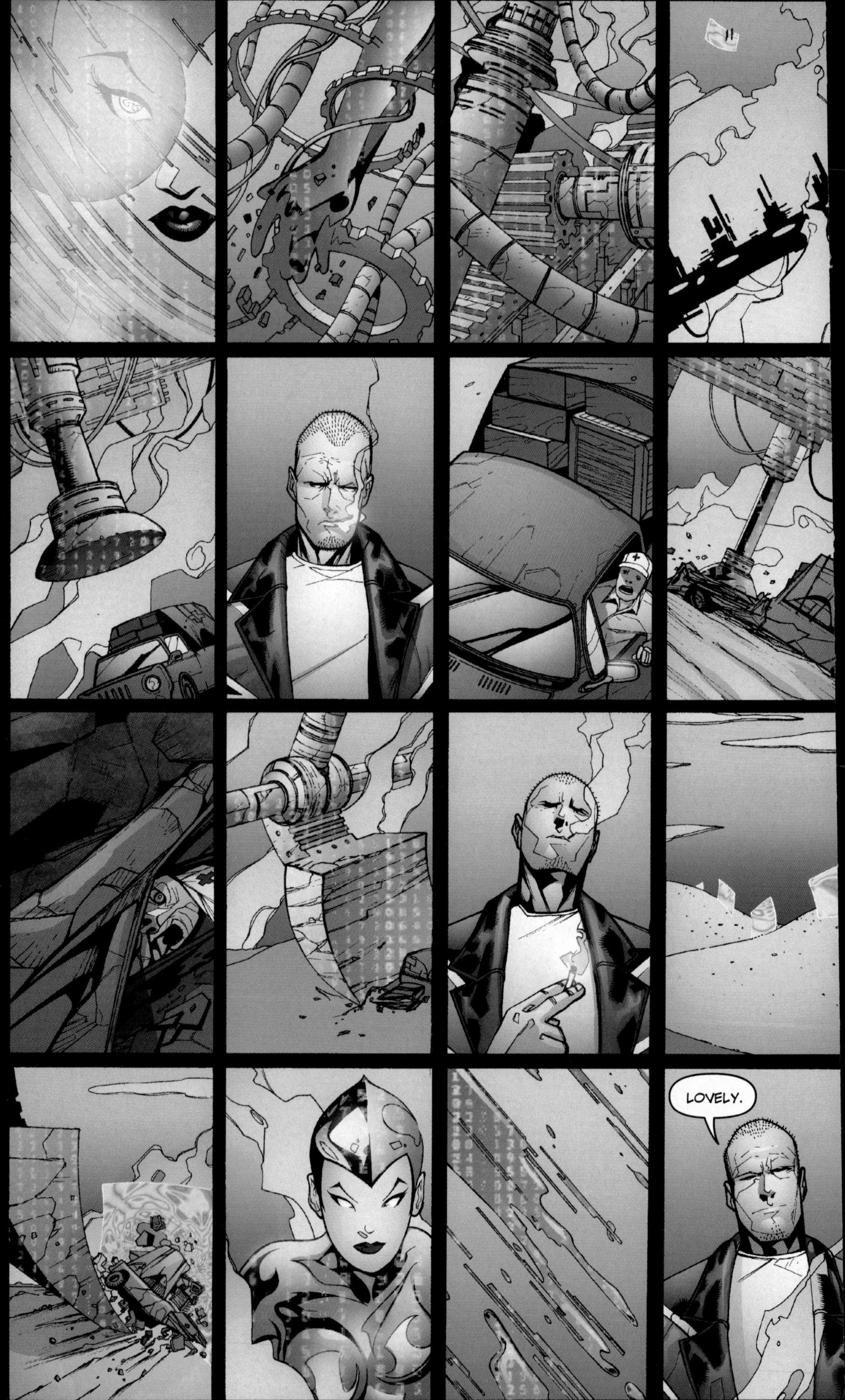
LOVELY.

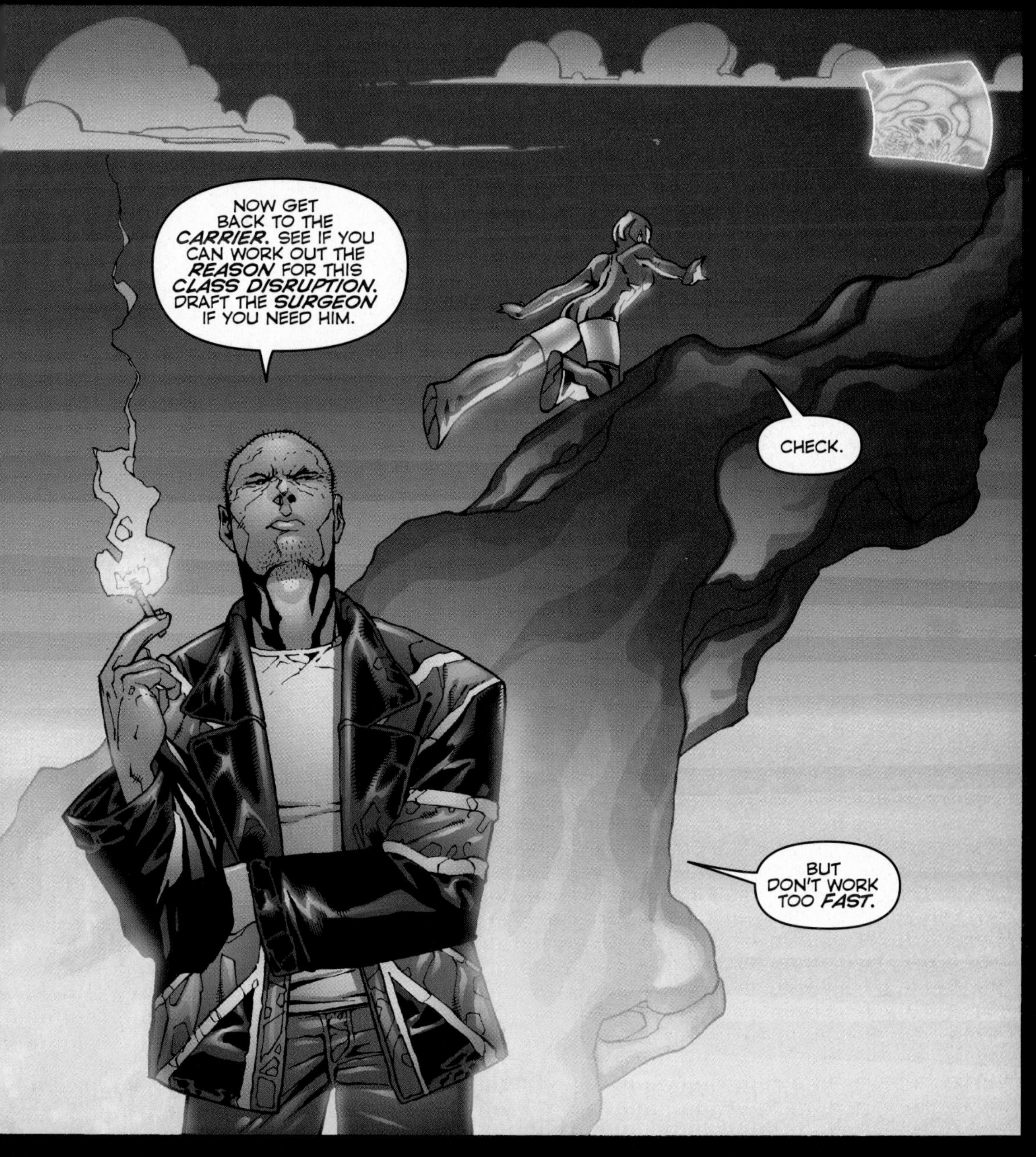
NOW GET BACK TO THE CARRIER. SEE IF YOU CAN WORK OUT THE REASON FOR THIS CLASS DISRUPTION. DRAFT THE SURGEON IF YOU NEED HIM.
CHECK.
BUT DON'T WORK TOO FAST.

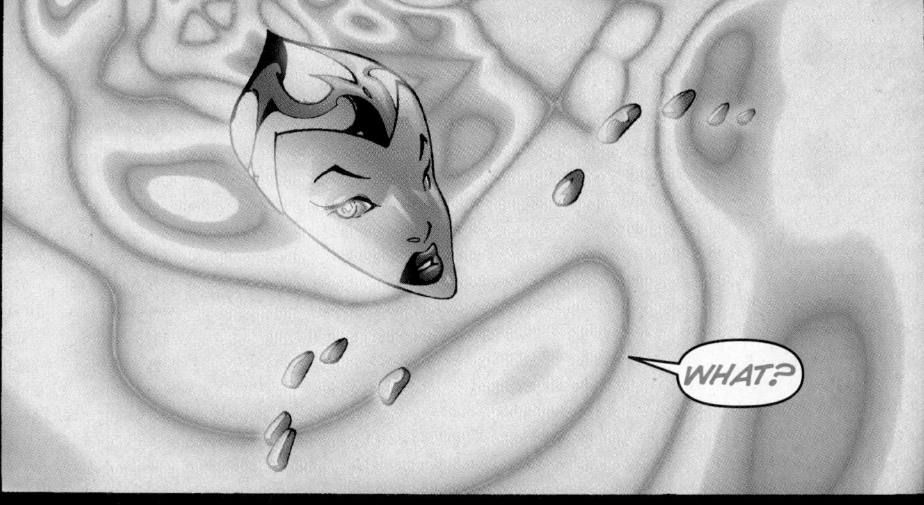
WHAT?

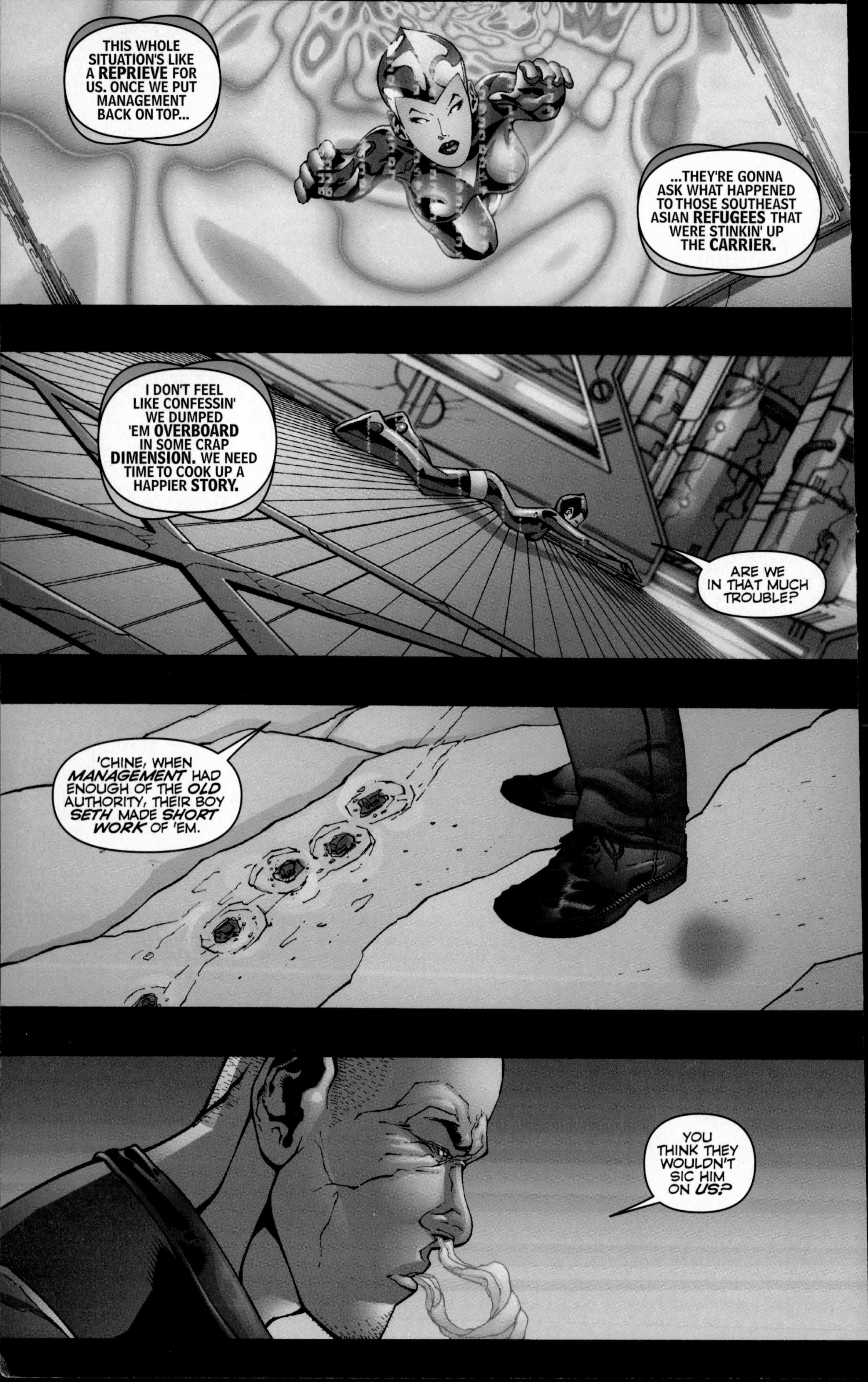
THIS WHOLE SITUATION'S LIKE A REPRIEVE FOR US. ONCE WE PUT MANAGEMENT BACK ON TOP...
...THEY'RE GONNA ASK WHAT HAPPENED TO THOSE SOUTHEAST ASIAN REFUGEES THAT WERE STINKIN' UP THE CARRIER.
I DON'T FEEL LIKE CONFESSIN' WE DUMPED 'EM OVERBOARD IN SOME CRAP DIMENSION. WE NEED TIME TO COOK UP A HAPPIER STORY.
ARE WE IN THAT MUCH TROUBLE?
'CHINE, WHEN MANAGEMENT HAD ENOUGH OF THE OLD AUTHORITY, THEIR BOY SETH MADE SHORT WORK OF 'EM.
YOU THINK THEY WOULDN'T SIC HIM ON US?

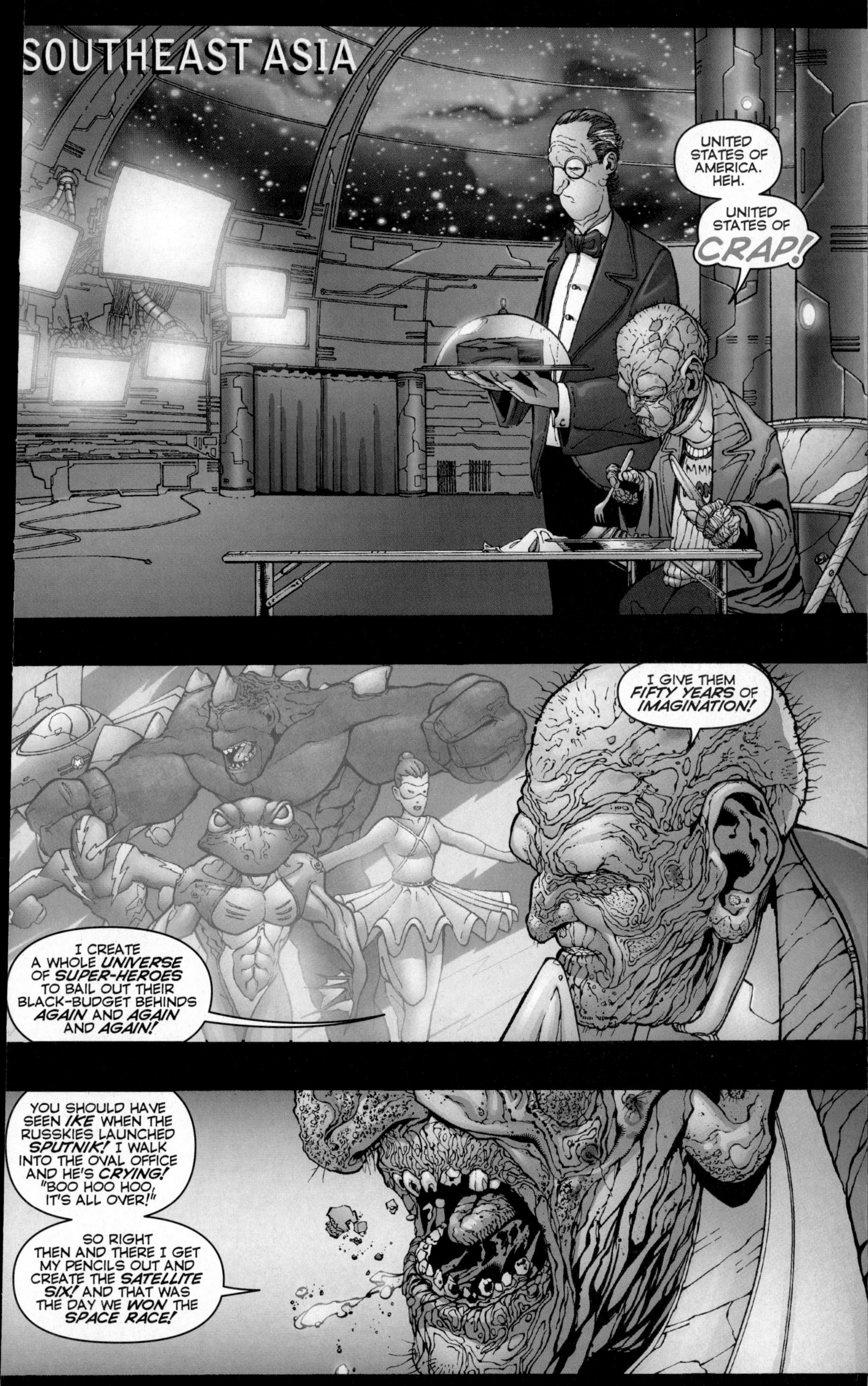
SOUTHEAST ASIA
UNITED STATES OF AMERICA. HEH.
UNITED STATES OF CRAP!
I GIVE THEM FIFTY YEARS OF IMAGINATION!
I CREATE A WHOLE UNIVERSE OF SUPER-HEROES TO BAIL OUT THEIR BLACK-BUDGET BEHINDS AGAIN AND AGAIN AND AGAIN!
YOU SHOULD HAVE SEEN IKE WHEN THE RUSSKIES LAUNCHED SPUTNIK! I WALK INTO THE OVAL OFFICE AND HE'S CRYING! "BOO HOO HOO, IT'S ALL OVER!"
SO RIGHT THEN AND THERE I GET MY PENCILS OUT AND CREATE THE SATELLITE SIX! AND THAT WAS THE DAY WE WON THE SPACE RACE!

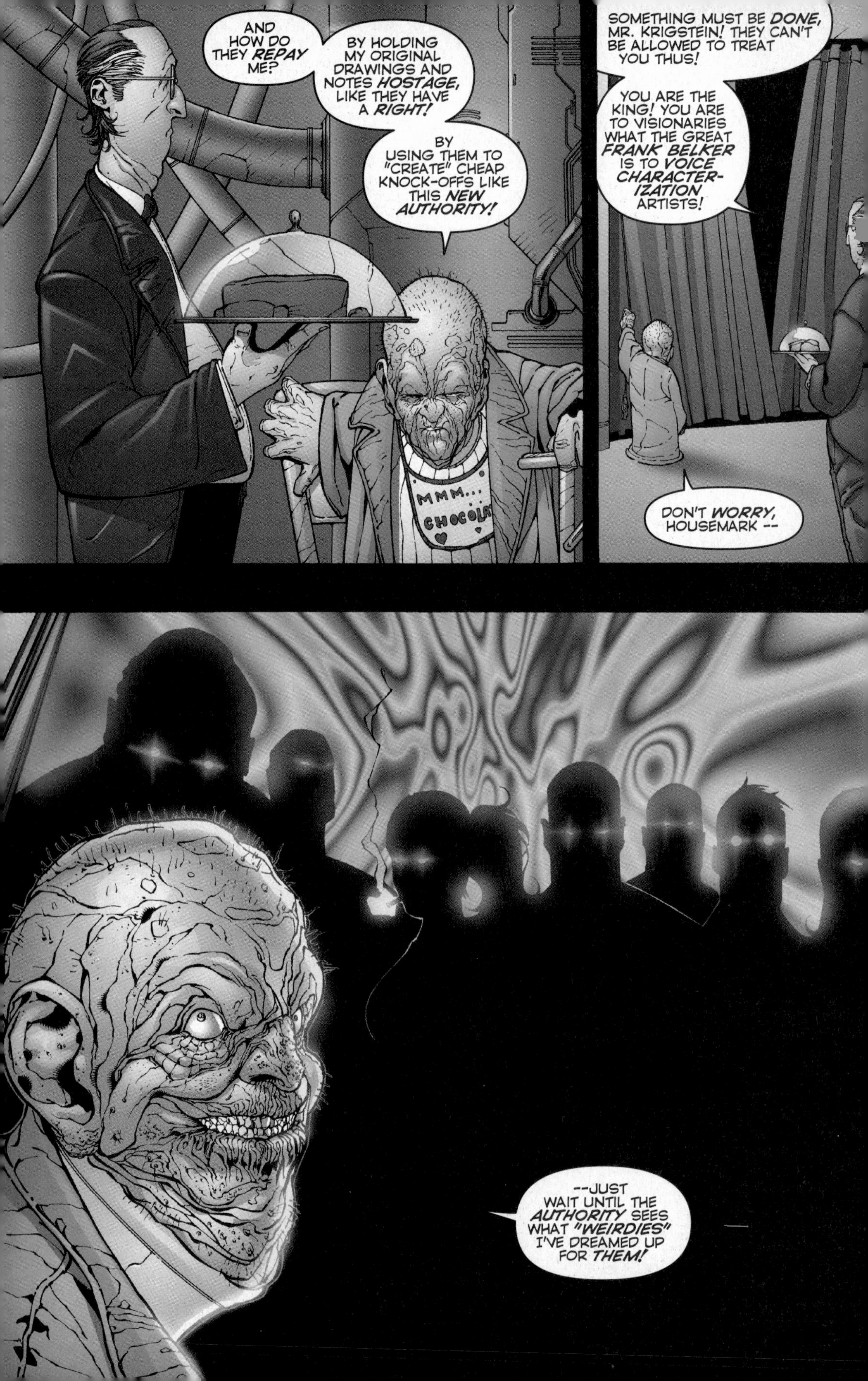
AND HOW DO THEY *REPAY* ME?
BY HOLDING MY ORIGINAL DRAWINGS AND NOTES *HOSTAGE,* LIKE THEY HAVE A *RIGHT!*
BY USING THEM TO "CREATE" CHEAP KNOCK-OFFS LIKE THIS *NEW AUTHORITY!*
MMM... CHOCOLA
SOMETHING MUST BE *DONE,* MR. KRIGSTEIN! THEY CAN'T BE ALLOWED TO TREAT YOU THUS!
YOU ARE THE KING! YOU ARE TO VISIONARIES WHAT THE GREAT *FRANK BELKER* IS TO *VOICE CHARACTERIZATION* ARTISTS!
DON'T *WORRY,* HOUSEMARK --
--JUST WAIT UNTIL THE *AUTHORITY* SEES WHAT *"WEIRDIES"* I'VE DREAMED UP FOR *THEM!*

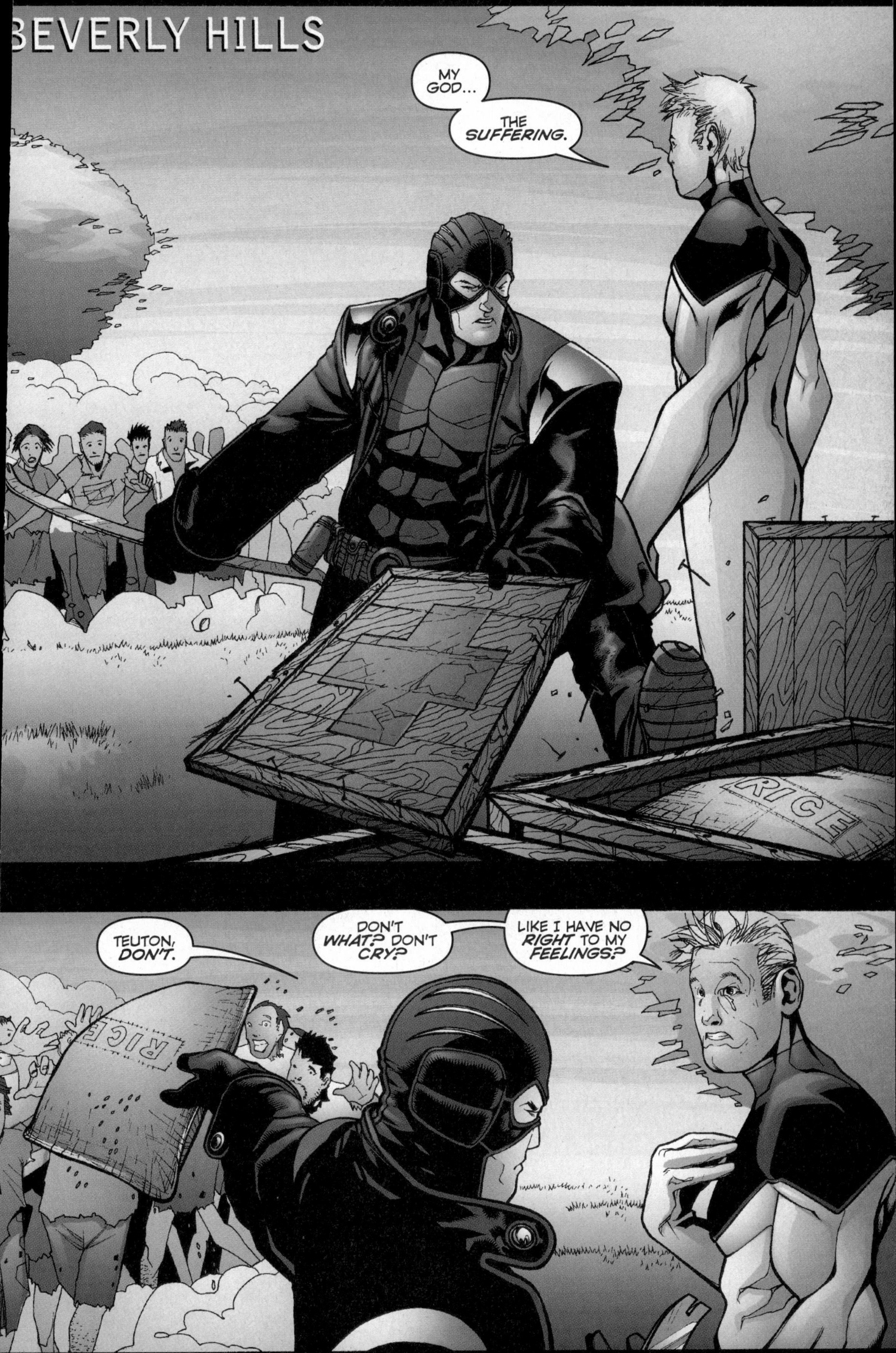
BEVERLY HILLS
MY GOD...
THE SUFFERING.
RICE
TEUTON, DON'T.
DON'T WHAT? DON'T CRY?
LIKE I HAVE NO RIGHT TO MY FEELINGS?
RICE

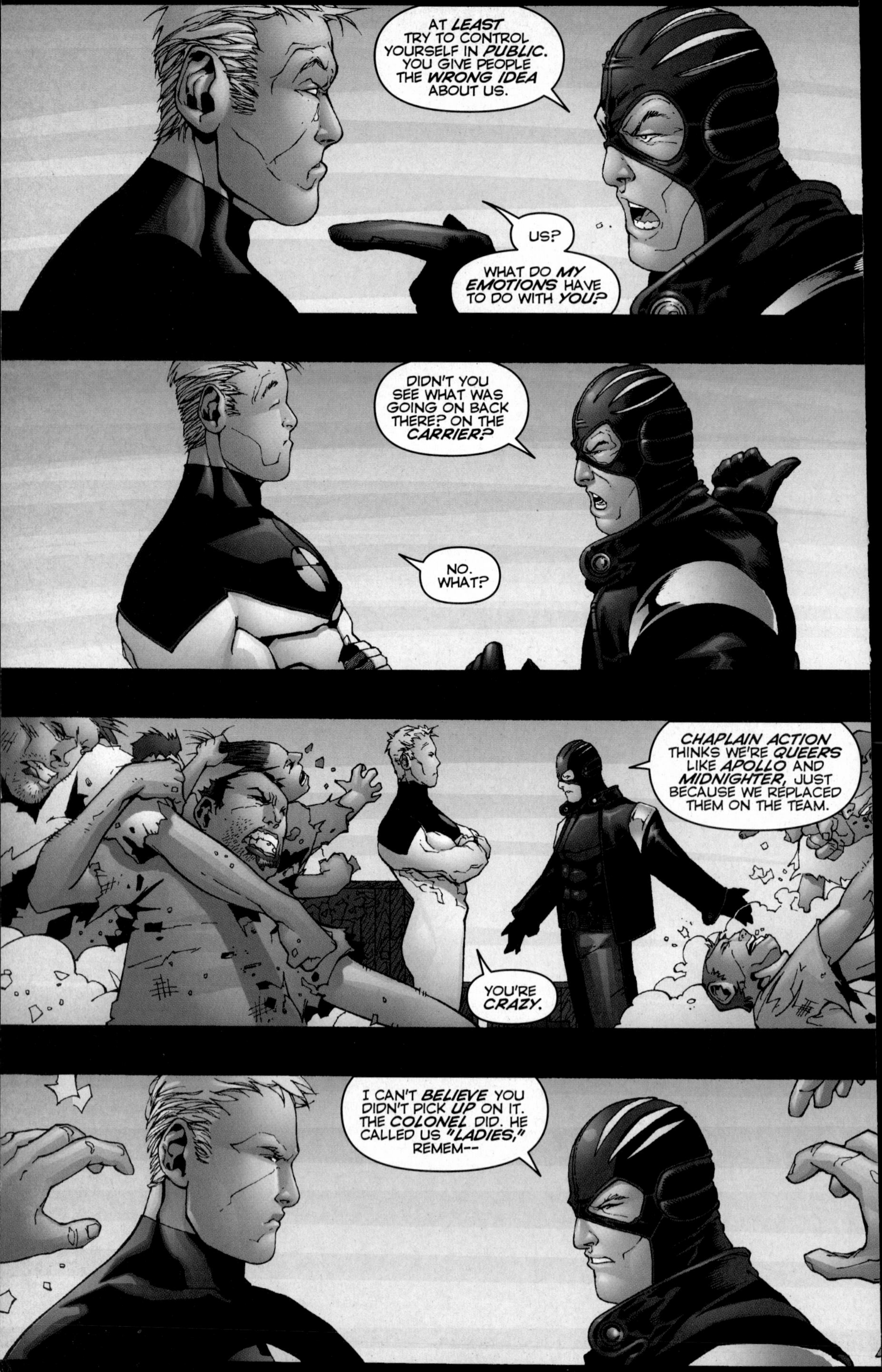
AT LEAST TRY TO CONTROL YOURSELF IN PUBLIC. YOU GIVE PEOPLE THE WRONG IDEA ABOUT US.
US?
WHAT DO MY EMOTIONS HAVE TO DO WITH YOU?
DIDN'T YOU SEE WHAT WAS GOING ON BACK THERE? ON THE CARRIER?
NO. WHAT?
CHAPLAIN ACTION THINKS WE'RE QUEERS LIKE APOLLO AND MIDNIGHTER, JUST BECAUSE WE REPLACED THEM ON THE TEAM.
YOU'RE CRAZY.
I CAN'T BELIEVE YOU DIDN'T PICK UP ON IT. THE COLONEL DID. HE CALLED US "LADIES," REMEM--

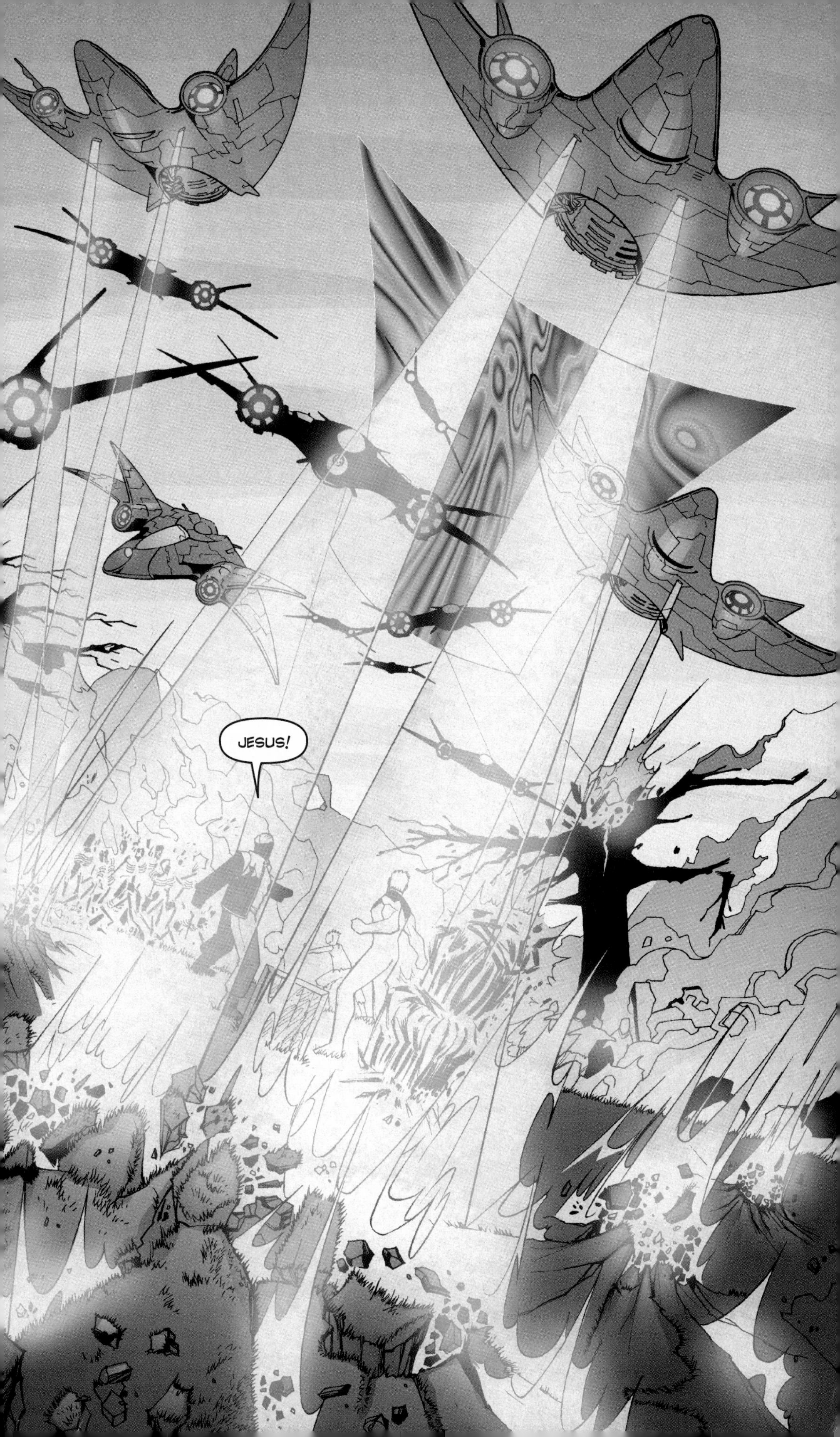
JESUS!

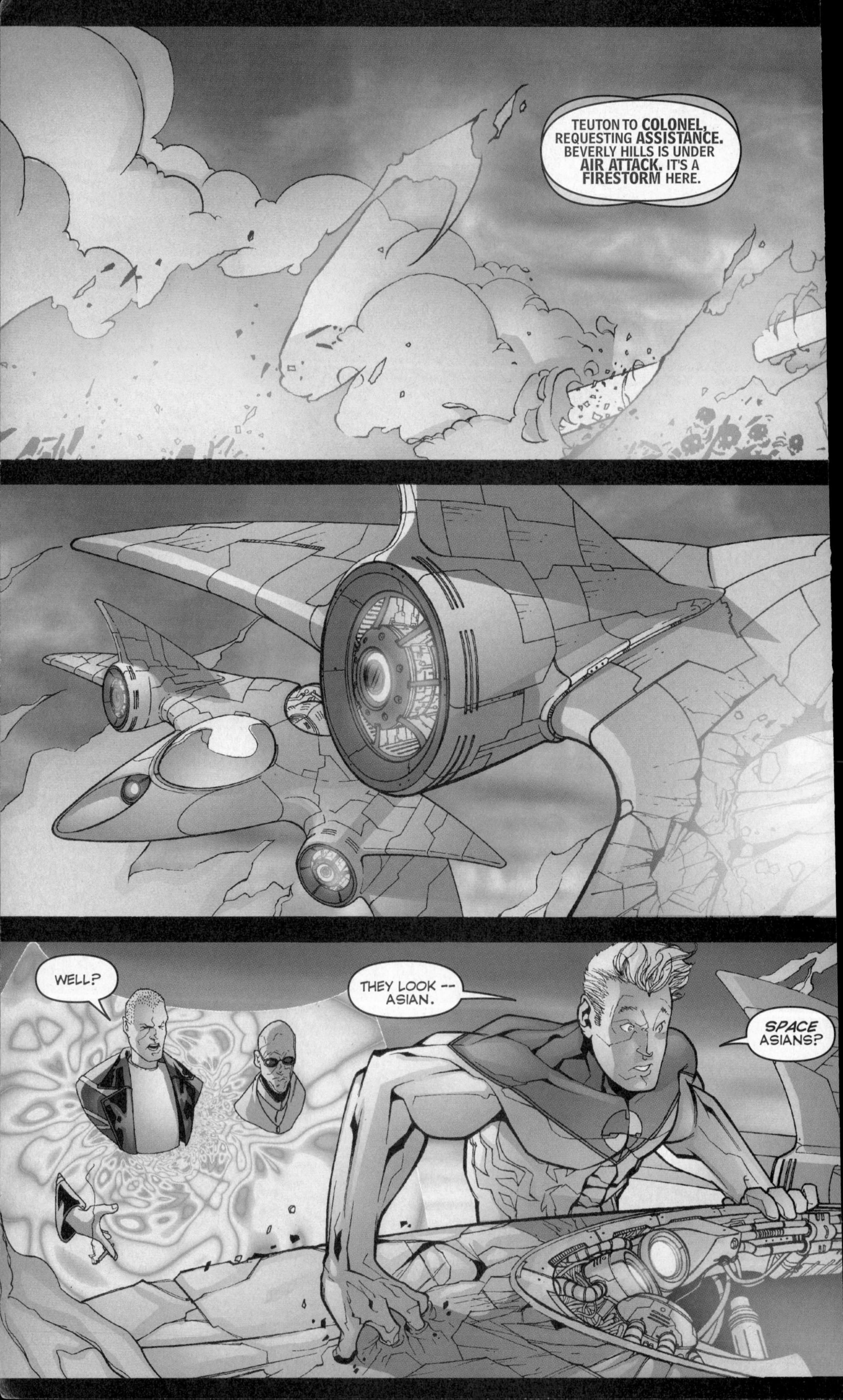

TEUTON TO COLONEL, REQUESTING ASSISTANCE. BEVERLY HILLS IS UNDER AIR ATTACK. IT'S A FIRESTORM HERE.
WELL?
THEY LOOK -- ASIAN.
SPACE ASIANS?

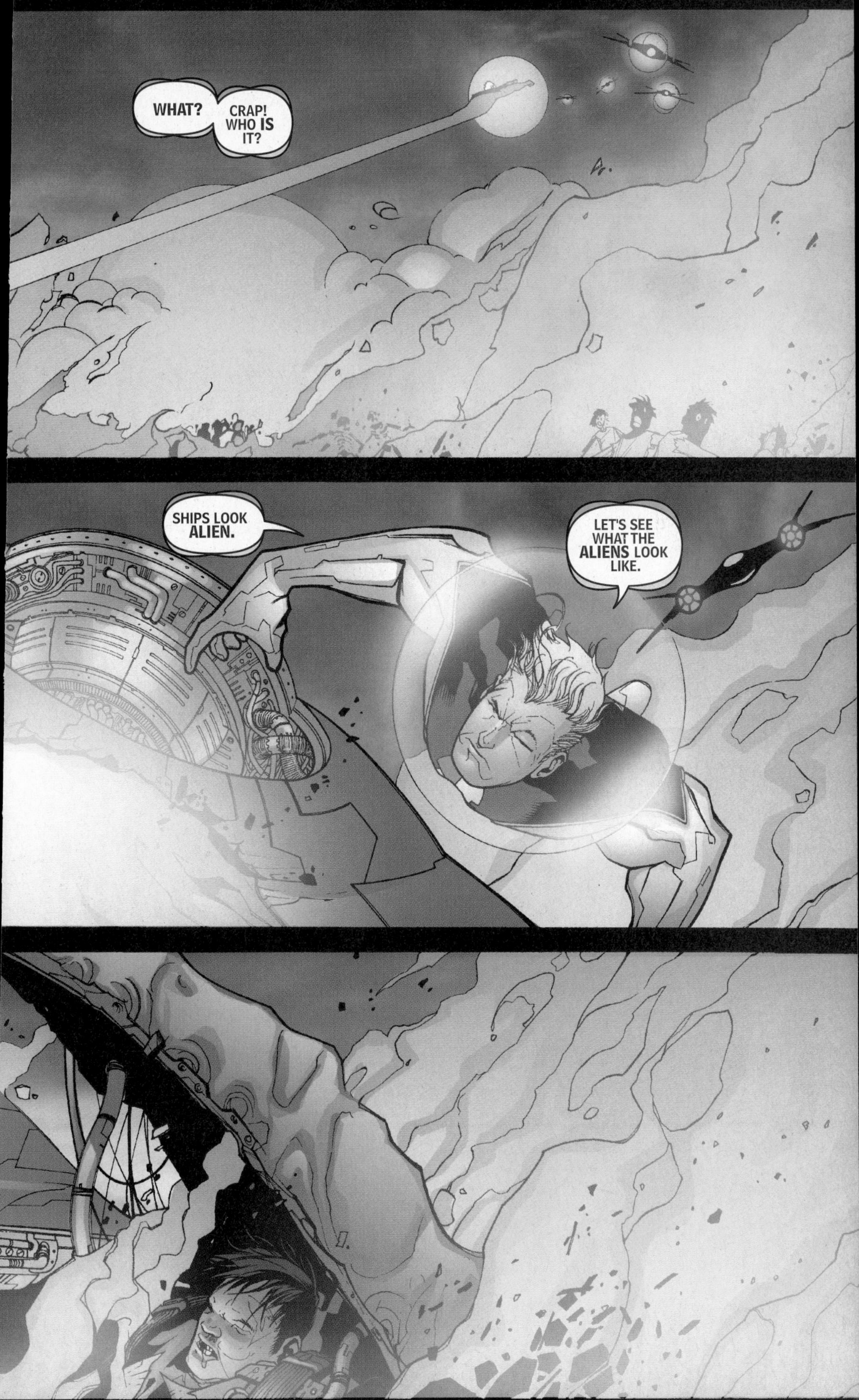
WHAT?
CRAP! WHO IS IT?
SHIPS LOOK ALIEN.
LET'S SEE WHAT THE ALIENS LOOK LIKE.

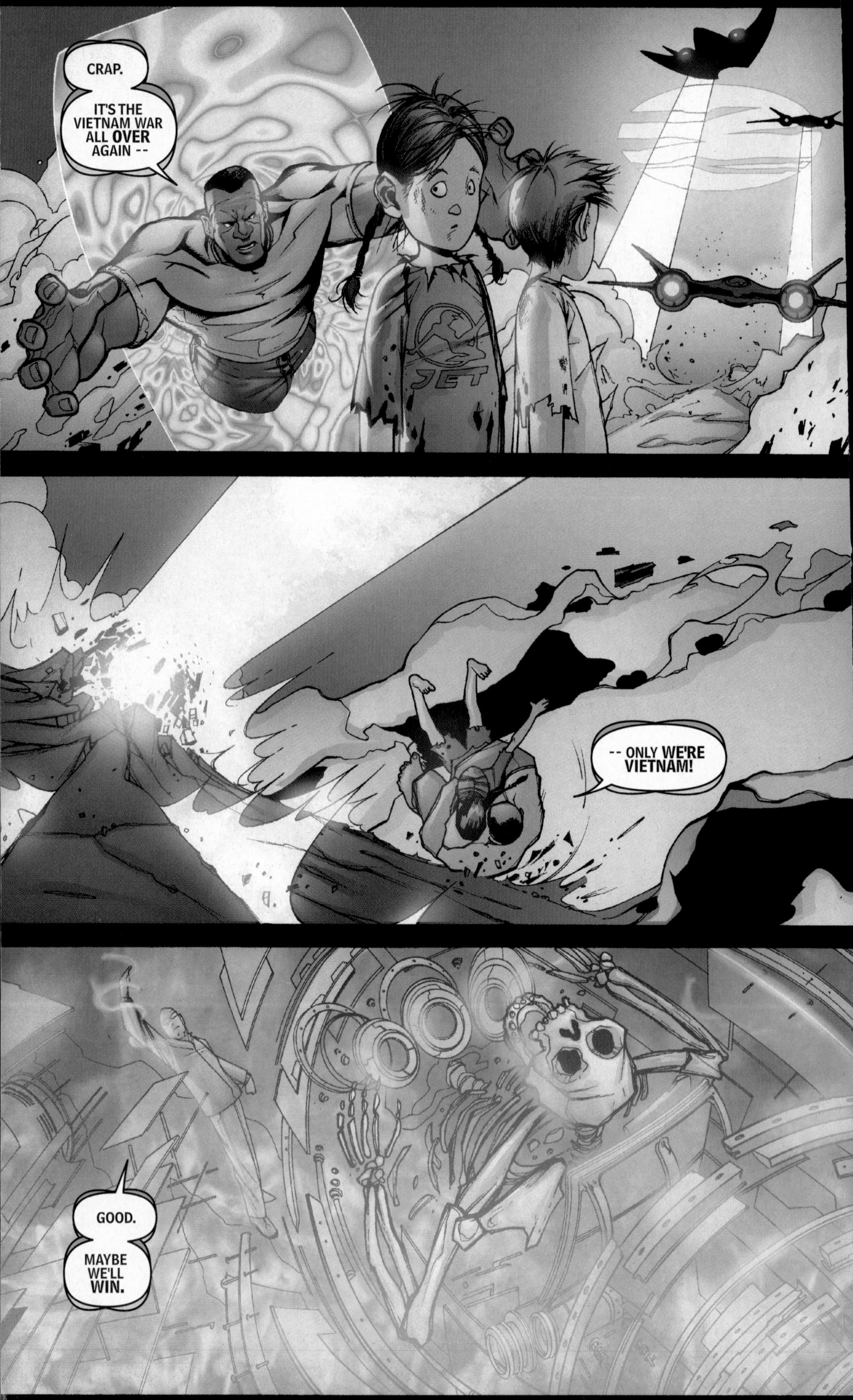
CRAP.
IT'S THE VIETNAM WAR ALL OVER AGAIN --
-- ONLY WE'RE VIETNAM!
GOOD.
MAYBE WE'LL WIN.

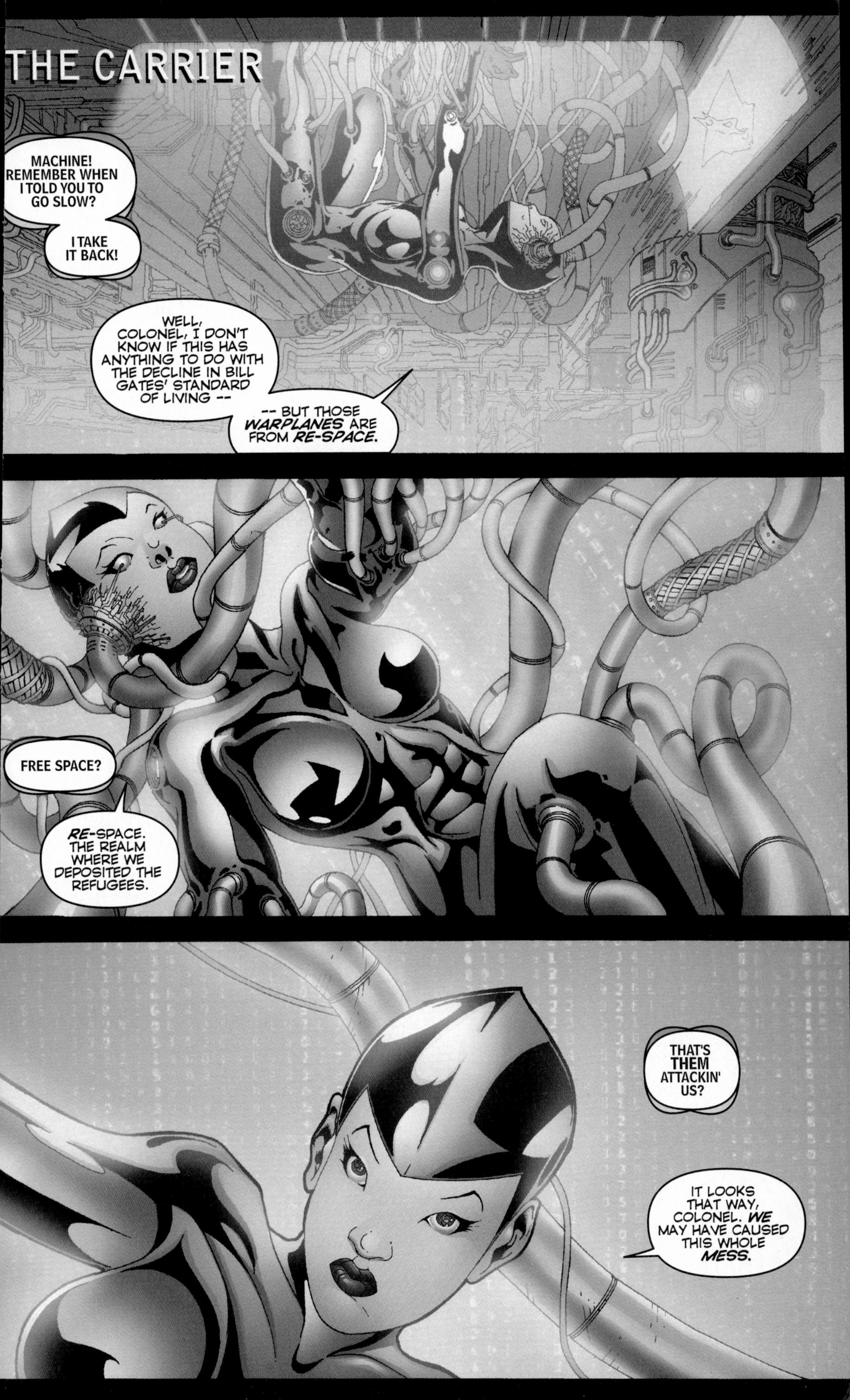
THE CARRIER
MACHINE! REMEMBER WHEN I TOLD YOU TO GO SLOW?
I TAKE IT BACK!
WELL, COLONEL, I DON'T KNOW IF THIS HAS ANYTHING TO DO WITH THE DECLINE IN BILL GATES' STANDARD OF LIVING --
-- BUT THOSE WARPLANES ARE FROM RE-SPACE.
FREE SPACE?
RE-SPACE. THE REALM WHERE WE DEPOSITED THE REFUGEES.
THAT'S THEM ATTACKIN' US?
IT LOOKS THAT WAY, COLONEL. WE MAY HAVE CAUSED THIS WHOLE MESS.

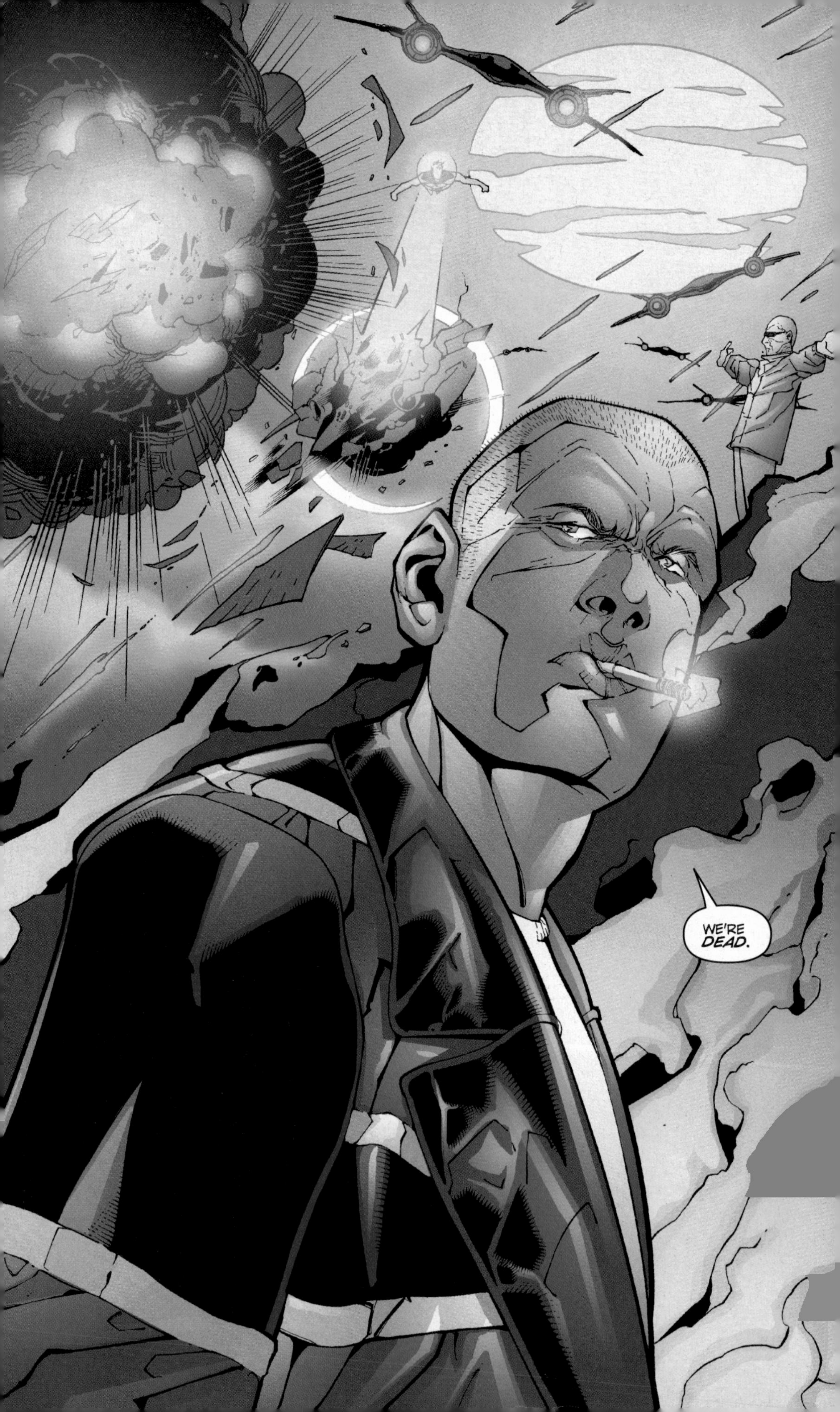
WE'RE DEAD.

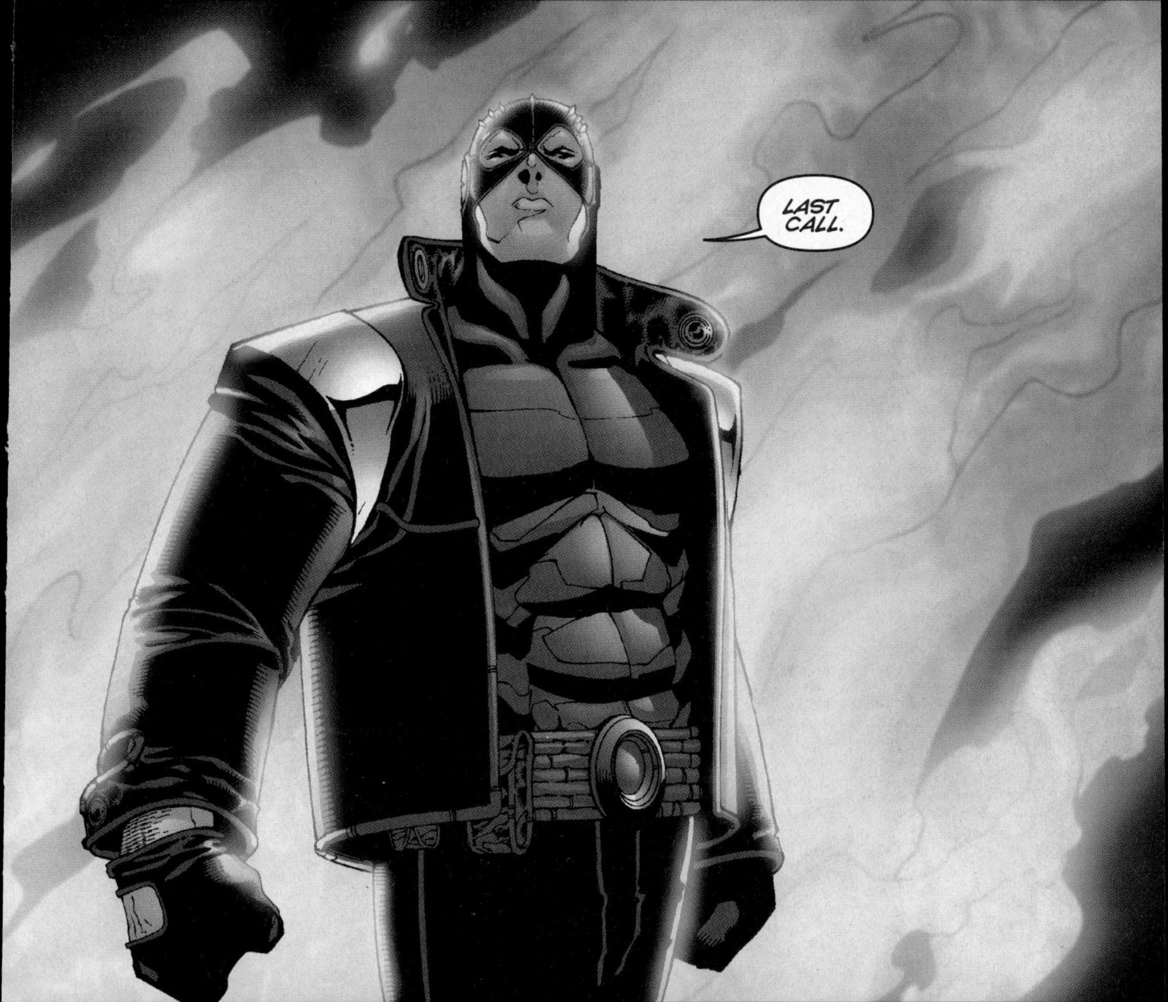
LAST CALL.

TRANSFER OF POWER

Three of Four

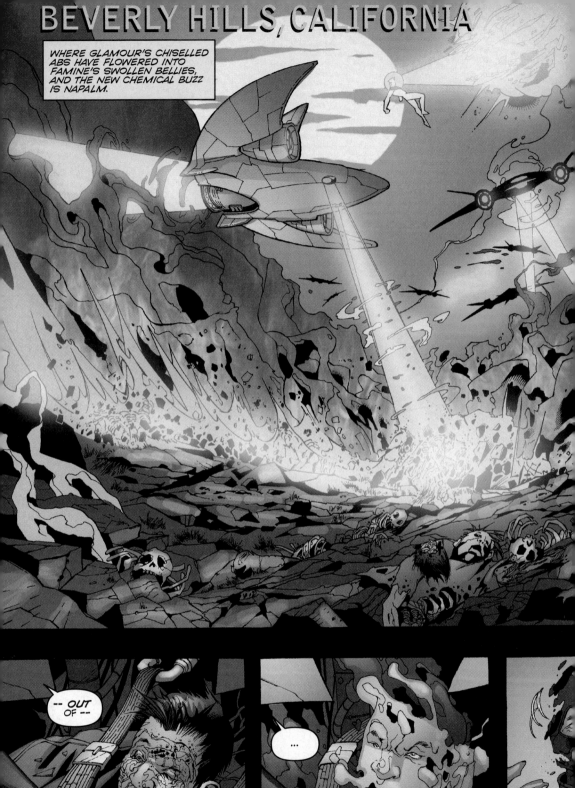

BEVERLY HILLS, CALIFORNIA

WHERE GLAMOUR'S CHISELLED ABS HAVE FLOWERED INTO FAMINE'S SWOLLEN BELLIES, AND THE NEW CHEMICAL BUZZ IS NAPALM.

-- OUT OF --

...

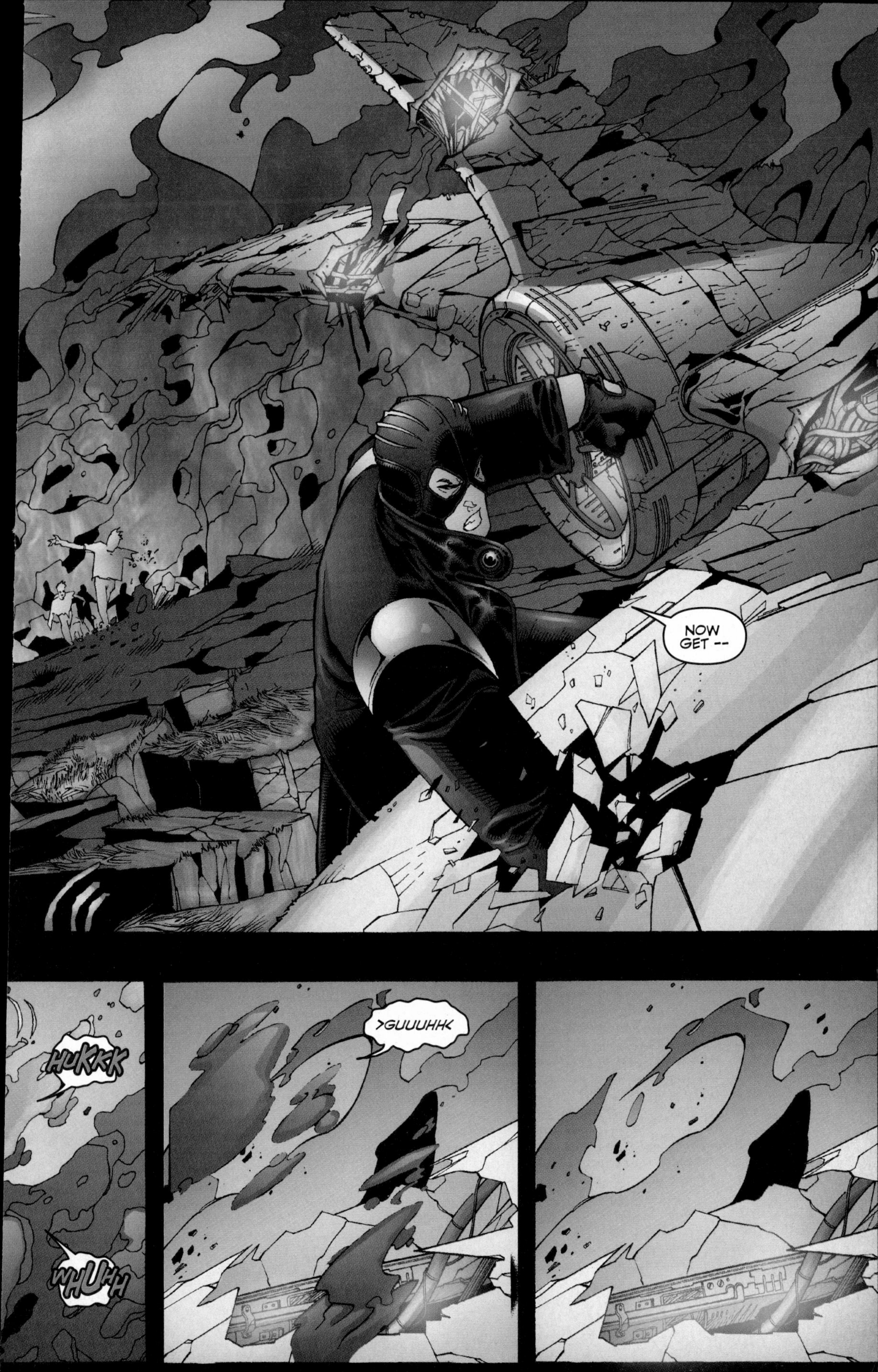
NOW GET --
HUKKK
WHUHH
>GUUUHH<

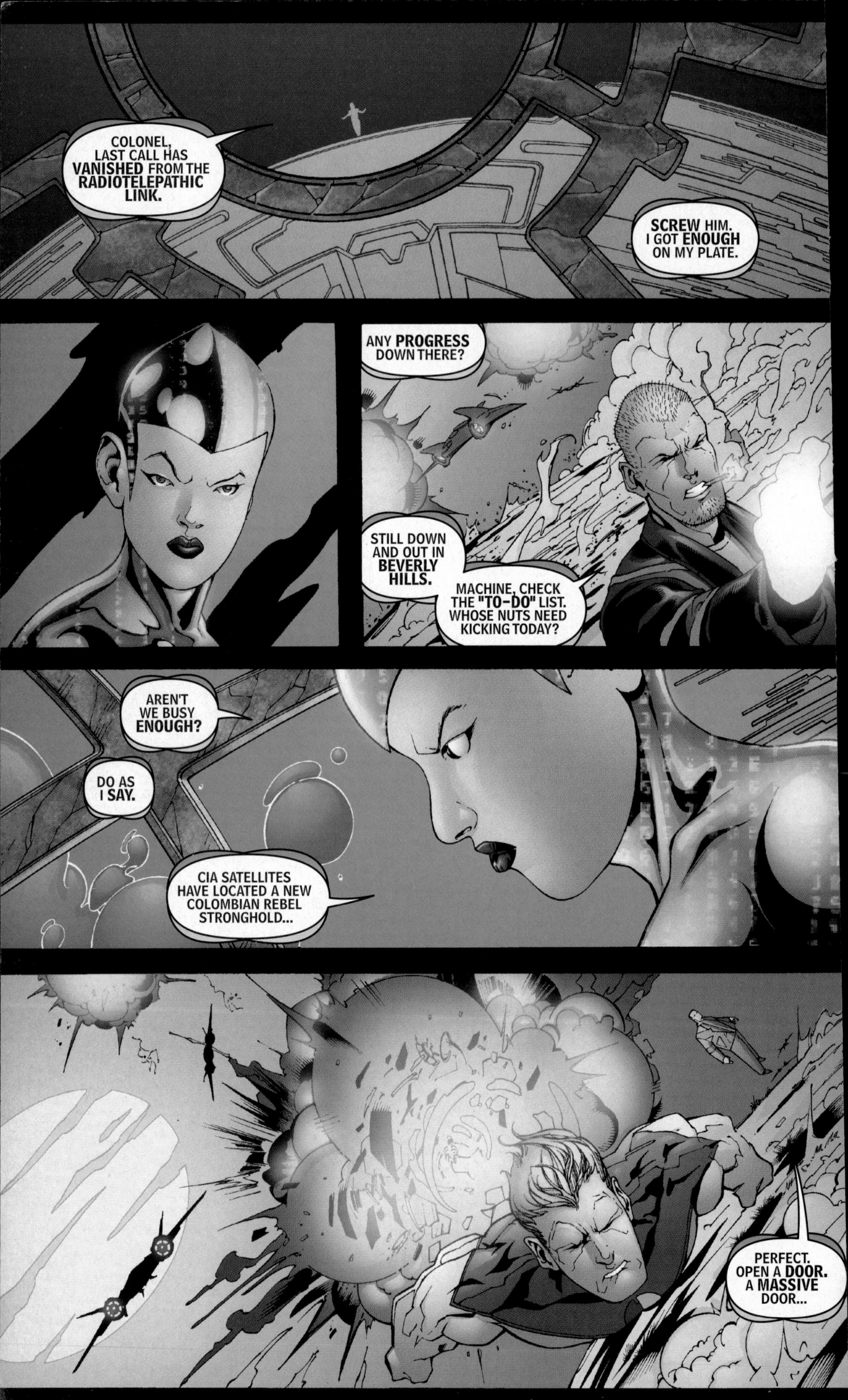
COLONEL, LAST CALL HAS VANISHED FROM THE RADIOTELEPATHIC LINK.
SCREW HIM. I GOT ENOUGH ON MY PLATE.
ANY PROGRESS DOWN THERE?
STILL DOWN AND OUT IN BEVERLY HILLS.
MACHINE, CHECK THE "TO-DO" LIST. WHOSE NUTS NEED KICKING TODAY?
AREN'T WE BUSY ENOUGH?
DO AS I SAY.
CIA SATELLITES HAVE LOCATED A NEW COLOMBIAN REBEL STRONGHOLD...
PERFECT. OPEN A DOOR. A MASSIVE DOOR...

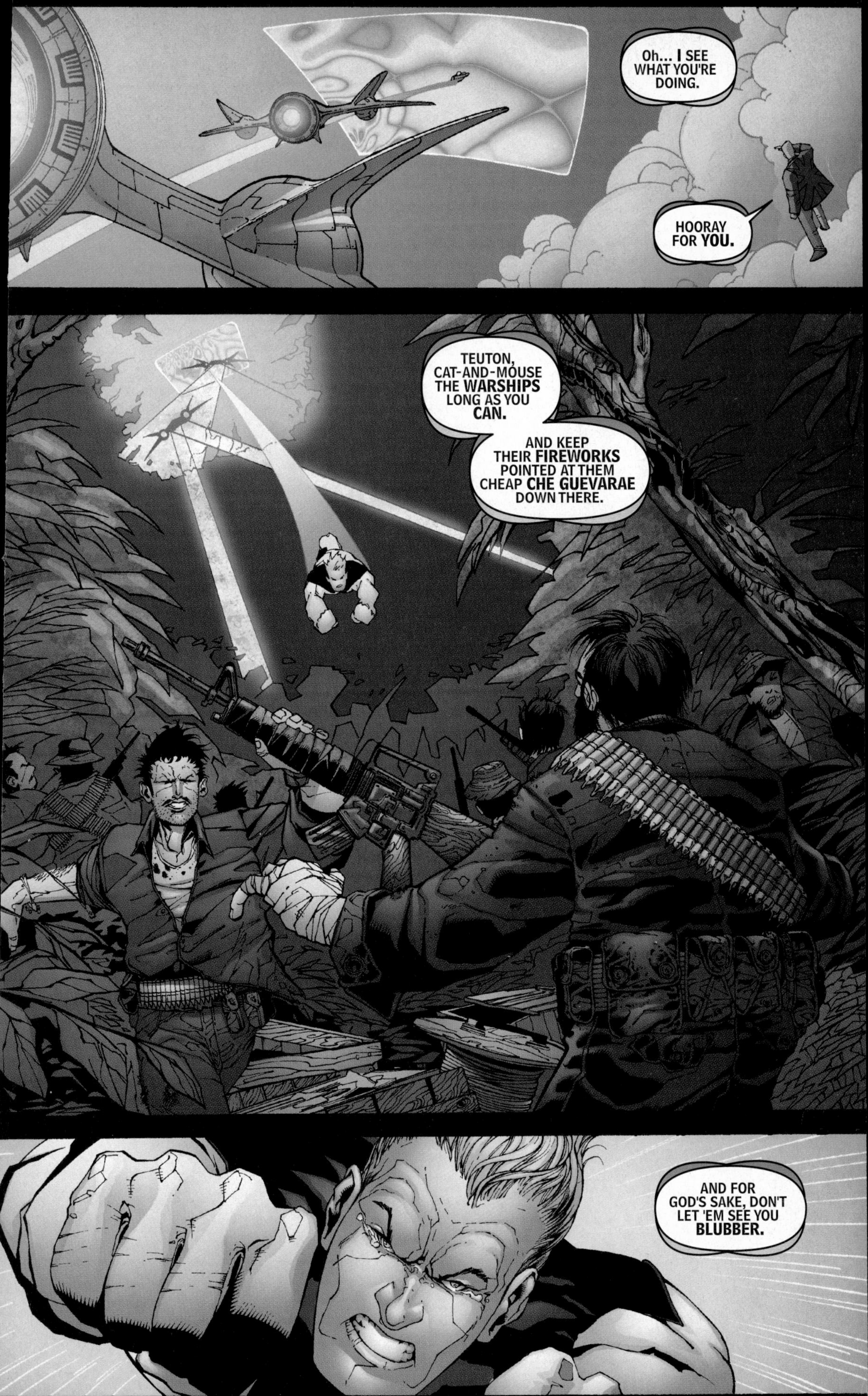

Oh... I SEE WHAT YOU'RE DOING.
HOORAY FOR YOU.
TEUTON, CAT-AND-MOUSE THE WARSHIPS LONG AS YOU CAN.
AND KEEP THEIR FIREWORKS POINTED AT THEM CHEAP CHE GUEVARAE DOWN THERE.
AND FOR GOD'S SAKE, DON'T LET 'EM SEE YOU BLUBBER.

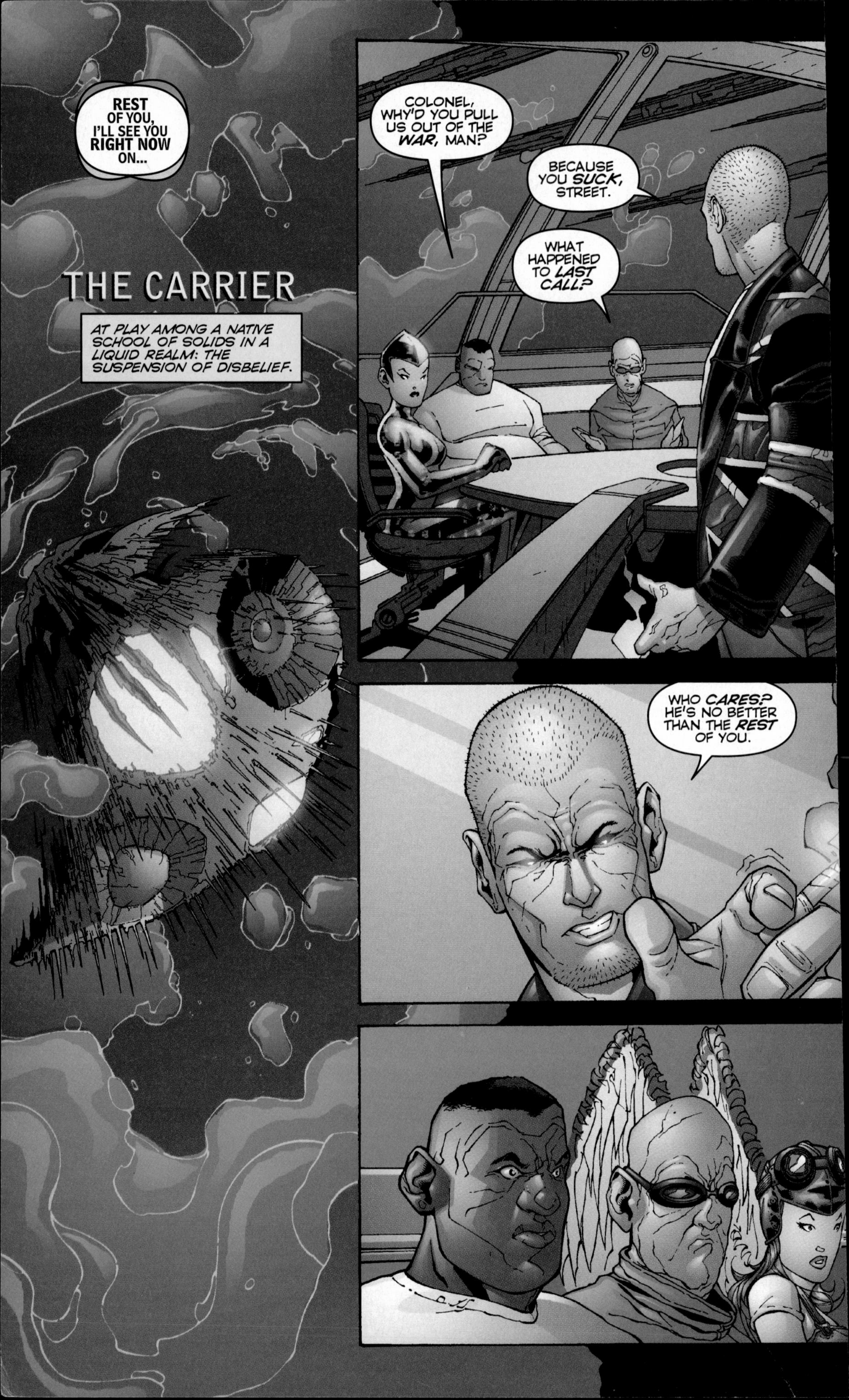
REST OF YOU, I'LL SEE YOU RIGHT NOW ON...
THE CARRIER
AT PLAY AMONG A NATIVE SCHOOL OF SOLIDS IN A LIQUID REALM: THE SUSPENSION OF DISBELIEF.
COLONEL, WHY'D YOU PULL US OUT OF THE WAR, MAN?
BECAUSE YOU SUCK, STREET.
WHAT HAPPENED TO LAST CALL?
WHO CARES? HE'S NO BETTER THAN THE REST OF YOU.

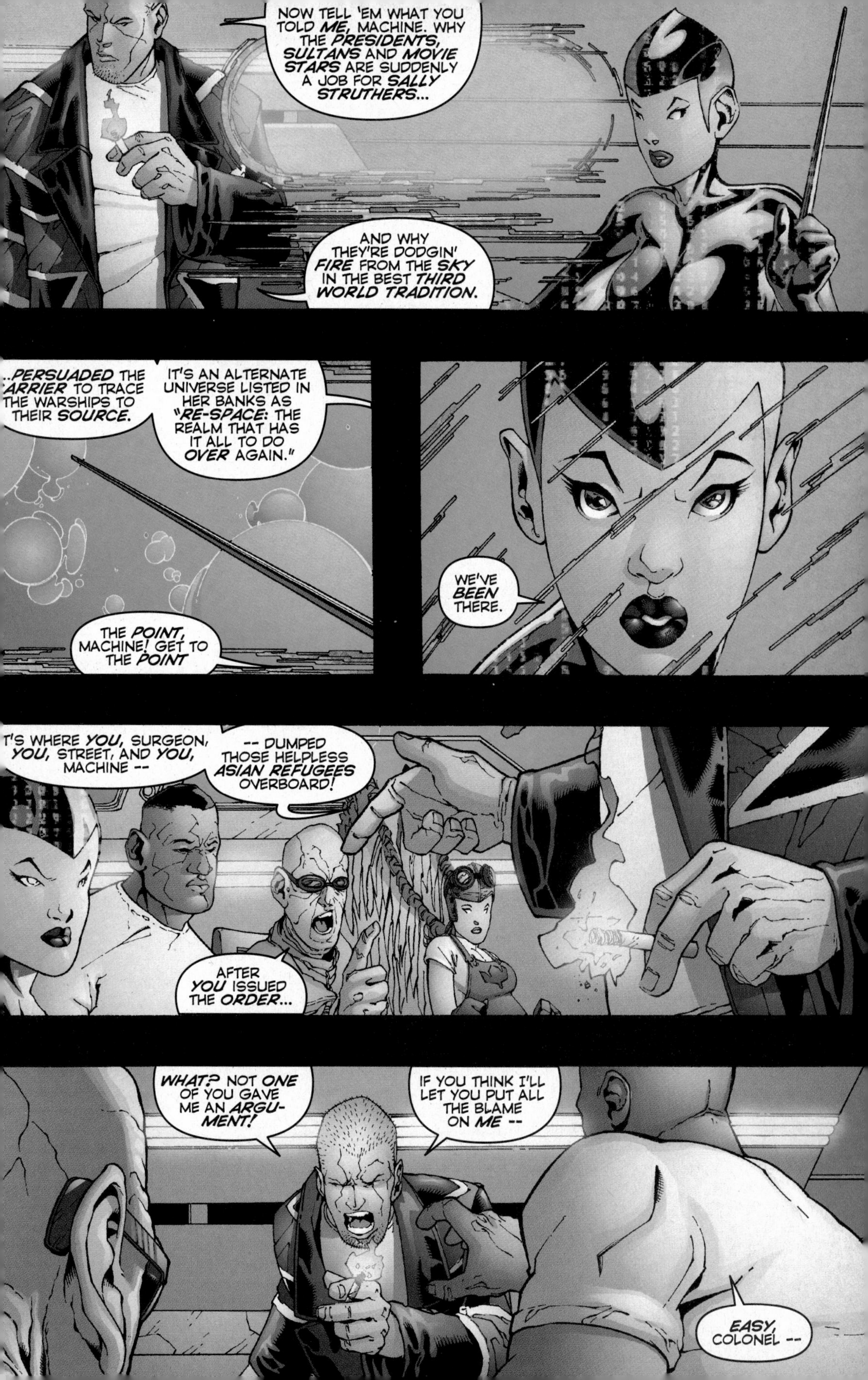
NOW TELL 'EM WHAT YOU TOLD ME, MACHINE. WHY THE PRESIDENTS, SULTANS AND MOVIE STARS ARE SUDDENLY A JOB FOR SALLY STRUTHERS...
AND WHY THEY'RE DODGIN' FIRE FROM THE SKY IN THE BEST THIRD WORLD TRADITION.
..PERSUADED THE CARRIER TO TRACE THE WARSHIPS TO THEIR SOURCE.
IT'S AN ALTERNATE UNIVERSE LISTED IN HER BANKS AS "RE-SPACE: THE REALM THAT HAS IT ALL TO DO OVER AGAIN."
THE POINT, MACHINE! GET TO THE POINT
WE'VE BEEN THERE.
IT'S WHERE YOU, SURGEON, YOU, STREET, AND YOU, MACHINE --
-- DUMPED THOSE HELPLESS ASIAN REFUGEES OVERBOARD!
AFTER YOU ISSUED THE ORDER...
WHAT? NOT ONE OF YOU GAVE ME AN ARGUMENT!
IF YOU THINK I'LL LET YOU PUT ALL THE BLAME ON ME --
EASY, COLONEL --

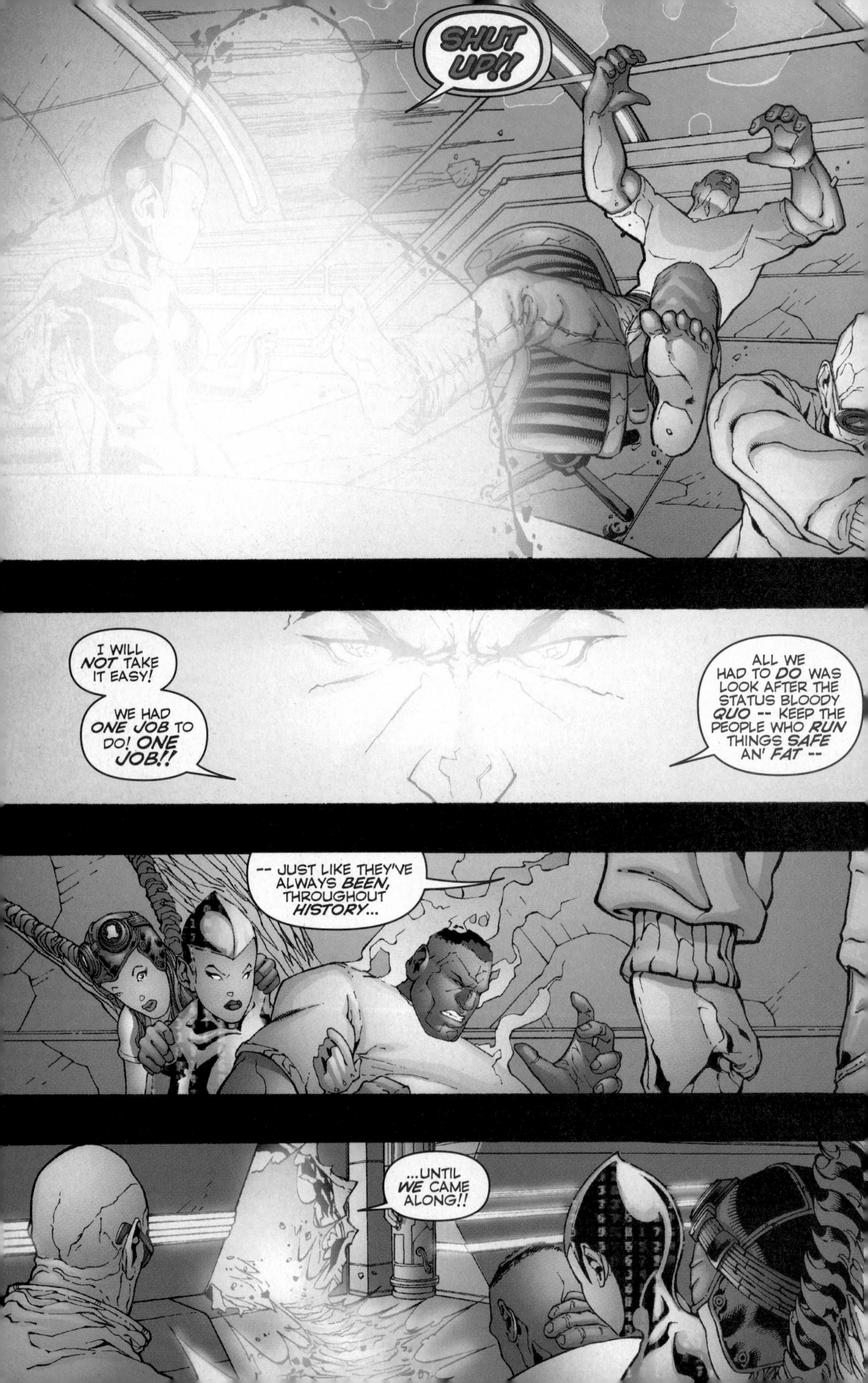
SHUT UP!!
I WILL NOT TAKE IT EASY!
WE HAD ONE JOB TO DO! ONE JOB!!
ALL WE HAD TO DO WAS LOOK AFTER THE STATUS BLOODY QUO -- KEEP THE PEOPLE WHO RUN THINGS SAFE AN' FAT --
-- JUST LIKE THEY'VE ALWAYS BEEN, THROUGHOUT HISTORY...
...UNTIL WE CAME ALONG!!

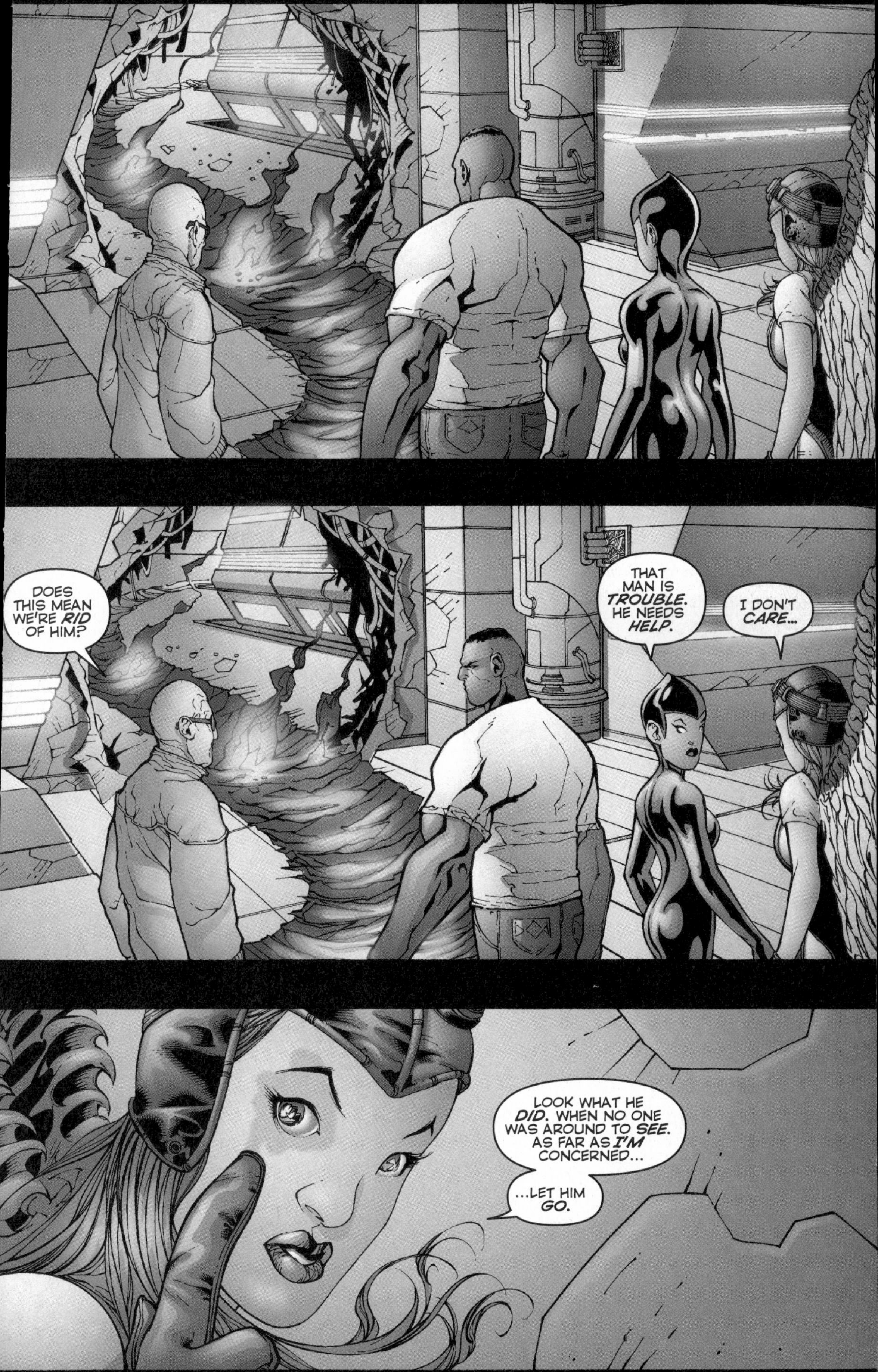
DOES THIS MEAN WE'RE RID OF HIM?
THAT MAN IS TROUBLE. HE NEEDS HELP.
I DON'T CARE...
LOOK WHAT HE DID. WHEN NO ONE WAS AROUND TO SEE. AS FAR AS I'M CONCERNED...
...LET HIM GO.

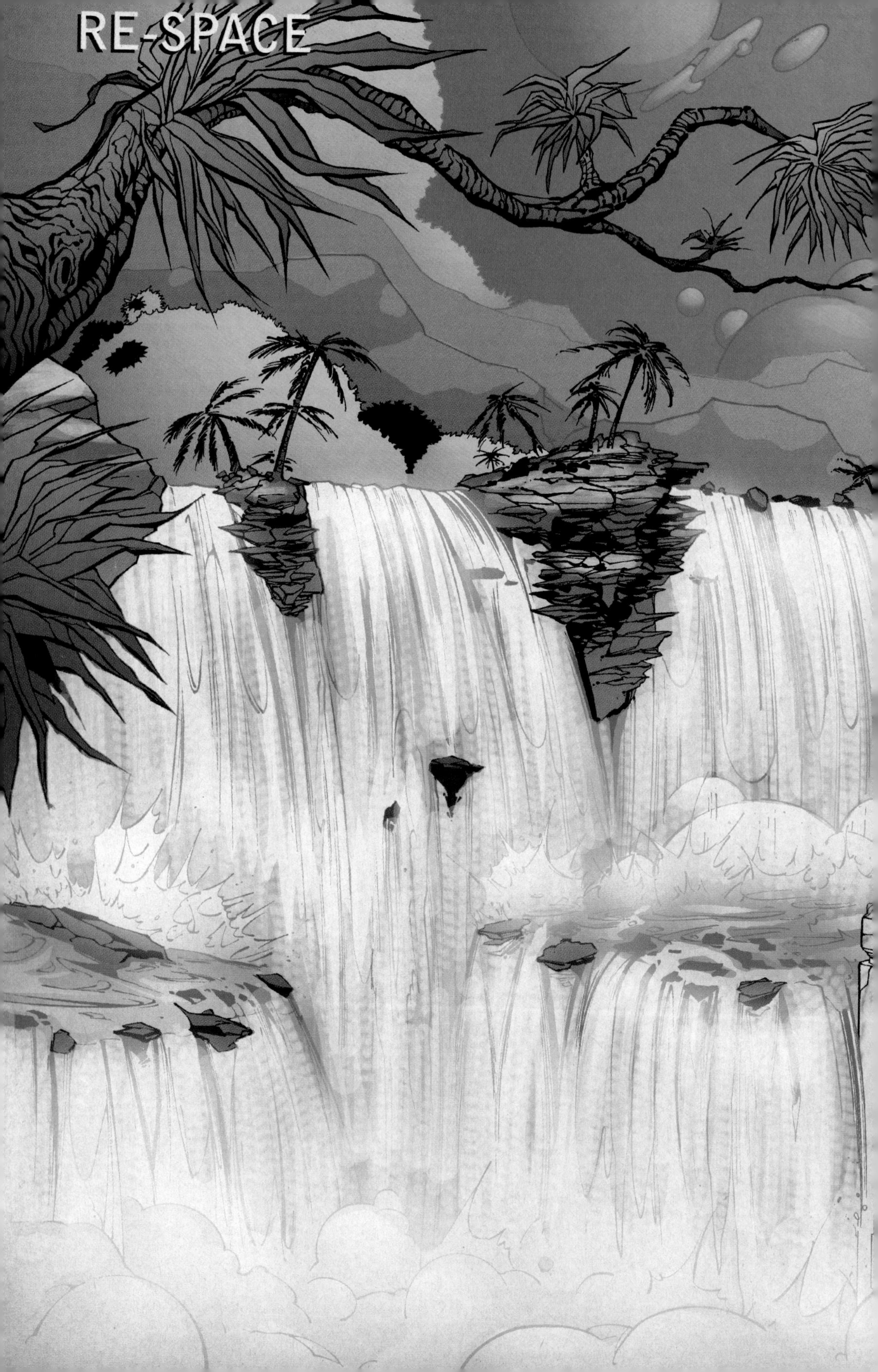
RE-SPACE

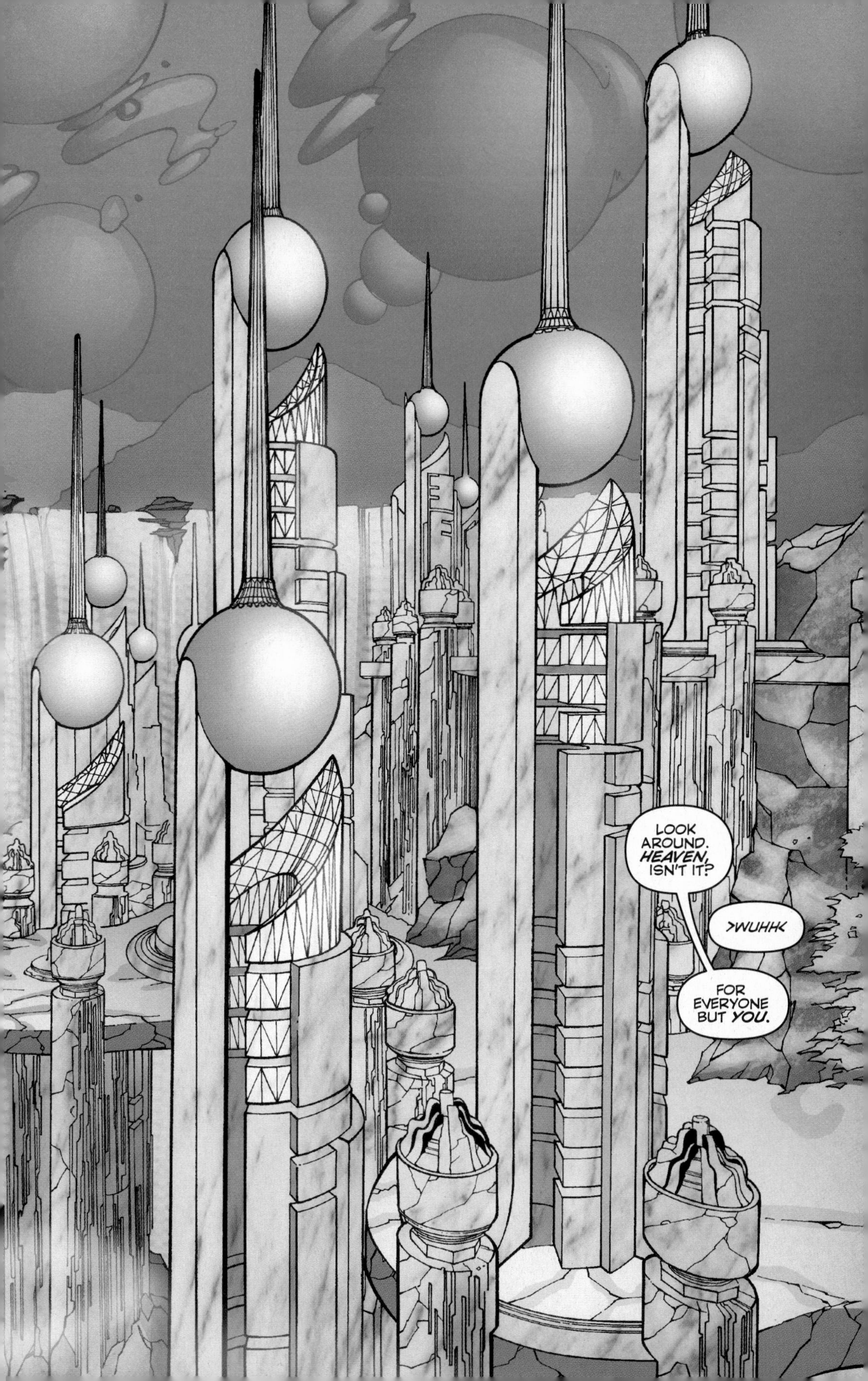
LOOK AROUND. *HEAVEN,* ISN'T IT?
>WUHH<
FOR EVERYONE BUT *YOU.*

THE HORROR OF EARTHLIFE IS *BEHIND* US. WE *IMAGINE* OUR SECOND CHANCE, AND RE-SPACE MAKES IT *TRUE.*

THE *REAL* AUTHORITY BELIEVED IN A FUTURE LIKE *THIS...* A FUTURE FOR *EVERYONE...*

WHICH IS WHY THE WEST *DESTROYED* THEM...REPLACED THEM WITH *YOU,* AS BOWEL-WASTE REPLACES *FOOD.*

BUT WE *DEALT* WITH YOUR *MASTERS...*

FOLLOWING THEIR EXAMPLE, WE MADE A WORLD OF VAST WEALTH FROM *SOMEWHERE ELSE.*

FROM WASHINGTON. PARIS. LONDON. TOKYO. WE REIMAGINE THEIR *TREASURE* AS *OURS,* TO FEED OUR *BODIES...*

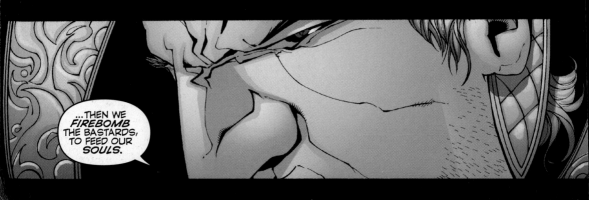

...THEN WE *FIREBOMB* THE BASTARDS, TO FEED OUR *SOULS.*

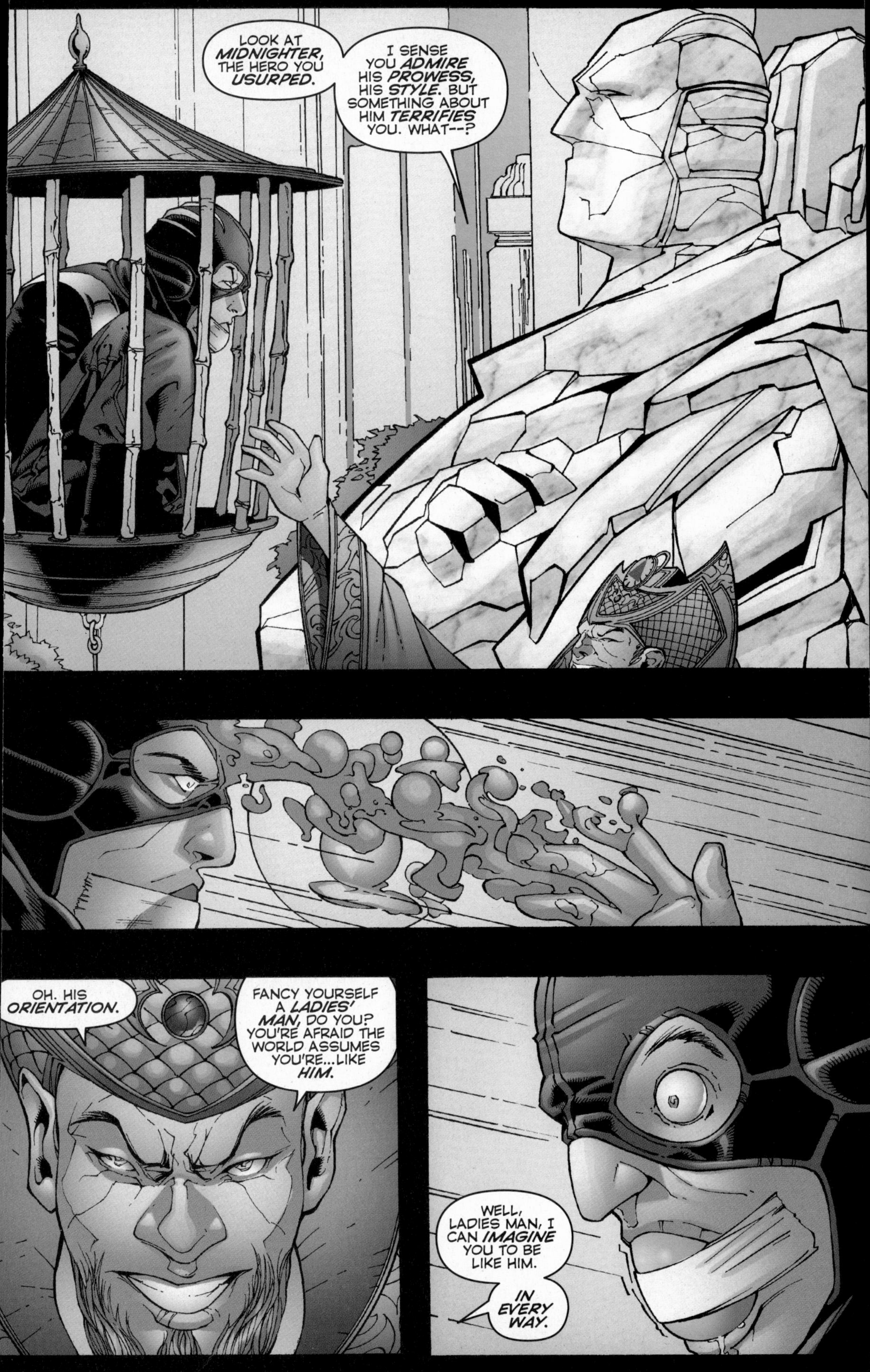
LOOK AT MIDNIGHTER, THE HERO YOU USURPED.
I SENSE YOU ADMIRE HIS PROWESS, HIS STYLE. BUT SOMETHING ABOUT HIM TERRIFIES YOU. WHAT--?
OH. HIS ORIENTATION.
FANCY YOURSELF A LADIES' MAN, DO YOU? YOU'RE AFRAID THE WORLD ASSUMES YOU'RE...LIKE HIM.
WELL, LADIES MAN, I CAN IMAGINE YOU TO BE LIKE HIM.
IN EVERY WAY.

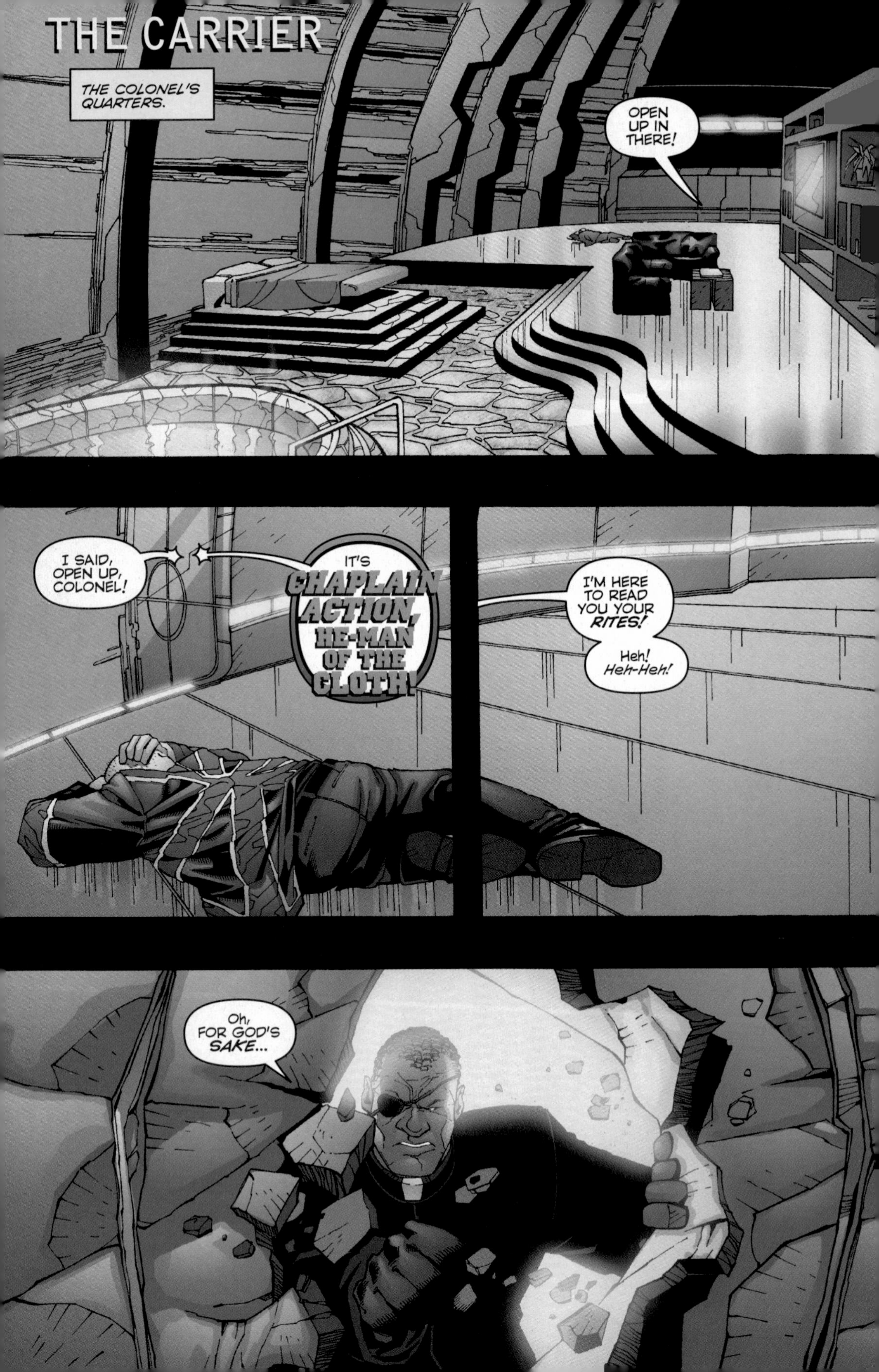
THE CARRIER
THE COLONEL'S QUARTERS.
OPEN UP IN THERE!
I SAID, OPEN UP, COLONEL!
IT'S CHAPLAIN ACTION, HE-MAN OF THE CLOTH!
I'M HERE TO READ YOU YOUR RITES!
Heh! Heh-Heh!
Oh, FOR GOD'S SAKE...

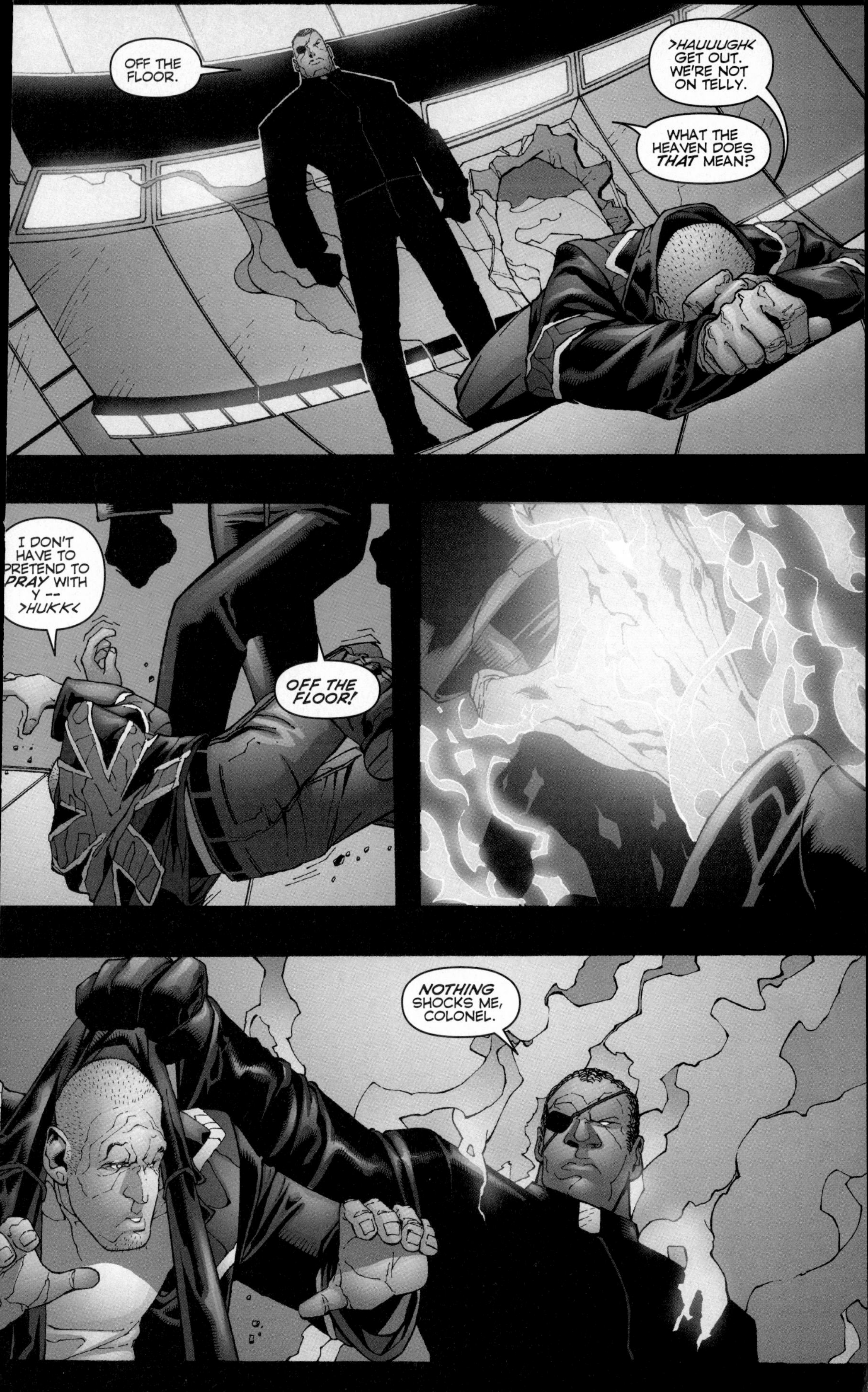
OFF THE FLOOR.
>HAUUUGH< GET OUT. WE'RE NOT ON TELLY.
WHAT THE HEAVEN DOES *THAT* MEAN?
I DON'T HAVE TO PRETEND TO *PRAY* WITH Y -- >HUKK<
OFF THE FLOOR!
NOTHING SHOCKS ME, COLONEL.

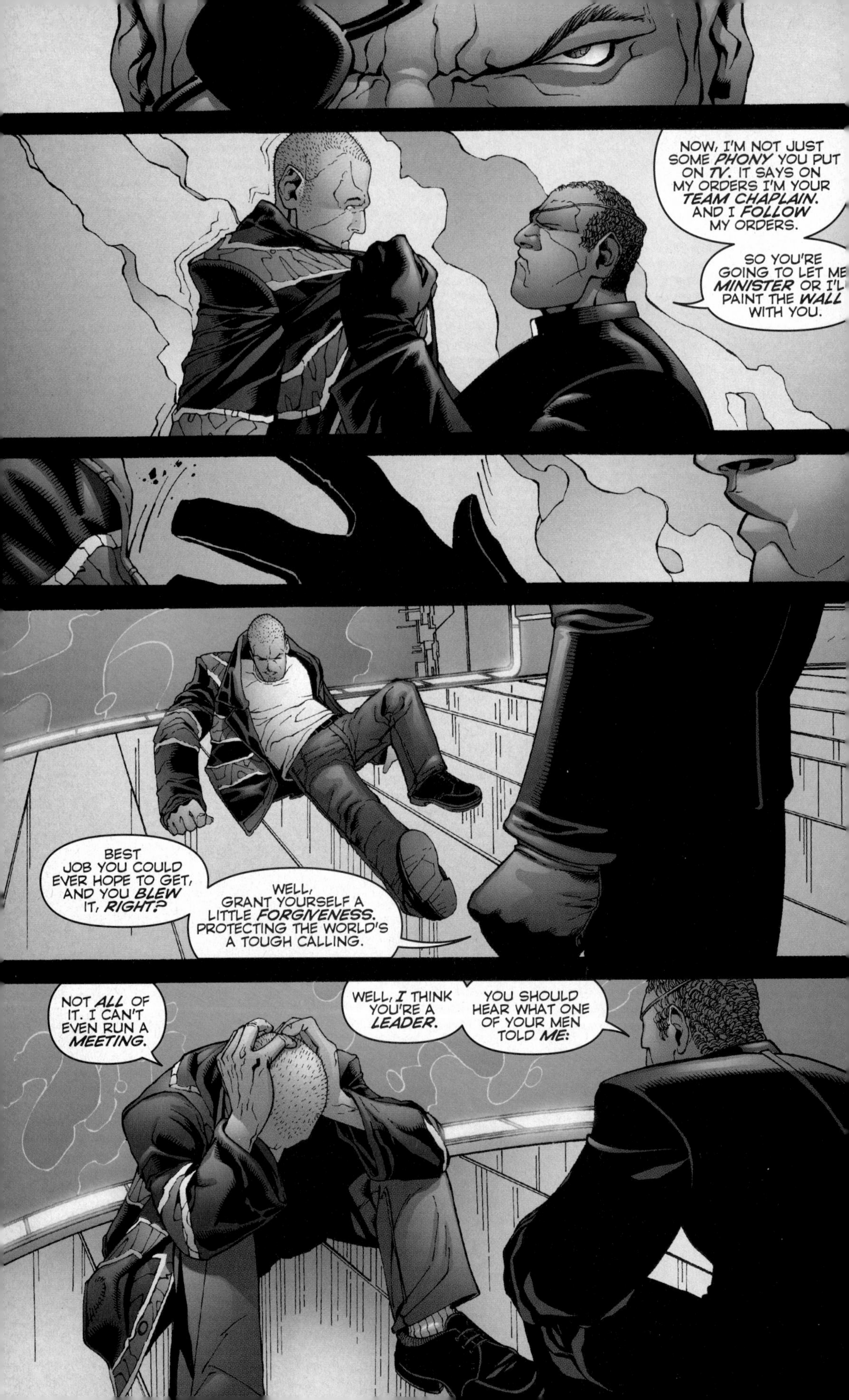
NOW, I'M NOT JUST SOME PHONY YOU PUT ON TV. IT SAYS ON MY ORDERS I'M YOUR TEAM CHAPLAIN. AND I FOLLOW MY ORDERS.
SO YOU'RE GOING TO LET ME MINISTER OR I'LL PAINT THE WALL WITH YOU.
BEST JOB YOU COULD EVER HOPE TO GET, AND YOU BLEW IT, RIGHT?
WELL, GRANT YOURSELF A LITTLE FORGIVENESS. PROTECTING THE WORLD'S A TOUGH CALLING.
NOT ALL OF IT. I CAN'T EVEN RUN A MEETING.
WELL, I THINK YOU'RE A LEADER.
YOU SHOULD HEAR WHAT ONE OF YOUR MEN TOLD ME:

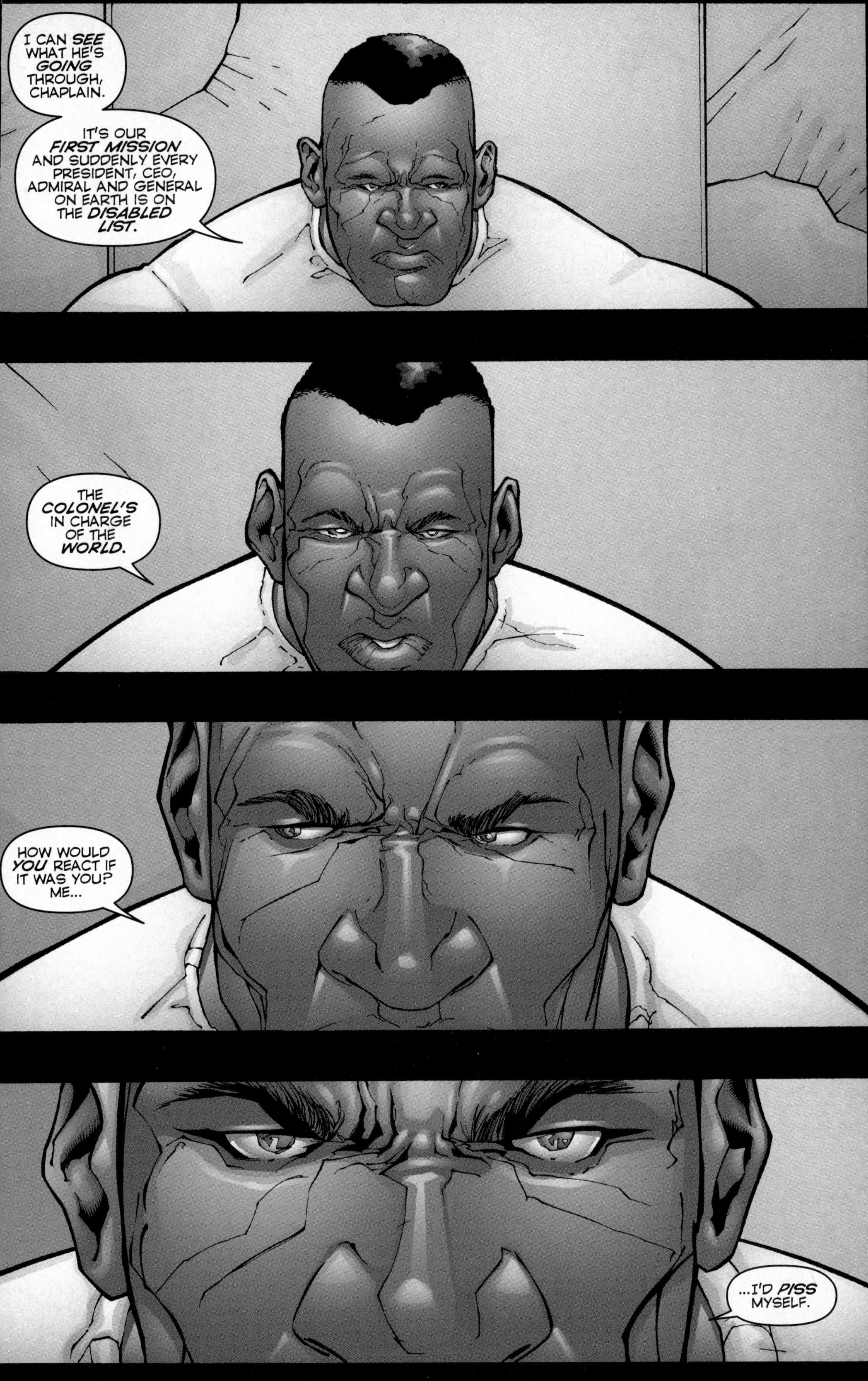
I CAN SEE WHAT HE'S GOING THROUGH, CHAPLAIN.
IT'S OUR FIRST MISSION AND SUDDENLY EVERY PRESIDENT, CEO, ADMIRAL AND GENERAL ON EARTH IS ON THE DISABLED LIST.
THE COLONEL'S IN CHARGE OF THE WORLD.
HOW WOULD YOU REACT IF IT WAS YOU? ME...
...I'D PISS MYSELF.

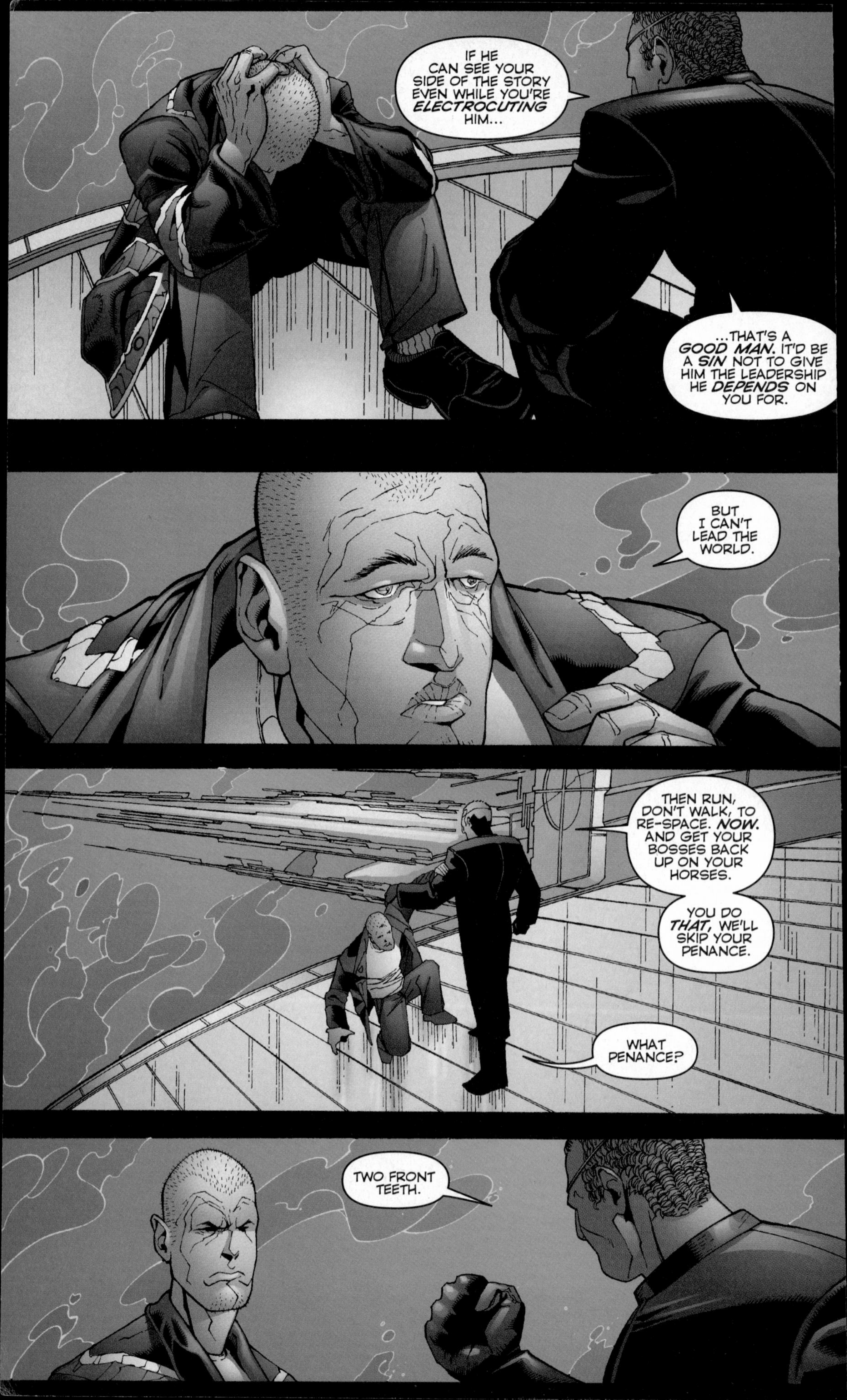
IF HE CAN SEE YOUR SIDE OF THE STORY EVEN WHILE YOU'RE ELECTROCUTING HIM...
...THAT'S A GOOD MAN. IT'D BE A SIN NOT TO GIVE HIM THE LEADERSHIP HE DEPENDS ON YOU FOR.
BUT I CAN'T LEAD THE WORLD.
THEN RUN, DON'T WALK, TO RE-SPACE. NOW. AND GET YOUR BOSSES BACK UP ON YOUR HORSES.
YOU DO THAT, WE'LL SKIP YOUR PENANCE.
WHAT PENANCE?
TWO FRONT TEETH.

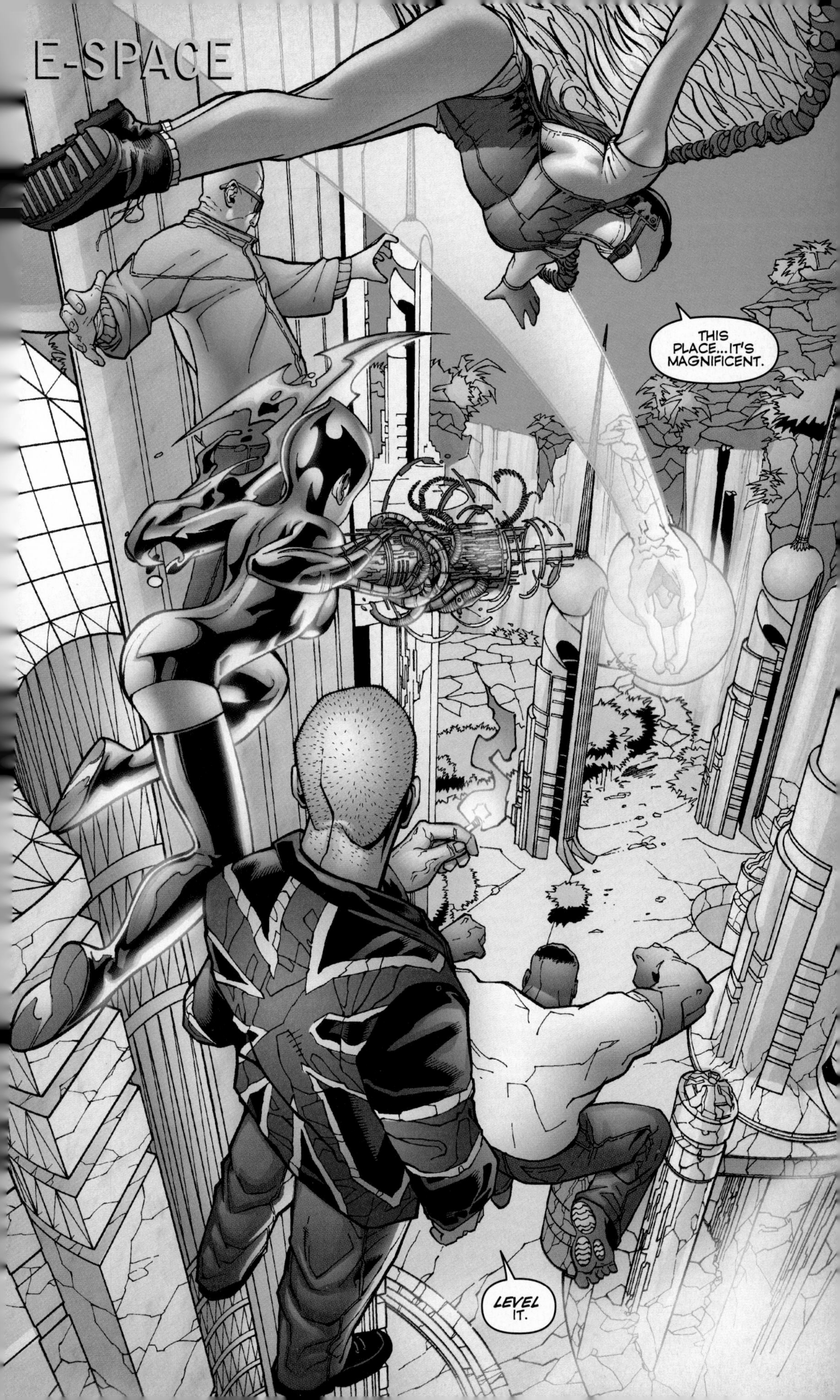
E-SPACE
THIS PLACE...IT'S MAGNIFICENT.
LEVEL IT.

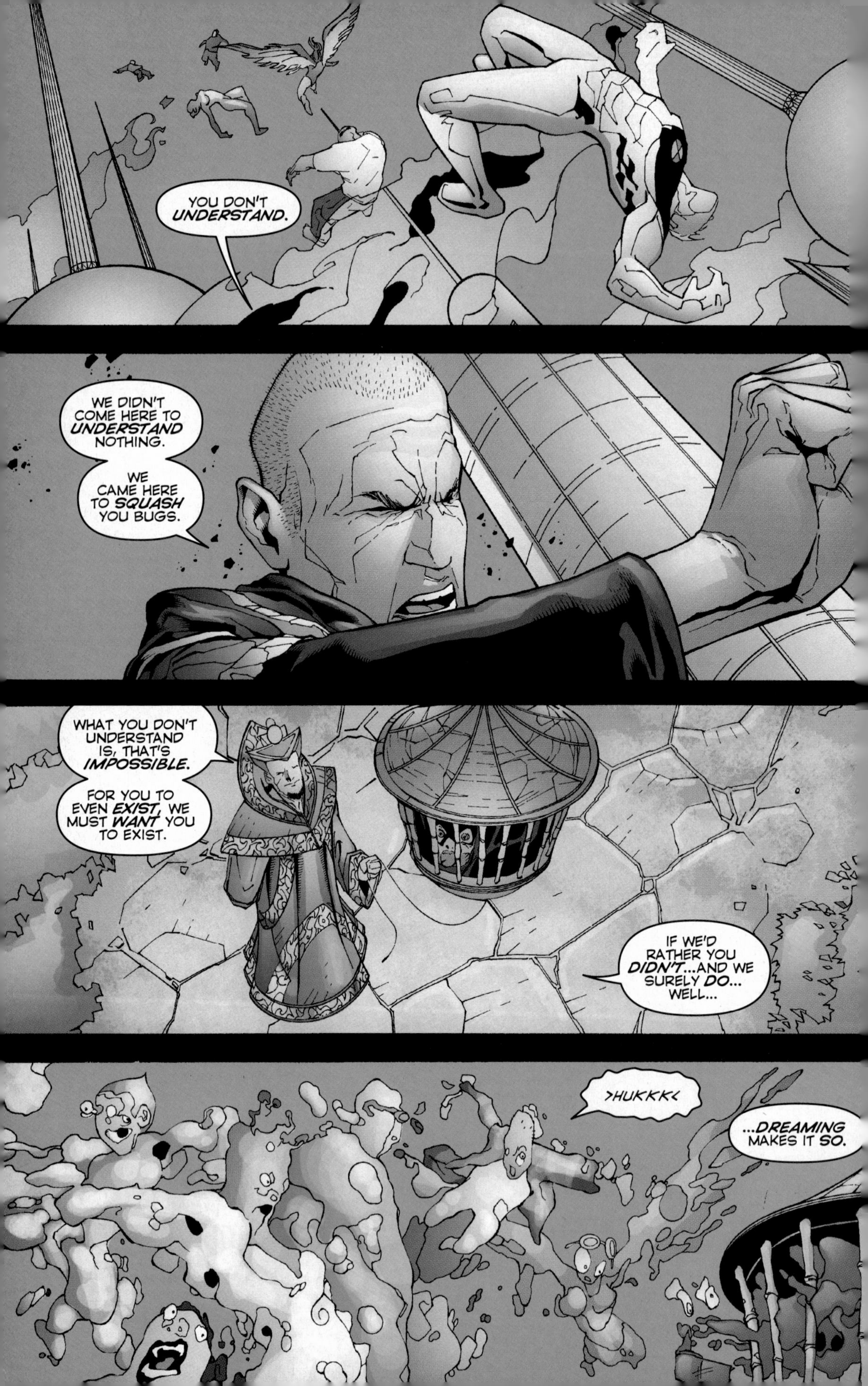
YOU DON'T UNDERSTAND.
WE DIDN'T COME HERE TO UNDERSTAND NOTHING.
WE CAME HERE TO SQUASH YOU BUGS.
WHAT YOU DON'T UNDERSTAND IS, THAT'S IMPOSSIBLE.
FOR YOU TO EVEN EXIST, WE MUST WANT YOU TO EXIST.
IF WE'D RATHER YOU DIDN'T...AND WE SURELY DO... WELL...
>HUKKK<
...DREAMING MAKES IT SO.

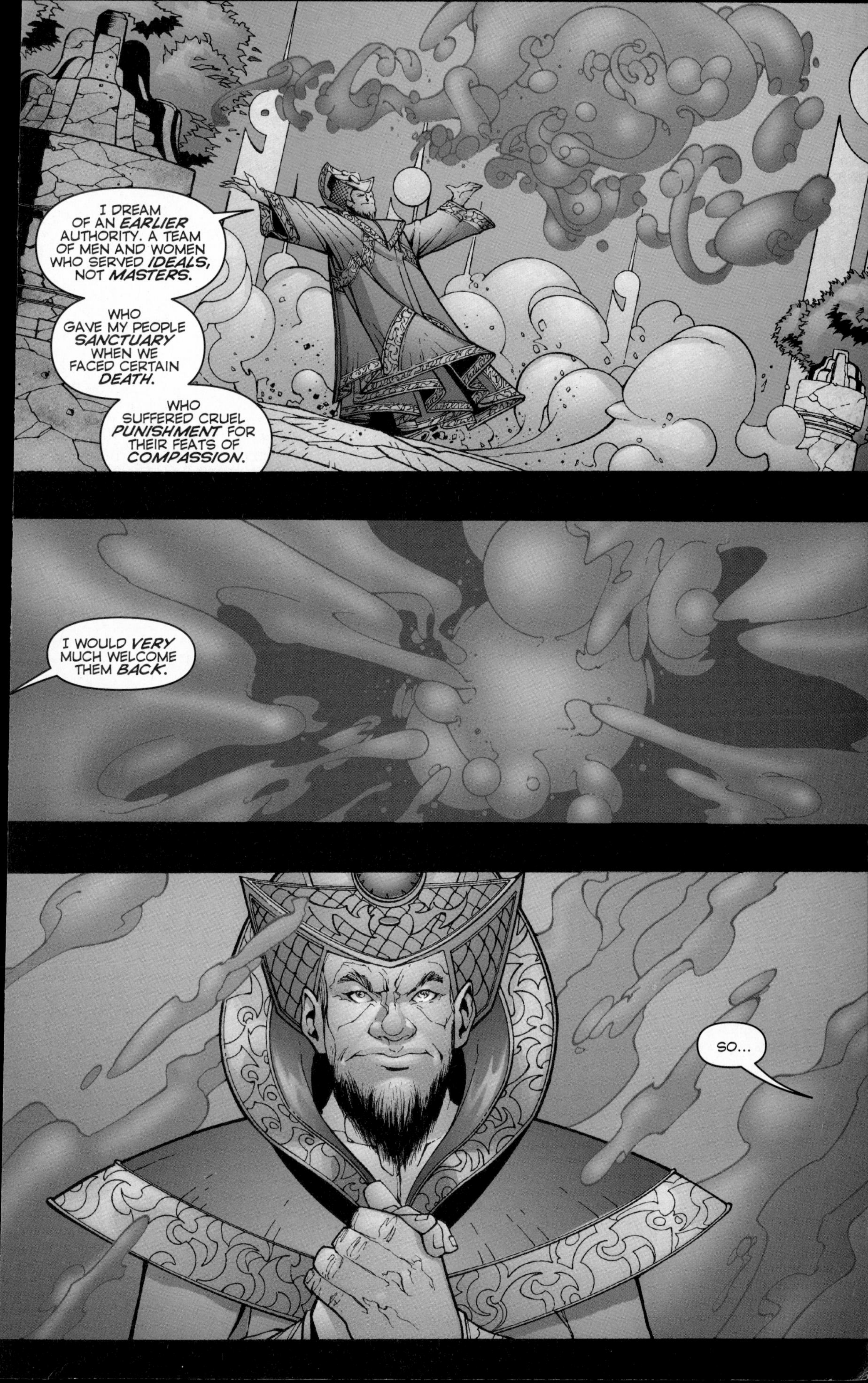
I DREAM OF AN EARLIER AUTHORITY. A TEAM OF MEN AND WOMEN WHO SERVED IDEALS, NOT MASTERS.
WHO GAVE MY PEOPLE SANCTUARY WHEN WE FACED CERTAIN DEATH.
WHO SUFFERED CRUEL PUNISHMENT FOR THEIR FEATS OF COMPASSION.
I WOULD VERY MUCH WELCOME THEM BACK.
SO...

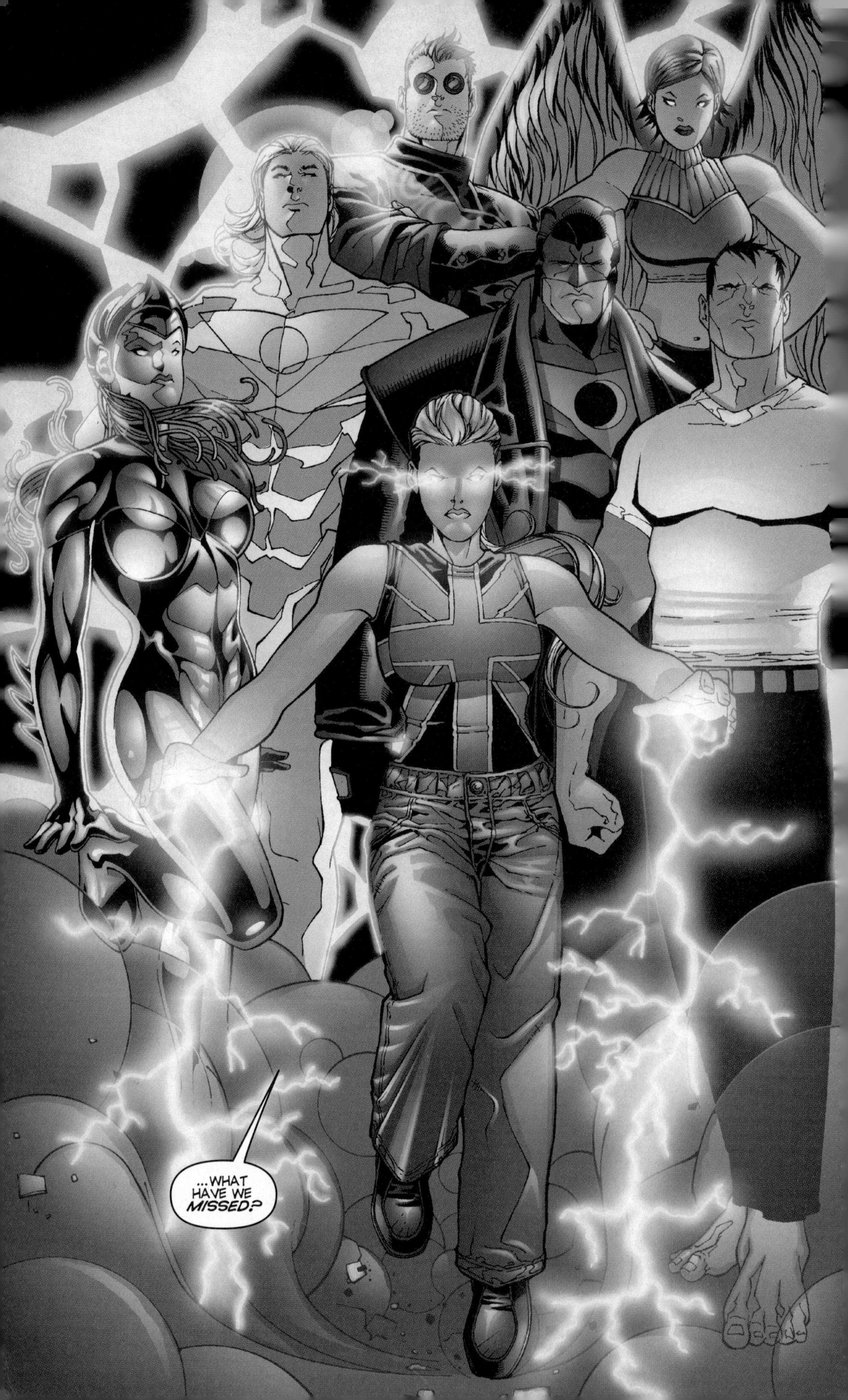
...WHAT HAVE WE MISSED?

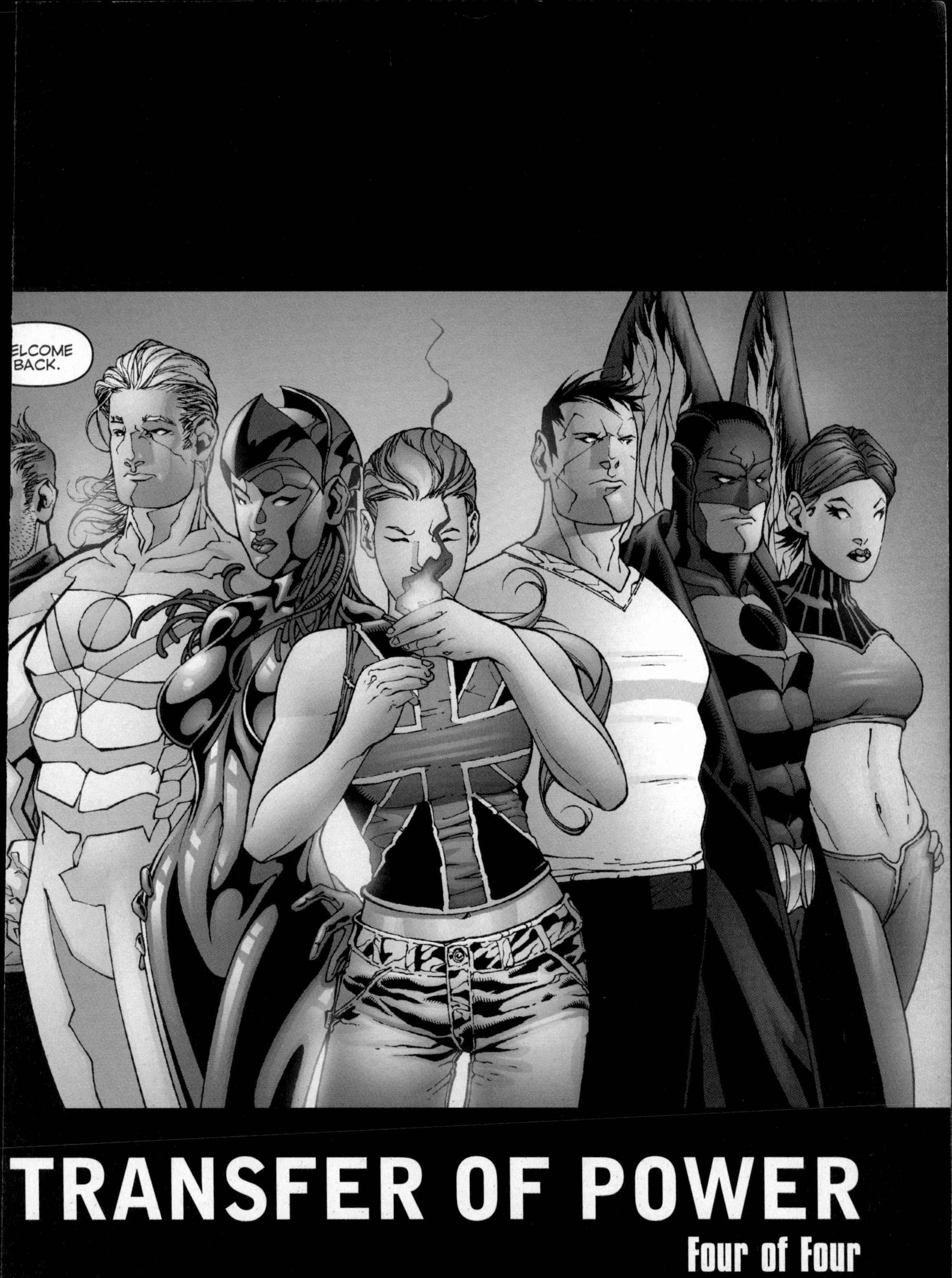
ELCOME BACK.

TRANSFER OF POWER

Four of Four

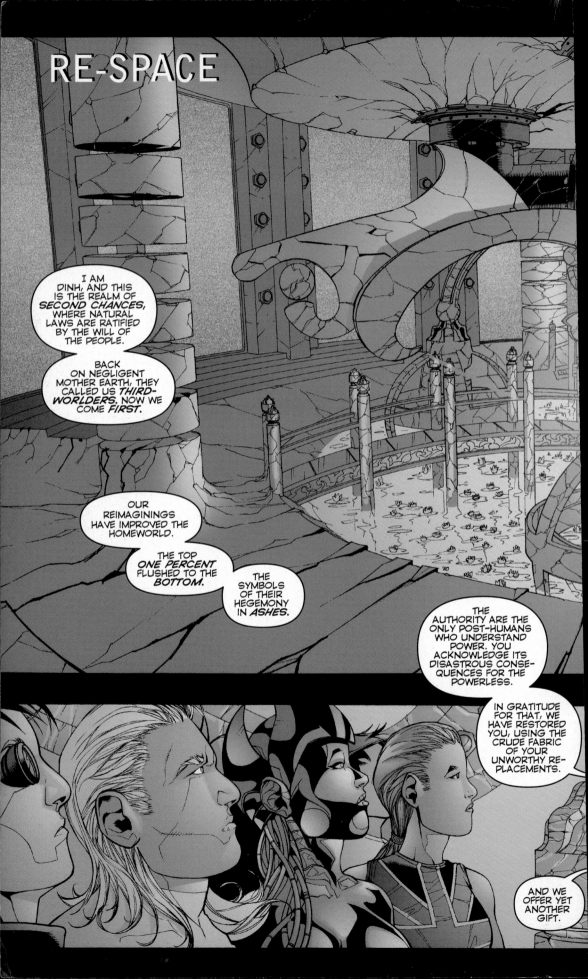

RE-SPACE

I AM DINH, AND THIS IS THE REALM OF *SECOND CHANCES*, WHERE NATURAL LAWS ARE RATIFIED BY THE WILL OF THE PEOPLE.

BACK ON NEGLIGENT MOTHER EARTH, THEY CALLED US *THIRD-WORLDERS*. NOW WE COME *FIRST*.

OUR REIMAGININGS HAVE IMPROVED THE HOMEWORLD.

THE TOP *ONE PERCENT* FLUSHED TO THE *BOTTOM*.

THE SYMBOLS OF THEIR HEGEMONY IN *ASHES*.

THE AUTHORITY ARE THE ONLY POST-HUMANS WHO UNDERSTAND POWER. YOU ACKNOWLEDGE ITS DISASTROUS CONSE-QUENCES FOR THE POWERLESS.

IN GRATITUDE FOR THAT, WE HAVE RESTORED YOU, USING THE CRUDE FABRIC OF YOUR UNWORTHY RE-PLACEMENTS.

AND WE OFFER YET ANOTHER GIFT.

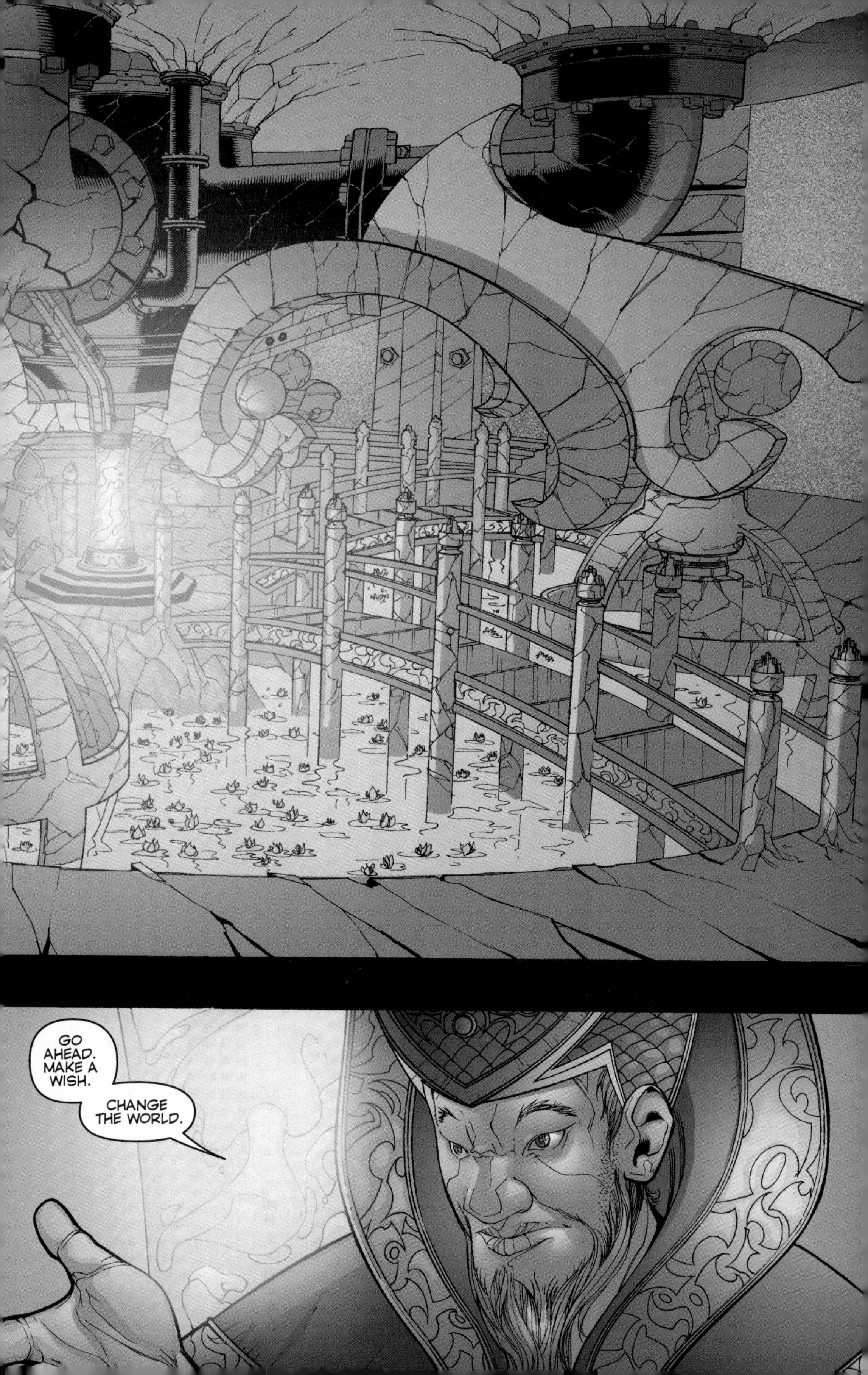
GO AHEAD. MAKE A WISH.
CHANGE THE WORLD.

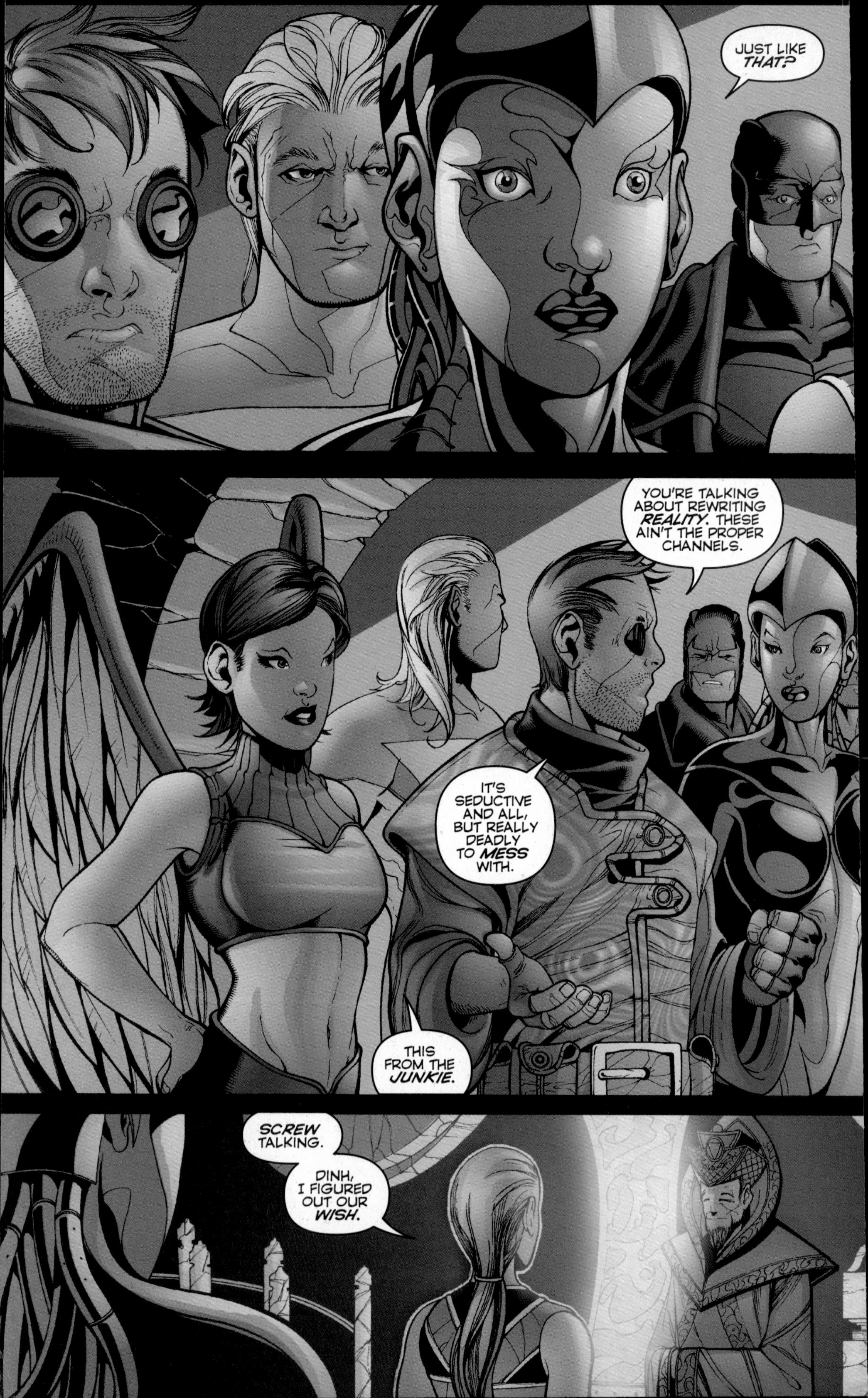
JUST LIKE *THAT?*
YOU'RE TALKING ABOUT REWRITING *REALITY*. THESE AIN'T THE PROPER CHANNELS.
IT'S SEDUCTIVE AND ALL, BUT REALLY DEADLY TO *MESS* WITH.
THIS FROM THE *JUNKIE*.
SCREW TALKING.
DINH, I FIGURED OUT OUR *WISH*.

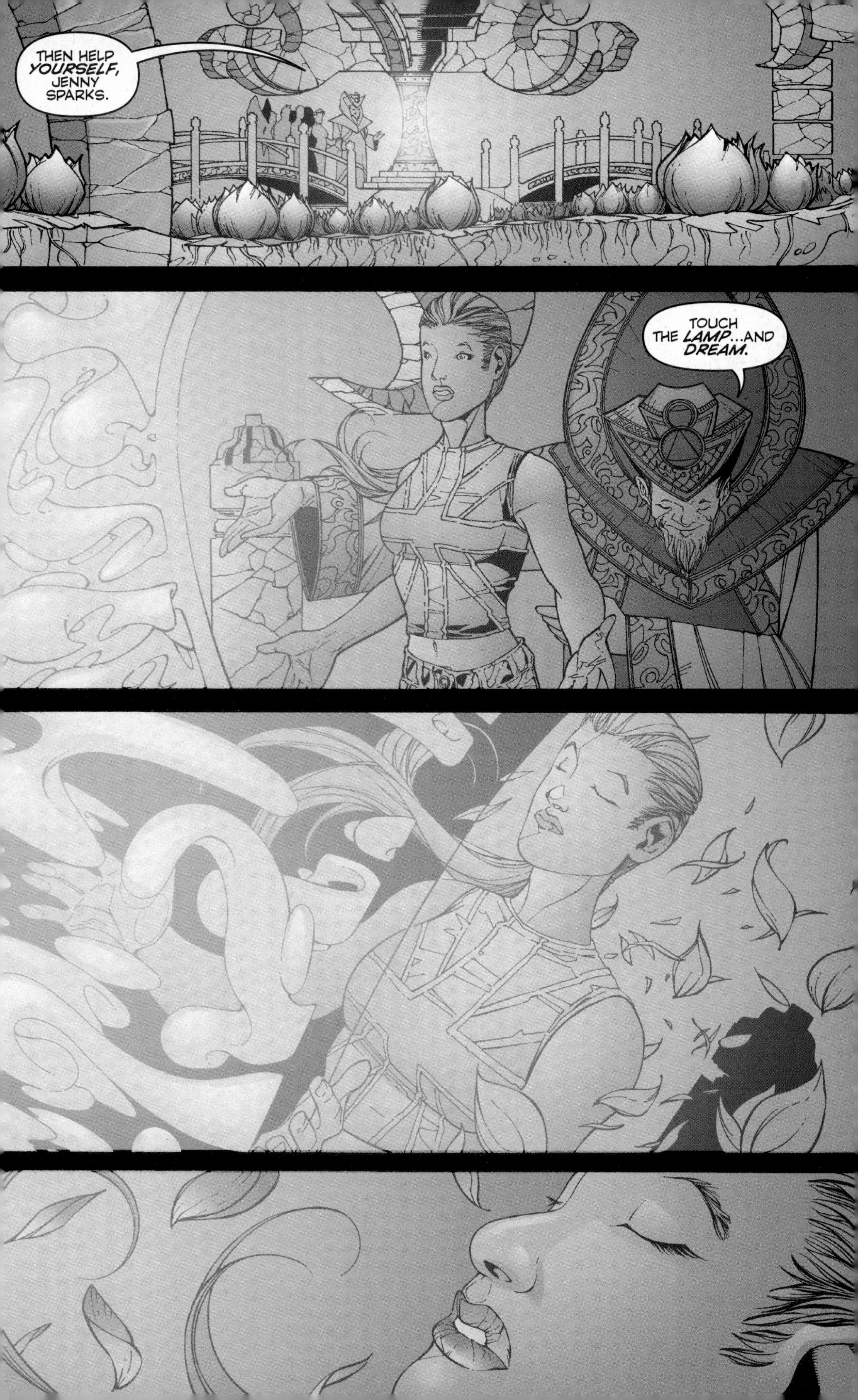
THEN HELP *YOURSELF,* JENNY SPARKS.
TOUCH THE *LAMP*...AND *DREAM.*

EARTH

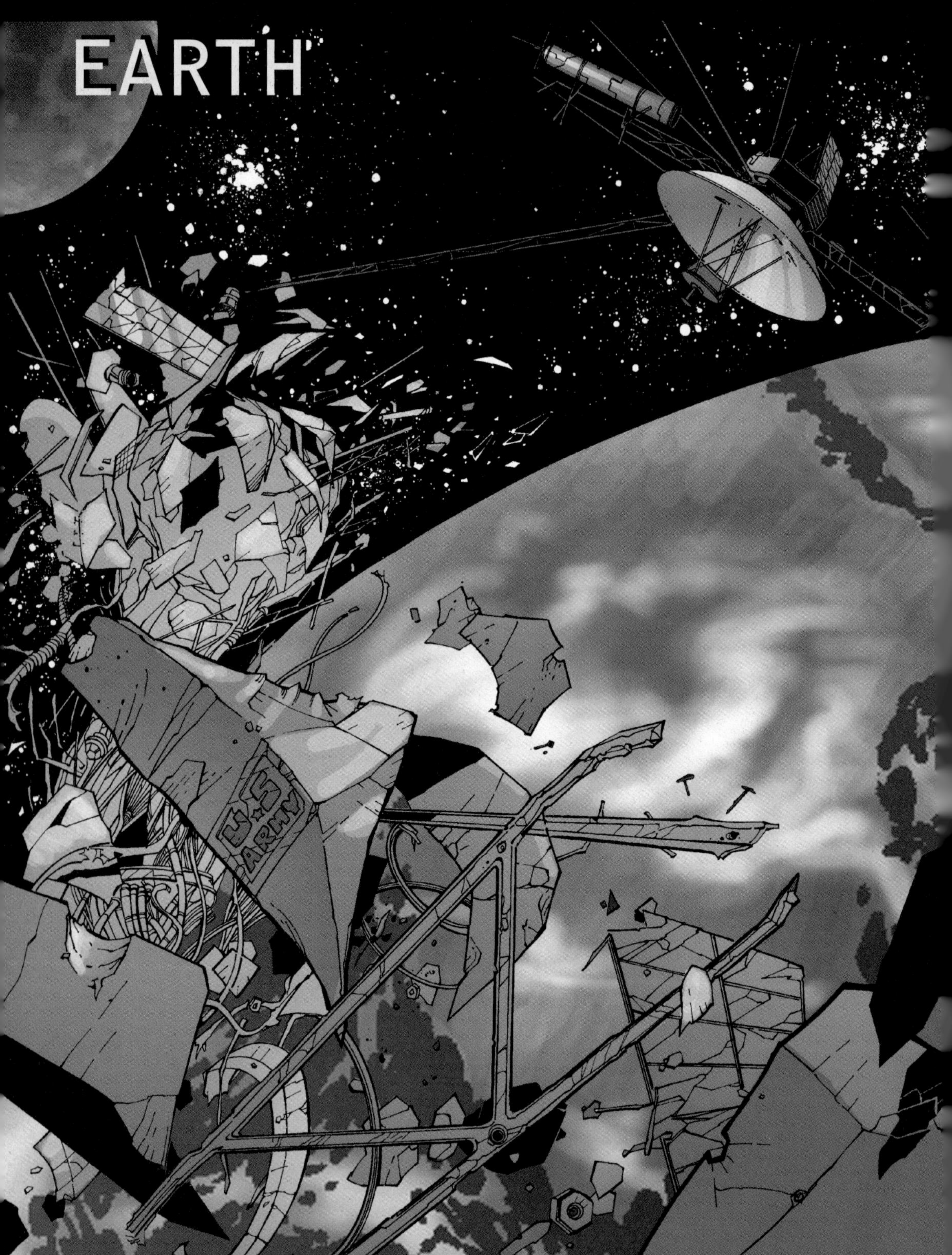

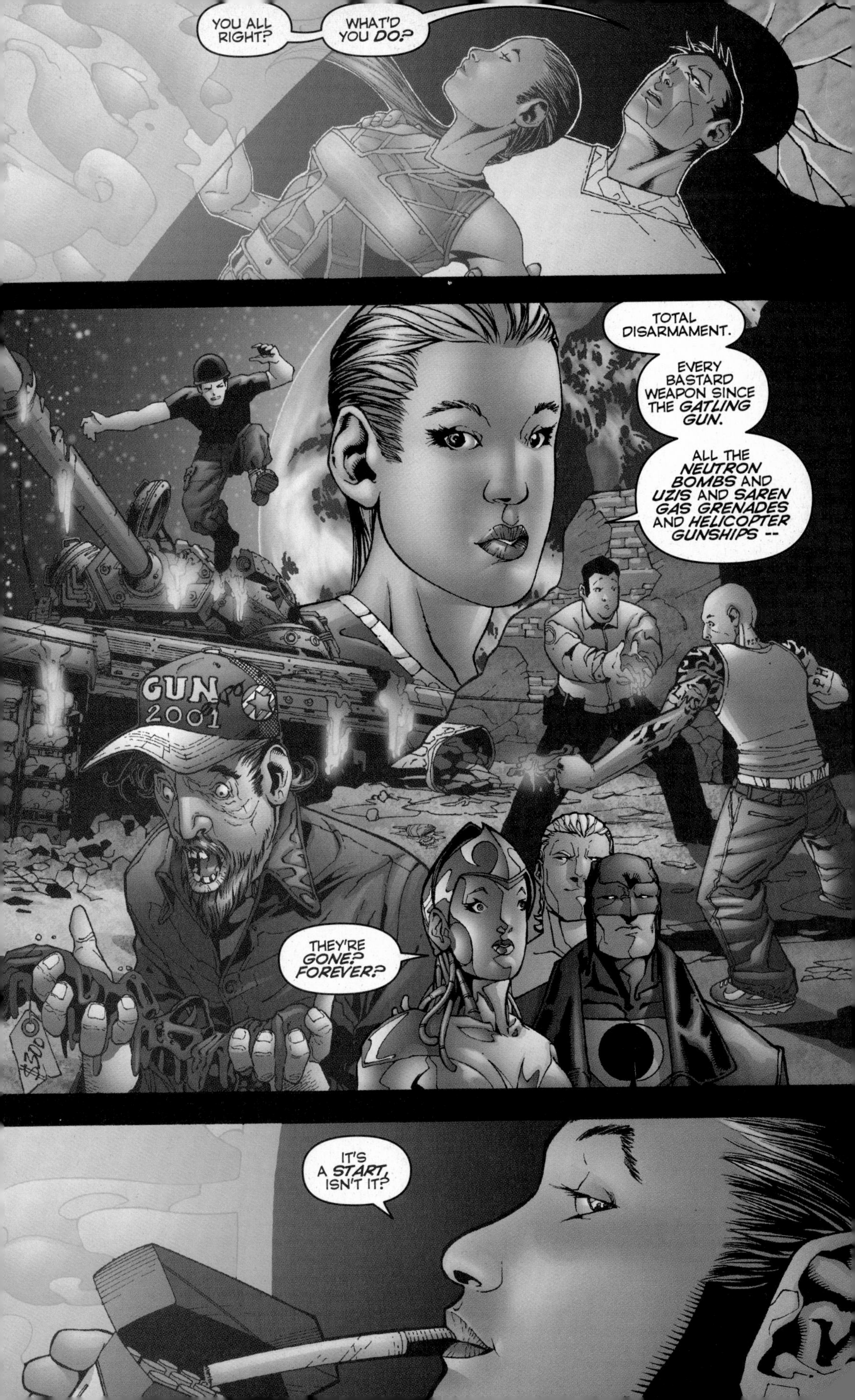
YOU ALL RIGHT?
WHAT'D YOU DO?
TOTAL DISARMAMENT.
EVERY BASTARD WEAPON SINCE THE GATLING GUN.
ALL THE NEUTRON BOMBS AND UZIS AND SAREN GAS GRENADES AND HELICOPTER GUNSHIPS --
GUN 2001
THEY'RE GONE? FOREVER?
IT'S A START, ISN'T IT?

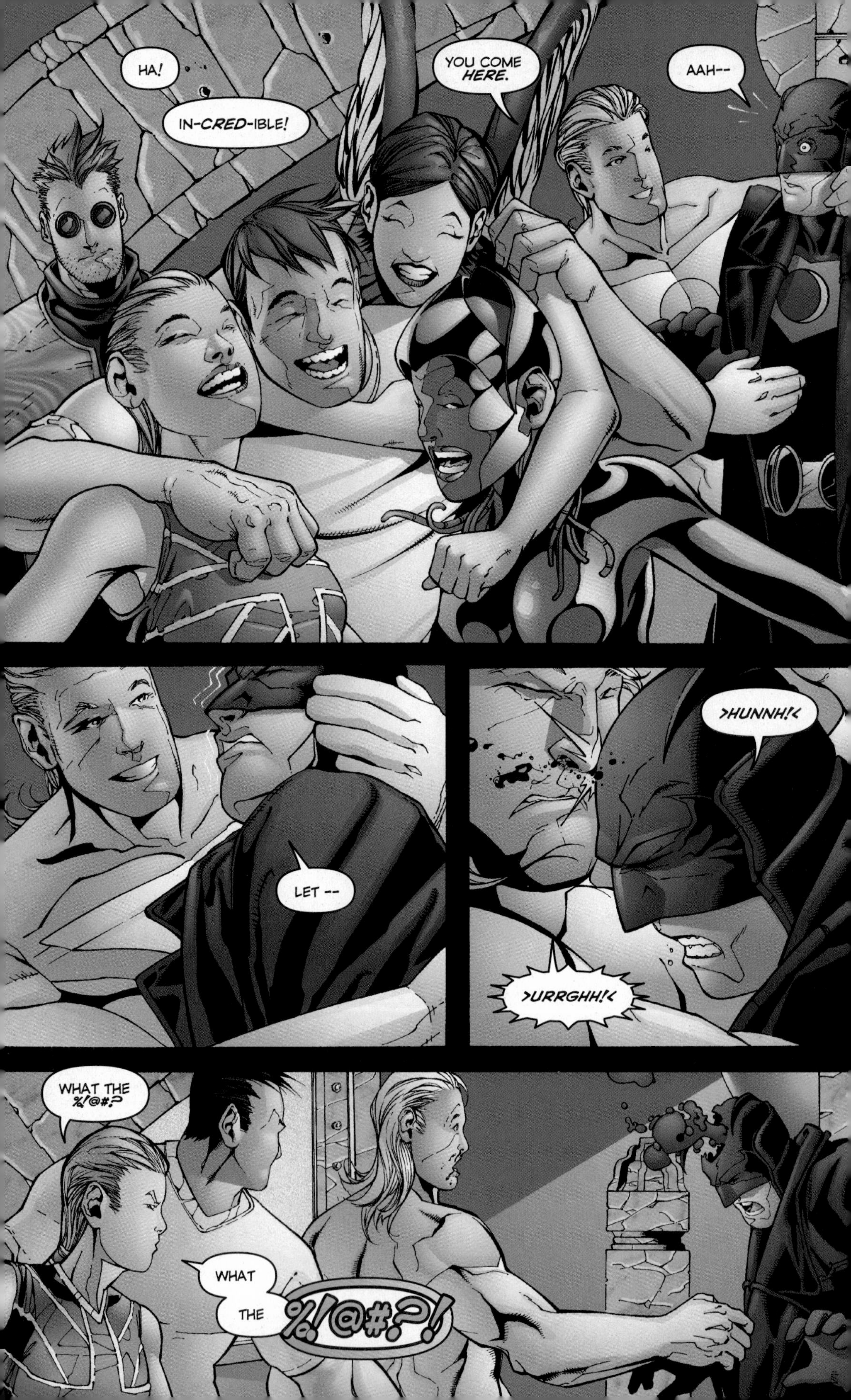

HA!
IN-CRED-IBLE!
YOU COME HERE.
AAH--
LET --
>HUNNH!<
>URRGHH!<
WHAT THE %!@#?
WHAT THE %!@#?!

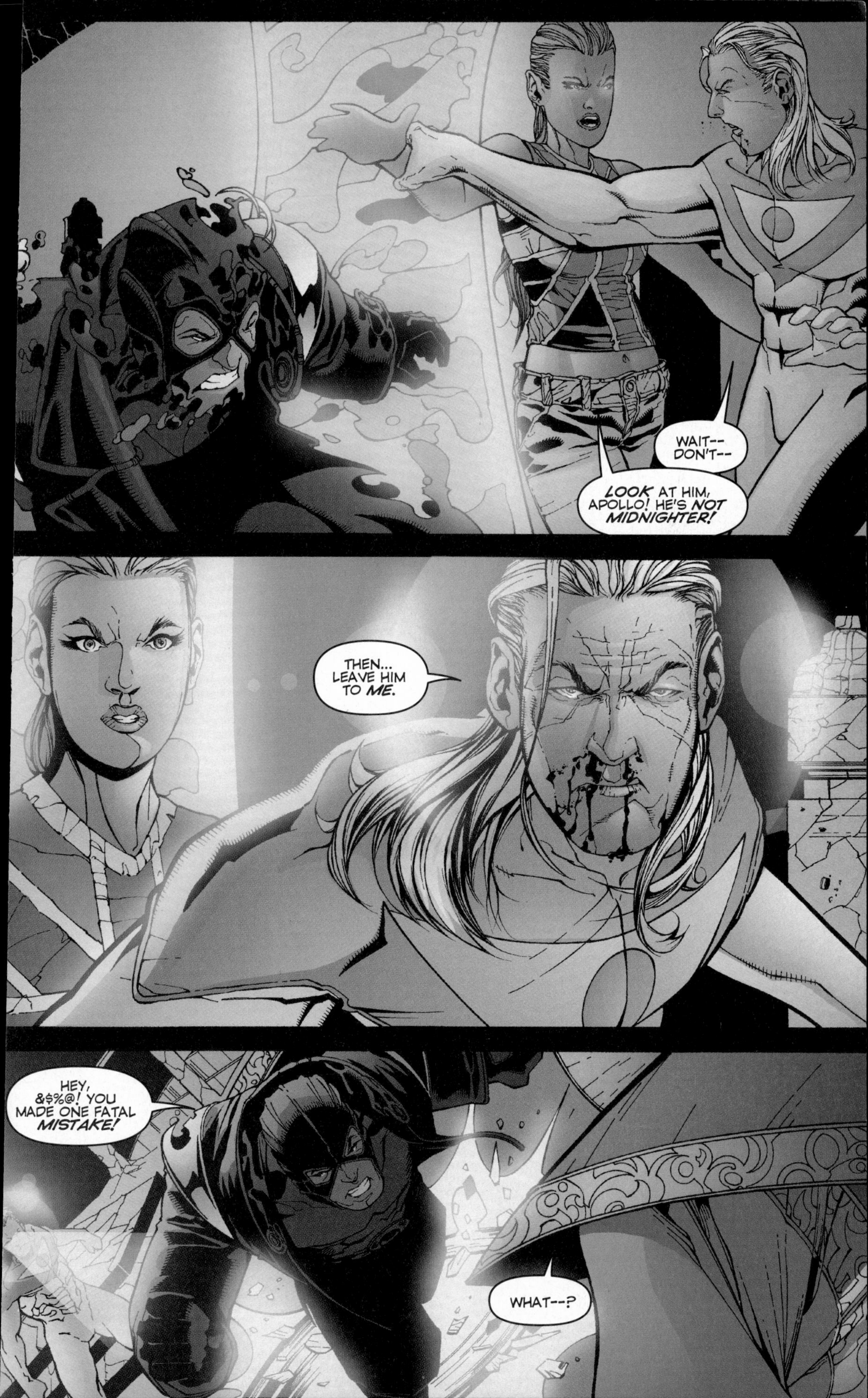
WAIT-- DON'T--
LOOK AT HIM, APOLLO! HE'S NOT MIDNIGHTER!
THEN... LEAVE HIM TO ME.
HEY, &$%@! YOU MADE ONE FATAL MISTAKE!
WHAT--?

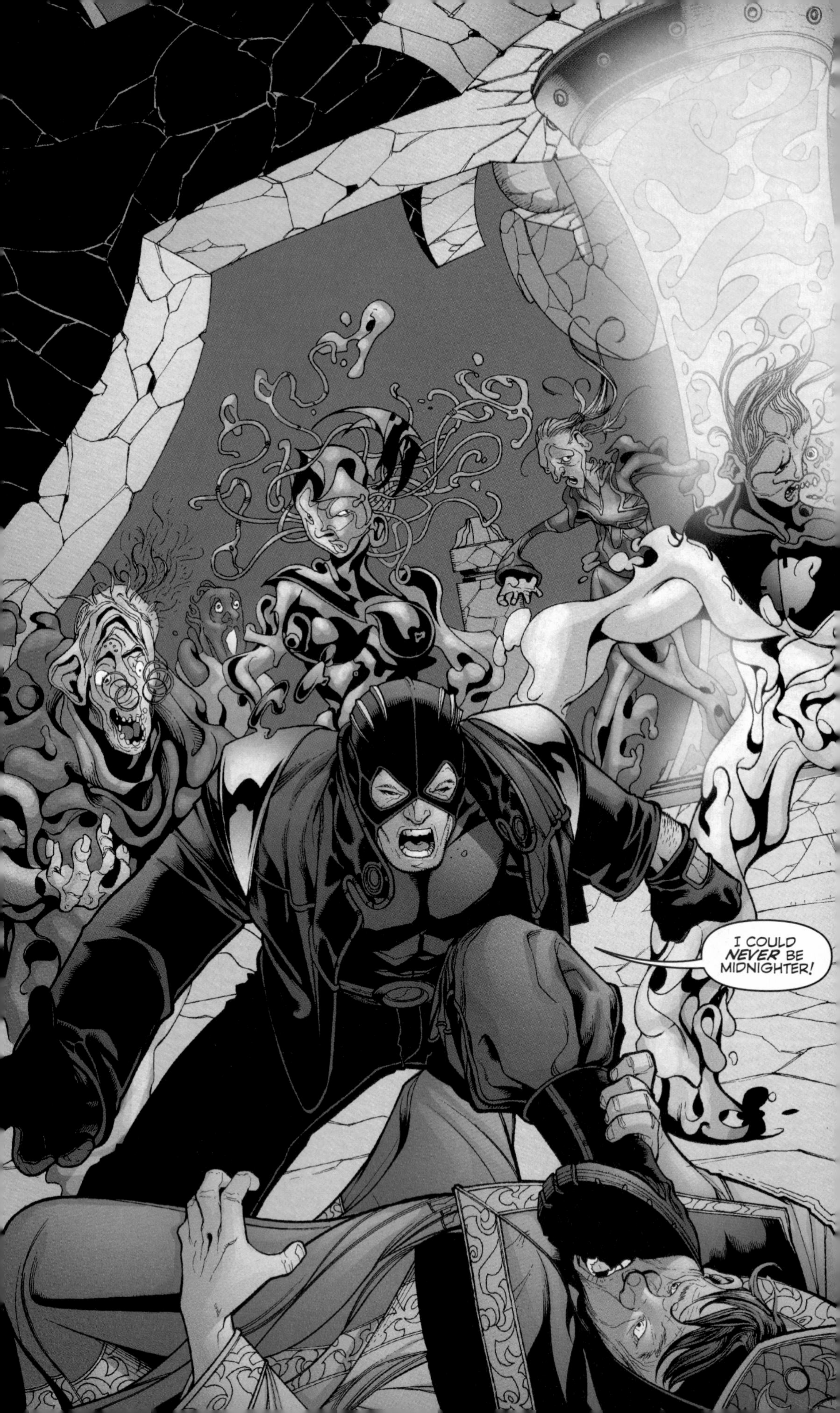
I COULD *NEVER* BE MIDNIGHTER!

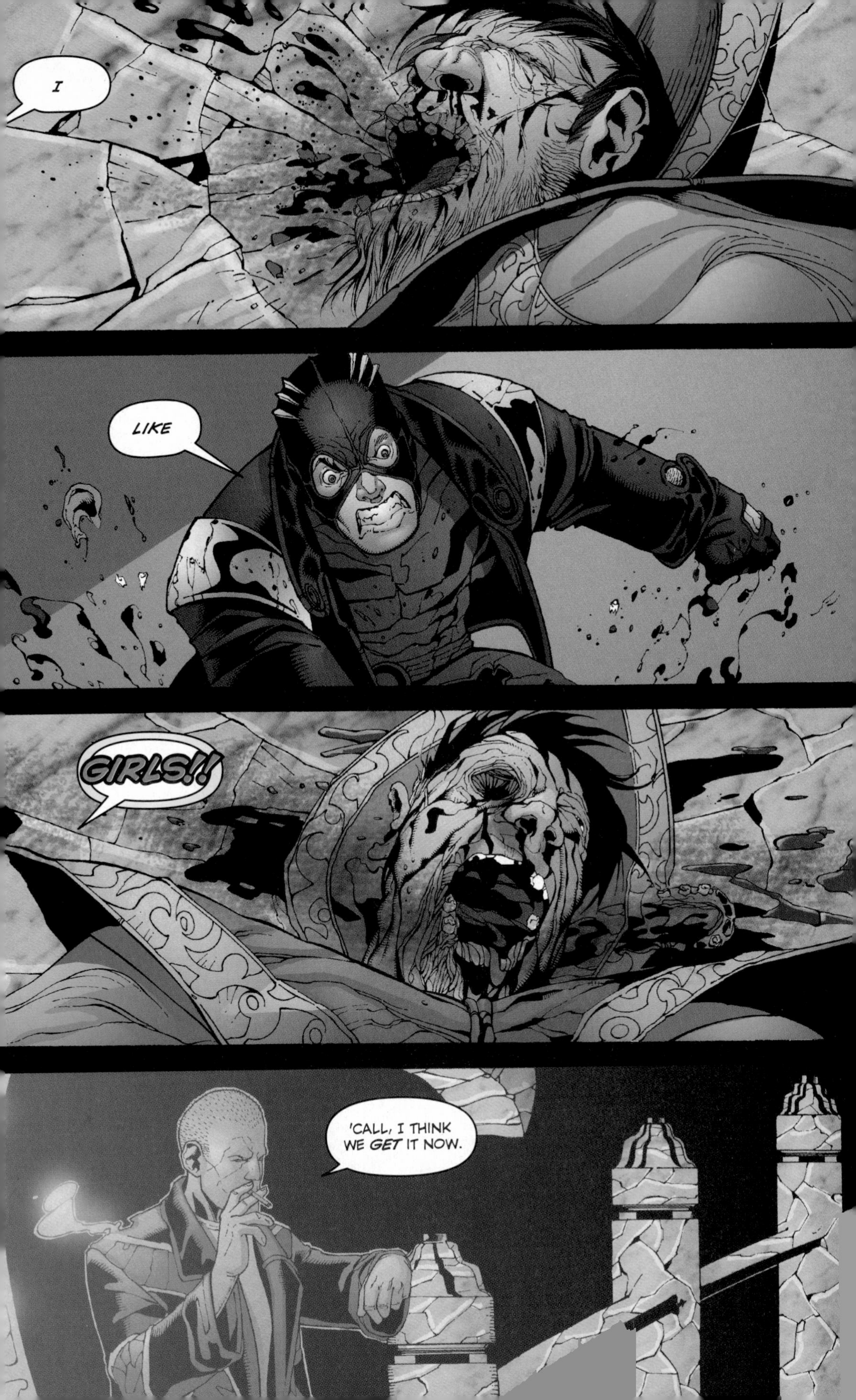
I
LIKE
GIRLS!!
'CALL, I THINK WE GET IT NOW.

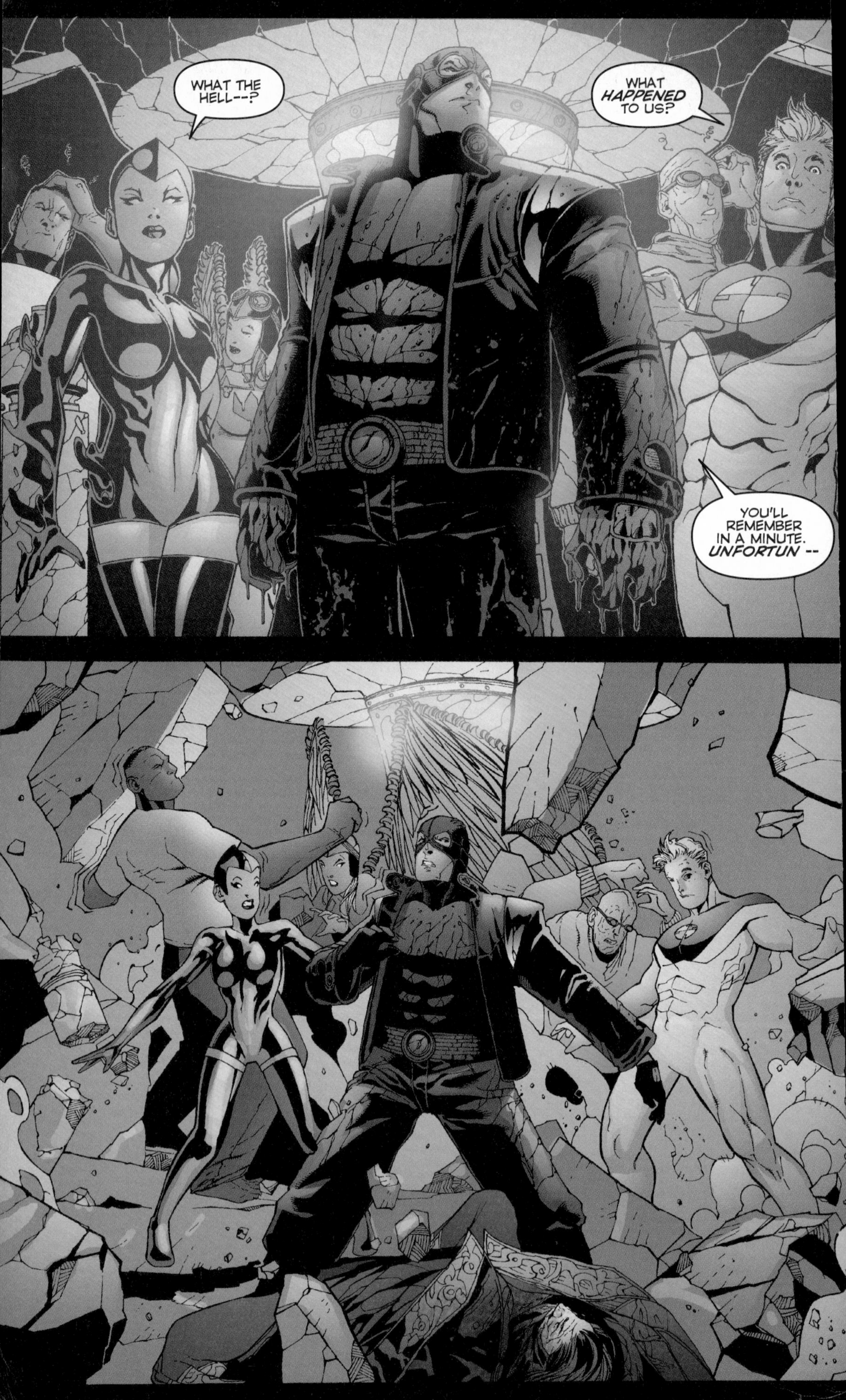
WHAT THE HELL--?
WHAT HAPPENED TO US?
YOU'LL REMEMBER IN A MINUTE. UNFORTUN --

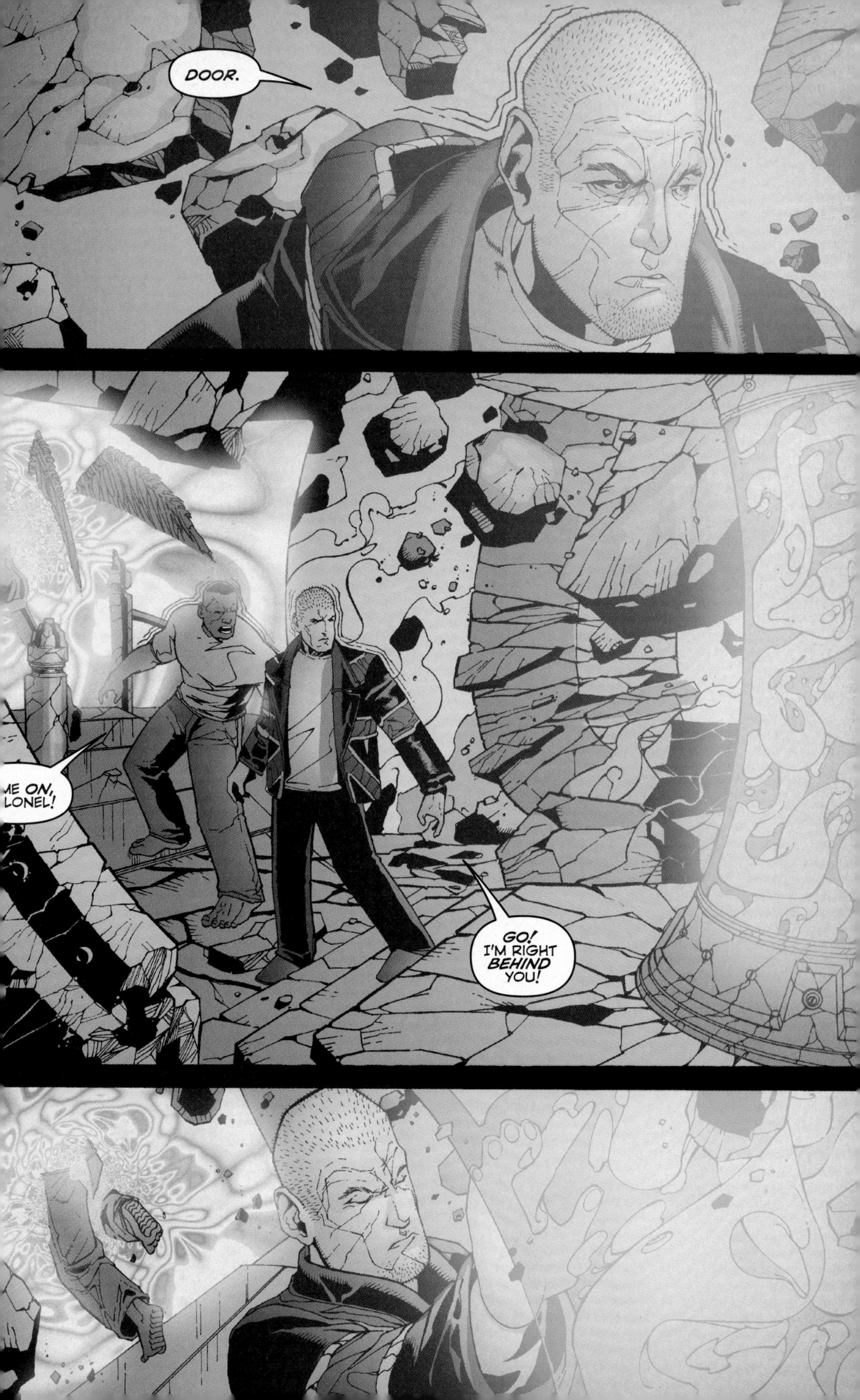
DOOR.
ME ON, LONEL!
GO! I'M RIGHT BEHIND YOU!

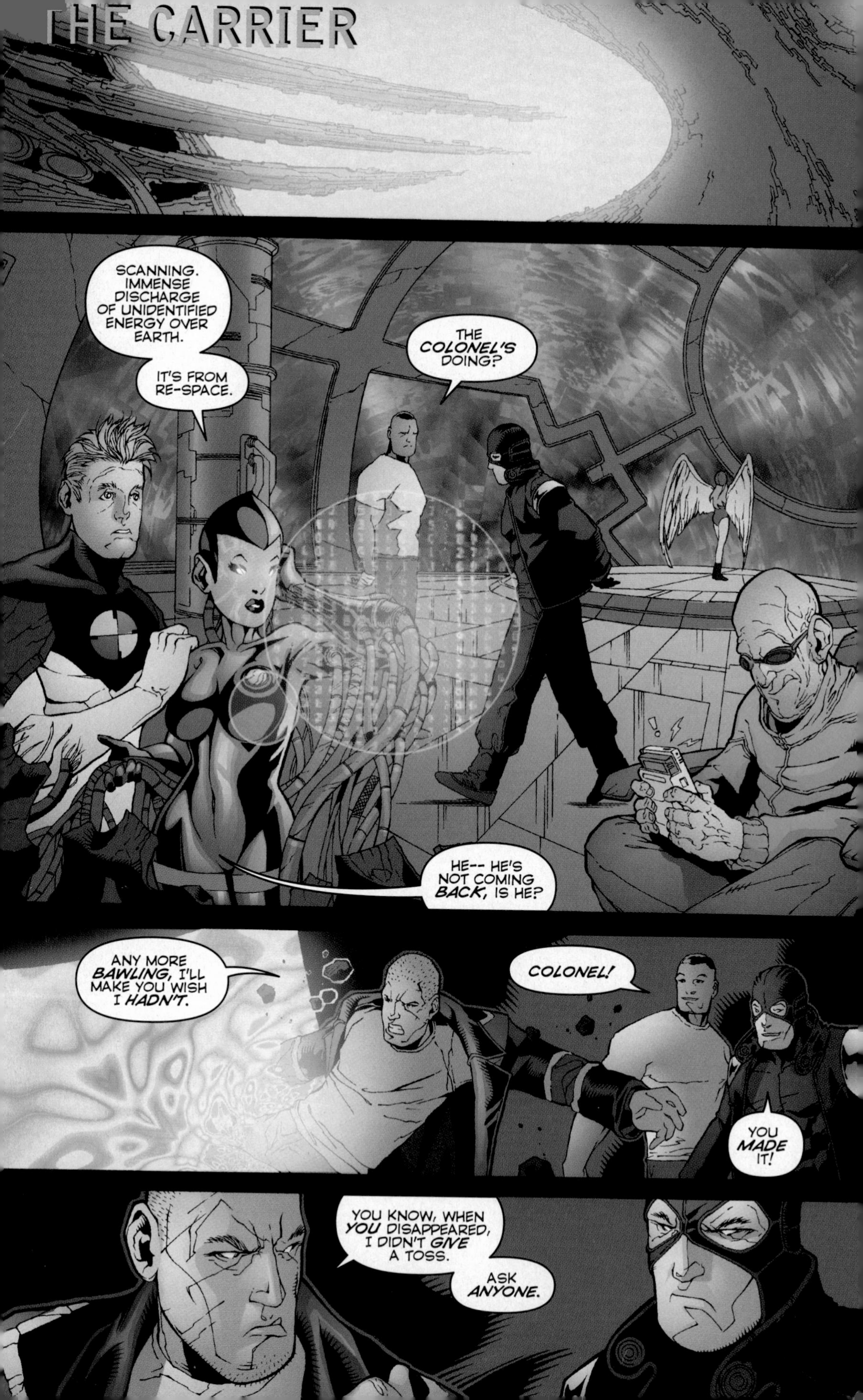

THE CARRIER
SCANNING. IMMENSE DISCHARGE OF UNIDENTIFIED ENERGY OVER EARTH.
IT'S FROM RE-SPACE.
THE COLONEL'S DOING?
HE-- HE'S NOT COMING BACK, IS HE?
ANY MORE BAWLING, I'LL MAKE YOU WISH I HADN'T.
COLONEL!
YOU MADE IT!
YOU KNOW, WHEN YOU DISAPPEARED, I DIDN'T GIVE A TOSS.
ASK ANYONE.

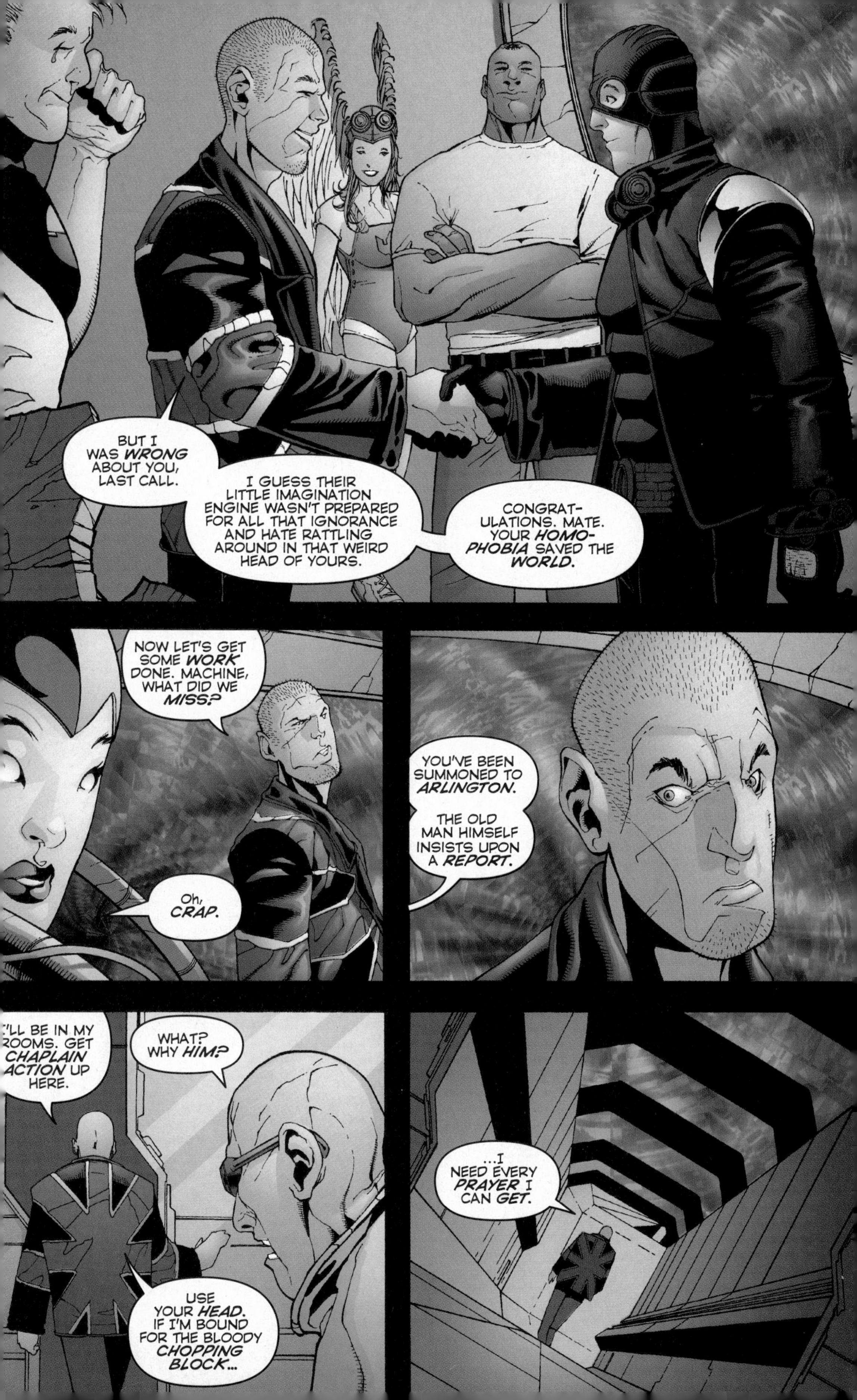
BUT I WAS *WRONG* ABOUT YOU, LAST CALL.
I GUESS THEIR LITTLE IMAGINATION ENGINE WASN'T PREPARED FOR ALL THAT IGNORANCE AND HATE RATTLING AROUND IN THAT WEIRD HEAD OF YOURS.
CONGRAT-ULATIONS. MATE. YOUR *HOMO-PHOBIA* SAVED THE *WORLD*.
NOW LET'S GET SOME *WORK* DONE. MACHINE, WHAT DID WE *MISS?*
Oh, *CRAP*.
YOU'VE BEEN SUMMONED TO *ARLINGTON*.
THE OLD MAN HIMSELF INSISTS UPON A *REPORT*.
I'LL BE IN MY ROOMS. GET *CHAPLAIN ACTION* UP HERE.
WHAT? WHY *HIM?*
USE YOUR *HEAD*. IF I'M BOUND FOR THE BLOODY *CHOPPING BLOCK*...
...I NEED EVERY *PRAYER* I CAN *GET*.

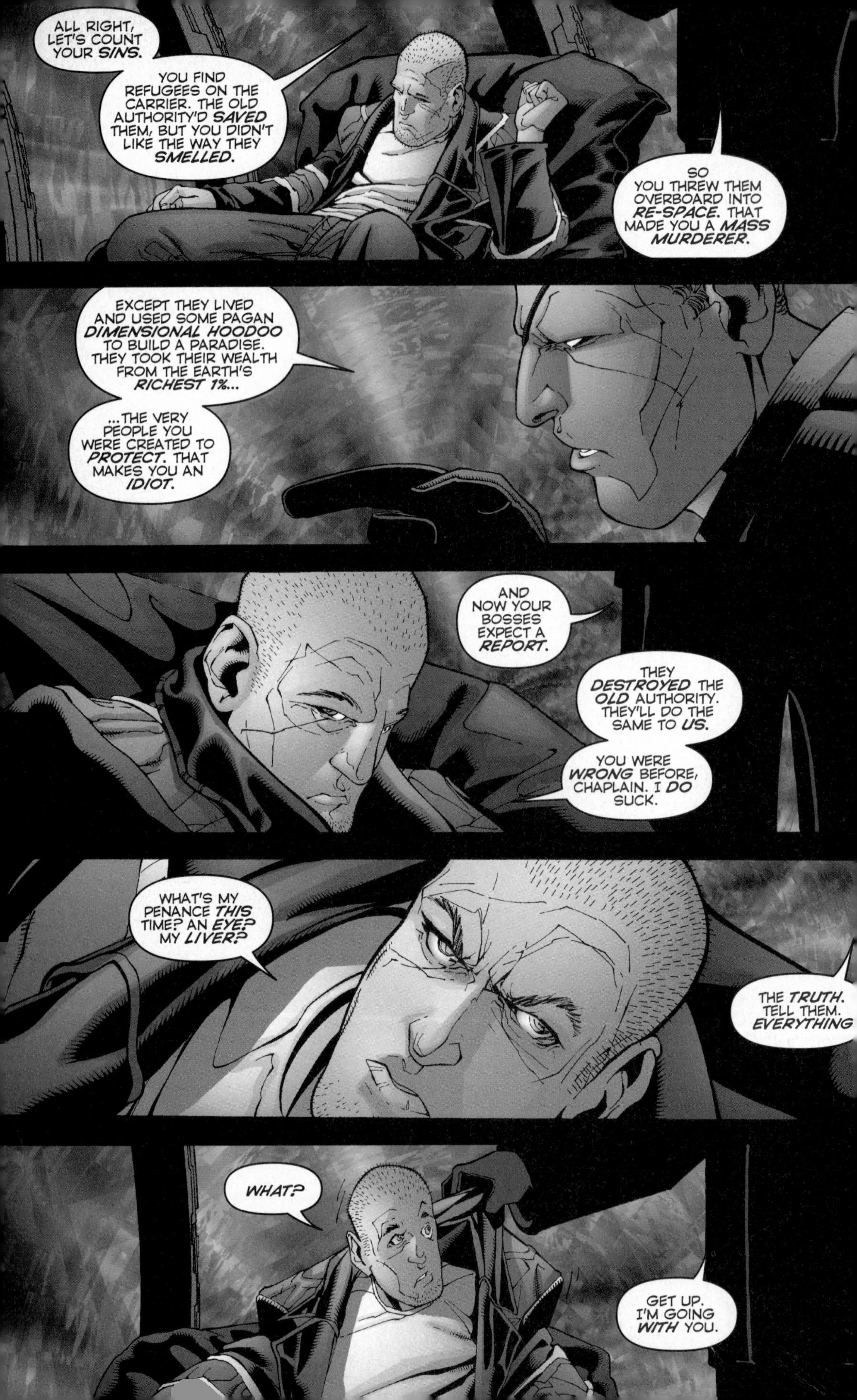
ALL RIGHT, LET'S COUNT YOUR SINS.
YOU FIND REFUGEES ON THE CARRIER. THE OLD AUTHORITY'D SAVED THEM, BUT YOU DIDN'T LIKE THE WAY THEY SMELLED.
SO YOU THREW THEM OVERBOARD INTO RE-SPACE. THAT MADE YOU A MASS MURDERER.
EXCEPT THEY LIVED AND USED SOME PAGAN DIMENSIONAL HOODOO TO BUILD A PARADISE. THEY TOOK THEIR WEALTH FROM THE EARTH'S RICHEST 1%...
...THE VERY PEOPLE YOU WERE CREATED TO PROTECT. THAT MAKES YOU AN IDIOT.
AND NOW YOUR BOSSES EXPECT A REPORT.
THEY DESTROYED THE OLD AUTHORITY. THEY'LL DO THE SAME TO US.
YOU WERE WRONG BEFORE, CHAPLAIN. I DO SUCK.
WHAT'S MY PENANCE THIS TIME? AN EYE? MY LIVER?
THE TRUTH. TELL THEM. EVERYTHING
WHAT?
GET UP. I'M GOING WITH YOU.

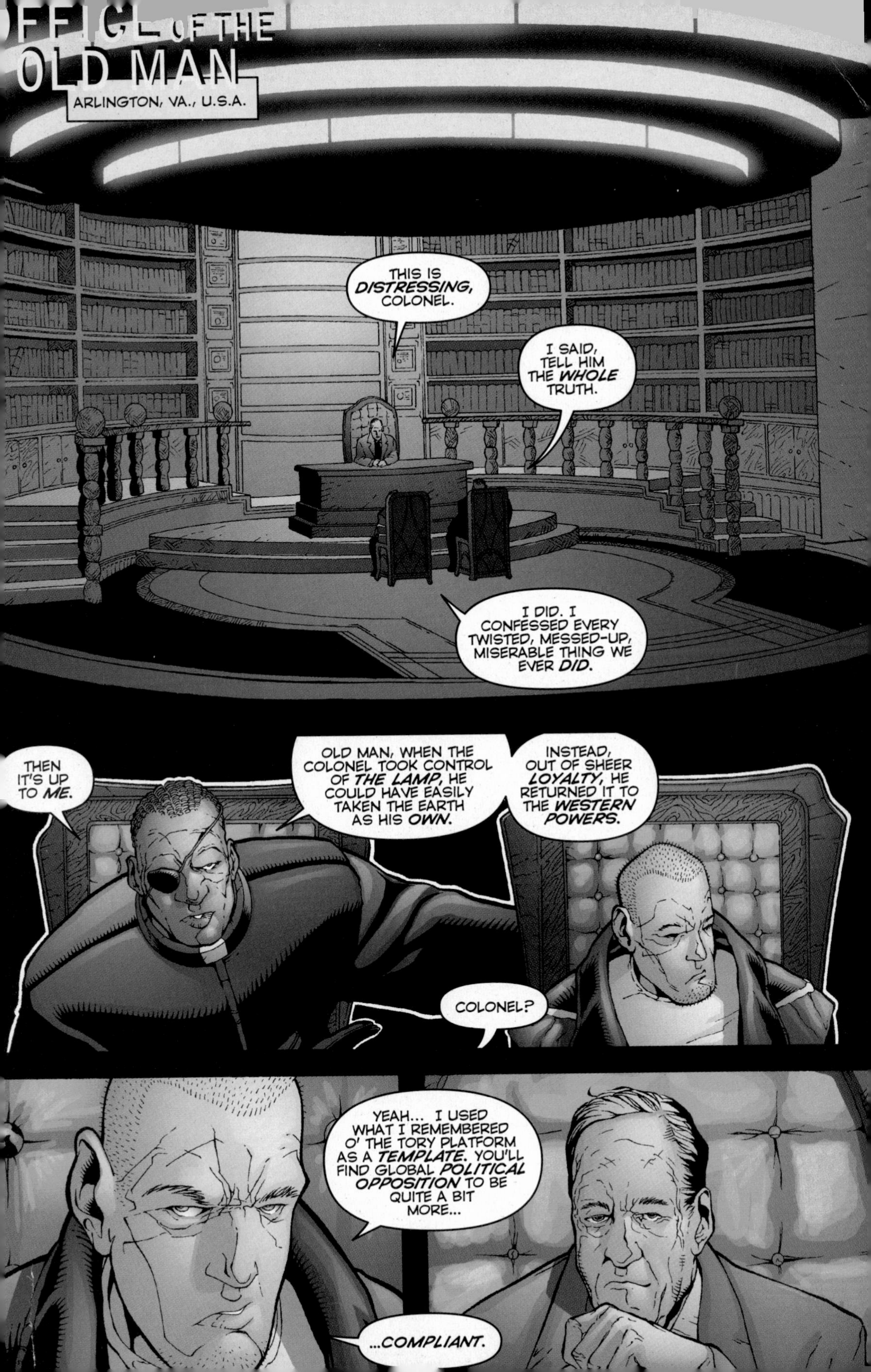

FFICE OF THE OLD MAN
ARLINGTON, VA., U.S.A.
THIS IS DISTRESSING, COLONEL.
I SAID, TELL HIM THE WHOLE TRUTH.
I DID. I CONFESSED EVERY TWISTED, MESSED-UP, MISERABLE THING WE EVER DID.
THEN IT'S UP TO ME.
OLD MAN, WHEN THE COLONEL TOOK CONTROL OF THE LAMP, HE COULD HAVE EASILY TAKEN THE EARTH AS HIS OWN.
INSTEAD, OUT OF SHEER LOYALTY, HE RETURNED IT TO THE WESTERN POWERS.
COLONEL?
YEAH... I USED WHAT I REMEMBERED O' THE TORY PLATFORM AS A TEMPLATE. YOU'LL FIND GLOBAL POLITICAL OPPOSITION TO BE QUITE A BIT MORE...
...COMPLIANT.

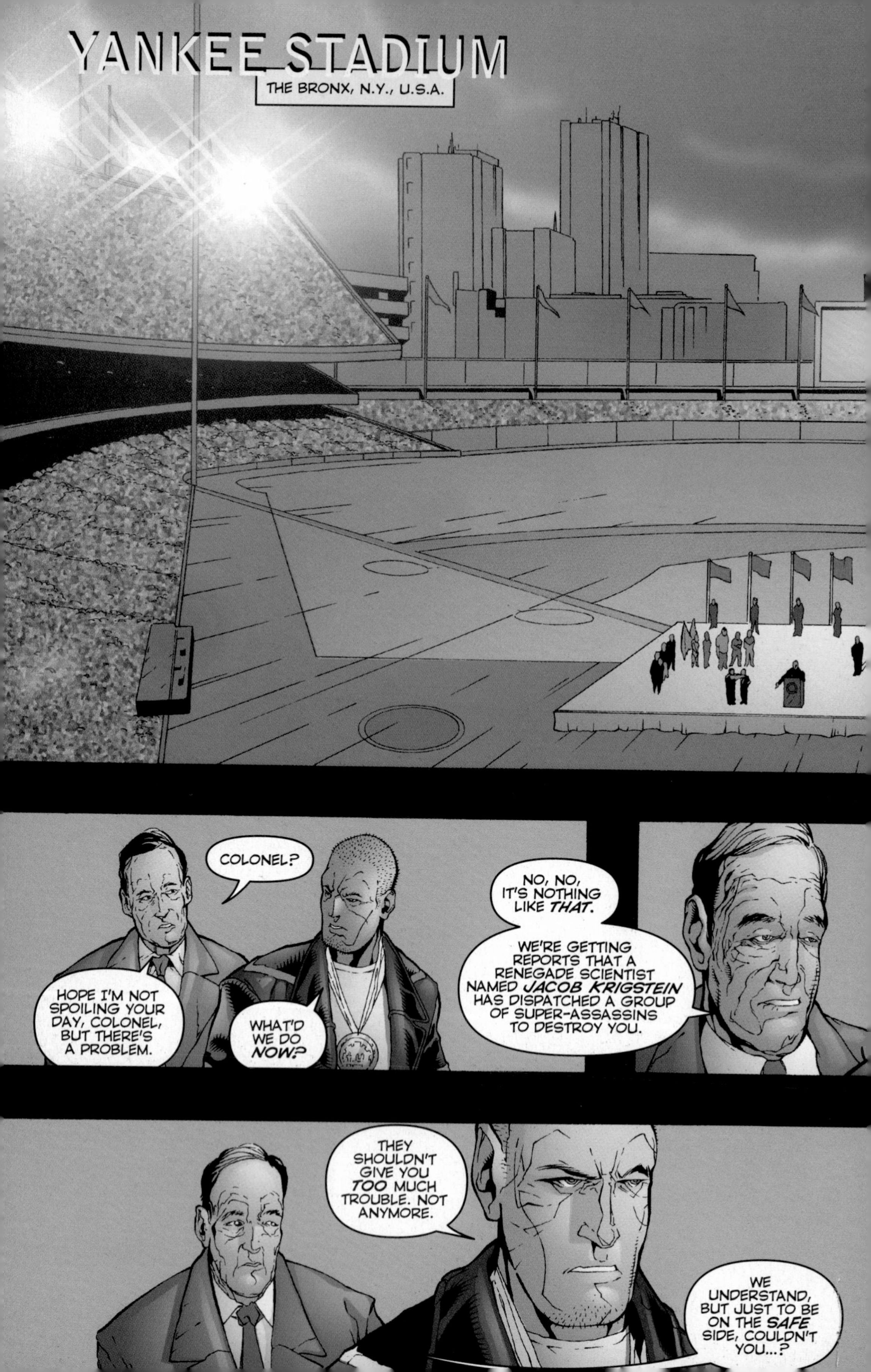
YANKEE STADIUM
THE BRONX, N.Y., U.S.A.
HOPE I'M NOT SPOILING YOUR DAY, COLONEL, BUT THERE'S A PROBLEM.
COLONEL?
WHAT'D WE DO NOW?
NO, NO, IT'S NOTHING LIKE THAT.
WE'RE GETTING REPORTS THAT A RENEGADE SCIENTIST NAMED JACOB KRIGSTEIN HAS DISPATCHED A GROUP OF SUPER-ASSASSINS TO DESTROY YOU.
THEY SHOULDN'T GIVE YOU TOO MUCH TROUBLE. NOT ANYMORE.
WE UNDERSTAND, BUT JUST TO BE ON THE SAFE SIDE, COULDN'T YOU...?

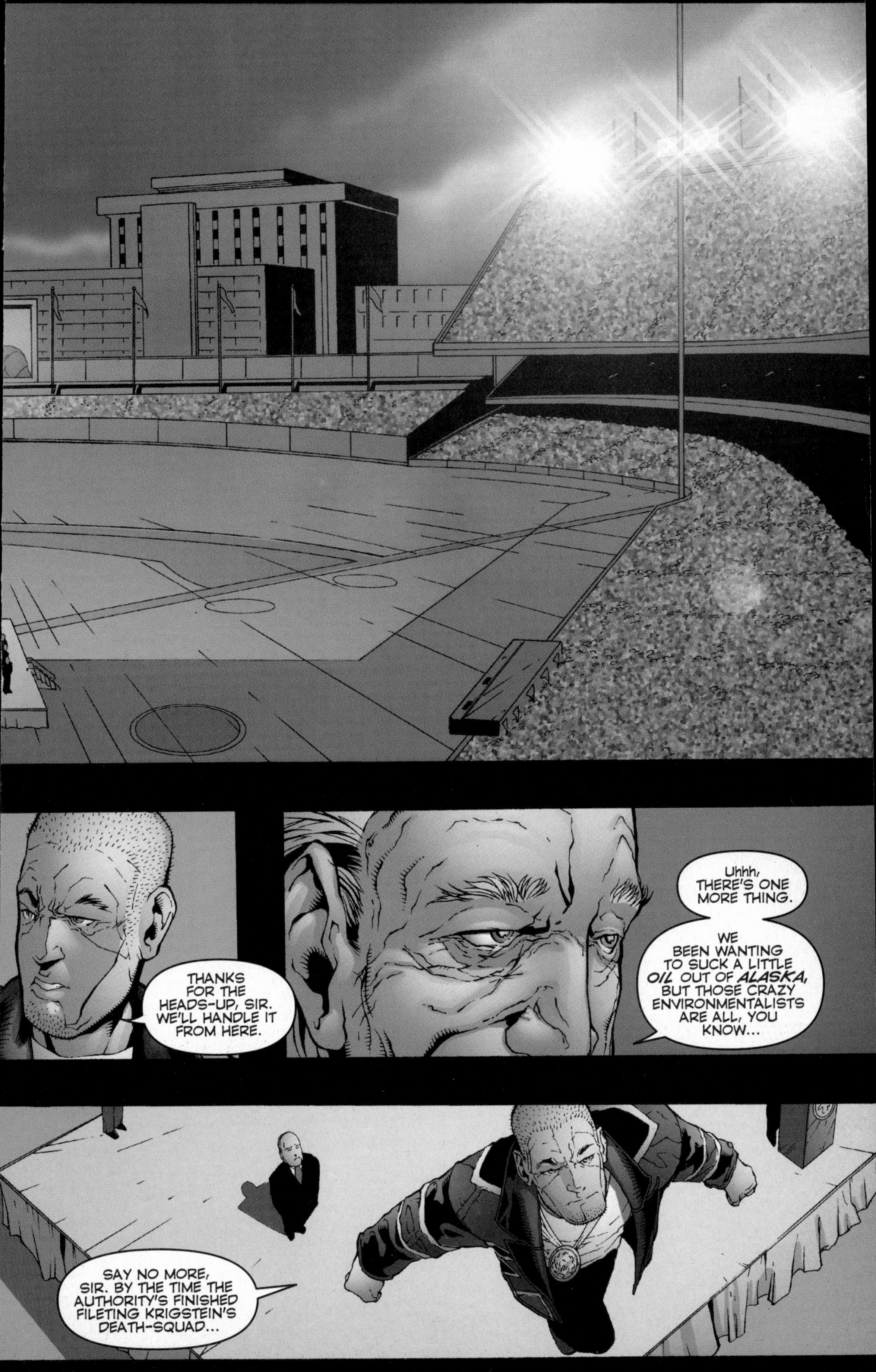
THANKS FOR THE HEADS-UP, SIR. WE'LL HANDLE IT FROM HERE.
Uhhh, THERE'S ONE MORE THING.
WE BEEN WANTING TO SUCK A LITTLE OIL OUT OF ALASKA, BUT THOSE CRAZY ENVIRONMENTALISTS ARE ALL, YOU KNOW...
SAY NO MORE, SIR. BY THE TIME THE AUTHORITY'S FINISHED FILETING KRIGSTEIN'S DEATH-SQUAD...

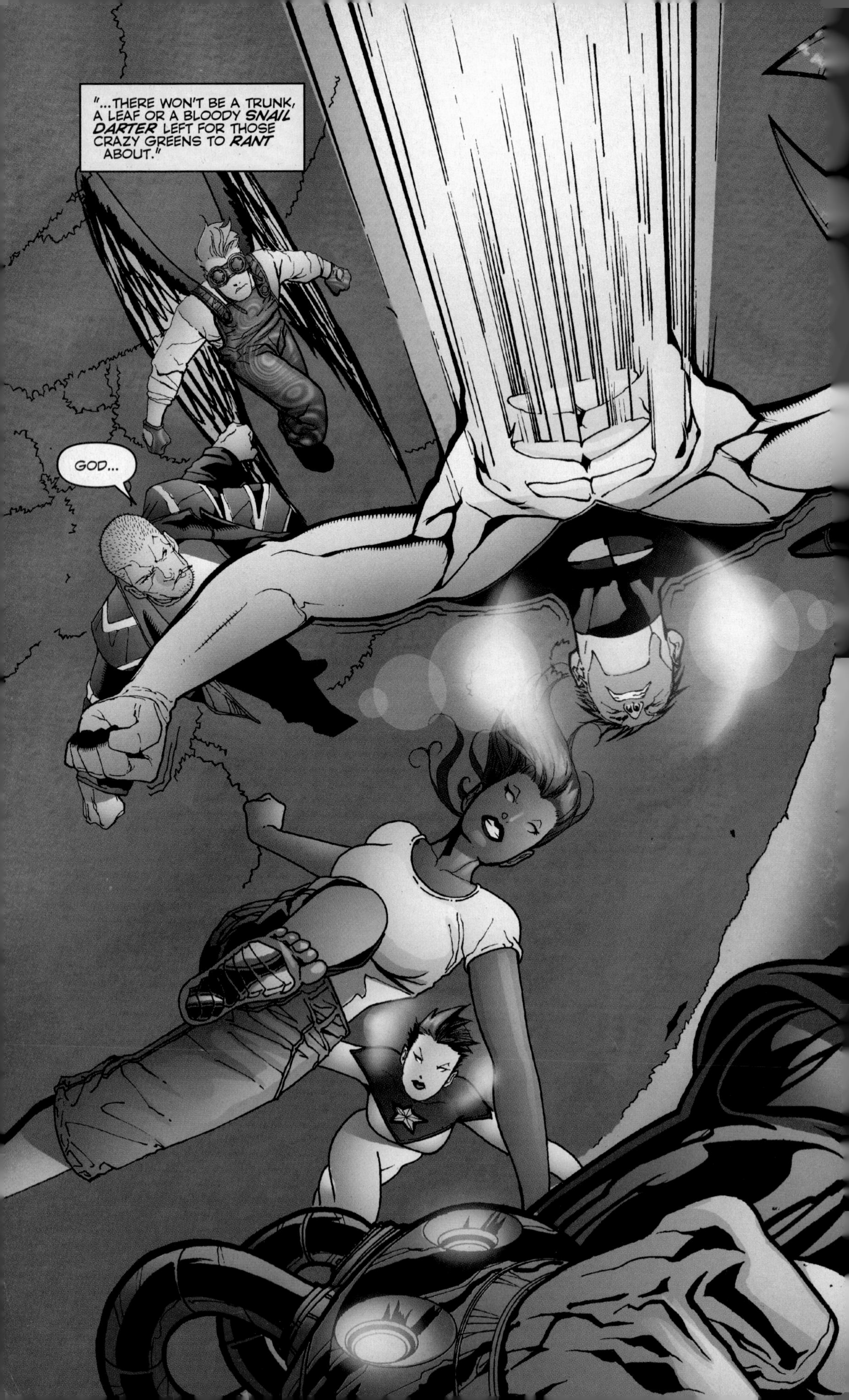
"...THERE WON'T BE A TRUNK, A LEAF OR A BLOODY SNAIL DARTER LEFT FOR THOSE CRAZY GREENS TO RANT ABOUT."
GOD...

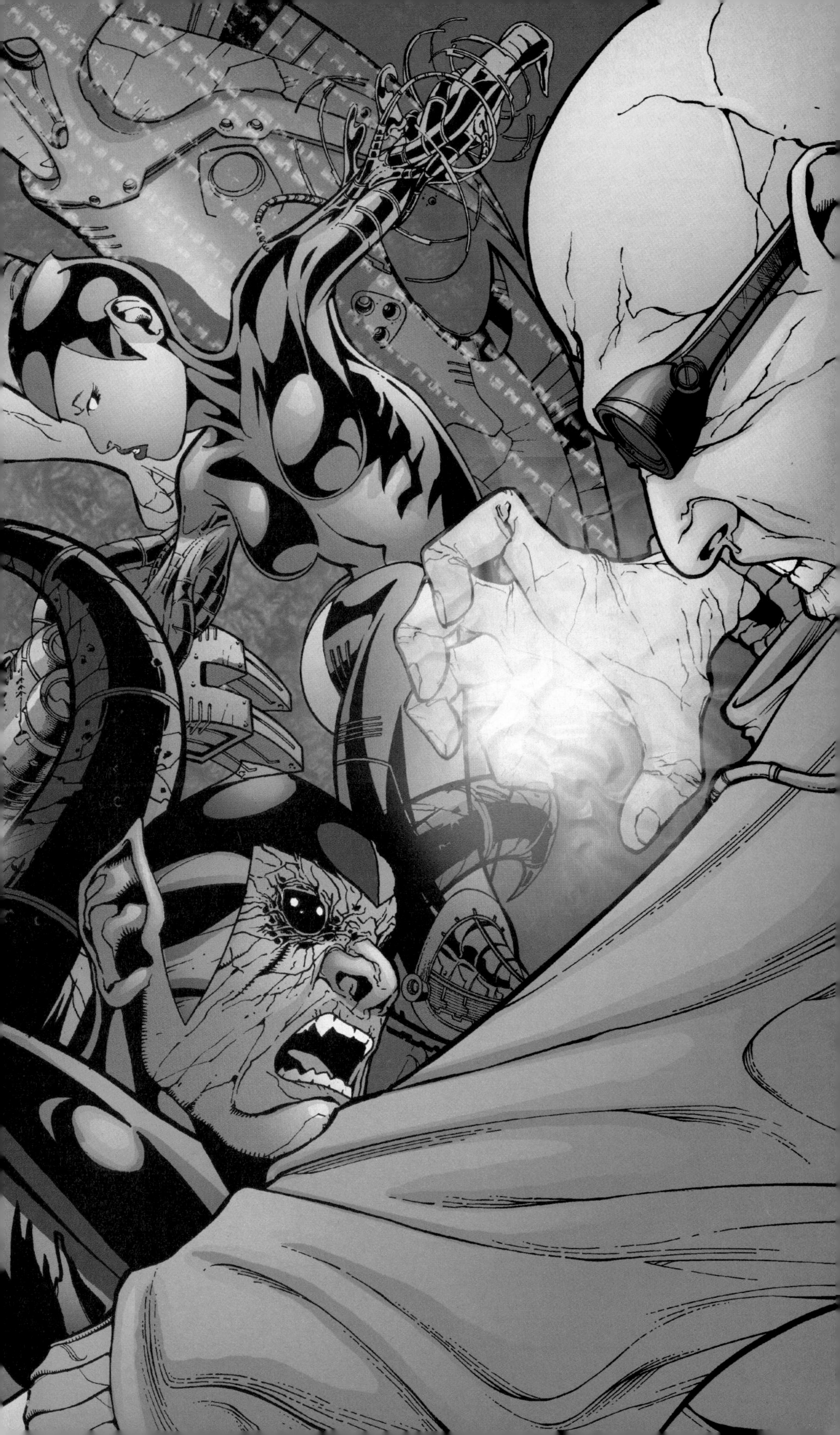

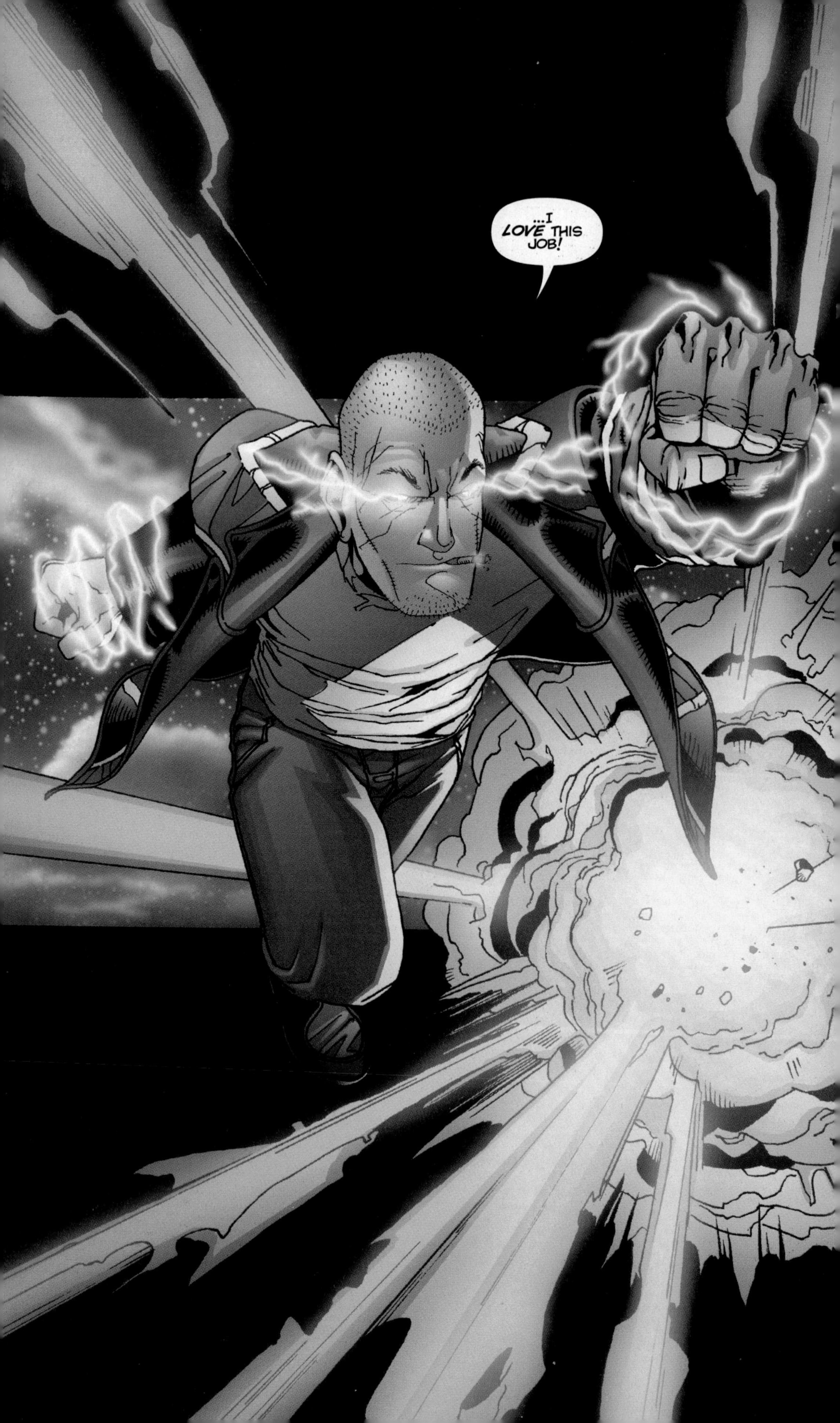
...I *LOVE* THIS JOB!

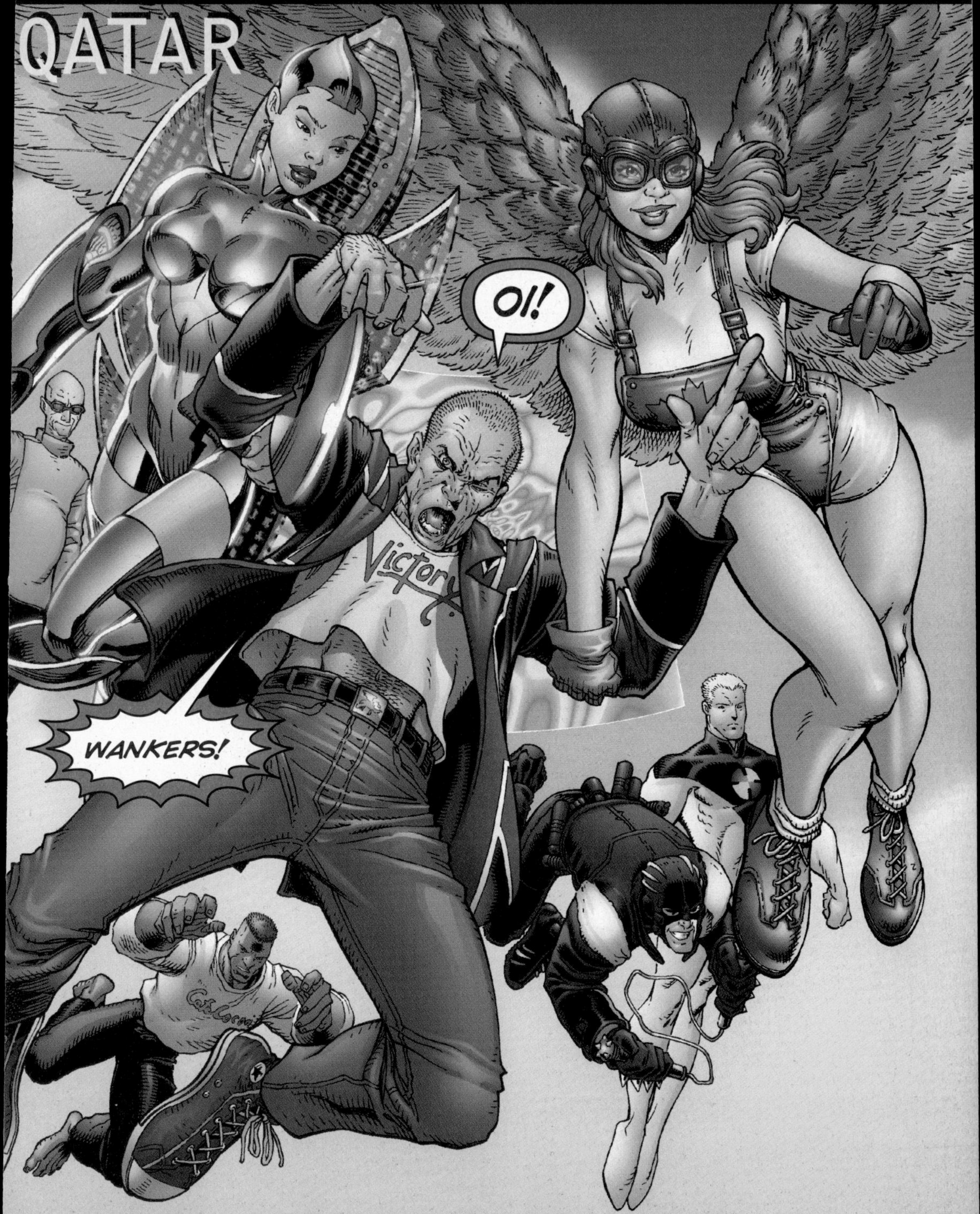
QATAR
OI!
WANKERS!
Victory

BRAVE NEW WORLD

Two of Four

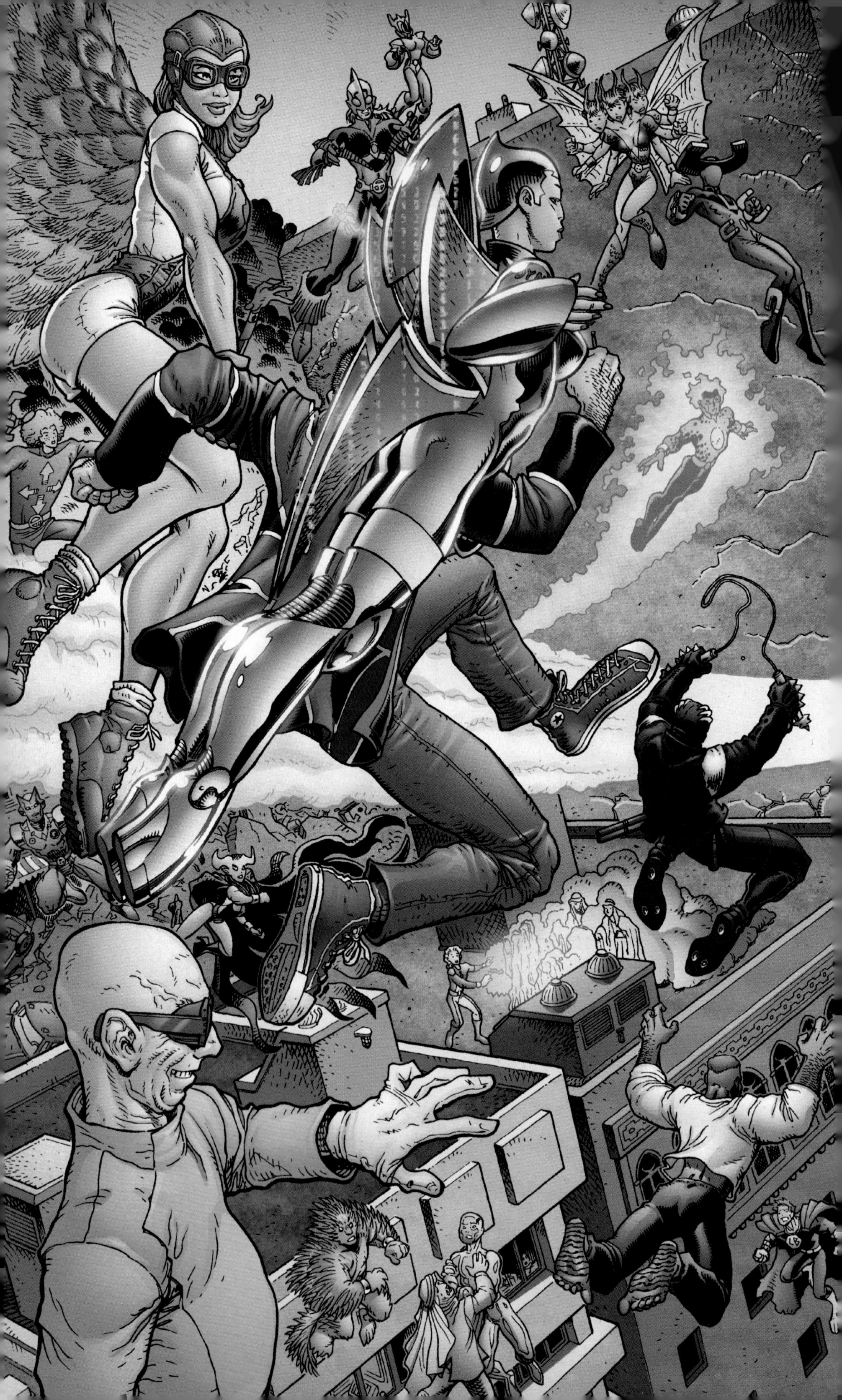

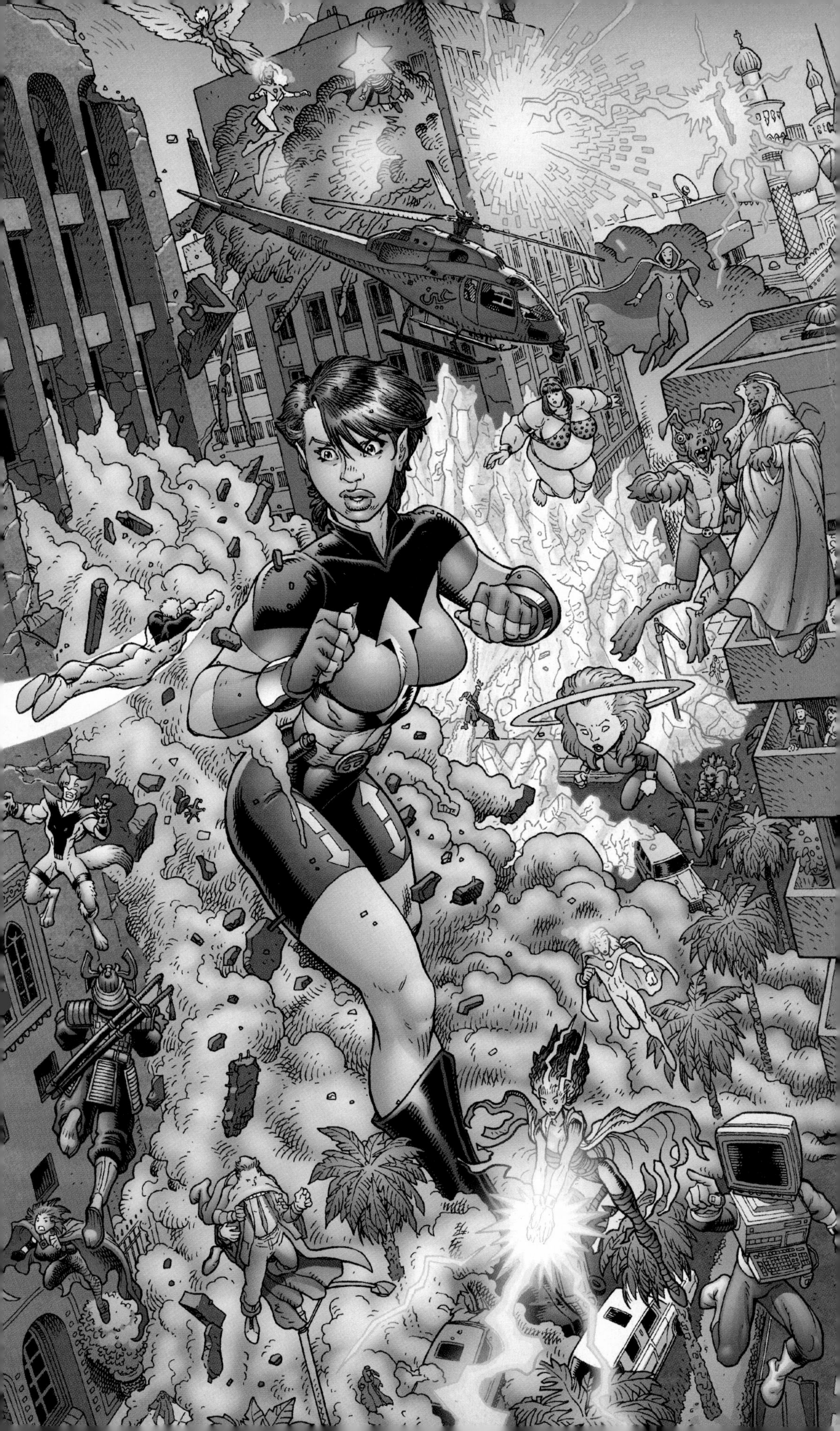

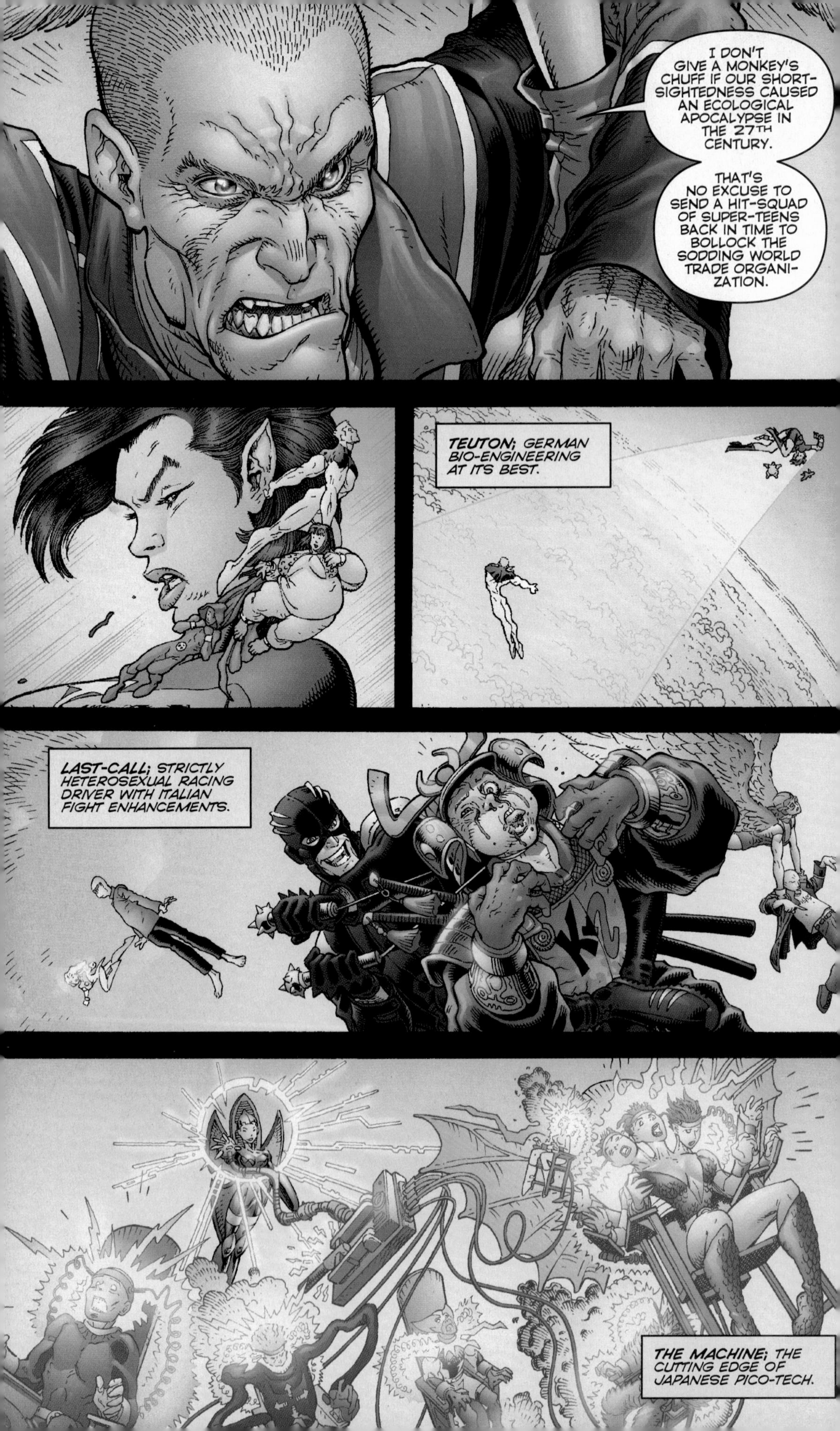
I DON'T GIVE A MONKEY'S CHUFF IF OUR SHORT-SIGHTEDNESS CAUSED AN ECOLOGICAL APOCALYPSE IN THE 27TH CENTURY.
THAT'S NO EXCUSE TO SEND A HIT-SQUAD OF SUPER-TEENS BACK IN TIME TO BOLLOCK THE SODDING WORLD TRADE ORGANI-ZATION.
TEUTON; GERMAN BIO-ENGINEERING AT ITS BEST.
LAST-CALL; STRICTLY HETEROSEXUAL RACING DRIVER WITH ITALIAN FIGHT ENHANCEMENTS.
THE MACHINE; THE CUTTING EDGE OF JAPANESE PICO-TECH.

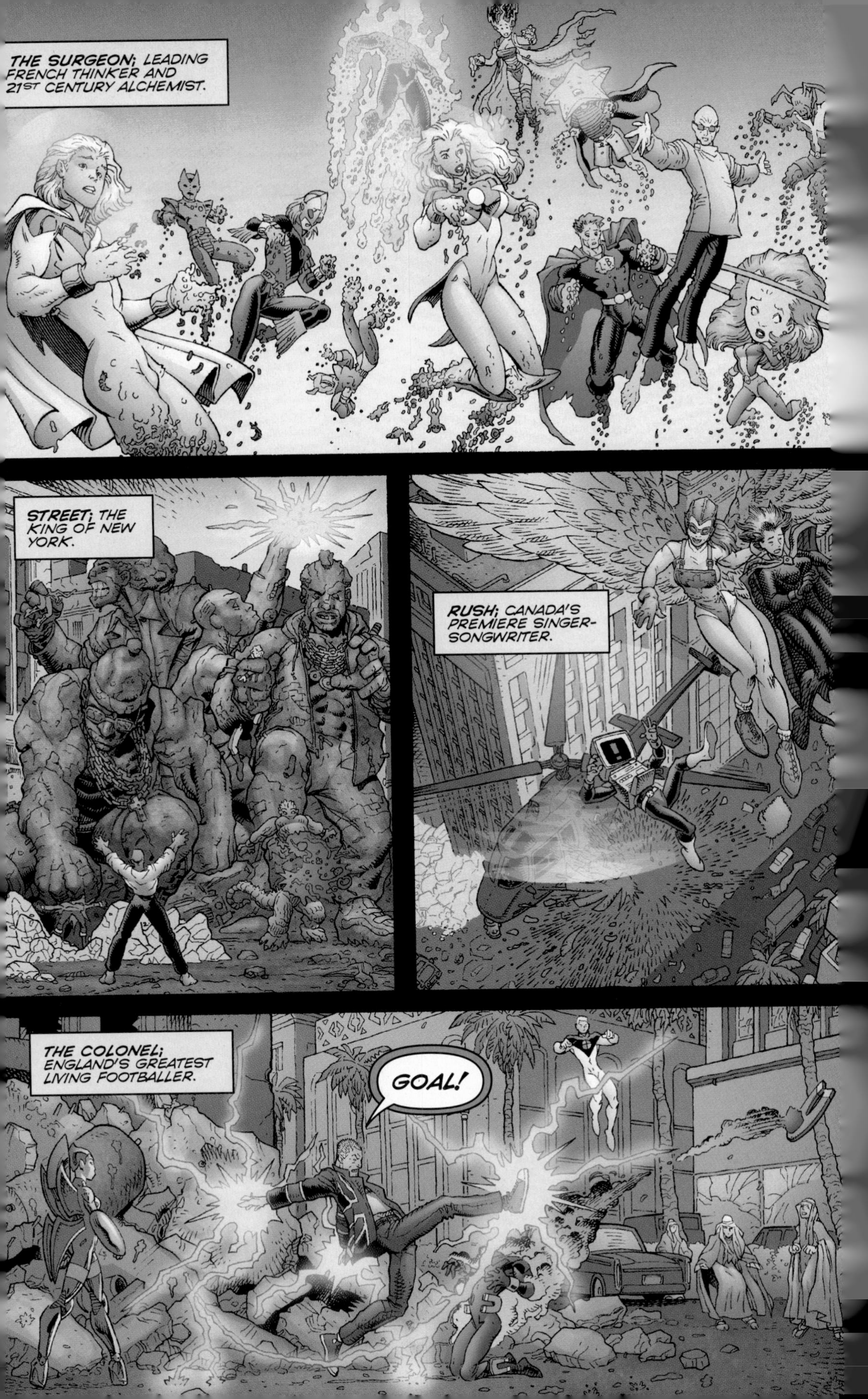
THE SURGEON; LEADING FRENCH THINKER AND 21ST CENTURY ALCHEMIST.
STREET; THE KING OF NEW YORK.
RUSH; CANADA'S PREMIERE SINGER-SONGWRITER.
THE COLONEL; ENGLAND'S GREATEST LIVING FOOTBALLER.
GOAL!

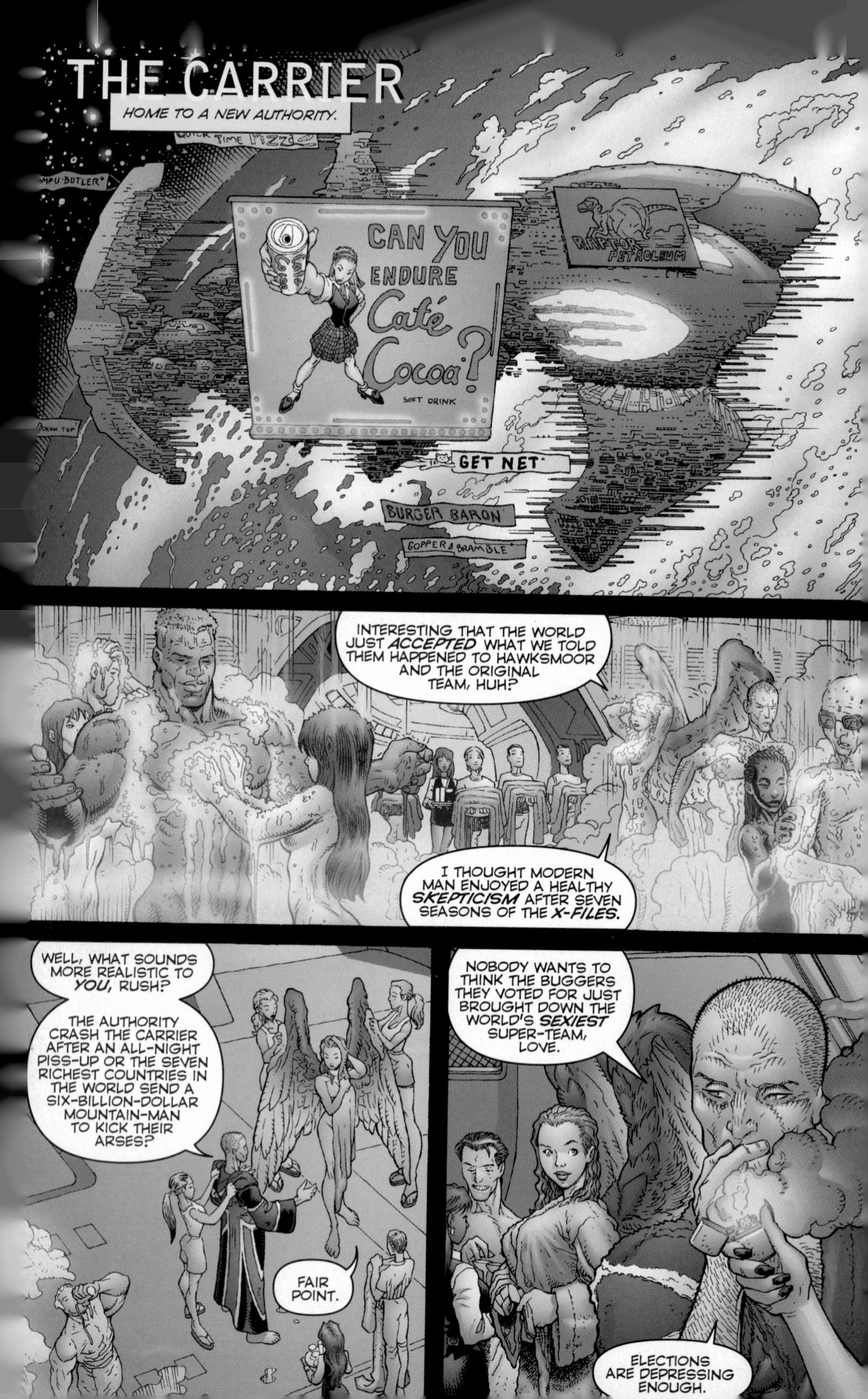
THE CARRIER
HOME TO A NEW AUTHORITY.
CAN YOU ENDURE Café Cocoa?
SOFT DRINK
RAPTOR PETROLEUM
GET NET
BURGER BARON
COPPER & BRAMBLE
INTERESTING THAT THE WORLD JUST ACCEPTED WHAT WE TOLD THEM HAPPENED TO HAWKSMOOR AND THE ORIGINAL TEAM, HUH?
I THOUGHT MODERN MAN ENJOYED A HEALTHY SKEPTICISM AFTER SEVEN SEASONS OF THE X-FILES.
WELL, WHAT SOUNDS MORE REALISTIC TO YOU, RUSH?
THE AUTHORITY CRASH THE CARRIER AFTER AN ALL-NIGHT PISS-UP OR THE SEVEN RICHEST COUNTRIES IN THE WORLD SEND A SIX-BILLION-DOLLAR MOUNTAIN-MAN TO KICK THEIR ARSES?
FAIR POINT.
NOBODY WANTS TO THINK THE BUGGERS THEY VOTED FOR JUST BROUGHT DOWN THE WORLD'S SEXIEST SUPER-TEAM, LOVE.
ELECTIONS ARE DEPRESSING ENOUGH.

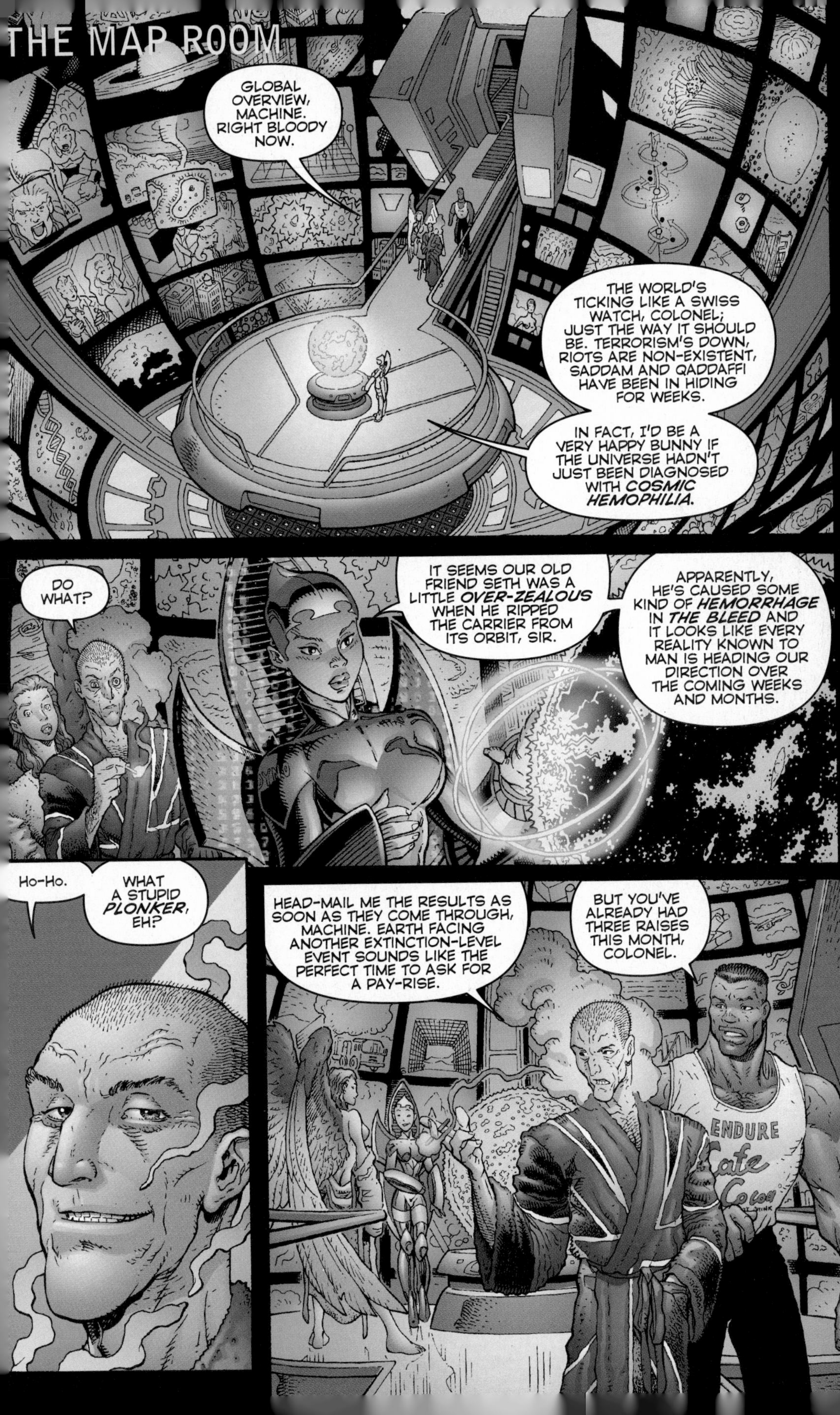
THE MAP ROOM
GLOBAL OVERVIEW, MACHINE. RIGHT BLOODY NOW.
THE WORLD'S TICKING LIKE A SWISS WATCH, COLONEL; JUST THE WAY IT SHOULD BE. TERRORISM'S DOWN, RIOTS ARE NON-EXISTENT, SADDAM AND QADDAFFI HAVE BEEN IN HIDING FOR WEEKS.
IN FACT, I'D BE A VERY HAPPY BUNNY IF THE UNIVERSE HADN'T JUST BEEN DIAGNOSED WITH *COSMIC HEMOPHILIA.*
DO WHAT?
IT SEEMS OUR OLD FRIEND SETH WAS A LITTLE *OVER-ZEALOUS* WHEN HE RIPPED THE CARRIER FROM ITS ORBIT, SIR.
APPARENTLY, HE'S CAUSED SOME KIND OF *HEMORRHAGE* IN *THE BLEED* AND IT LOOKS LIKE EVERY REALITY KNOWN TO MAN IS HEADING OUR DIRECTION OVER THE COMING WEEKS AND MONTHS.
Ho-Ho.
WHAT A STUPID *PLONKER*, EH?
HEAD-MAIL ME THE RESULTS AS SOON AS THEY COME THROUGH, MACHINE. EARTH FACING ANOTHER EXTINCTION-LEVEL EVENT SOUNDS LIKE THE PERFECT TIME TO ASK FOR A PAY-RISE.
BUT YOU'VE ALREADY HAD THREE RAISES THIS MONTH, COLONEL.
ENDURE
Cafe Cocoa

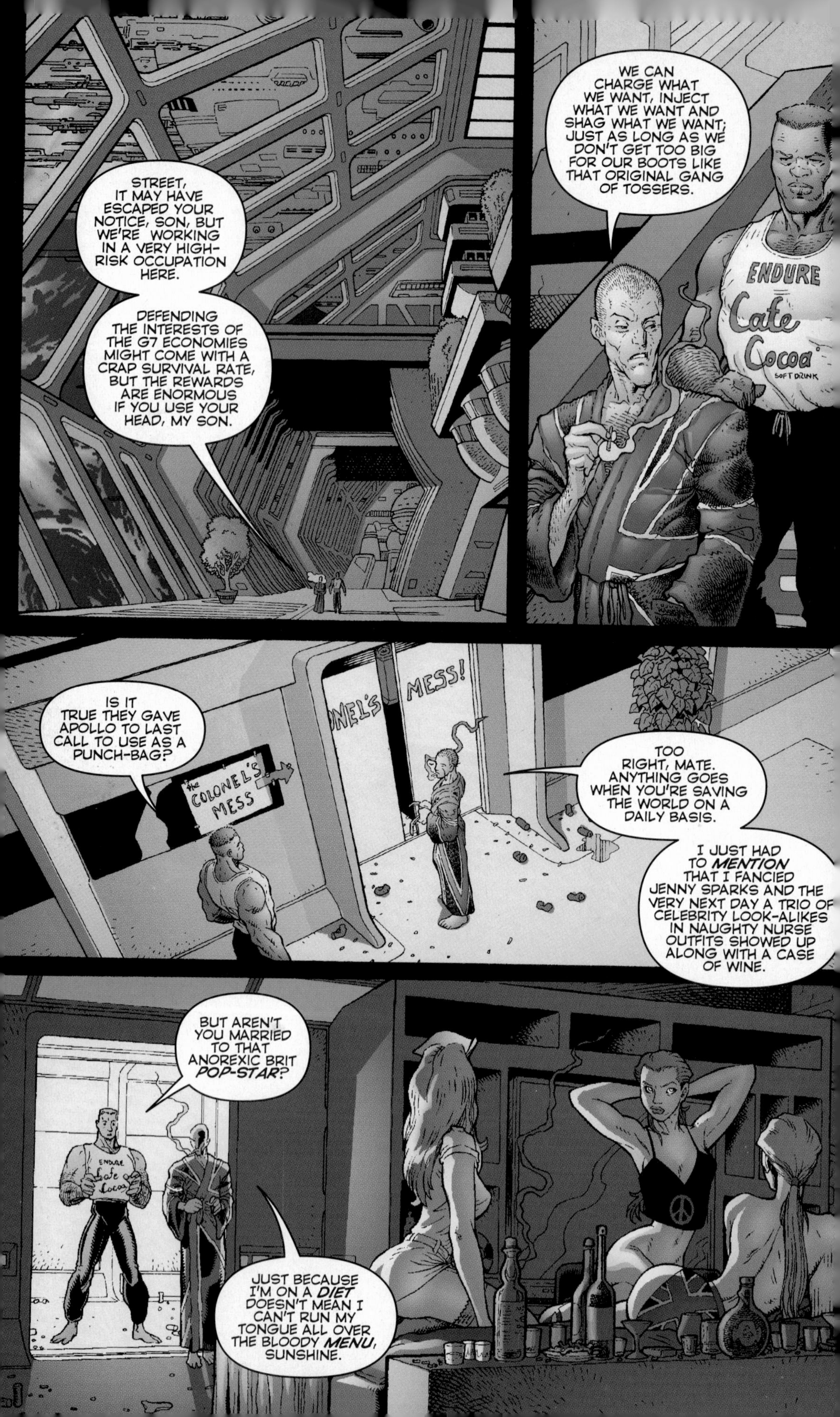
STREET, IT MAY HAVE ESCAPED YOUR NOTICE, SON, BUT WE'RE WORKING IN A VERY HIGH-RISK OCCUPATION HERE.
DEFENDING THE INTERESTS OF THE G7 ECONOMIES MIGHT COME WITH A CRAP SURVIVAL RATE, BUT THE REWARDS ARE ENORMOUS IF YOU USE YOUR HEAD, MY SON.
WE CAN CHARGE WHAT WE WANT, INJECT WHAT WE WANT AND SHAG WHAT WE WANT; JUST AS LONG AS WE DON'T GET TOO BIG FOR OUR BOOTS LIKE THAT ORIGINAL GANG OF TOSSERS.
ENDURE
Cafe Cocoa
SOFT DRINK
IS IT TRUE THEY GAVE APOLLO TO LAST CALL TO USE AS A PUNCH-BAG?
the COLONEL'S MESS
ONEL'S MESS!
TOO RIGHT, MATE. ANYTHING GOES WHEN YOU'RE SAVING THE WORLD ON A DAILY BASIS.
I JUST HAD TO MENTION THAT I FANCIED JENNY SPARKS AND THE VERY NEXT DAY A TRIO OF CELEBRITY LOOK-ALIKES IN NAUGHTY NURSE OUTFITS SHOWED UP ALONG WITH A CASE OF WINE.
BUT AREN'T YOU MARRIED TO THAT ANOREXIC BRIT POP-STAR?
JUST BECAUSE I'M ON A DIET DOESN'T MEAN I CAN'T RUN MY TONGUE ALL OVER THE BLOODY MENU, SUNSHINE.

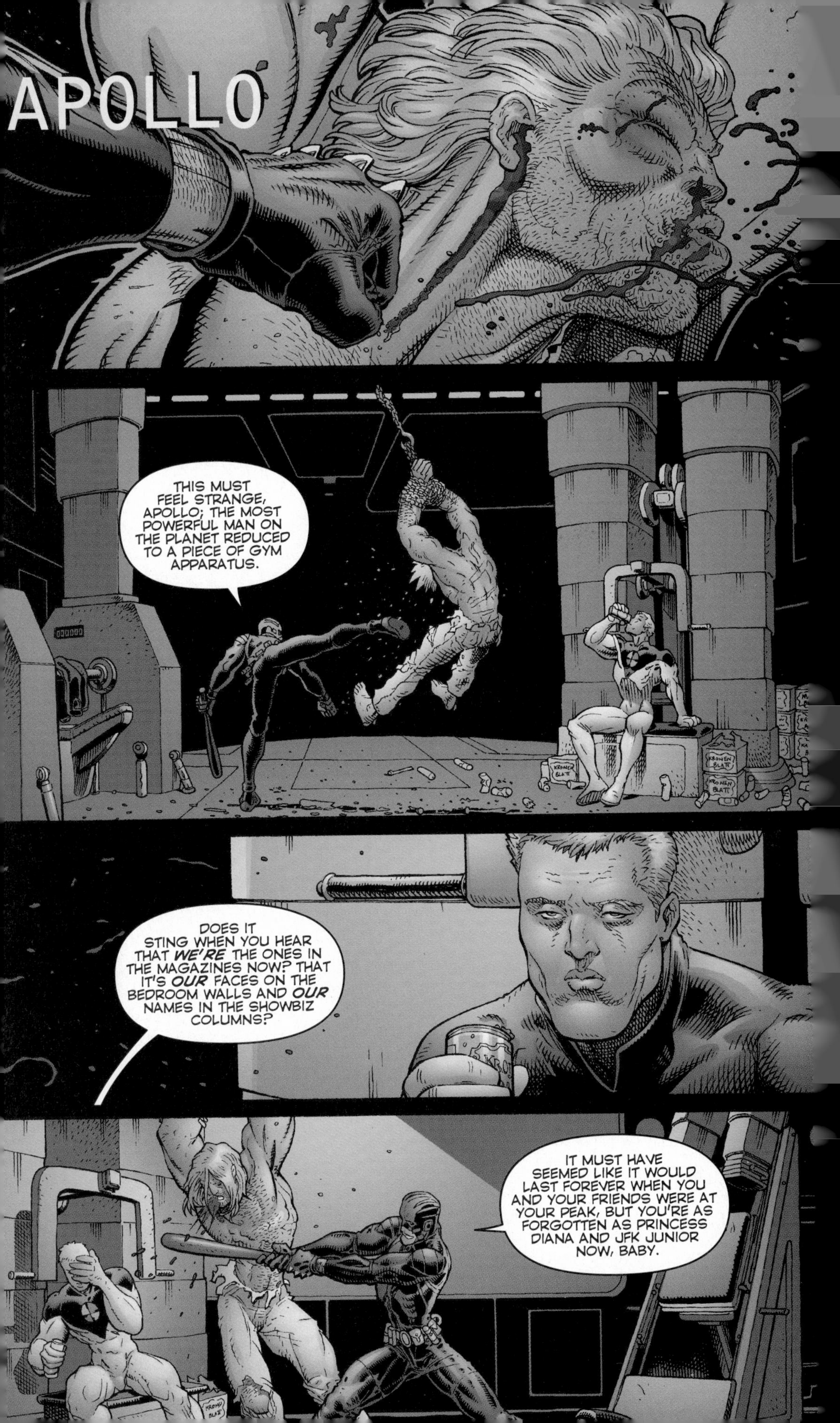
APOLLO
THIS MUST FEEL STRANGE, APOLLO; THE MOST POWERFUL MAN ON THE PLANET REDUCED TO A PIECE OF GYM APPARATUS.
DOES IT STING WHEN YOU HEAR THAT WE'RE THE ONES IN THE MAGAZINES NOW? THAT IT'S OUR FACES ON THE BEDROOM WALLS AND OUR NAMES IN THE SHOWBIZ COLUMNS?
IT MUST HAVE SEEMED LIKE IT WOULD LAST FOREVER WHEN YOU AND YOUR FRIENDS WERE AT YOUR PEAK, BUT YOU'RE AS FORGOTTEN AS PRINCESS DIANA AND JFK JUNIOR NOW, BABY.

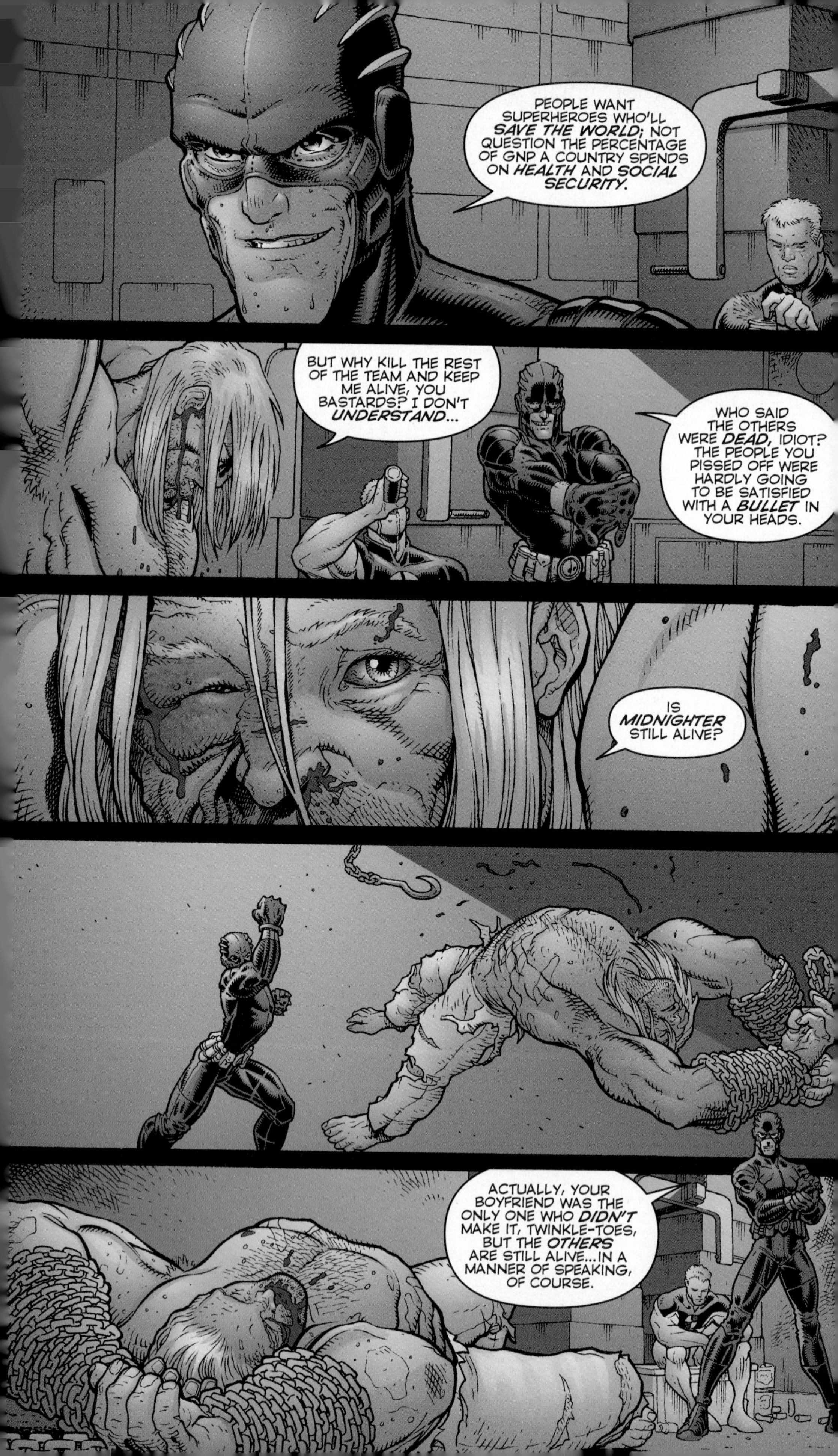
PEOPLE WANT SUPERHEROES WHO'LL *SAVE THE WORLD*; NOT QUESTION THE PERCENTAGE OF GNP A COUNTRY SPENDS ON *HEALTH* AND *SOCIAL SECURITY*.
BUT WHY KILL THE REST OF THE TEAM AND KEEP ME ALIVE, YOU BASTARDS? I DON'T *UNDERSTAND*...
WHO SAID THE OTHERS WERE *DEAD*, IDIOT? THE PEOPLE YOU PISSED OFF WERE HARDLY GOING TO BE SATISFIED WITH A *BULLET* IN YOUR HEADS.
IS *MIDNIGHTER* STILL ALIVE?
ACTUALLY, YOUR BOYFRIEND WAS THE ONLY ONE WHO *DIDN'T* MAKE IT, TWINKLE-TOES, BUT THE *OTHERS* ARE STILL ALIVE...IN A MANNER OF SPEAKING, OF COURSE.

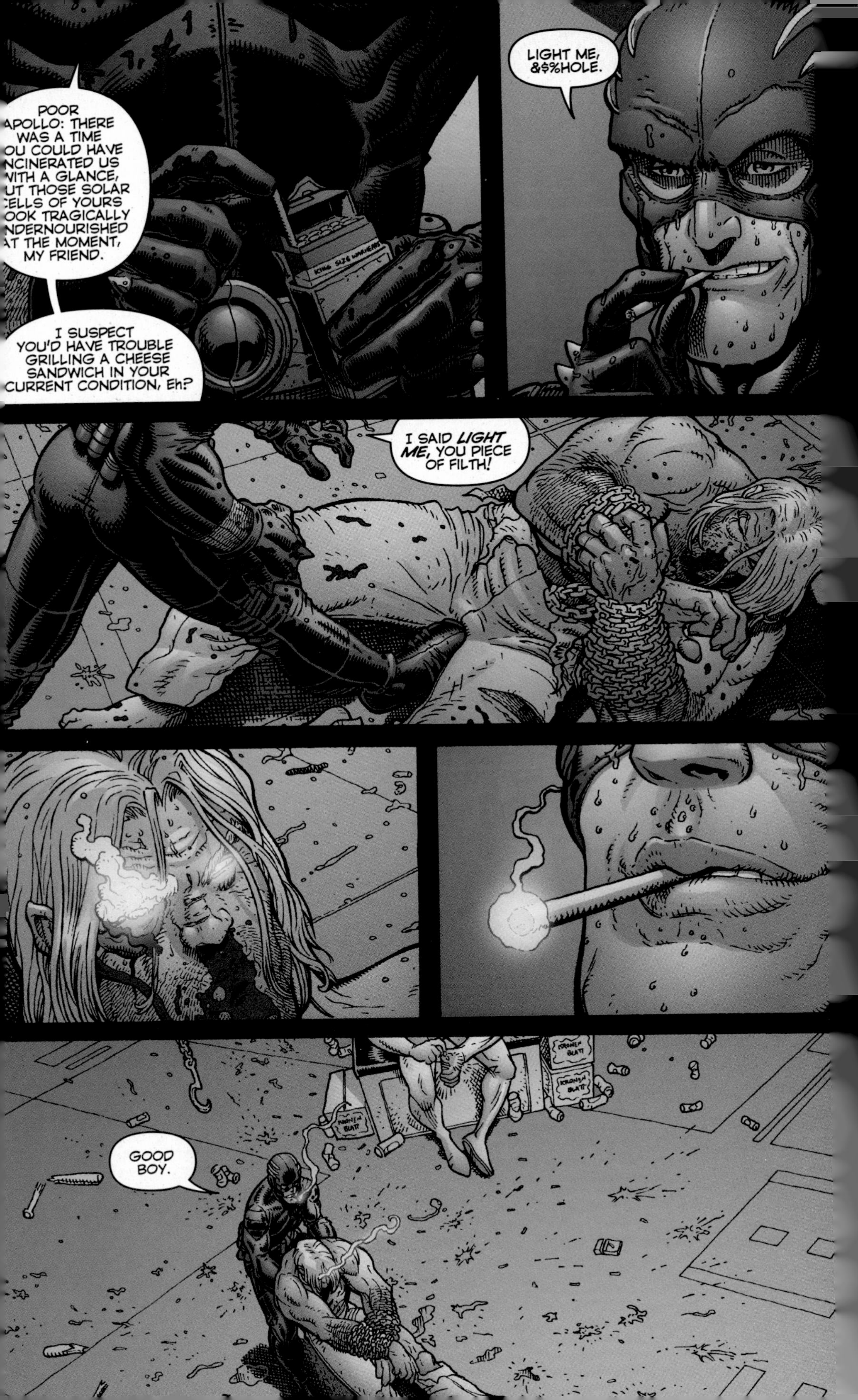
POOR APOLLO: THERE WAS A TIME OU COULD HAVE NCINERATED US WITH A GLANCE, UT THOSE SOLAR CELLS OF YOURS OOK TRAGICALLY NDERNOURISHED AT THE MOMENT, MY FRIEND.
I SUSPECT YOU'D HAVE TROUBLE GRILLING A CHEESE SANDWICH IN YOUR CURRENT CONDITION, Eh?
LIGHT ME, &$%HOLE.
I SAID *LIGHT ME,* YOU PIECE OF FILTH!
GOOD BOY.

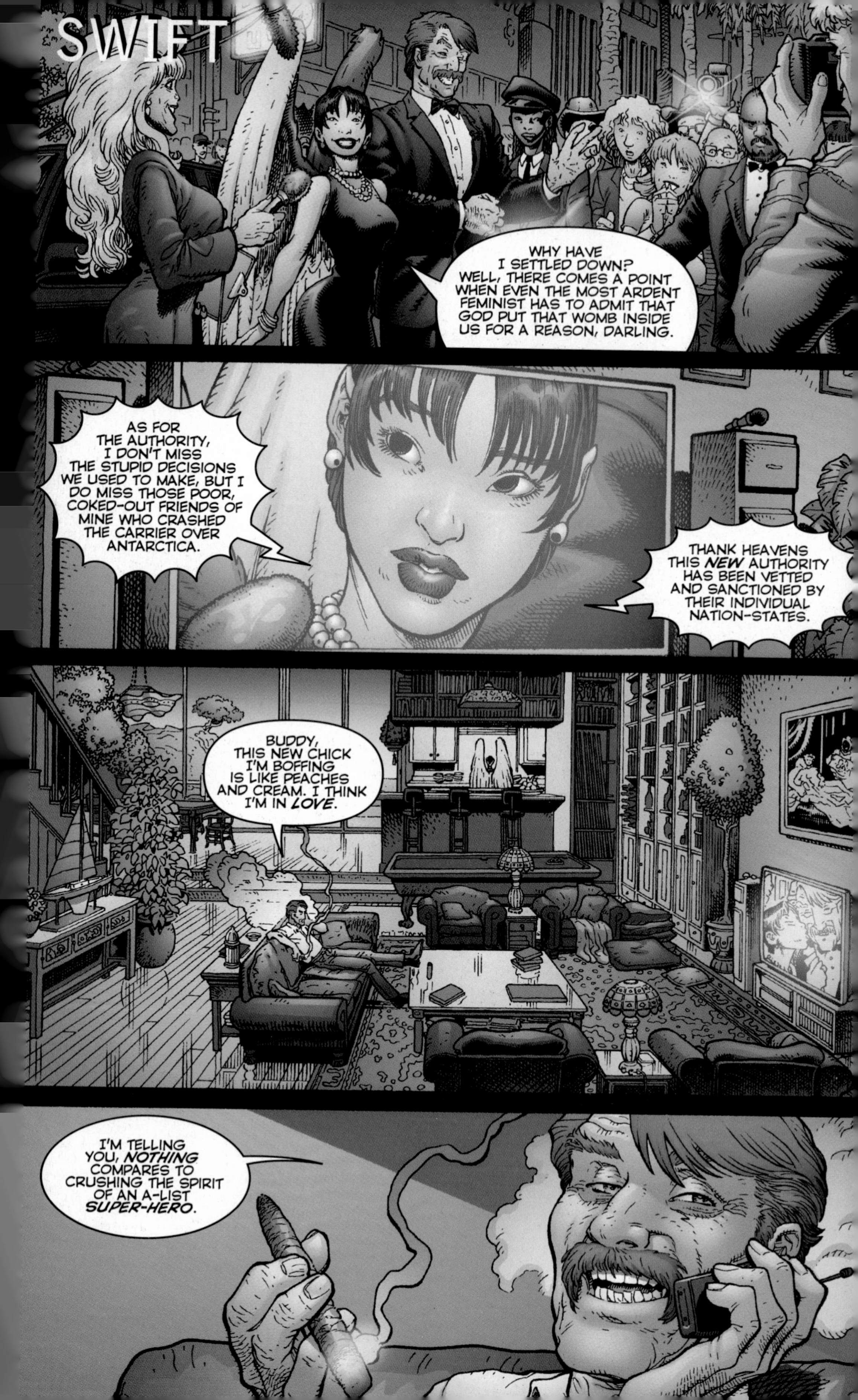
SWIFT
WHY HAVE I SETTLED DOWN? WELL, THERE COMES A POINT WHEN EVEN THE MOST ARDENT FEMINIST HAS TO ADMIT THAT GOD PUT THAT WOMB INSIDE US FOR A REASON, DARLING.
AS FOR THE AUTHORITY, I DON'T MISS THE STUPID DECISIONS WE USED TO MAKE, BUT I DO MISS THOSE POOR, COKED-OUT FRIENDS OF MINE WHO CRASHED THE CARRIER OVER ANTARCTICA.
THANK HEAVENS THIS NEW AUTHORITY HAS BEEN VETTED AND SANCTIONED BY THEIR INDIVIDUAL NATION-STATES.
BUDDY, THIS NEW CHICK I'M BOFFING IS LIKE PEACHES AND CREAM. I THINK I'M IN LOVE.
I'M TELLING YOU, NOTHING COMPARES TO CRUSHING THE SPIRIT OF AN A-LIST SUPER-HERO.

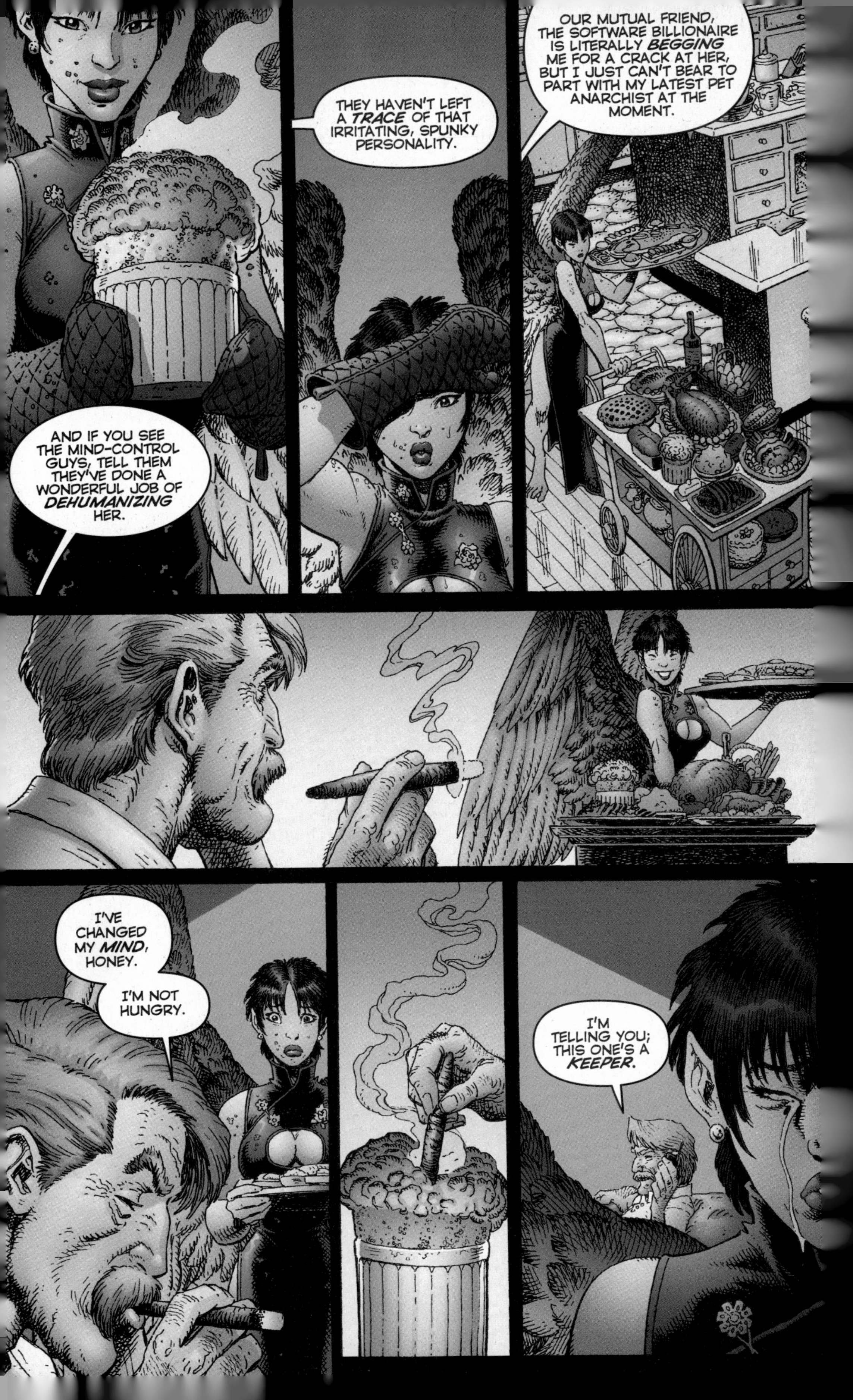
AND IF YOU SEE THE MIND-CONTROL GUYS, TELL THEM THEY'VE DONE A WONDERFUL JOB OF DEHUMANIZING HER.
THEY HAVEN'T LEFT A TRACE OF THAT IRRITATING, SPUNKY PERSONALITY.
OUR MUTUAL FRIEND, THE SOFTWARE BILLIONAIRE IS LITERALLY BEGGING ME FOR A CRACK AT HER, BUT I JUST CAN'T BEAR TO PART WITH MY LATEST PET ANARCHIST AT THE MOMENT.
I'VE CHANGED MY MIND, HONEY.
I'M NOT HUNGRY.
I'M TELLING YOU; THIS ONE'S A KEEPER.

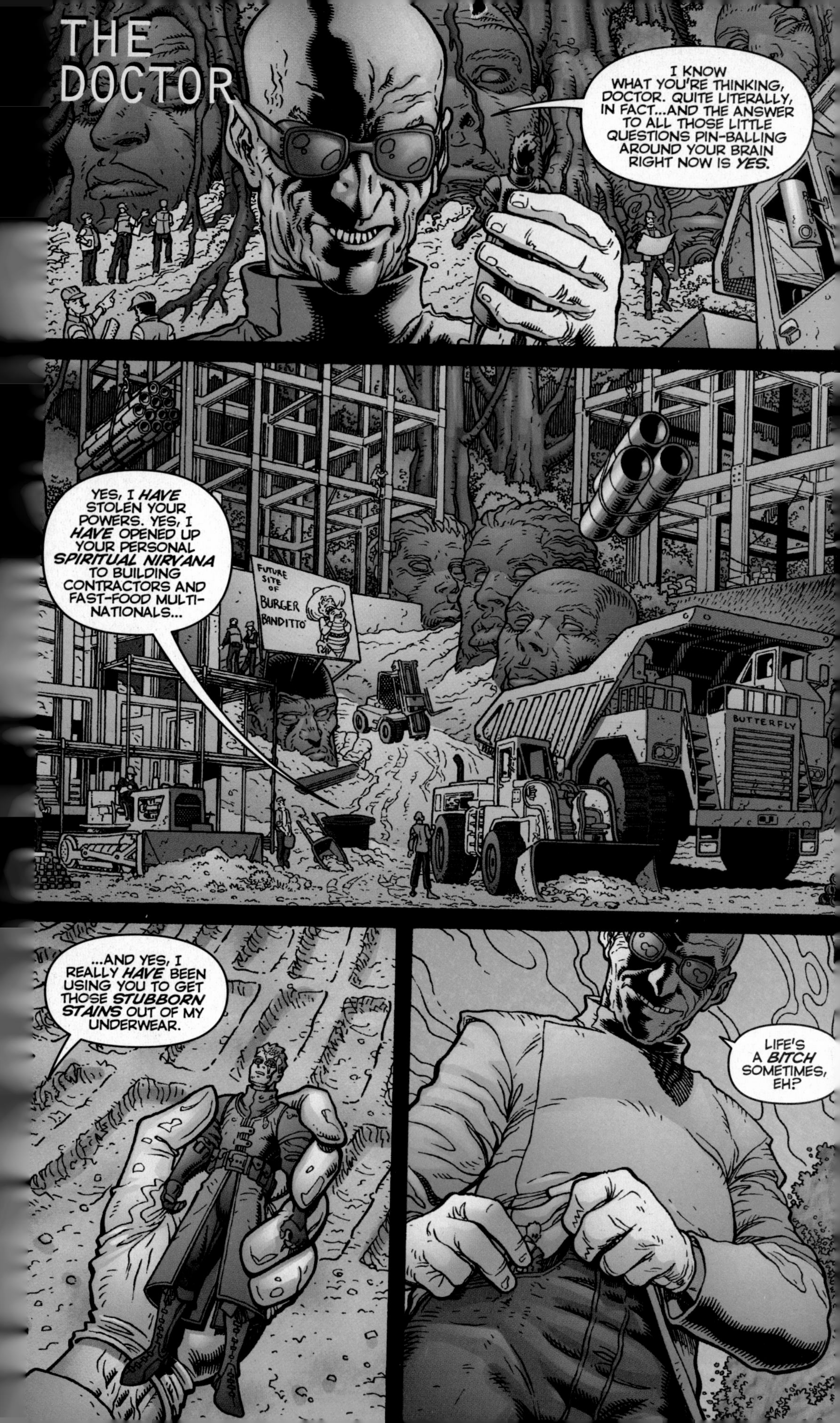
THE DOCTOR
I KNOW WHAT YOU'RE THINKING, DOCTOR. QUITE LITERALLY, IN FACT...AND THE ANSWER TO ALL THOSE LITTLE QUESTIONS PIN-BALLING AROUND YOUR BRAIN RIGHT NOW IS YES.
YES, I HAVE STOLEN YOUR POWERS. YES, I HAVE OPENED UP YOUR PERSONAL SPIRITUAL NIRVANA TO BUILDING CONTRACTORS AND FAST-FOOD MULTI-NATIONALS...
FUTURE SITE OF BURGER BANDITTO
BUTTERFLY
...AND YES, I REALLY HAVE BEEN USING YOU TO GET THOSE STUBBORN STAINS OUT OF MY UNDERWEAR.
LIFE'S A BITCH SOMETIMES, EH?

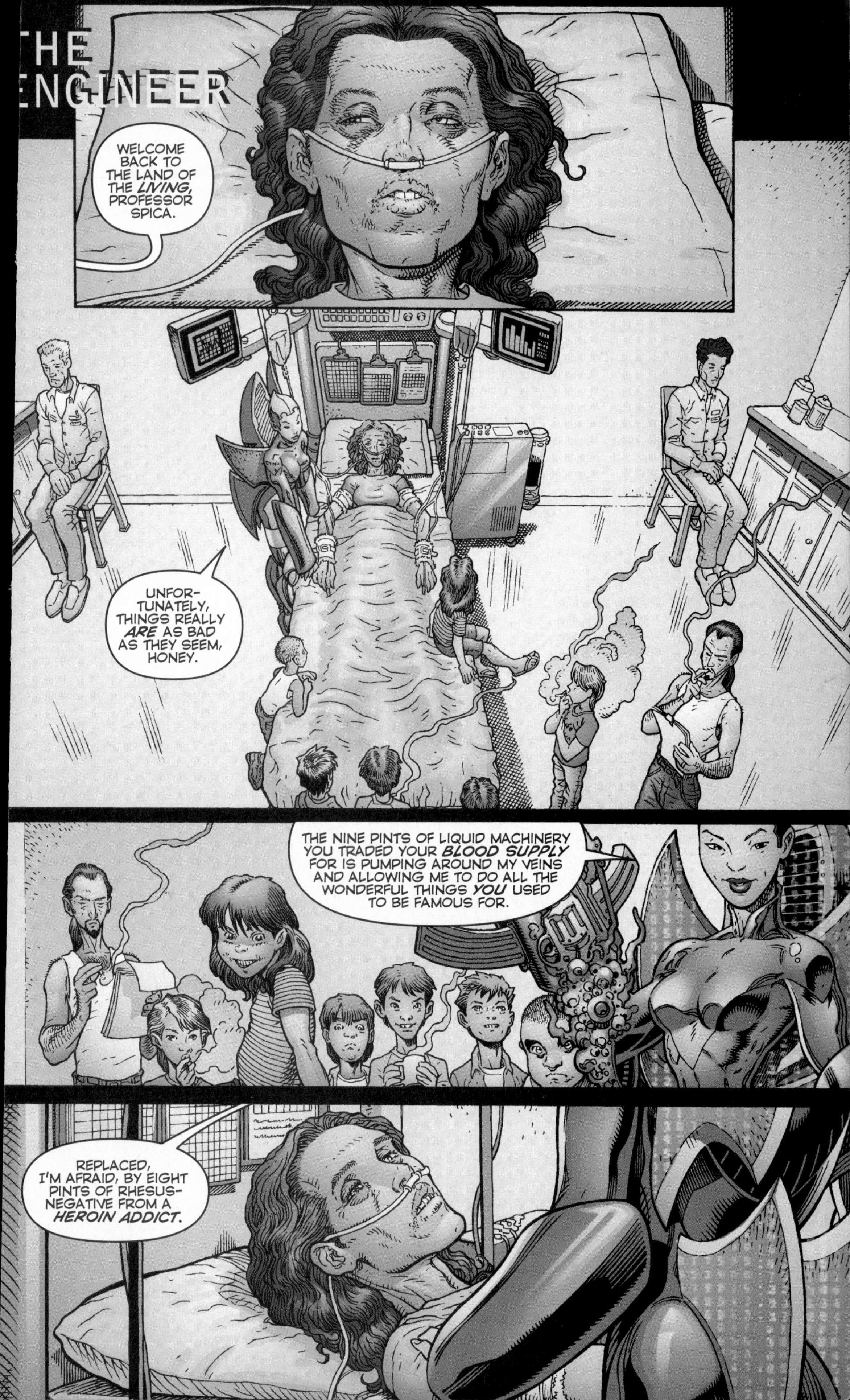
THE ENGINEER
WELCOME BACK TO THE LAND OF THE *LIVING,* PROFESSOR SPICA.
UNFOR-TUNATELY, THINGS REALLY *ARE* AS BAD AS THEY SEEM, HONEY.
THE NINE PINTS OF LIQUID MACHINERY YOU TRADED YOUR *BLOOD SUPPLY* FOR IS PUMPING AROUND MY VEINS AND ALLOWING ME TO DO ALL THE WONDERFUL THINGS *YOU* USED TO BE FAMOUS FOR.
REPLACED, I'M AFRAID, BY EIGHT PINTS OF RHESUS-NEGATIVE FROM A *HEROIN ADDICT*.

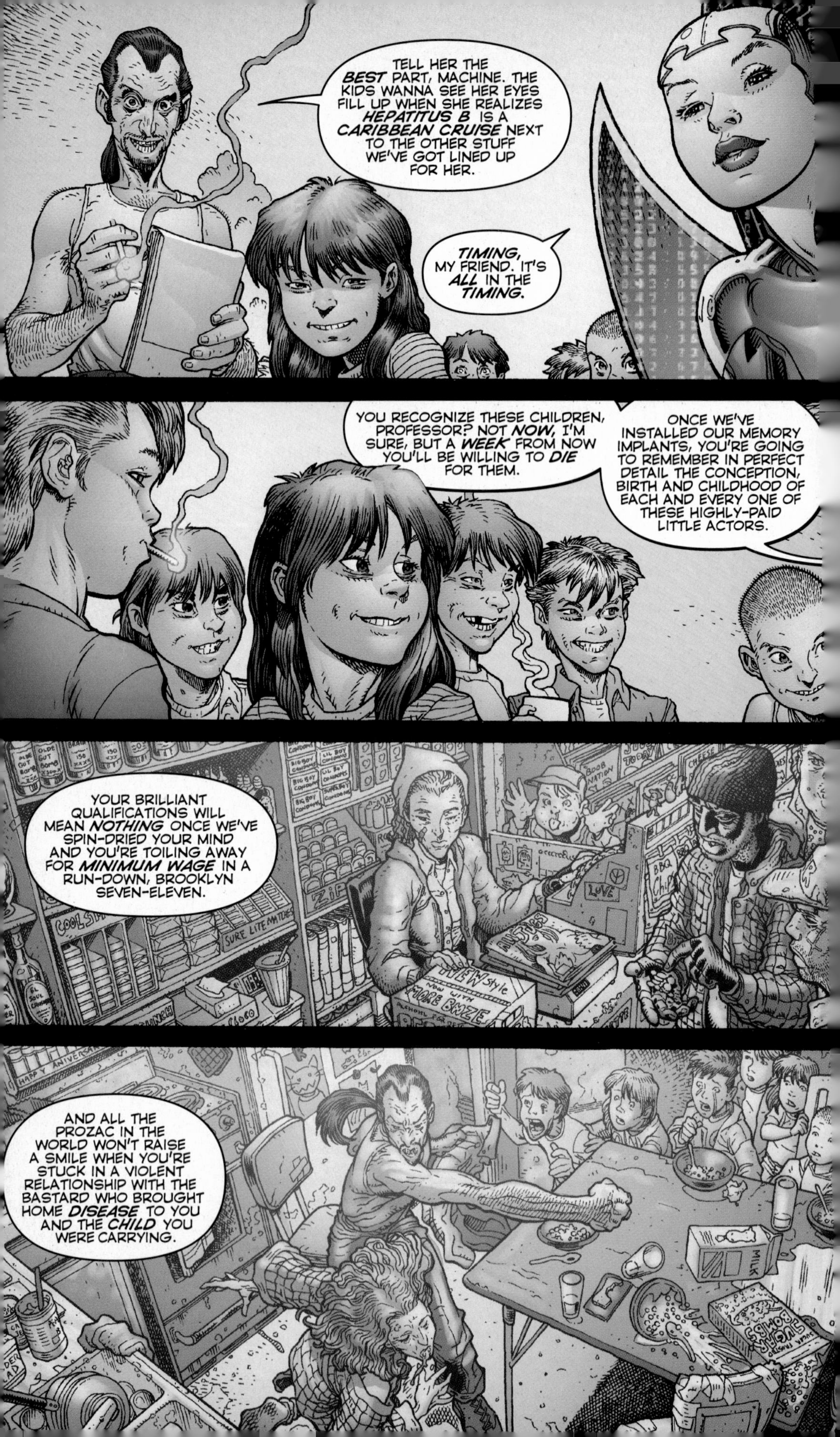
TELL HER THE BEST PART, MACHINE. THE KIDS WANNA SEE HER EYES FILL UP WHEN SHE REALIZES HEPATITUS B IS A CARIBBEAN CRUISE NEXT TO THE OTHER STUFF WE'VE GOT LINED UP FOR HER.
TIMING, MY FRIEND. IT'S ALL IN THE TIMING.
YOU RECOGNIZE THESE CHILDREN, PROFESSOR? NOT NOW, I'M SURE, BUT A WEEK FROM NOW YOU'LL BE WILLING TO DIE FOR THEM.
ONCE WE'VE INSTALLED OUR MEMORY IMPLANTS, YOU'RE GOING TO REMEMBER IN PERFECT DETAIL THE CONCEPTION, BIRTH AND CHILDHOOD OF EACH AND EVERY ONE OF THESE HIGHLY-PAID LITTLE ACTORS.
YOUR BRILLIANT QUALIFICATIONS WILL MEAN NOTHING ONCE WE'VE SPIN-DRIED YOUR MIND AND YOU'RE TOILING AWAY FOR MINIMUM WAGE IN A RUN-DOWN, BROOKLYN SEVEN-ELEVEN.
AND ALL THE PROZAC IN THE WORLD WON'T RAISE A SMILE WHEN YOU'RE STUCK IN A VIOLENT RELATIONSHIP WITH THE BASTARD WHO BROUGHT HOME DISEASE TO YOU AND THE CHILD YOU WERE CARRYING.
MILK
SUGAR FROSTED SUGAR BOMBS

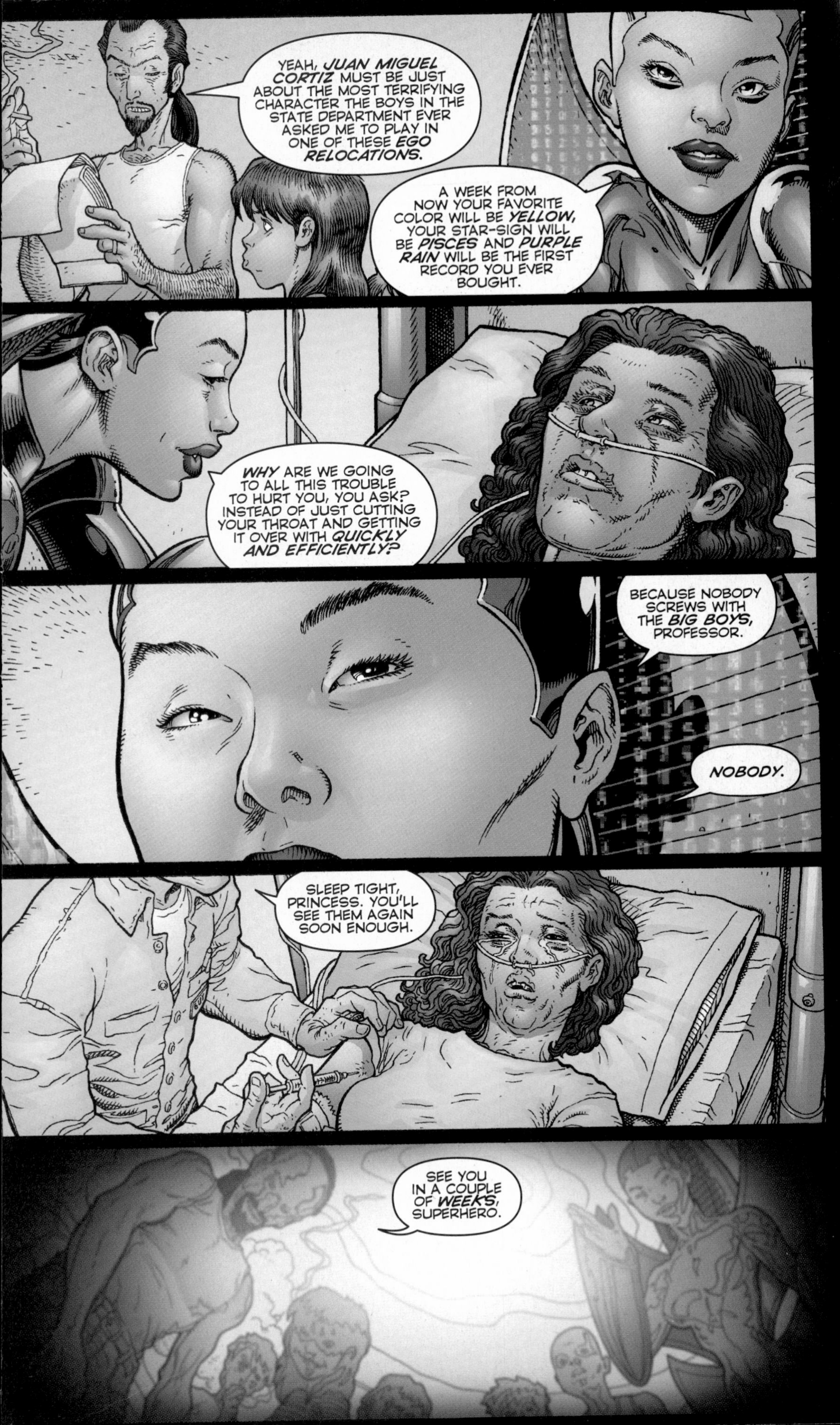
YEAH, JUAN MIGUEL CORTIZ MUST BE JUST ABOUT THE MOST TERRIFYING CHARACTER THE BOYS IN THE STATE DEPARTMENT EVER ASKED ME TO PLAY IN ONE OF THESE EGO RELOCATIONS.
A WEEK FROM NOW YOUR FAVORITE COLOR WILL BE YELLOW, YOUR STAR-SIGN WILL BE PISCES AND PURPLE RAIN WILL BE THE FIRST RECORD YOU EVER BOUGHT.
WHY ARE WE GOING TO ALL THIS TROUBLE TO HURT YOU, YOU ASK? INSTEAD OF JUST CUTTING YOUR THROAT AND GETTING IT OVER WITH QUICKLY AND EFFICIENTLY?
BECAUSE NOBODY SCREWS WITH THE BIG BOYS, PROFESSOR.
NOBODY.
SLEEP TIGHT, PRINCESS. YOU'LL SEE THEM AGAIN SOON ENOUGH.
SEE YOU IN A COUPLE OF WEEKS, SUPERHERO.

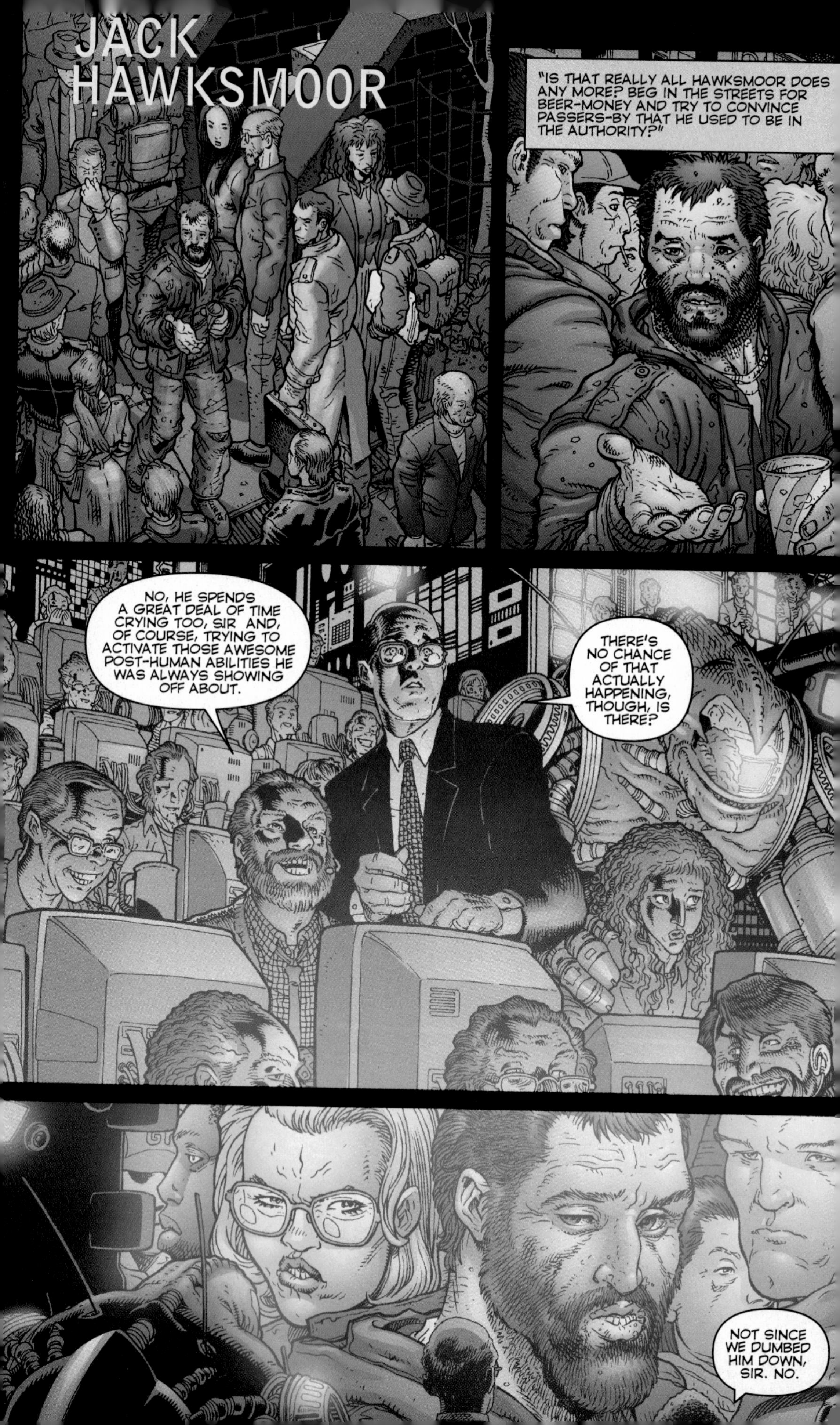
JACK HAWKSMOOR
"IS THAT REALLY ALL HAWKSMOOR DOES ANY MORE? BEG IN THE STREETS FOR BEER-MONEY AND TRY TO CONVINCE PASSERS-BY THAT HE USED TO BE IN THE AUTHORITY?"
NO, HE SPENDS A GREAT DEAL OF TIME CRYING TOO, SIR AND, OF COURSE, TRYING TO ACTIVATE THOSE AWESOME POST-HUMAN ABILITIES HE WAS ALWAYS SHOWING OFF ABOUT.
THERE'S NO CHANCE OF THAT ACTUALLY HAPPENING, THOUGH, IS THERE?
NOT SINCE WE DUMBED HIM DOWN, SIR. NO.

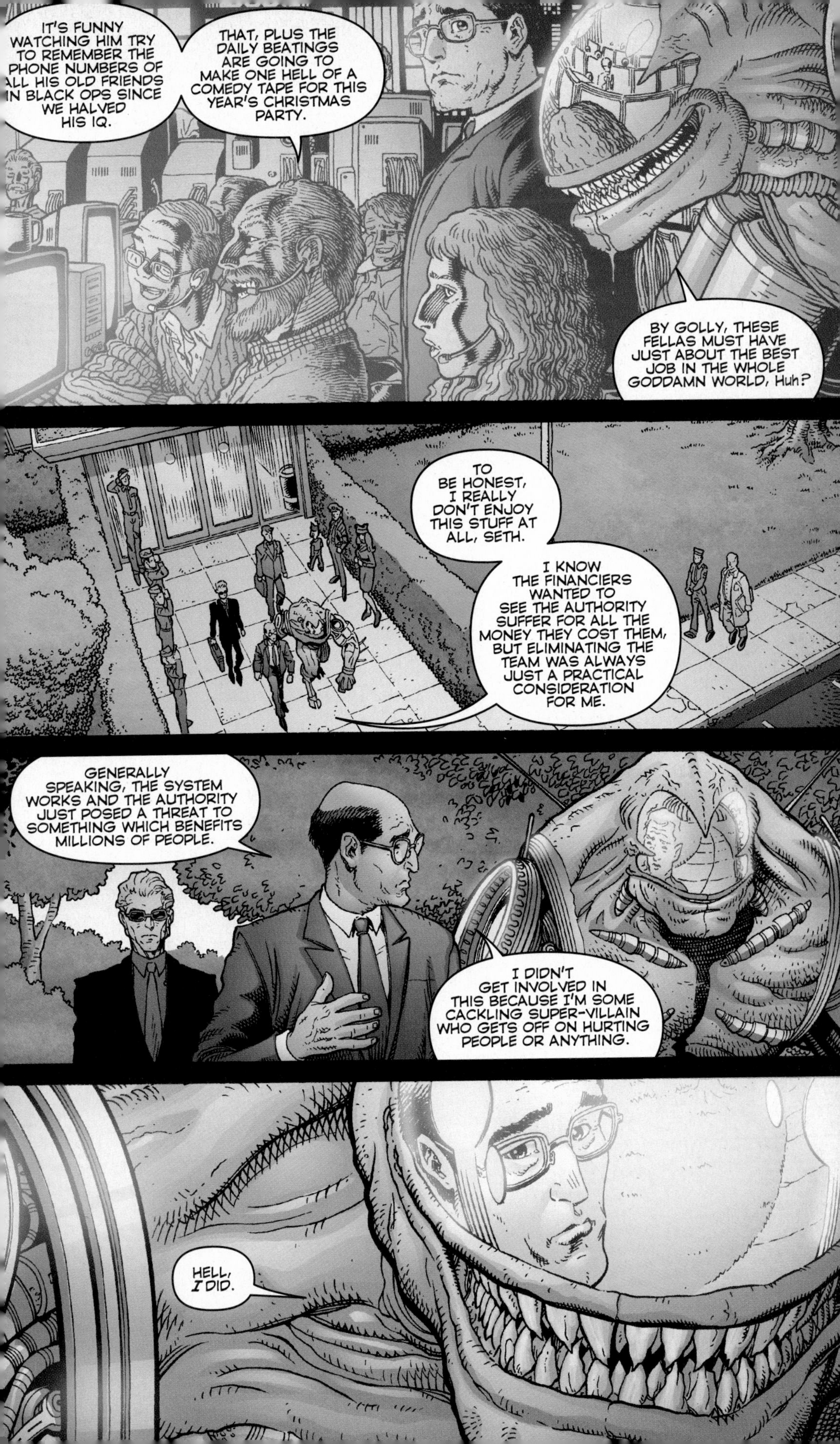
IT'S FUNNY WATCHING HIM TRY TO REMEMBER THE PHONE NUMBERS OF ALL HIS OLD FRIENDS IN BLACK OPS SINCE WE HALVED HIS IQ.
THAT, PLUS THE DAILY BEATINGS ARE GOING TO MAKE ONE HELL OF A COMEDY TAPE FOR THIS YEAR'S CHRISTMAS PARTY.
BY GOLLY, THESE FELLAS MUST HAVE JUST ABOUT THE BEST JOB IN THE WHOLE GODDAMN WORLD, Huh?
TO BE HONEST, I REALLY DON'T ENJOY THIS STUFF AT ALL, SETH.
I KNOW THE FINANCIERS WANTED TO SEE THE AUTHORITY SUFFER FOR ALL THE MONEY THEY COST THEM, BUT ELIMINATING THE TEAM WAS ALWAYS JUST A PRACTICAL CONSIDERATION FOR ME.
GENERALLY SPEAKING, THE SYSTEM WORKS AND THE AUTHORITY JUST POSED A THREAT TO SOMETHING WHICH BENEFITS MILLIONS OF PEOPLE.
I DIDN'T GET INVOLVED IN THIS BECAUSE I'M SOME CACKLING SUPER-VILLAIN WHO GETS OFF ON HURTING PEOPLE OR ANYTHING.
HELL, I DID.

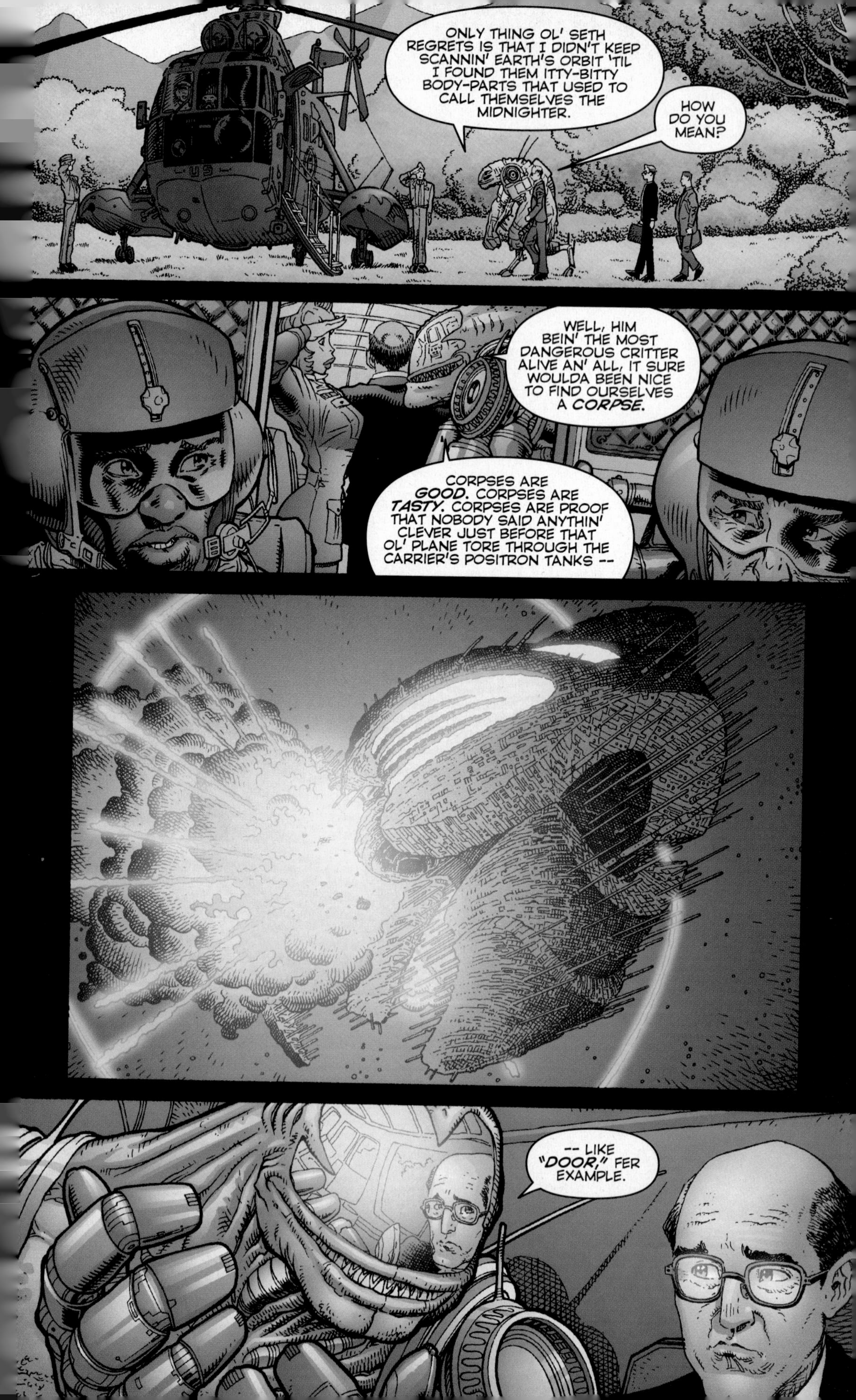
ONLY THING OL' SETH REGRETS IS THAT I DIDN'T KEEP SCANNIN' EARTH'S ORBIT 'TIL I FOUND THEM ITTY-BITTY BODY-PARTS THAT USED TO CALL THEMSELVES THE MIDNIGHTER.
HOW DO YOU MEAN?
WELL, HIM BEIN' THE MOST DANGEROUS CRITTER ALIVE AN' ALL, IT SURE WOULDA BEEN NICE TO FIND OURSELVES A *CORPSE*.
CORPSES ARE *GOOD*. CORPSES ARE *TASTY*. CORPSES ARE PROOF THAT NOBODY SAID ANYTHIN' CLEVER JUST BEFORE THAT OL' PLANE TORE THROUGH THE CARRIER'S POSITRON TANKS --
-- LIKE *"DOOR,"* FER EXAMPLE.

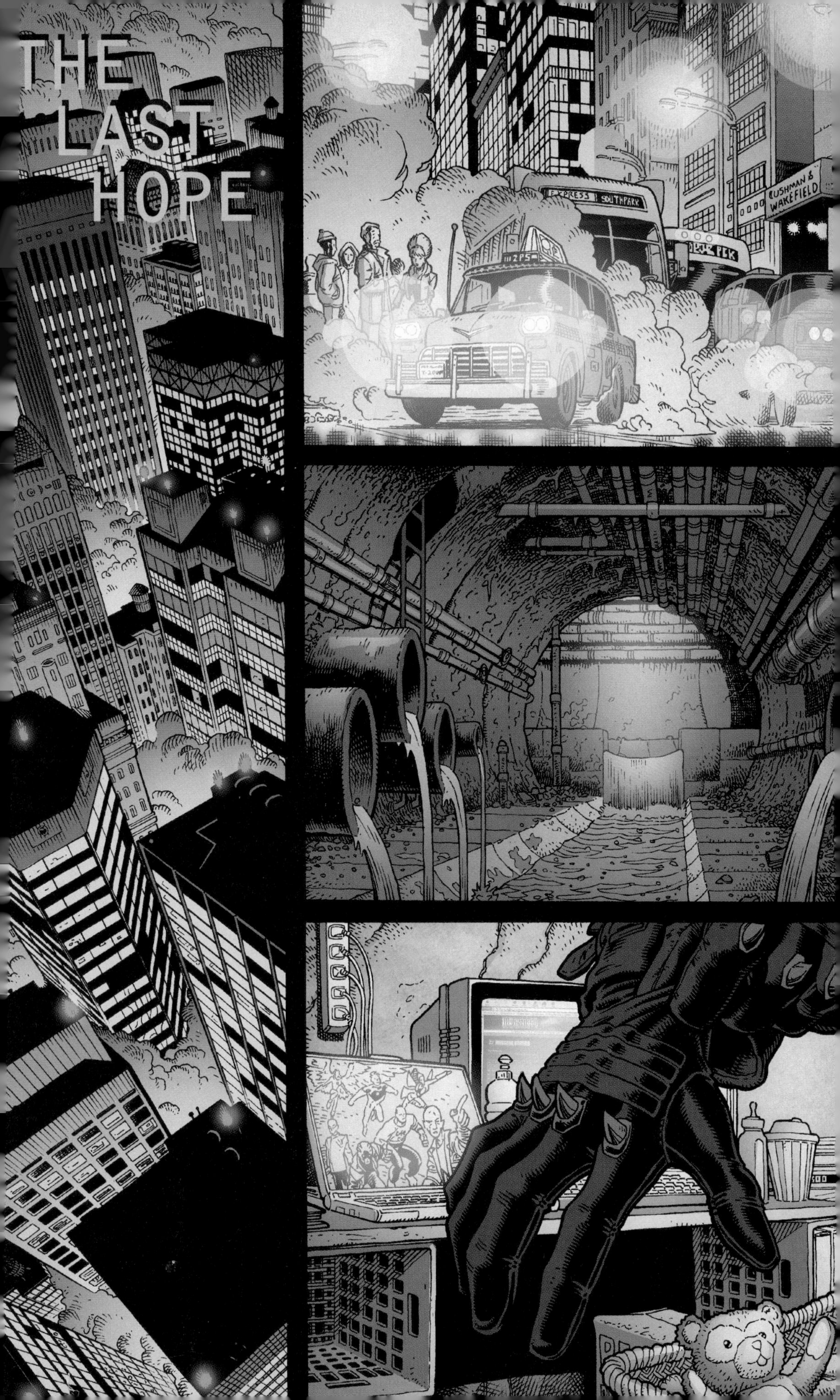
THE LAST HOPE
EXPRESS SOUTHPARK
CUSHMAN & WAKEFIELD

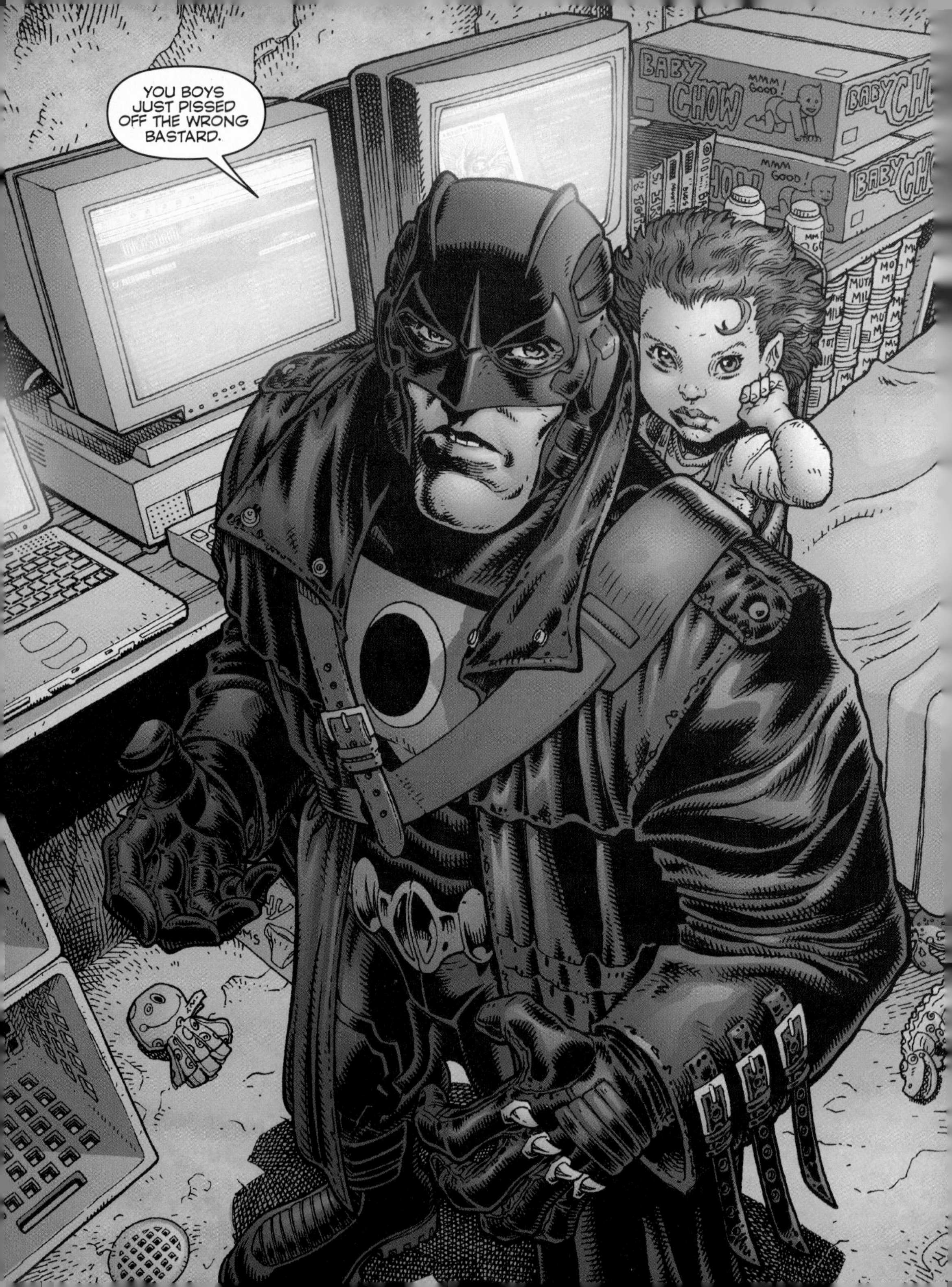
YOU BOYS JUST PISSED OFF THE WRONG BASTARD.

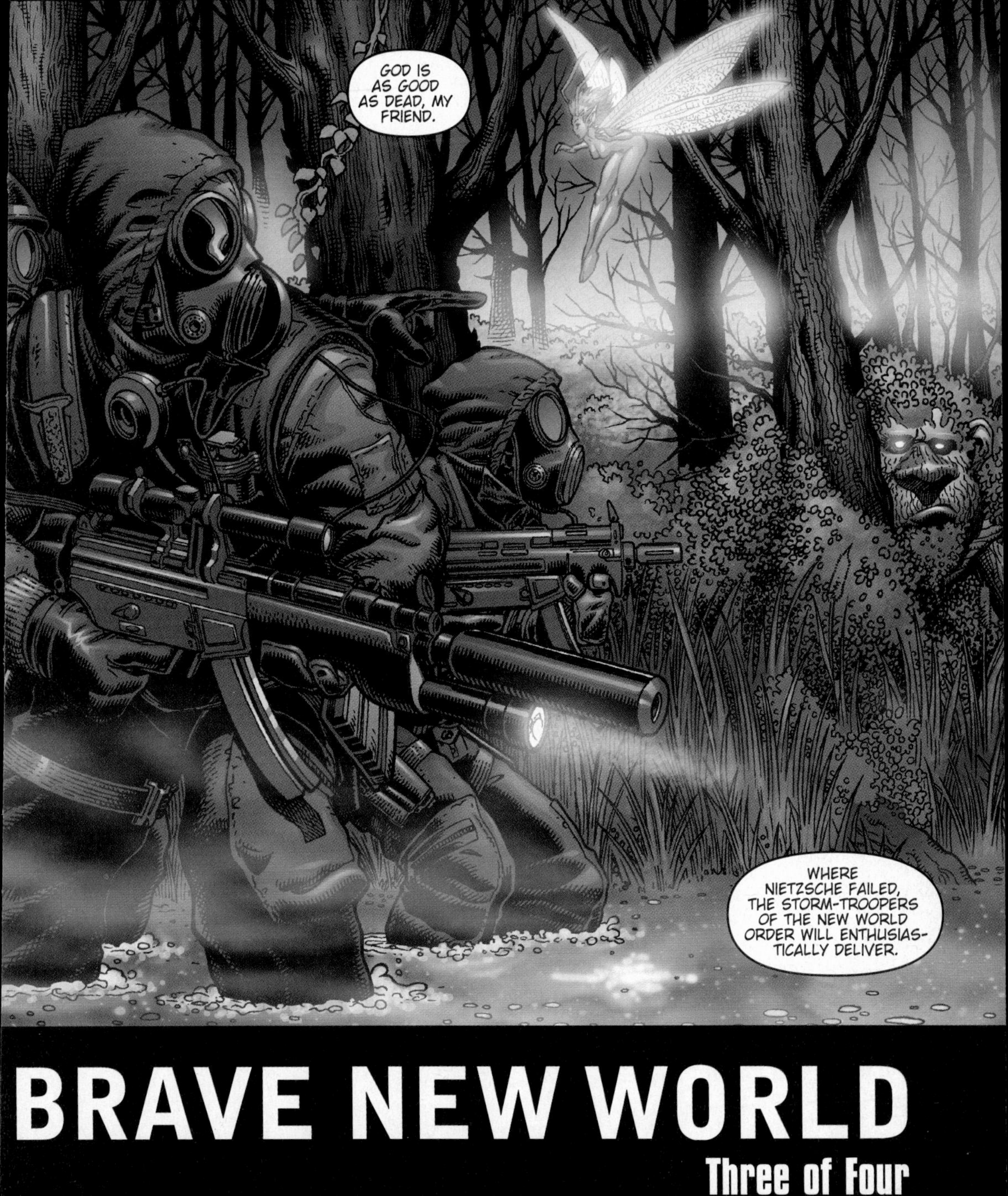
GOD IS AS GOOD AS DEAD, MY FRIEND.
WHERE NIETZSCHE FAILED, THE STORM-TROOPERS OF THE NEW WORLD ORDER WILL ENTHUSIAS-TICALLY DELIVER.

BRAVE NEW WORLD

Three of Four

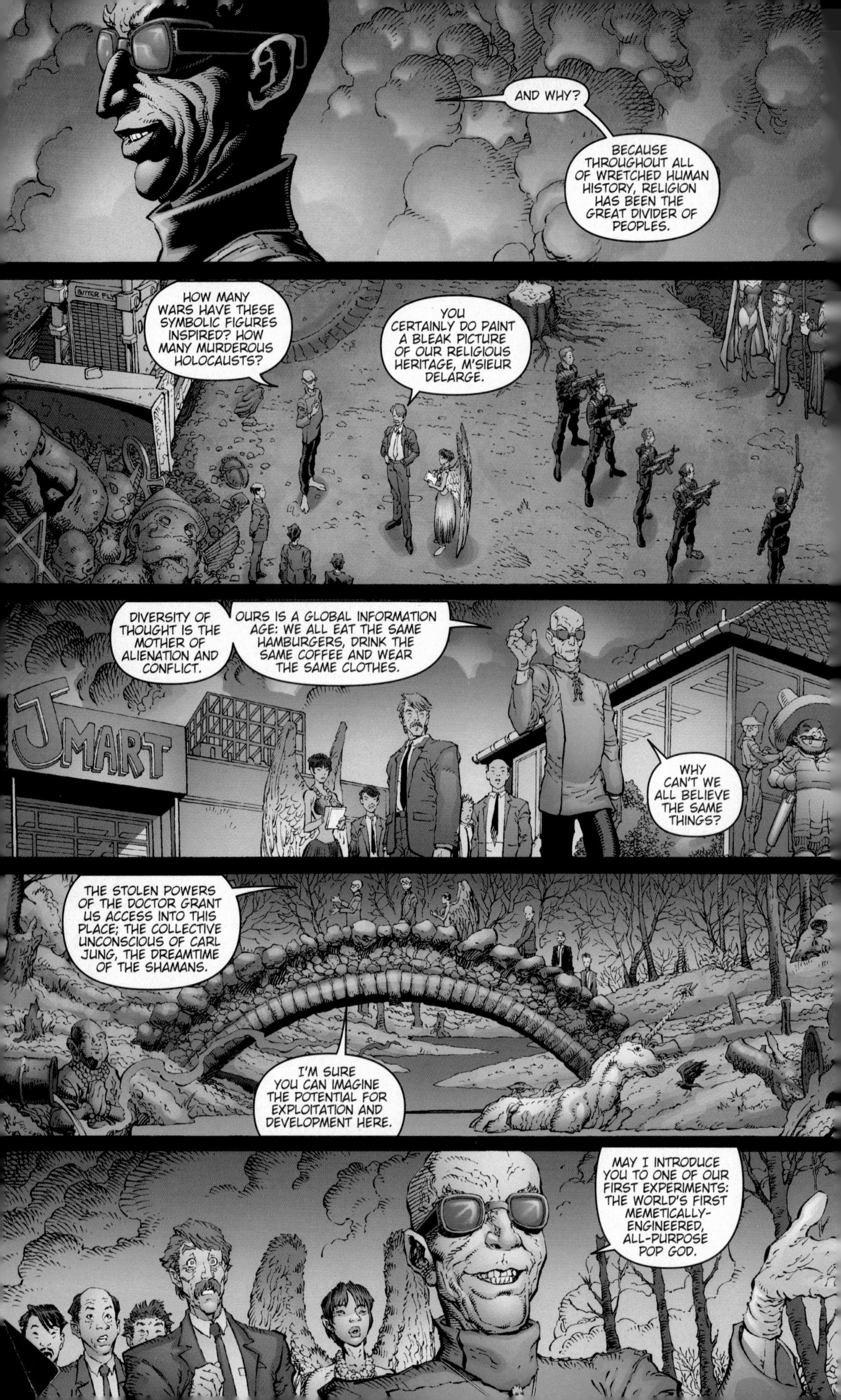
AND WHY?
BECAUSE THROUGHOUT ALL OF WRETCHED HUMAN HISTORY, RELIGION HAS BEEN THE GREAT DIVIDER OF PEOPLES.
HOW MANY WARS HAVE THESE SYMBOLIC FIGURES INSPIRED? HOW MANY MURDEROUS HOLOCAUSTS?
YOU CERTAINLY DO PAINT A BLEAK PICTURE OF OUR RELIGIOUS HERITAGE, M'SIEUR DELARGE.
DIVERSITY OF THOUGHT IS THE MOTHER OF ALIENATION AND CONFLICT.
OURS IS A GLOBAL INFORMATION AGE: WE ALL EAT THE SAME HAMBURGERS, DRINK THE SAME COFFEE AND WEAR THE SAME CLOTHES.
JMART
WHY CAN'T WE ALL BELIEVE THE SAME THINGS?
THE STOLEN POWERS OF THE DOCTOR GRANT US ACCESS INTO THIS PLACE; THE COLLECTIVE UNCONSCIOUS OF CARL JUNG, THE DREAMTIME OF THE SHAMANS.
I'M SURE YOU CAN IMAGINE THE POTENTIAL FOR EXPLOITATION AND DEVELOPMENT HERE.
MAY I INTRODUCE YOU TO ONE OF OUR FIRST EXPERIMENTS: THE WORLD'S FIRST MEMETICALLY-ENGINEERED, ALL-PURPOSE POP GOD.

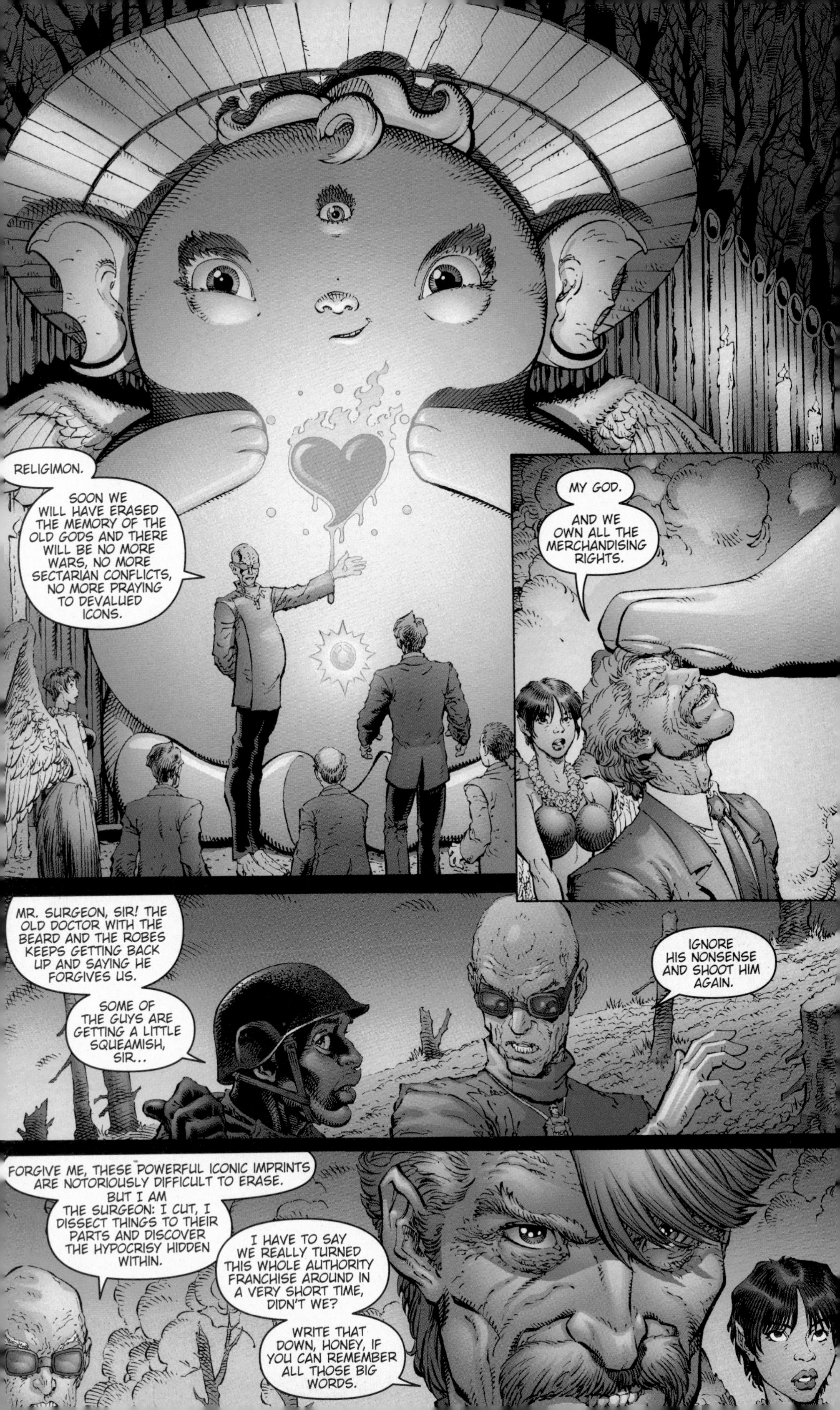
RELIGIMON.
SOON WE WILL HAVE ERASED THE MEMORY OF THE OLD GODS AND THERE WILL BE NO MORE WARS, NO MORE SECTARIAN CONFLICTS, NO MORE PRAYING TO DEVALUED ICONS.
MY GOD.
AND WE OWN ALL THE MERCHANDISING RIGHTS.
MR. SURGEON, SIR! THE OLD DOCTOR WITH THE BEARD AND THE ROBES KEEPS GETTING BACK UP AND SAYING HE FORGIVES US.
SOME OF THE GUYS ARE GETTING A LITTLE SQUEAMISH, SIR...
IGNORE HIS NONSENSE AND SHOOT HIM AGAIN.
FORGIVE ME, THESE POWERFUL ICONIC IMPRINTS ARE NOTORIOUSLY DIFFICULT TO ERASE.
BUT I AM THE SURGEON: I CUT, I DISSECT THINGS TO THEIR PARTS AND DISCOVER THE HYPOCRISY HIDDEN WITHIN.
I HAVE TO SAY WE REALLY TURNED THIS WHOLE AUTHORITY FRANCHISE AROUND IN A VERY SHORT TIME, DIDN'T WE?
WRITE THAT DOWN, HONEY, IF YOU CAN REMEMBER ALL THOSE BIG WORDS.

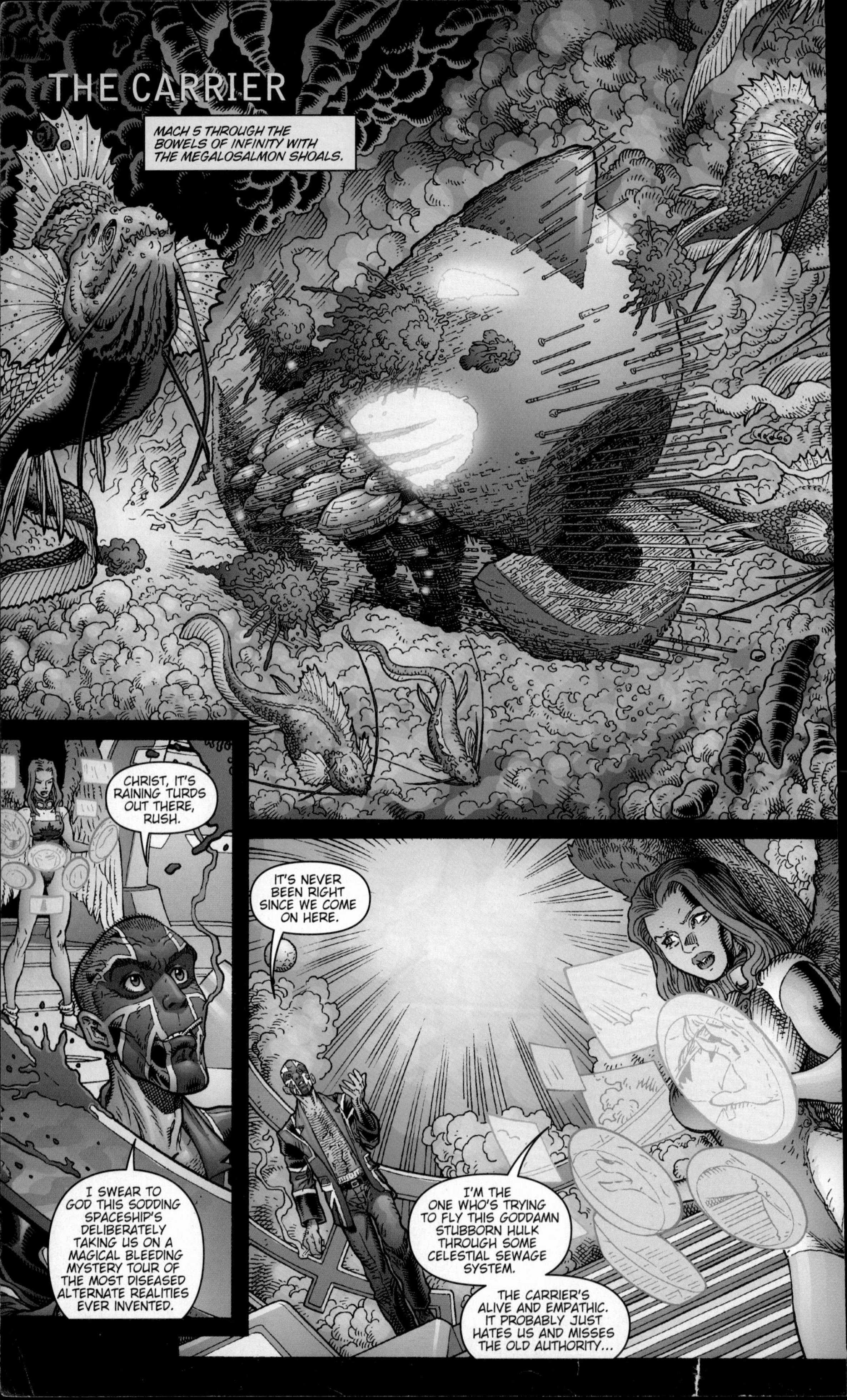
THE CARRIER
MACH 5 THROUGH THE BOWELS OF INFINITY WITH THE MEGALOSALMON SHOALS.
CHRIST, IT'S RAINING TURDS OUT THERE, RUSH.
I SWEAR TO GOD THIS SODDING SPACESHIP'S DELIBERATELY TAKING US ON A MAGICAL BLEEDING MYSTERY TOUR OF THE MOST DISEASED ALTERNATE REALITIES EVER INVENTED.
IT'S NEVER BEEN RIGHT SINCE WE COME ON HERE.
I'M THE ONE WHO'S TRYING TO FLY THIS GODDAMN STUBBORN HULK THROUGH SOME CELESTIAL SEWAGE SYSTEM.
THE CARRIER'S ALIVE AND EMPATHIC. IT PROBABLY JUST HATES US AND MISSES THE OLD AUTHORITY...

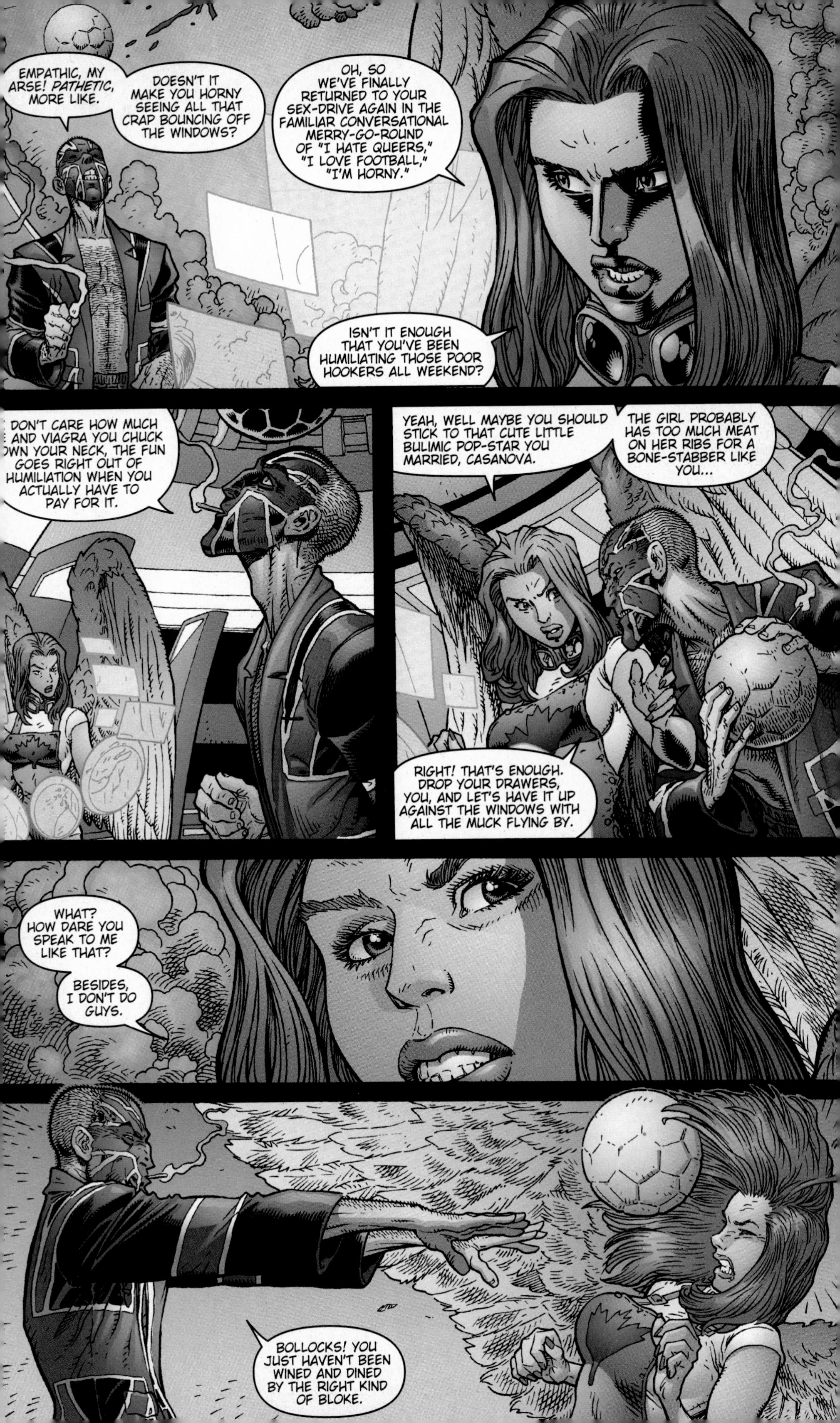
EMPATHIC, MY ARSE! *PATHETIC*, MORE LIKE.
DOESN'T IT MAKE YOU HORNY SEEING ALL THAT CRAP BOUNCING OFF THE WINDOWS?
OH, SO WE'VE FINALLY RETURNED TO YOUR SEX-DRIVE AGAIN IN THE FAMILIAR CONVERSATIONAL MERRY-GO-ROUND OF "I HATE QUEERS," "I LOVE FOOTBALL," "I'M HORNY."
ISN'T IT ENOUGH THAT YOU'VE BEEN HUMILIATING THOSE POOR HOOKERS ALL WEEKEND?
DON'T CARE HOW MUCH E AND VIAGRA YOU CHUCK OWN YOUR NECK, THE FUN GOES RIGHT OUT OF HUMILIATION WHEN YOU ACTUALLY HAVE TO PAY FOR IT.
YEAH, WELL MAYBE YOU SHOULD STICK TO THAT CUTE LITTLE BULIMIC POP-STAR YOU MARRIED, CASANOVA.
THE GIRL PROBABLY HAS TOO MUCH MEAT ON HER RIBS FOR A BONE-STABBER LIKE YOU...
RIGHT! THAT'S ENOUGH. DROP YOUR DRAWERS, YOU, AND LET'S HAVE IT UP AGAINST THE WINDOWS WITH ALL THE MUCK FLYING BY.
WHAT? HOW DARE YOU SPEAK TO ME LIKE THAT?
BESIDES, I DON'T DO GUYS.
BOLLOCKS! YOU JUST HAVEN'T BEEN WINED AND DINED BY THE RIGHT KIND OF BLOKE.

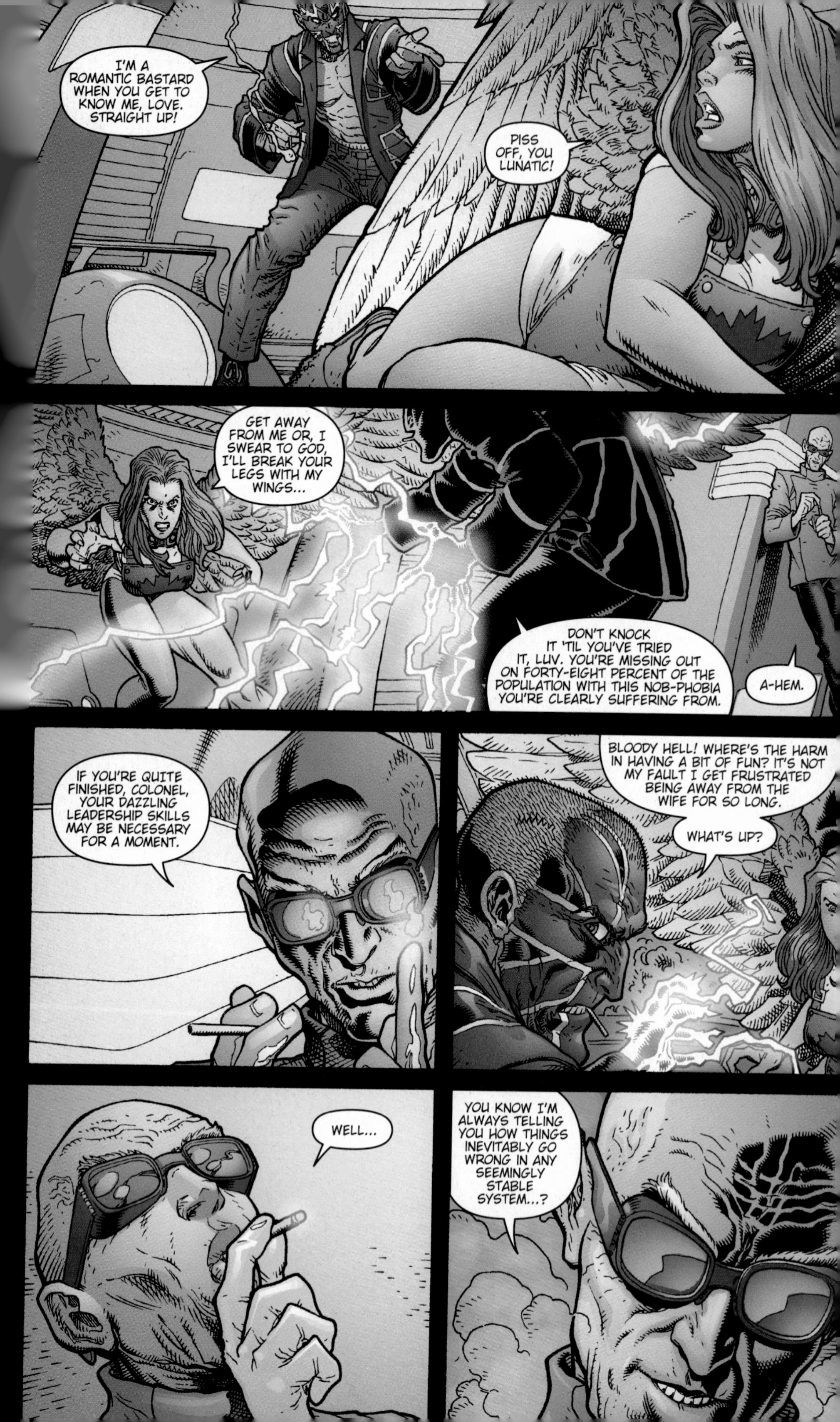

I'M A ROMANTIC BASTARD WHEN YOU GET TO KNOW ME, LOVE. STRAIGHT UP!
PISS OFF, YOU LUNATIC!
GET AWAY FROM ME OR, I SWEAR TO GOD, I'LL BREAK YOUR LEGS WITH MY WINGS...
DON'T KNOCK IT 'TIL YOU'VE TRIED IT, LUV. YOU'RE MISSING OUT ON FORTY-EIGHT PERCENT OF THE POPULATION WITH THIS NOB-PHOBIA YOU'RE CLEARLY SUFFERING FROM.
A-HEM.
IF YOU'RE QUITE FINISHED, COLONEL, YOUR DAZZLING LEADERSHIP SKILLS MAY BE NECESSARY FOR A MOMENT.
BLOODY HELL! WHERE'S THE HARM IN HAVING A BIT OF FUN? IT'S NOT MY FAULT I GET FRUSTRATED BEING AWAY FROM THE WIFE FOR SO LONG.
WHAT'S UP?
WELL...
YOU KNOW I'M ALWAYS TELLING YOU HOW THINGS INEVITABLY GO WRONG IN ANY SEEMINGLY STABLE SYSTEM...?

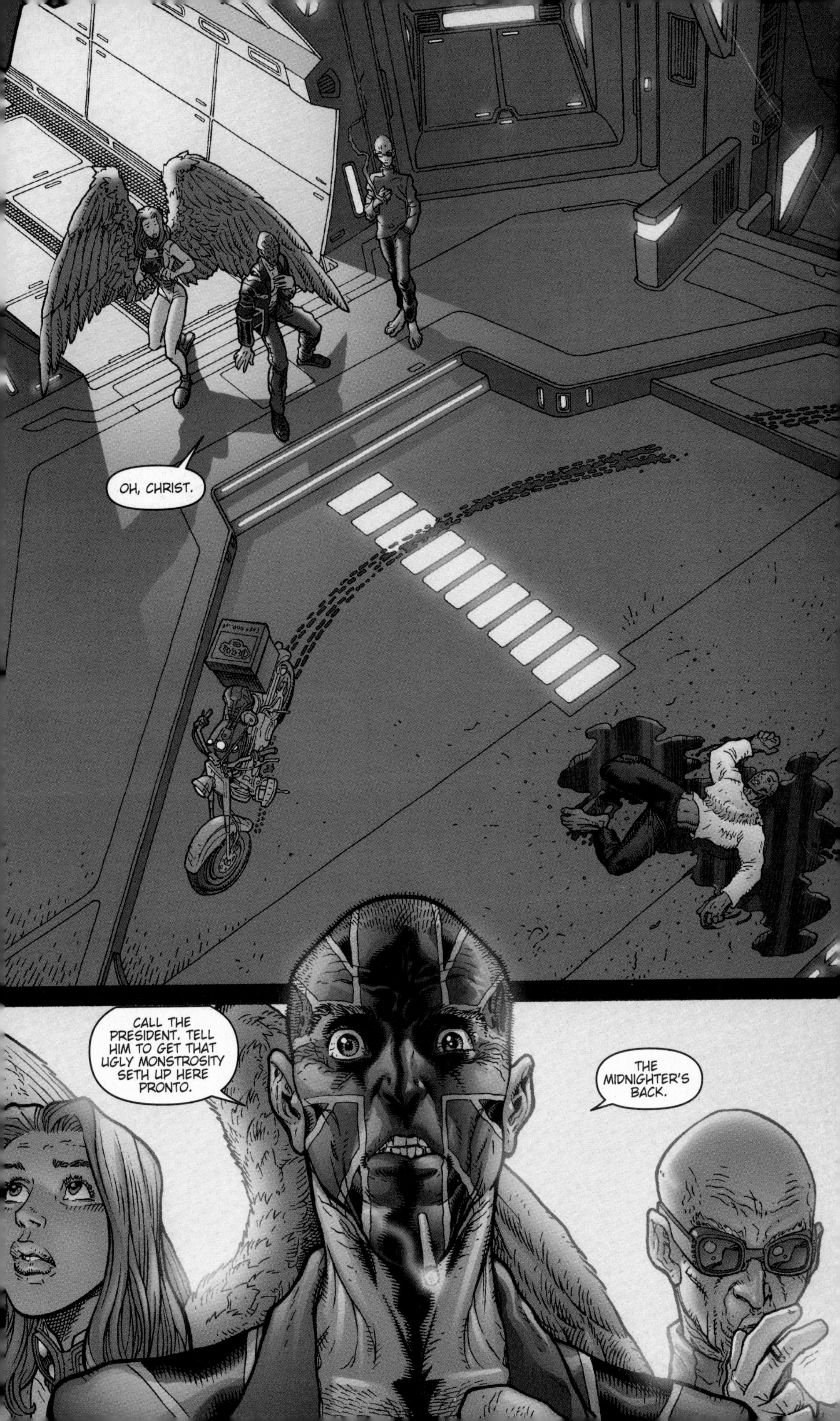
OH, CHRIST.
CALL THE PRESIDENT. TELL HIM TO GET THAT UGLY MONSTROSITY SETH UP HERE PRONTO.
THE MIDNIGHTER'S BACK.

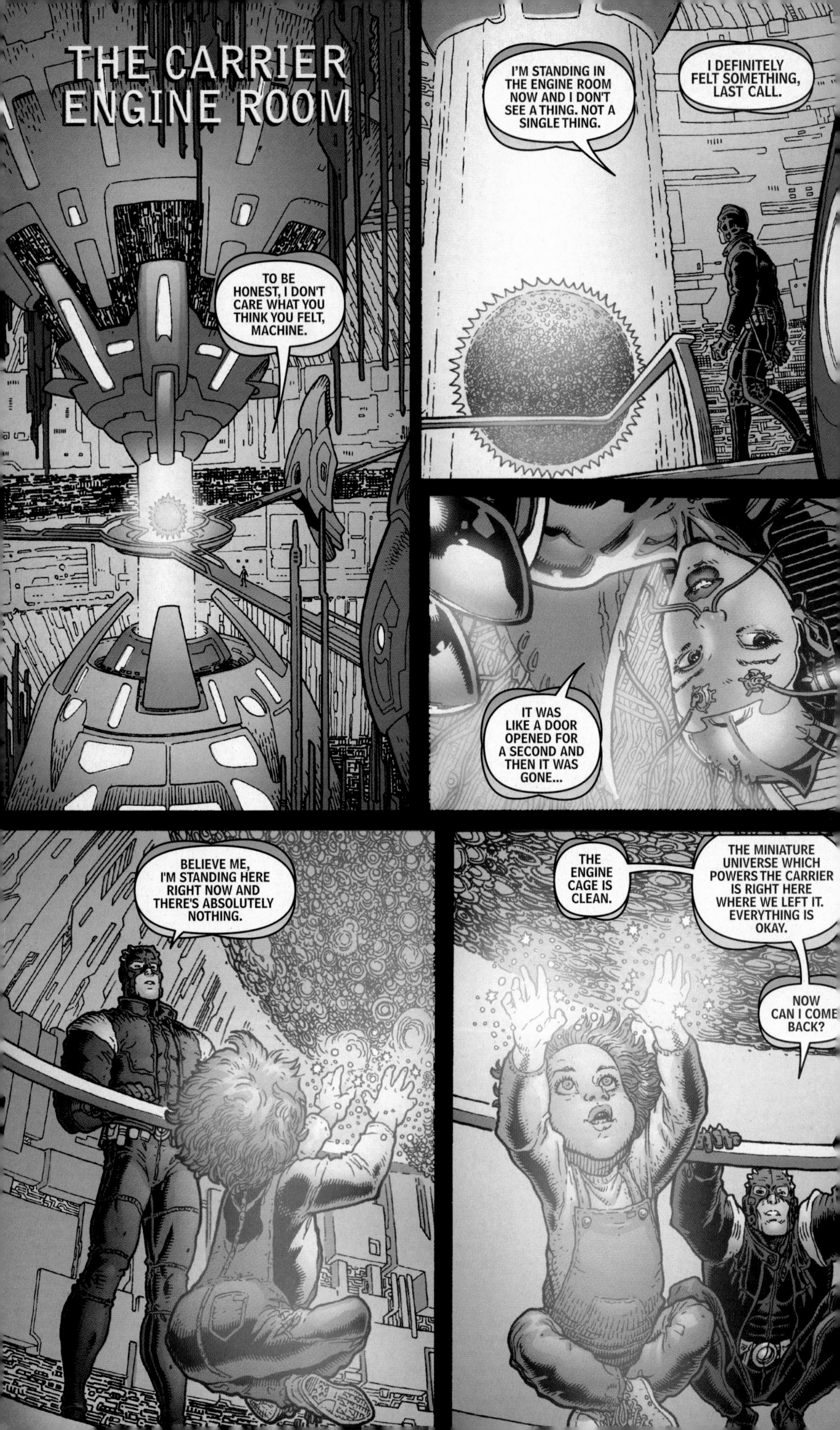
THE CARRIER ENGINE ROOM
I'M STANDING IN THE ENGINE ROOM NOW AND I DON'T SEE A THING. NOT A SINGLE THING.
I DEFINITELY FELT SOMETHING, LAST CALL.
TO BE HONEST, I DON'T CARE WHAT YOU THINK YOU FELT, MACHINE.
IT WAS LIKE A DOOR OPENED FOR A SECOND AND THEN IT WAS GONE...
BELIEVE ME, I'M STANDING HERE RIGHT NOW AND THERE'S ABSOLUTELY NOTHING.
THE ENGINE CAGE IS CLEAN.
THE MINIATURE UNIVERSE WHICH POWERS THE CARRIER IS RIGHT HERE WHERE WE LEFT IT. EVERYTHING IS OKAY.
NOW CAN I COME BACK?

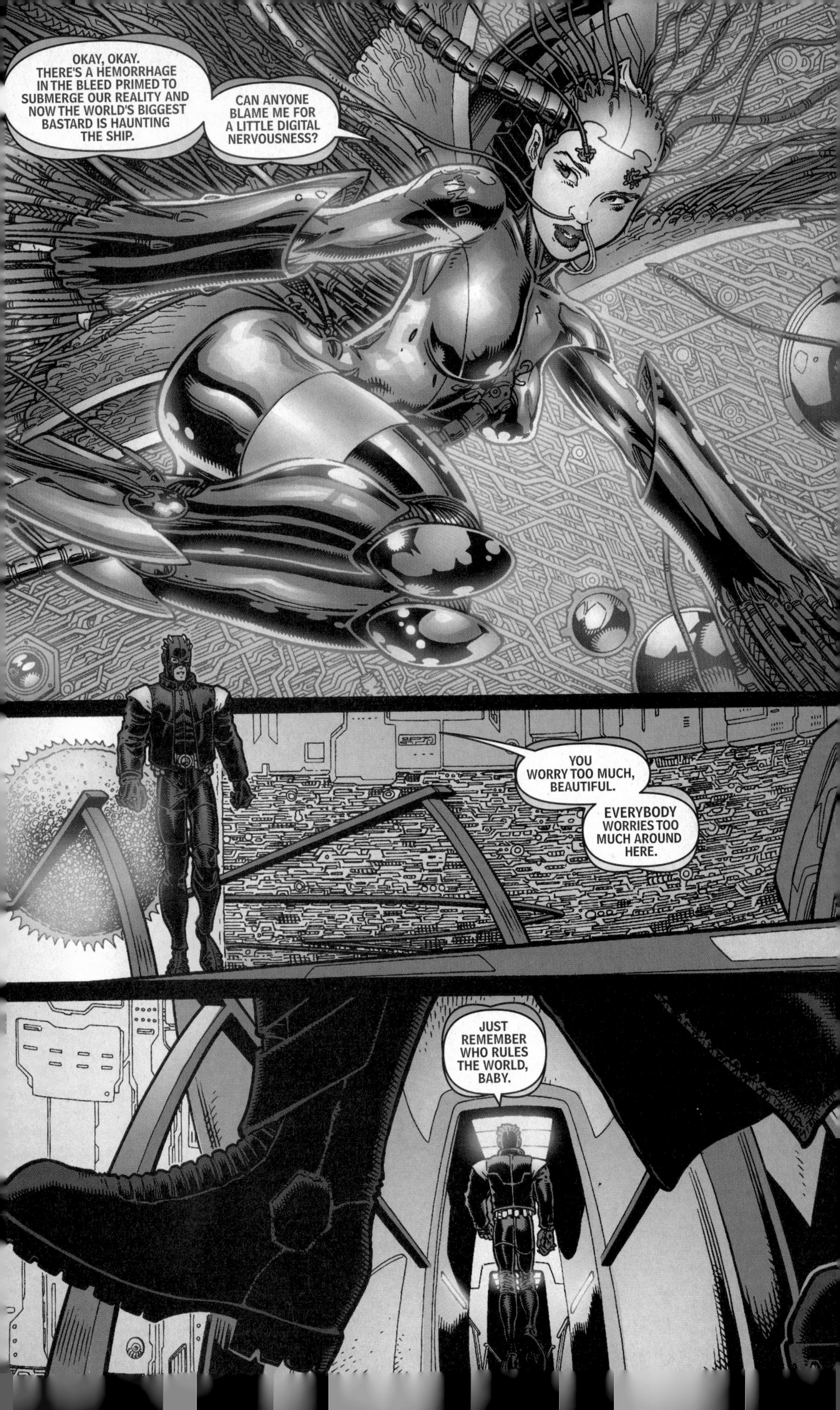
OKAY, OKAY. THERE'S A HEMORRHAGE IN THE BLEED PRIMED TO SUBMERGE OUR REALITY AND NOW THE WORLD'S BIGGEST BASTARD IS HAUNTING THE SHIP.
CAN ANYONE BLAME ME FOR A LITTLE DIGITAL NERVOUSNESS?
YOU WORRY TOO MUCH, BEAUTIFUL.
EVERYBODY WORRIES TOO MUCH AROUND HERE.
JUST REMEMBER WHO RULES THE WORLD, BABY.

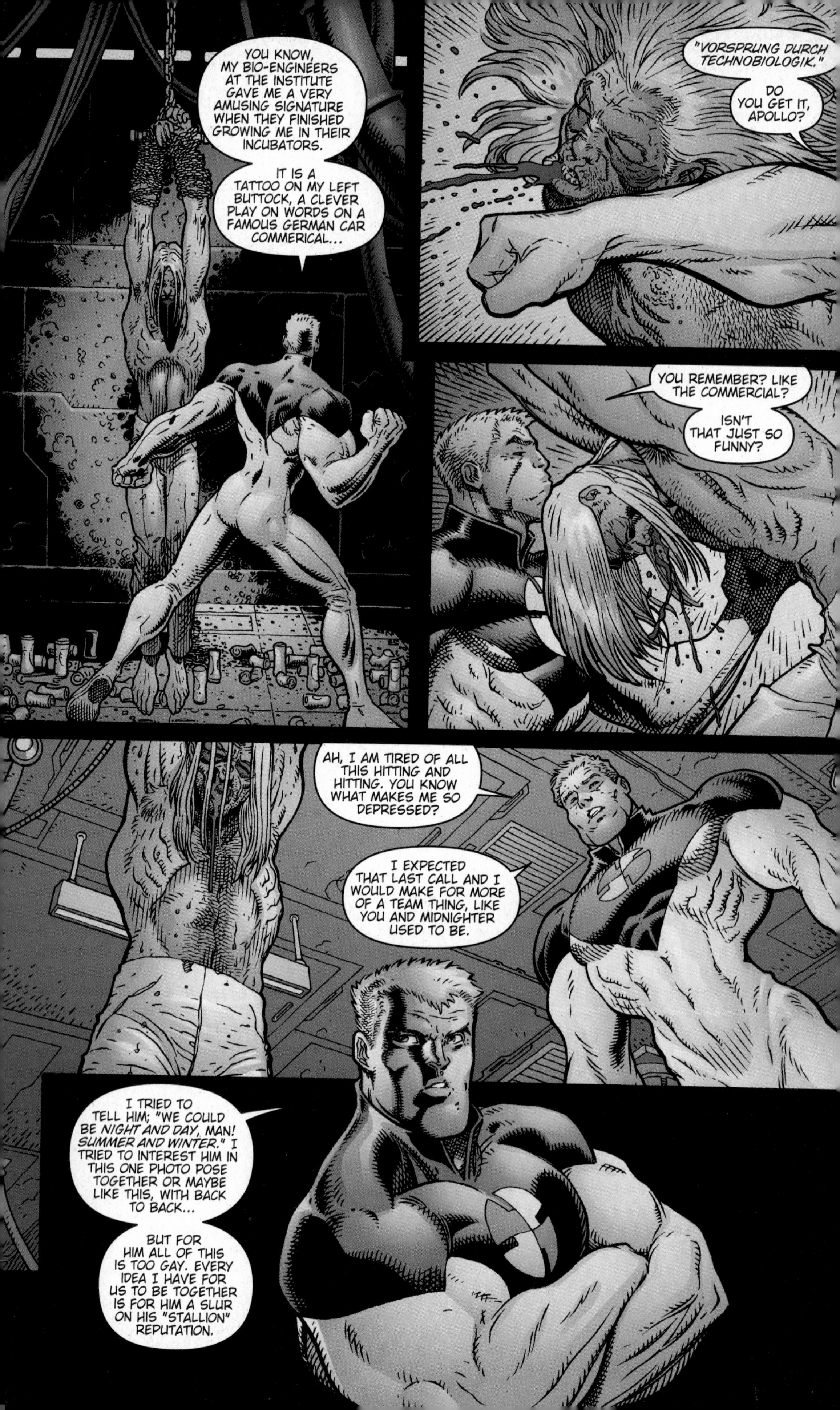

YOU KNOW, MY BIO-ENGINEERS AT THE INSTITUTE GAVE ME A VERY AMUSING SIGNATURE WHEN THEY FINISHED GROWING ME IN THEIR INCUBATORS.
IT IS A TATTOO ON MY LEFT BUTTOCK, A CLEVER PLAY ON WORDS ON A FAMOUS GERMAN CAR COMMERICAL...
"VORSPRUNG DURCH TECHNOBIOLOGIK."
DO YOU GET IT, APOLLO?
YOU REMEMBER? LIKE THE COMMERCIAL?
ISN'T THAT JUST SO FUNNY?
AH, I AM TIRED OF ALL THIS HITTING AND HITTING. YOU KNOW WHAT MAKES ME SO DEPRESSED?
I EXPECTED THAT LAST CALL AND I WOULD MAKE FOR MORE OF A TEAM THING, LIKE YOU AND MIDNIGHTER USED TO BE.
I TRIED TO TELL HIM; "WE COULD BE *NIGHT AND DAY, MAN! SUMMER AND WINTER.*" I TRIED TO INTEREST HIM IN THIS ONE PHOTO POSE TOGETHER OR MAYBE LIKE THIS, WITH BACK TO BACK...
BUT FOR HIM ALL OF THIS IS TOO GAY. EVERY IDEA I HAVE FOR US TO BE TOGETHER IS FOR HIM A SLUR ON HIS "STALLION" REPUTATION.

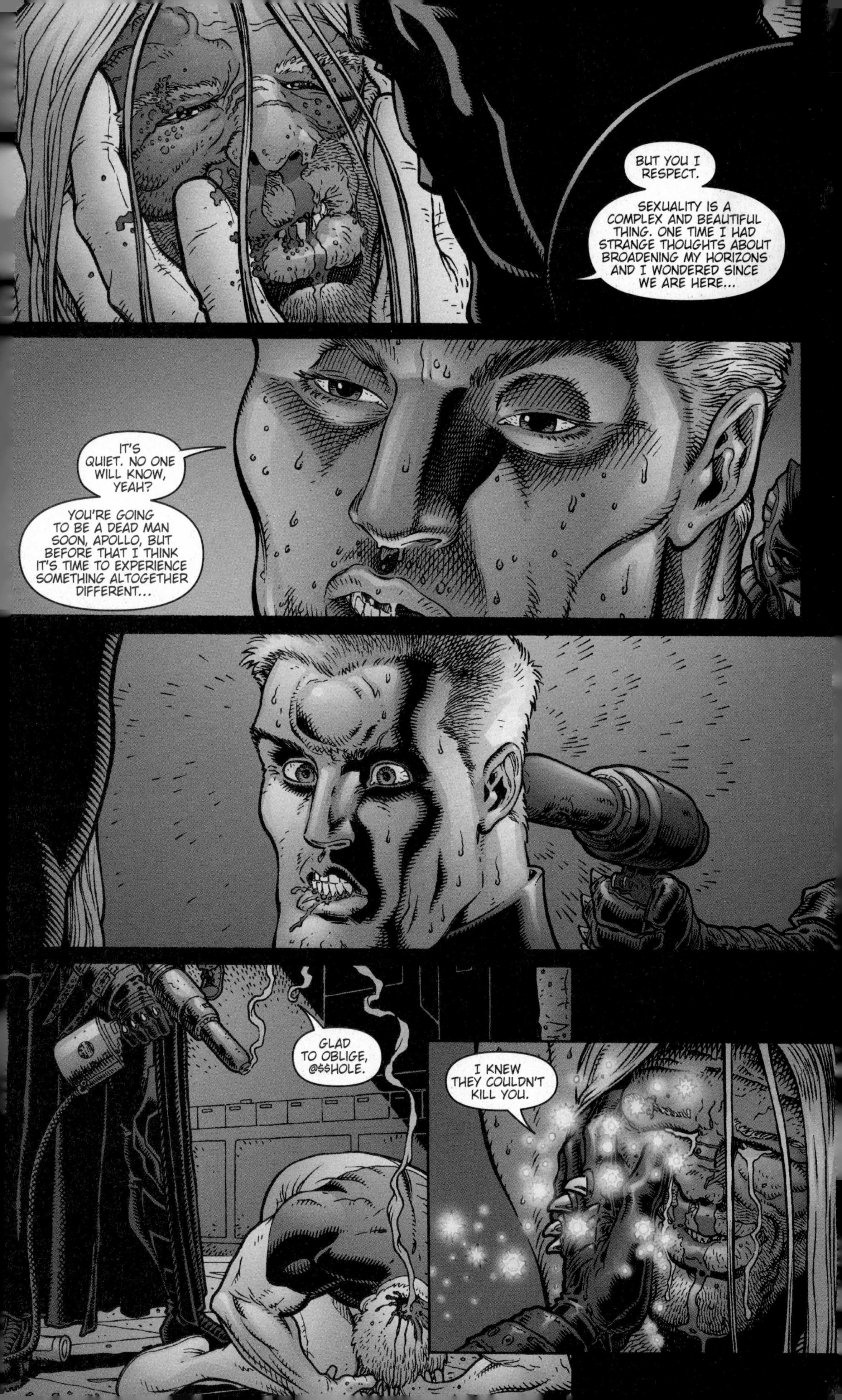

BUT YOU I RESPECT.
SEXUALITY IS A COMPLEX AND BEAUTIFUL THING. ONE TIME I HAD STRANGE THOUGHTS ABOUT BROADENING MY HORIZONS AND I WONDERED SINCE WE ARE HERE...
IT'S QUIET. NO ONE WILL KNOW, YEAH?
YOU'RE GOING TO BE A DEAD MAN SOON, APOLLO, BUT BEFORE THAT I THINK IT'S TIME TO EXPERIENCE SOMETHING ALTOGETHER DIFFERENT...
GLAD TO OBLIGE, @$$HOLE.
I KNEW THEY COULDN'T KILL YOU.

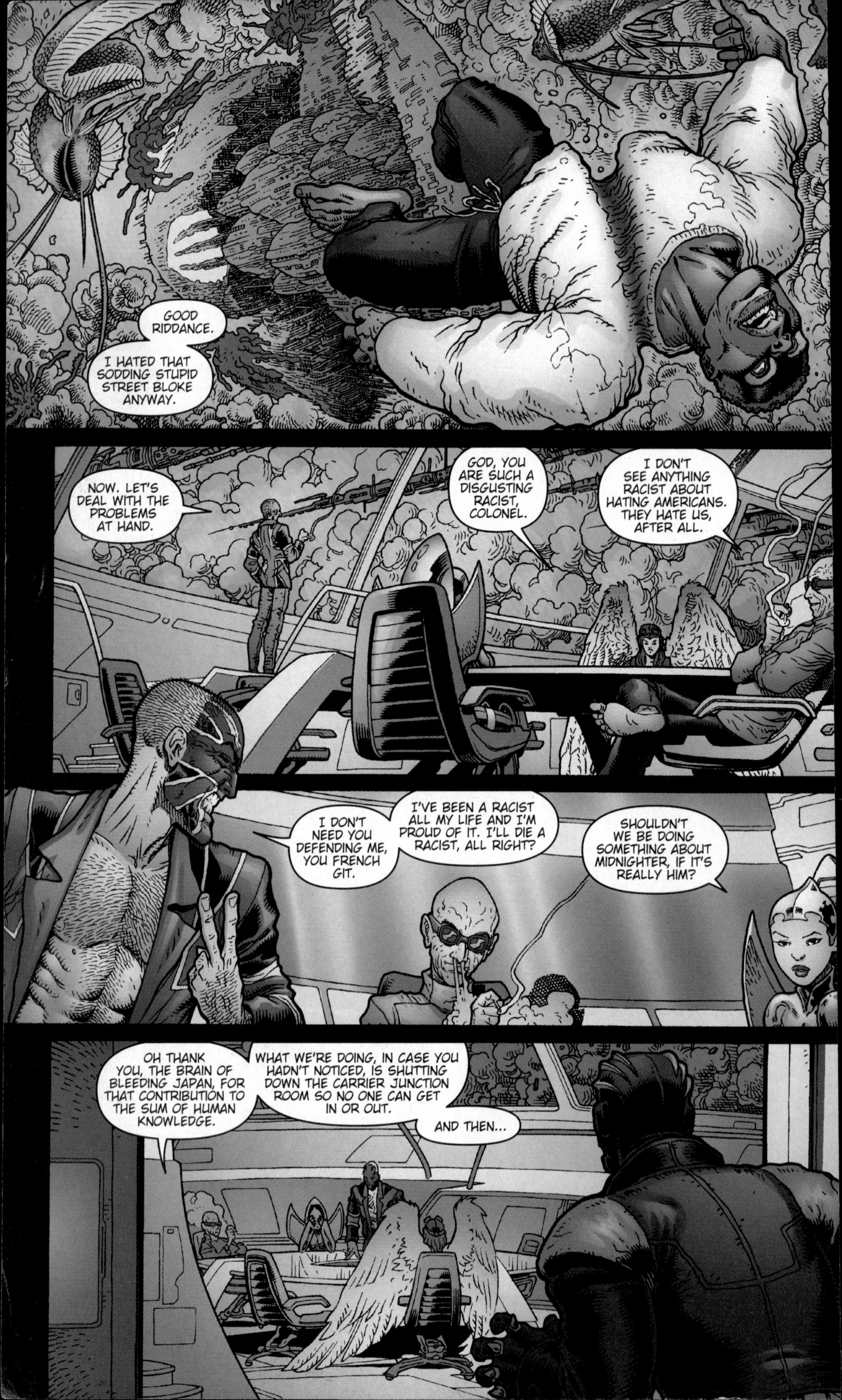
GOOD RIDDANCE.
I HATED THAT SODDING STUPID STREET BLOKE ANYWAY.
NOW. LET'S DEAL WITH THE PROBLEMS AT HAND.
GOD, YOU ARE SUCH A DISGUSTING RACIST, COLONEL.
I DON'T SEE ANYTHING RACIST ABOUT HATING AMERICANS. THEY HATE US, AFTER ALL.
I DON'T NEED YOU DEFENDING ME, YOU FRENCH GIT.
I'VE BEEN A RACIST ALL MY LIFE AND I'M PROUD OF IT. I'LL DIE A RACIST, ALL RIGHT?
SHOULDN'T WE BE DOING SOMETHING ABOUT MIDNIGHTER, IF IT'S REALLY HIM?
OH THANK YOU, THE BRAIN OF BLEEDING JAPAN, FOR THAT CONTRIBUTION TO THE SUM OF HUMAN KNOWLEDGE.
WHAT WE'RE DOING, IN CASE YOU HADN'T NOTICED, IS SHUTTING DOWN THE CARRIER JUNCTION ROOM SO NO ONE CAN GET IN OR OUT.
AND THEN...

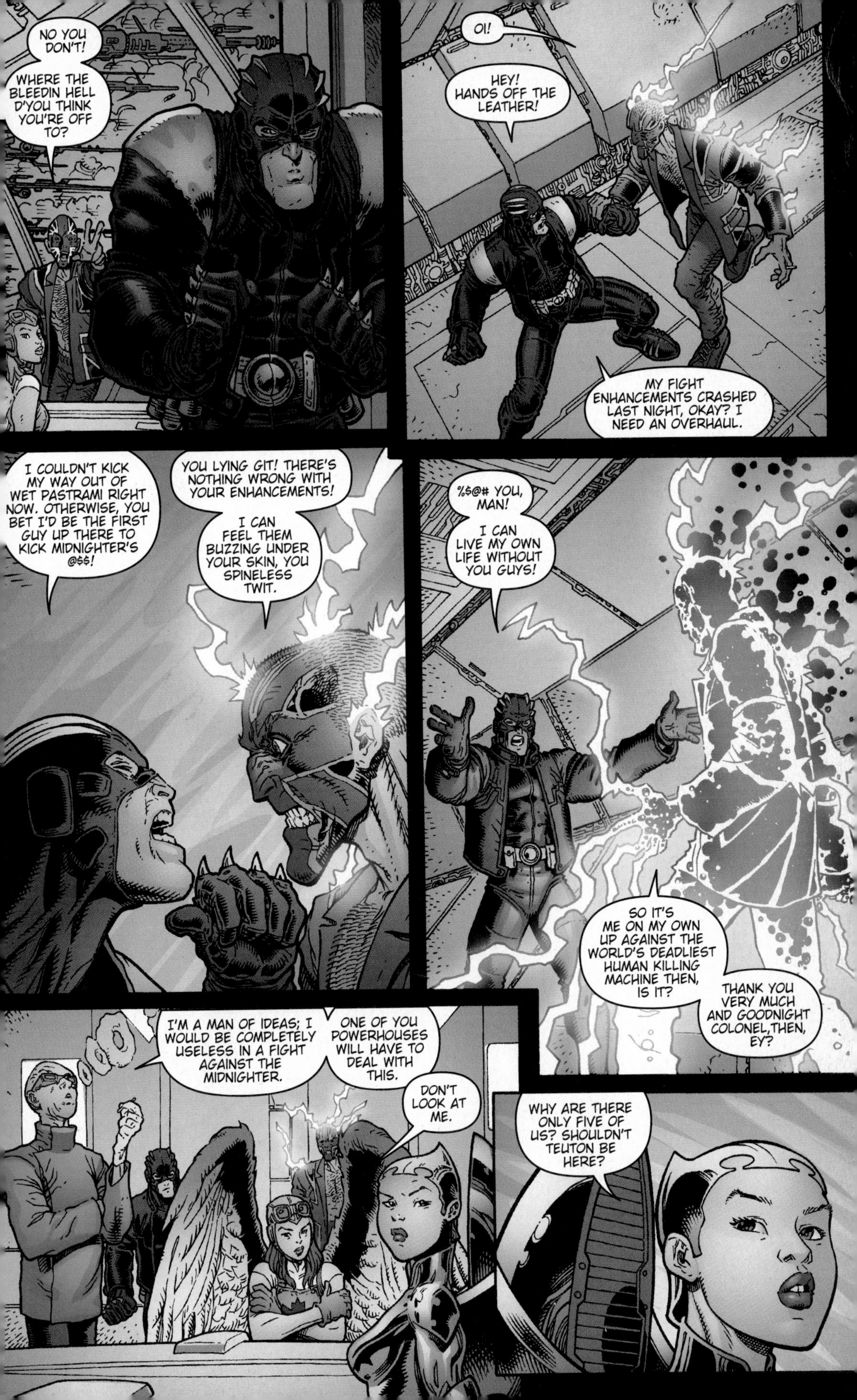
NO YOU DON'T!
WHERE THE BLEEDIN HELL D'YOU THINK YOU'RE OFF TO?
OI!
HEY! HANDS OFF THE LEATHER!
MY FIGHT ENHANCEMENTS CRASHED LAST NIGHT, OKAY? I NEED AN OVERHAUL.
I COULDN'T KICK MY WAY OUT OF WET PASTRAMI RIGHT NOW. OTHERWISE, YOU BET I'D BE THE FIRST GUY UP THERE TO KICK MIDNIGHTER'S @$$!
YOU LYING GIT! THERE'S NOTHING WRONG WITH YOUR ENHANCEMENTS!
I CAN FEEL THEM BUZZING UNDER YOUR SKIN, YOU SPINELESS TWIT.
%$@# YOU, MAN!
I CAN LIVE MY OWN LIFE WITHOUT YOU GUYS!
SO IT'S ME ON MY OWN UP AGAINST THE WORLD'S DEADLIEST HUMAN KILLING MACHINE THEN, IS IT?
THANK YOU VERY MUCH AND GOODNIGHT COLONEL,THEN, EY?
I'M A MAN OF IDEAS; I WOULD BE COMPLETELY USELESS IN A FIGHT AGAINST THE MIDNIGHTER.
ONE OF YOU POWERHOUSES WILL HAVE TO DEAL WITH THIS.
DON'T LOOK AT ME.
WHY ARE THERE ONLY FIVE OF US? SHOULDN'T TEUTON BE HERE?

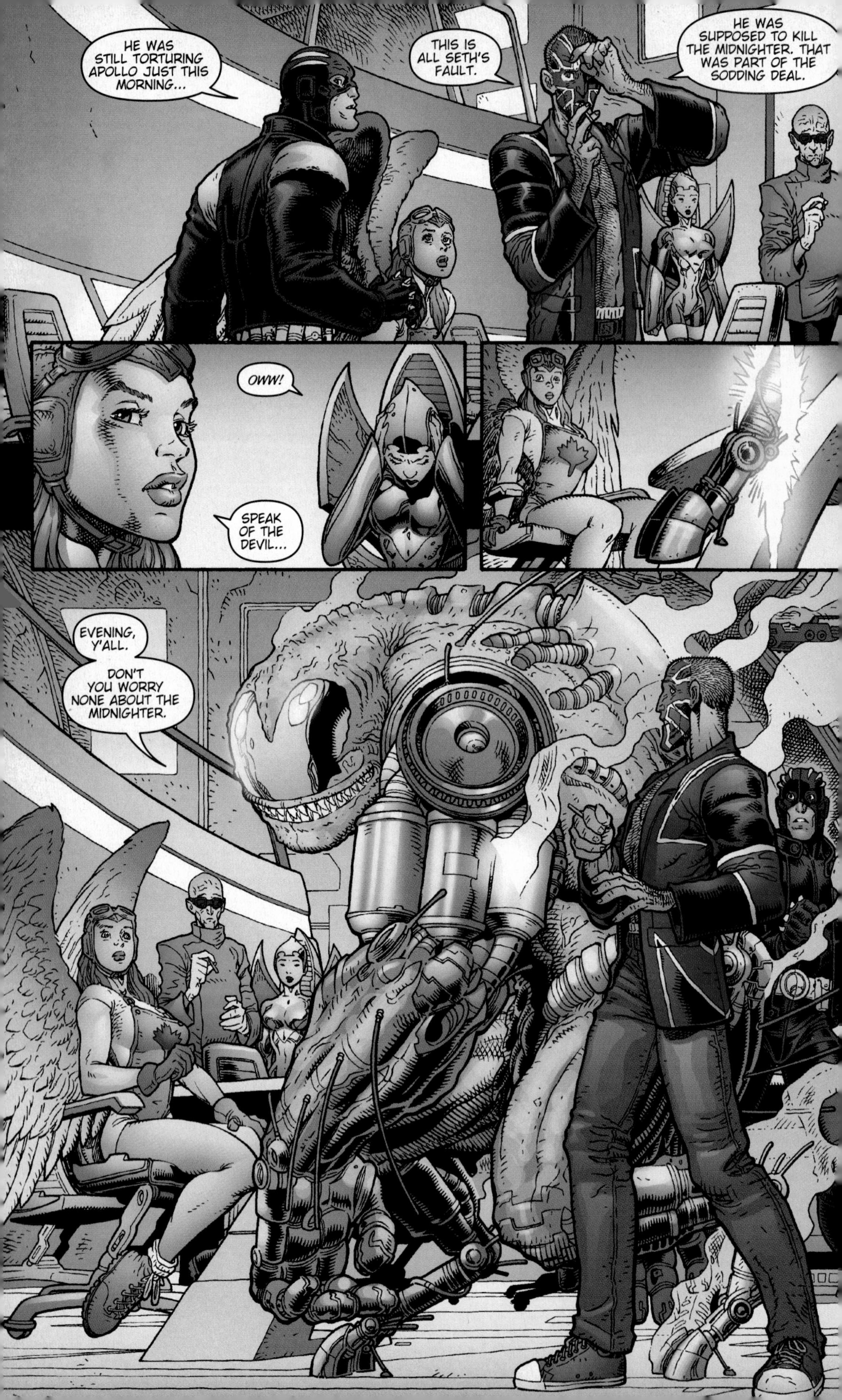
HE WAS STILL TORTURING APOLLO JUST THIS MORNING...
THIS IS ALL SETH'S FAULT.
HE WAS SUPPOSED TO KILL THE MIDNIGHTER. THAT WAS PART OF THE SODDING DEAL.
OWW!
SPEAK OF THE DEVIL...
EVENING, Y'ALL.
DON'T YOU WORRY NONE ABOUT THE MIDNIGHTER.

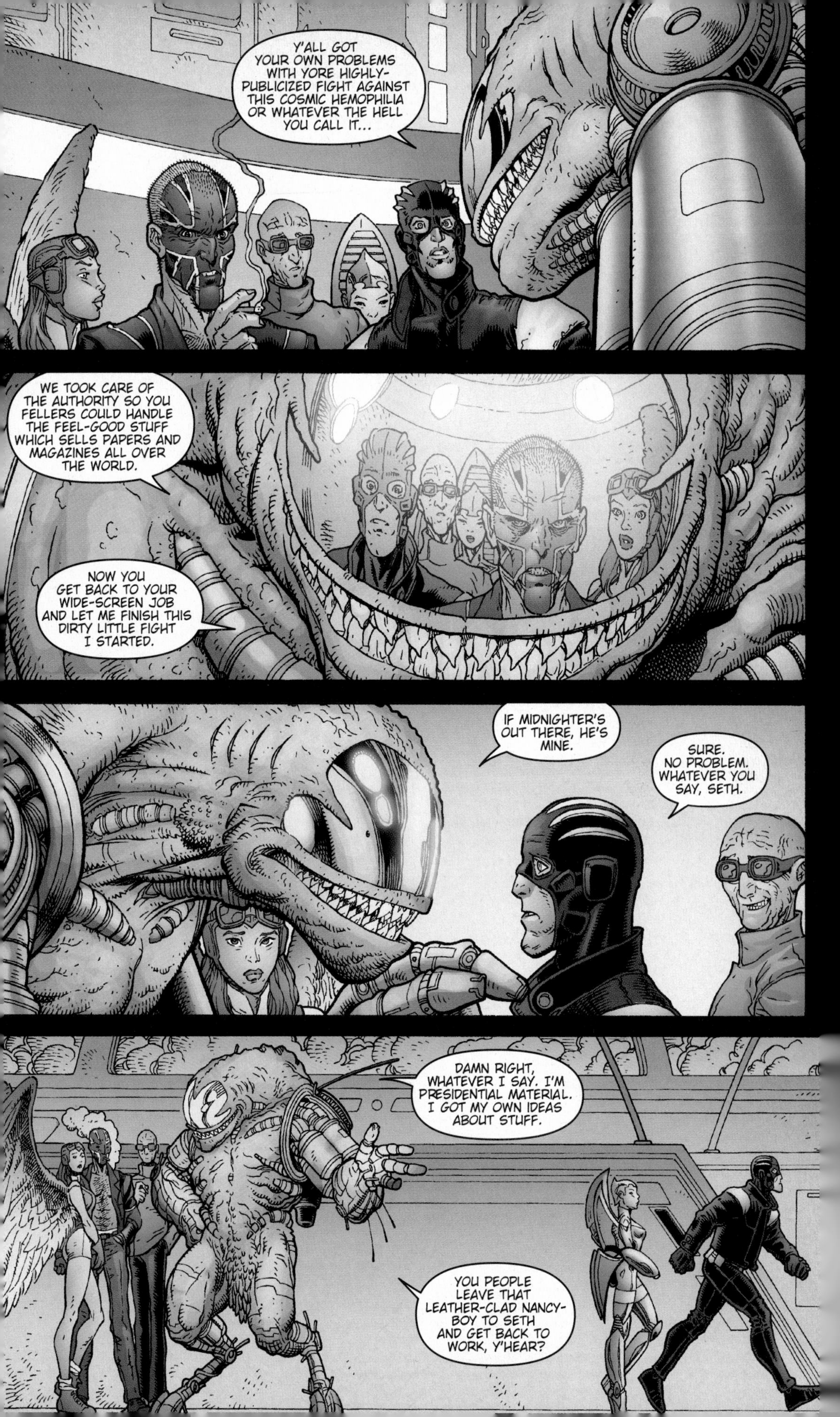
Y'ALL GOT YOUR OWN PROBLEMS WITH YORE HIGHLY-PUBLICIZED FIGHT AGAINST THIS COSMIC HEMOPHILIA OR WHATEVER THE HELL YOU CALL IT...
WE TOOK CARE OF THE AUTHORITY SO YOU FELLERS COULD HANDLE THE FEEL-GOOD STUFF WHICH SELLS PAPERS AND MAGAZINES ALL OVER THE WORLD.
NOW YOU GET BACK TO YOUR WIDE-SCREEN JOB AND LET ME FINISH THIS DIRTY LITTLE FIGHT I STARTED.
IF MIDNIGHTER'S OUT THERE, HE'S MINE.
SURE. NO PROBLEM. WHATEVER YOU SAY, SETH.
DAMN RIGHT, WHATEVER I SAY. I'M PRESIDENTIAL MATERIAL. I GOT MY OWN IDEAS ABOUT STUFF.
YOU PEOPLE LEAVE THAT LEATHER-CLAD NANCY-BOY TO SETH AND GET BACK TO WORK, Y'HEAR?

STOP TRYING TO PRETEND YOU'RE UNCONSCIOUS SO YOU DON'T HAVE TO DO ANY WORK.

LIGHT ME, YOU LAZY BASTARD.

HEY, APOLLO. WAS TEUTON TRYING TO FEEL YOU UP AGAIN?

MY PLEASURE.

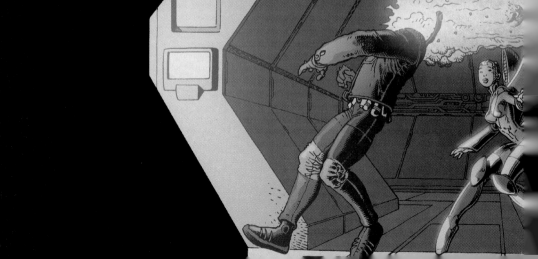

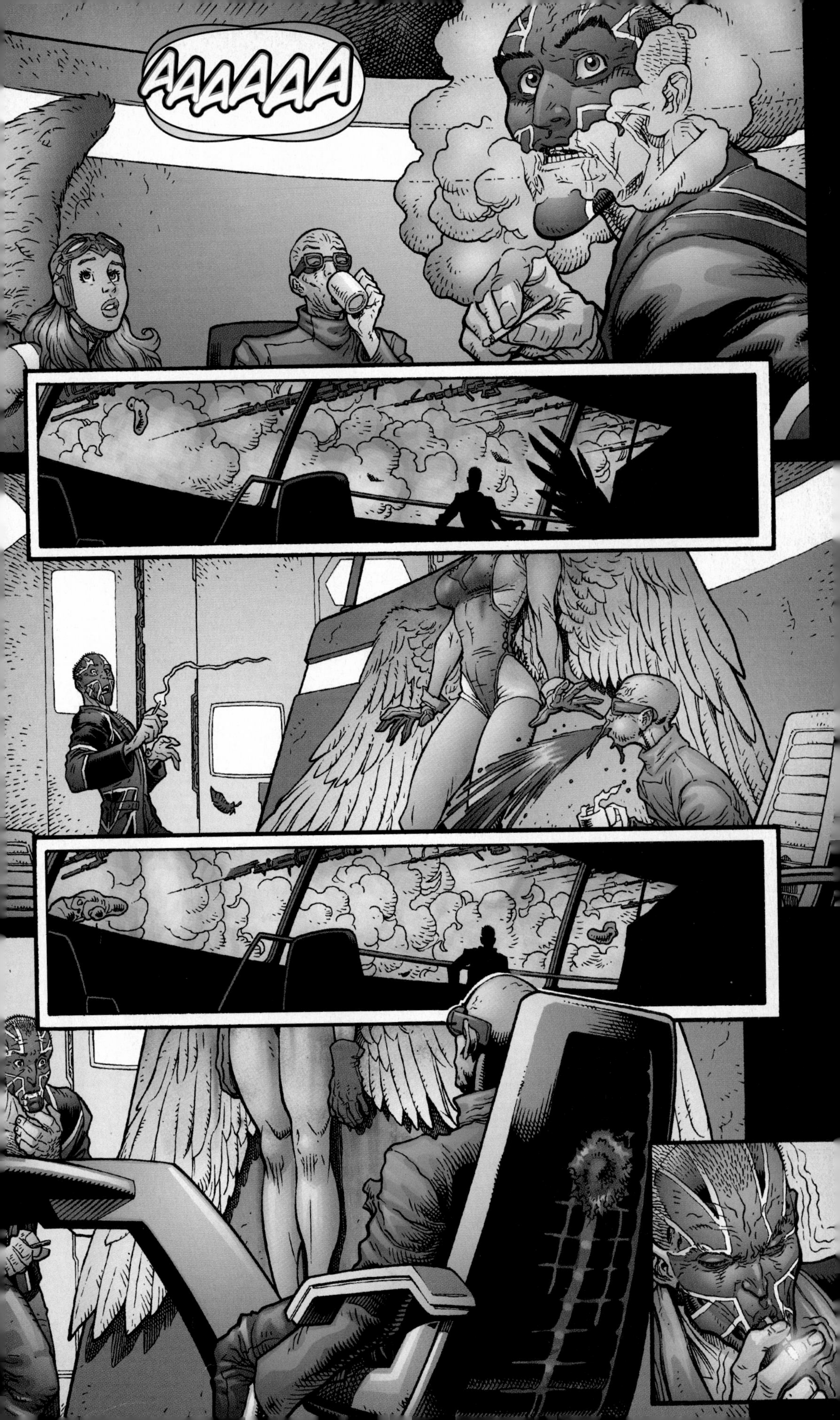
AAAAAA

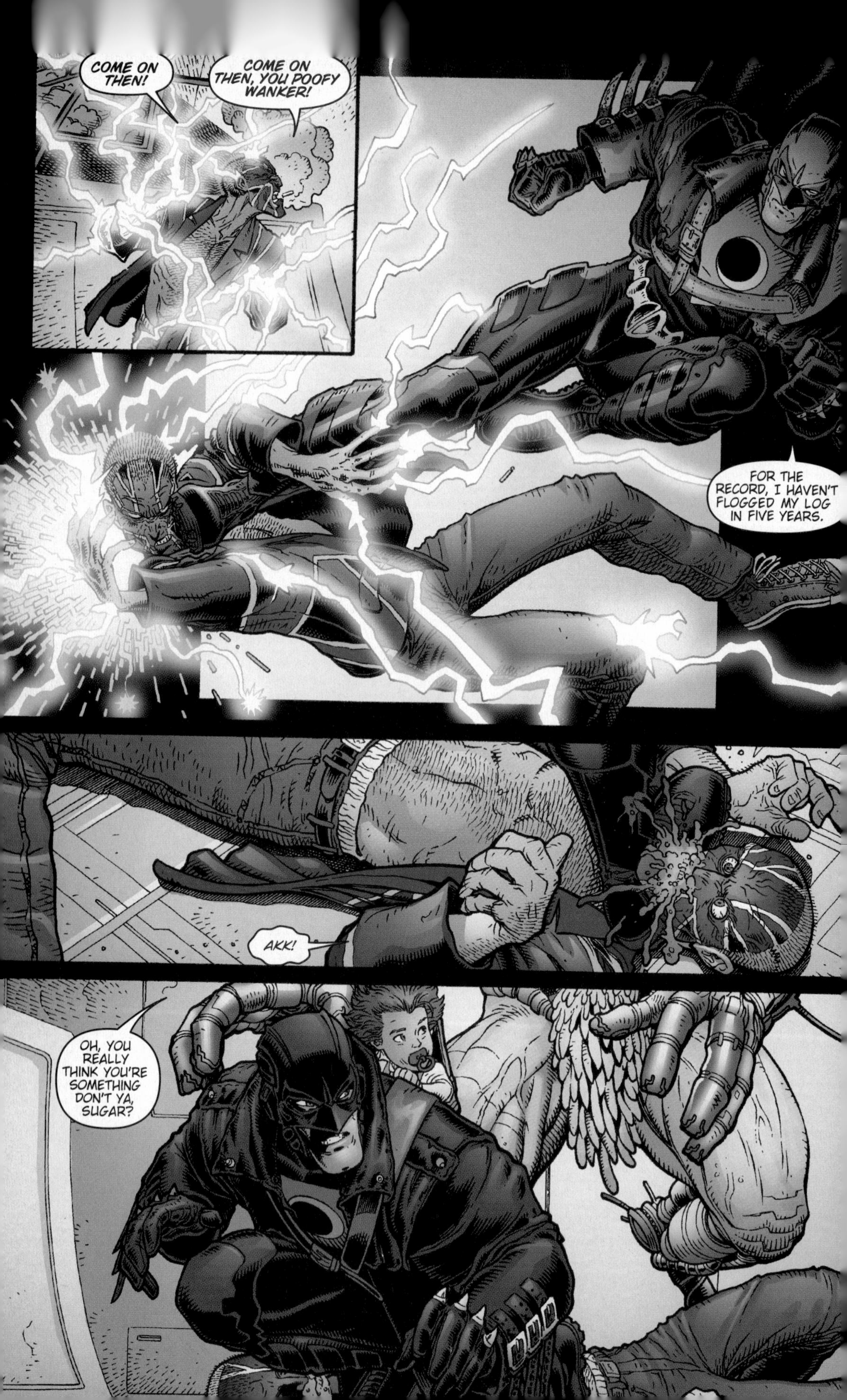
COME ON THEN!
COME ON THEN, YOU POOFY WANKER!
FOR THE RECORD, I HAVEN'T FLOGGED MY LOG IN FIVE YEARS.
AKK!
OH, YOU REALLY THINK YOU'RE SOMETHING DON'T YA, SUGAR?

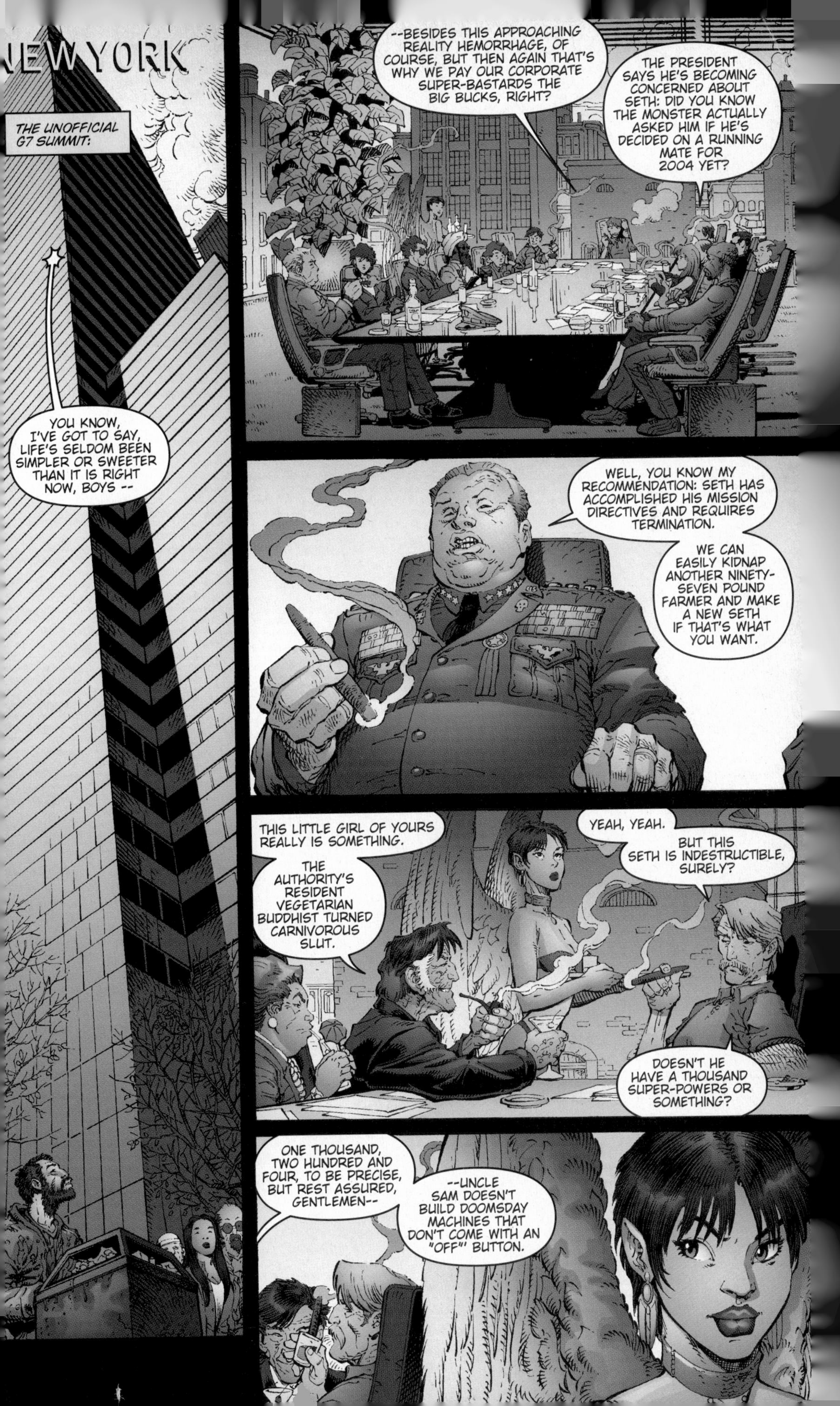
NEW YORK
THE UNOFFICIAL G7 SUMMIT:
YOU KNOW, I'VE GOT TO SAY, LIFE'S SELDOM BEEN SIMPLER OR SWEETER THAN IT IS RIGHT NOW, BOYS --
--BESIDES THIS APPROACHING REALITY HEMORRHAGE, OF COURSE, BUT THEN AGAIN THAT'S WHY WE PAY OUR CORPORATE SUPER-BASTARDS THE BIG BUCKS, RIGHT?
THE PRESIDENT SAYS HE'S BECOMING CONCERNED ABOUT SETH: DID YOU KNOW THE MONSTER ACTUALLY ASKED HIM IF HE'S DECIDED ON A RUNNING MATE FOR 2004 YET?
WELL, YOU KNOW MY RECOMMENDATION: SETH HAS ACCOMPLISHED HIS MISSION DIRECTIVES AND REQUIRES TERMINATION.
WE CAN EASILY KIDNAP ANOTHER NINETY-SEVEN POUND FARMER AND MAKE A NEW SETH IF THAT'S WHAT YOU WANT.
THIS LITTLE GIRL OF YOURS REALLY IS SOMETHING.
THE AUTHORITY'S RESIDENT VEGETARIAN BUDDHIST TURNED CARNIVOROUS SLUT.
YEAH, YEAH.
BUT THIS SETH IS INDESTRUCTIBLE, SURELY?
DOESN'T HE HAVE A THOUSAND SUPER-POWERS OR SOMETHING?
ONE THOUSAND, TWO HUNDRED AND FOUR, TO BE PRECISE, BUT REST ASSURED, GENTLEMEN--
--UNCLE SAM DOESN'T BUILD DOOMSDAY MACHINES THAT DON'T COME WITH AN "OFF" BUTTON.

THE CARRIER

NEEEEEIIIIIII

NO...

YOU'RE GOING TO BE OKAY.

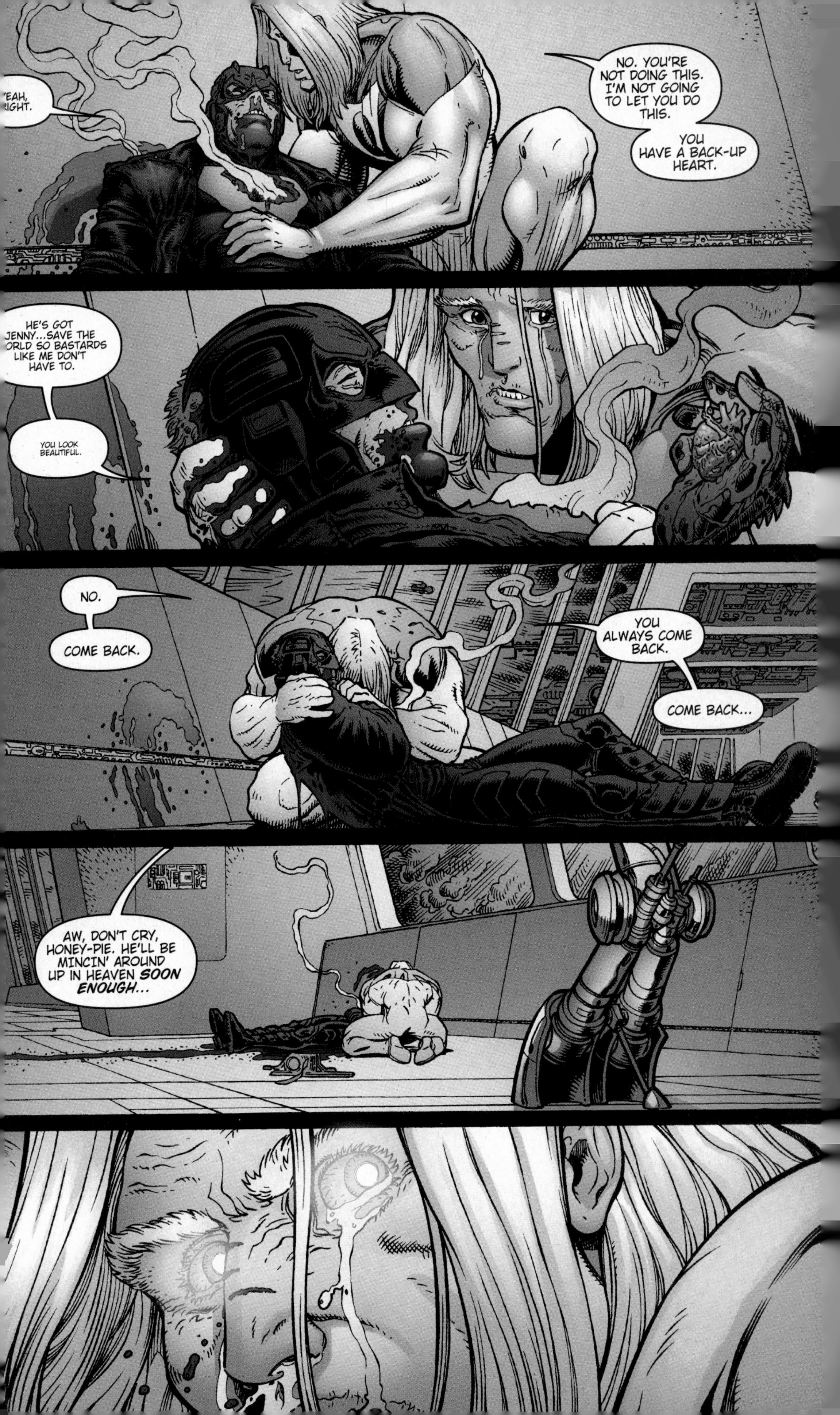
YEAH, RIGHT.
NO. YOU'RE NOT DOING THIS. I'M NOT GOING TO LET YOU DO THIS.
YOU HAVE A BACK-UP HEART.
HE'S GOT JENNY...SAVE THE WORLD SO BASTARDS LIKE ME DON'T HAVE TO.
YOU LOOK BEAUTIFUL.
NO.
COME BACK.
YOU ALWAYS COME BACK.
COME BACK...
AW, DON'T CRY, HONEY-PIE. HE'LL BE MINCIN' AROUND UP IN HEAVEN **SOON ENOUGH...**

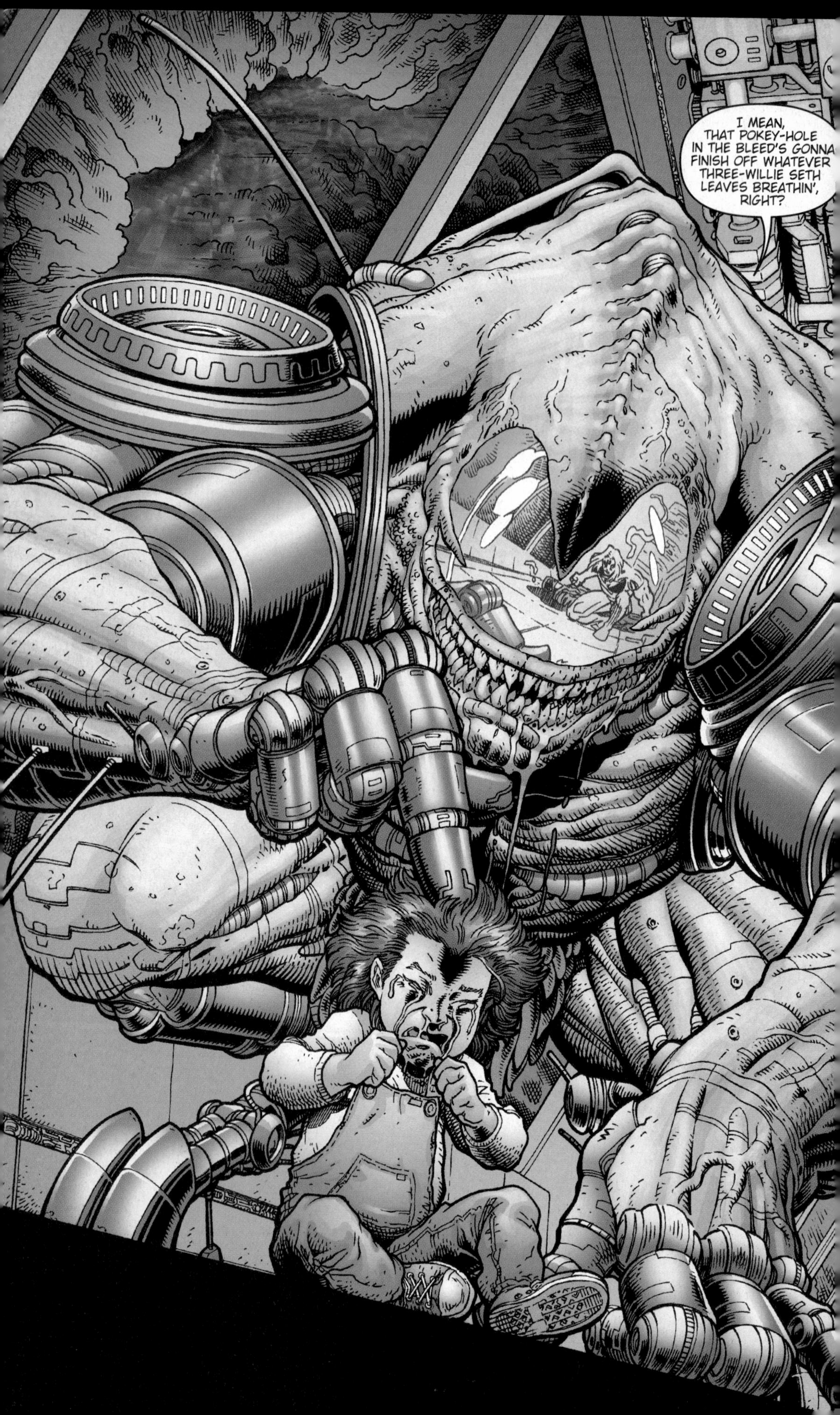
I MEAN, THAT POKEY-HOLE IN THE BLEED'S GONNA FINISH OFF WHATEVER THREE-WILLIE SETH LEAVES BREATHIN', RIGHT?

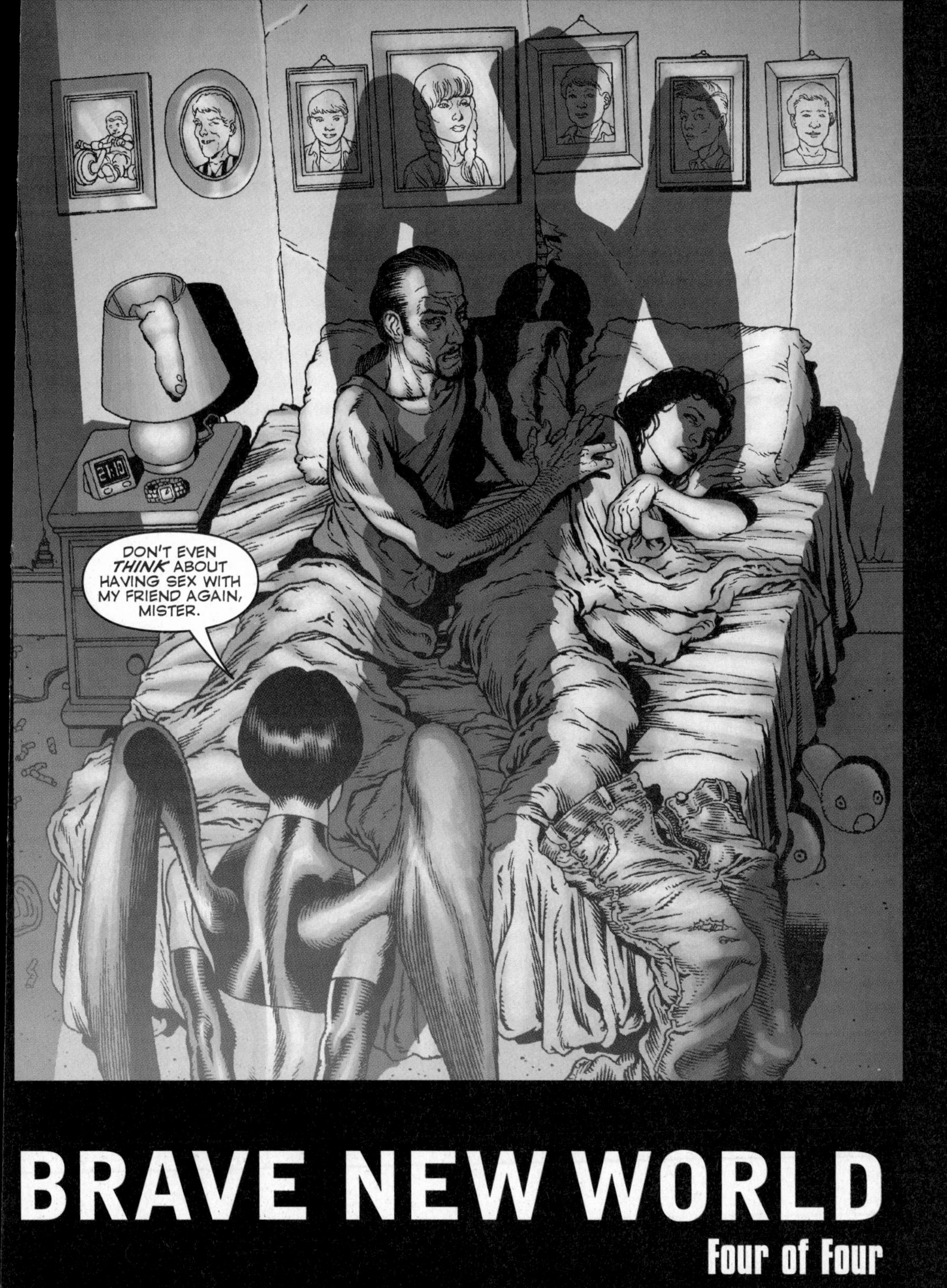

21:10
DON'T EVEN THINK ABOUT HAVING SEX WITH MY FRIEND AGAIN, MISTER.

BRAVE NEW WORLD

Four of Four

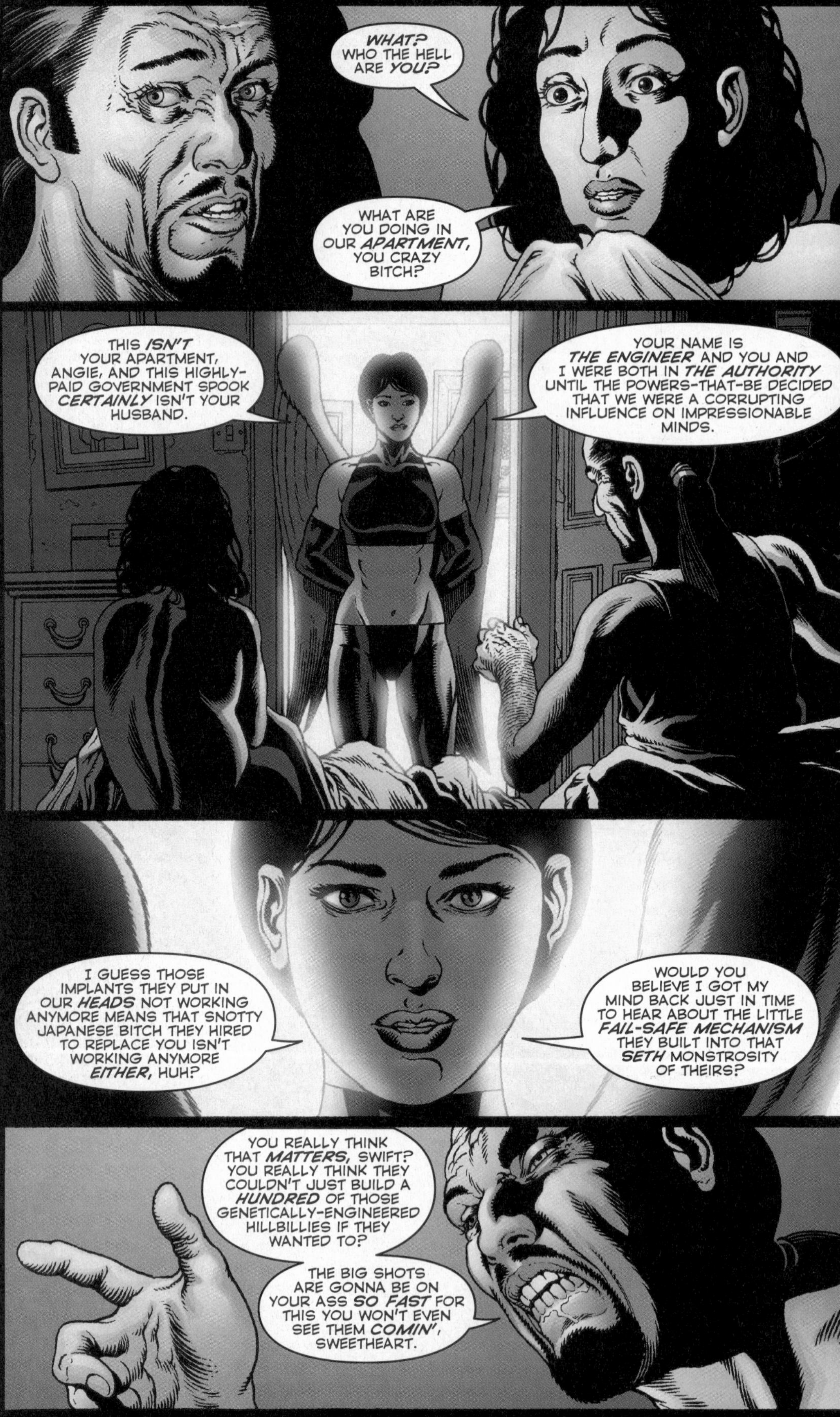
WHAT? WHO THE HELL ARE YOU?
WHAT ARE YOU DOING IN OUR APARTMENT, YOU CRAZY BITCH?
THIS ISN'T YOUR APARTMENT, ANGIE, AND THIS HIGHLY-PAID GOVERNMENT SPOOK CERTAINLY ISN'T YOUR HUSBAND.
YOUR NAME IS THE ENGINEER AND YOU AND I WERE BOTH IN THE AUTHORITY UNTIL THE POWERS-THAT-BE DECIDED THAT WE WERE A CORRUPTING INFLUENCE ON IMPRESSIONABLE MINDS.
I GUESS THOSE IMPLANTS THEY PUT IN OUR HEADS NOT WORKING ANYMORE MEANS THAT SNOTTY JAPANESE BITCH THEY HIRED TO REPLACE YOU ISN'T WORKING ANYMORE EITHER, HUH?
WOULD YOU BELIEVE I GOT MY MIND BACK JUST IN TIME TO HEAR ABOUT THE LITTLE FAIL-SAFE MECHANISM THEY BUILT INTO THAT SETH MONSTROSITY OF THEIRS?
YOU REALLY THINK THAT MATTERS, SWIFT? YOU REALLY THINK THEY COULDN'T JUST BUILD A HUNDRED OF THOSE GENETICALLY-ENGINEERED HILLBILLIES IF THEY WANTED TO?
THE BIG SHOTS ARE GONNA BE ON YOUR ASS SO FAST FOR THIS YOU WON'T EVEN SEE THEM COMIN', SWEETHEART.

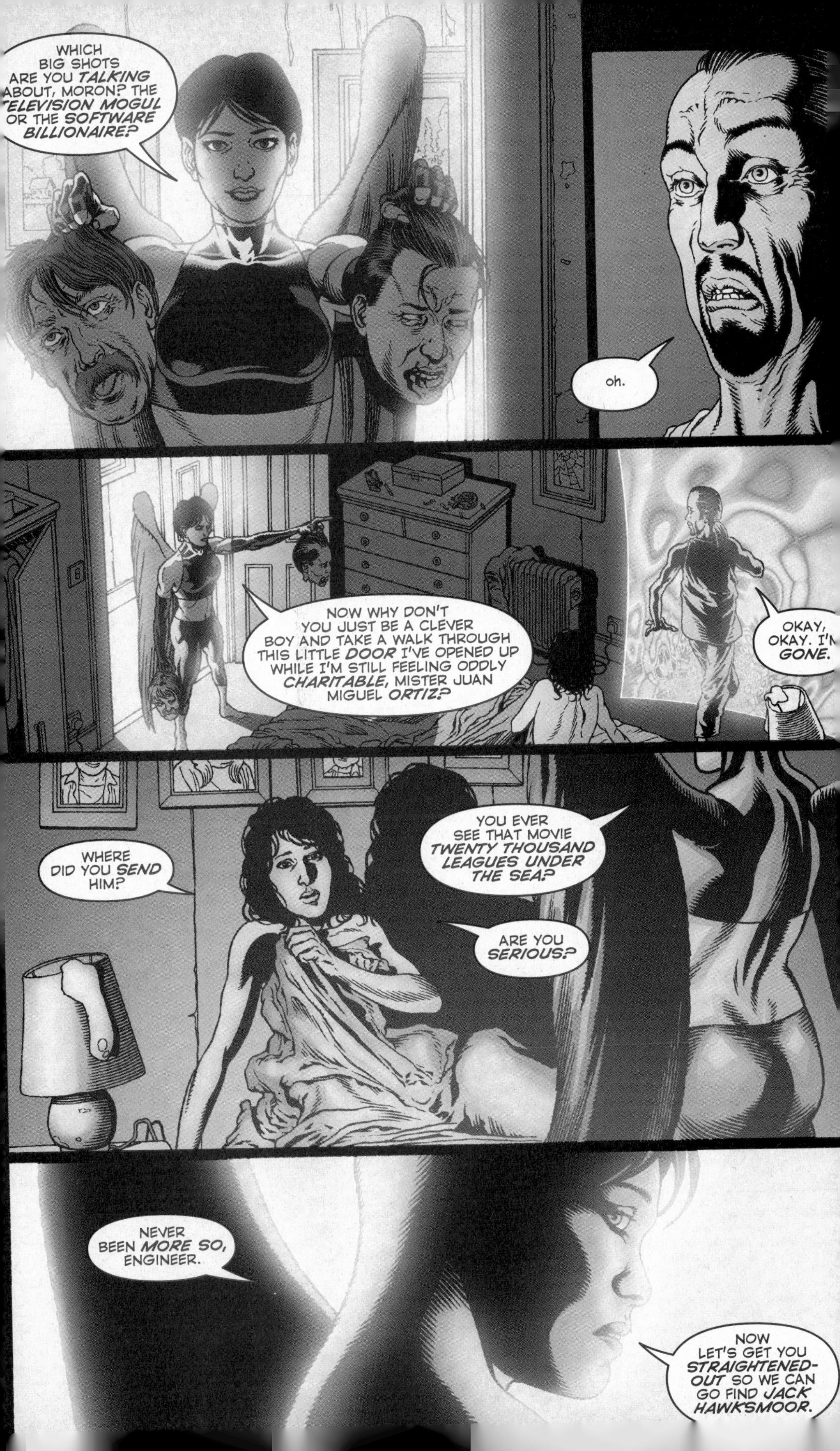
WHICH BIG SHOTS ARE YOU TALKING ABOUT, MORON? THE TELEVISION MOGUL OR THE SOFTWARE BILLIONAIRE?
oh.
NOW WHY DON'T YOU JUST BE A CLEVER BOY AND TAKE A WALK THROUGH THIS LITTLE DOOR I'VE OPENED UP WHILE I'M STILL FEELING ODDLY CHARITABLE, MISTER JUAN MIGUEL ORTIZ?
OKAY, OKAY. I'M GONE.
WHERE DID YOU SEND HIM?
YOU EVER SEE THAT MOVIE TWENTY THOUSAND LEAGUES UNDER THE SEA?
ARE YOU SERIOUS?
NEVER BEEN MORE SO, ENGINEER.
NOW LET'S GET YOU STRAIGHTENED-OUT SO WE CAN GO FIND JACK HAWKSMOOR.

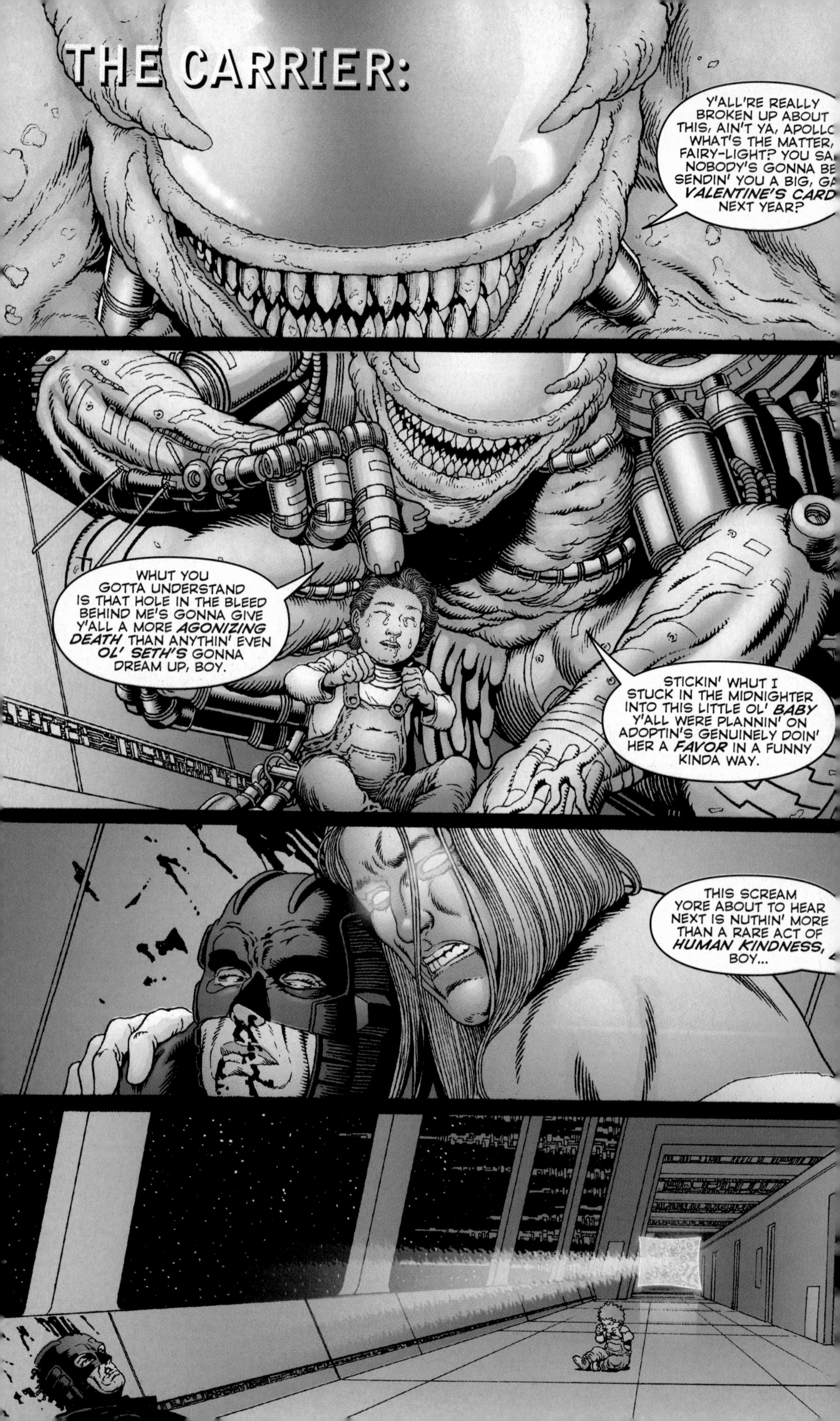
THE CARRIER:
Y'ALL'RE REALLY BROKEN UP ABOUT THIS, AIN'T YA, APOLLO WHAT'S THE MATTER, FAIRY-LIGHT? YOU SA NOBODY'S GONNA BE SENDIN' YOU A BIG, GA VALENTINE'S CARD NEXT YEAR?
WHUT YOU GOTTA UNDERSTAND IS THAT HOLE IN THE BLEED BEHIND ME'S GONNA GIVE Y'ALL A MORE AGONIZING DEATH THAN ANYTHIN' EVEN OL' SETH'S GONNA DREAM UP, BOY.
STICKIN' WHUT I STUCK IN THE MIDNIGHTER INTO THIS LITTLE OL' BABY Y'ALL WERE PLANNIN' ON ADOPTIN'S GENUINELY DOIN' HER A FAVOR IN A FUNNY KINDA WAY.
THIS SCREAM YORE ABOUT TO HEAR NEXT IS NUTHIN' MORE THAN A RARE ACT OF HUMAN KINDNESS, BOY...

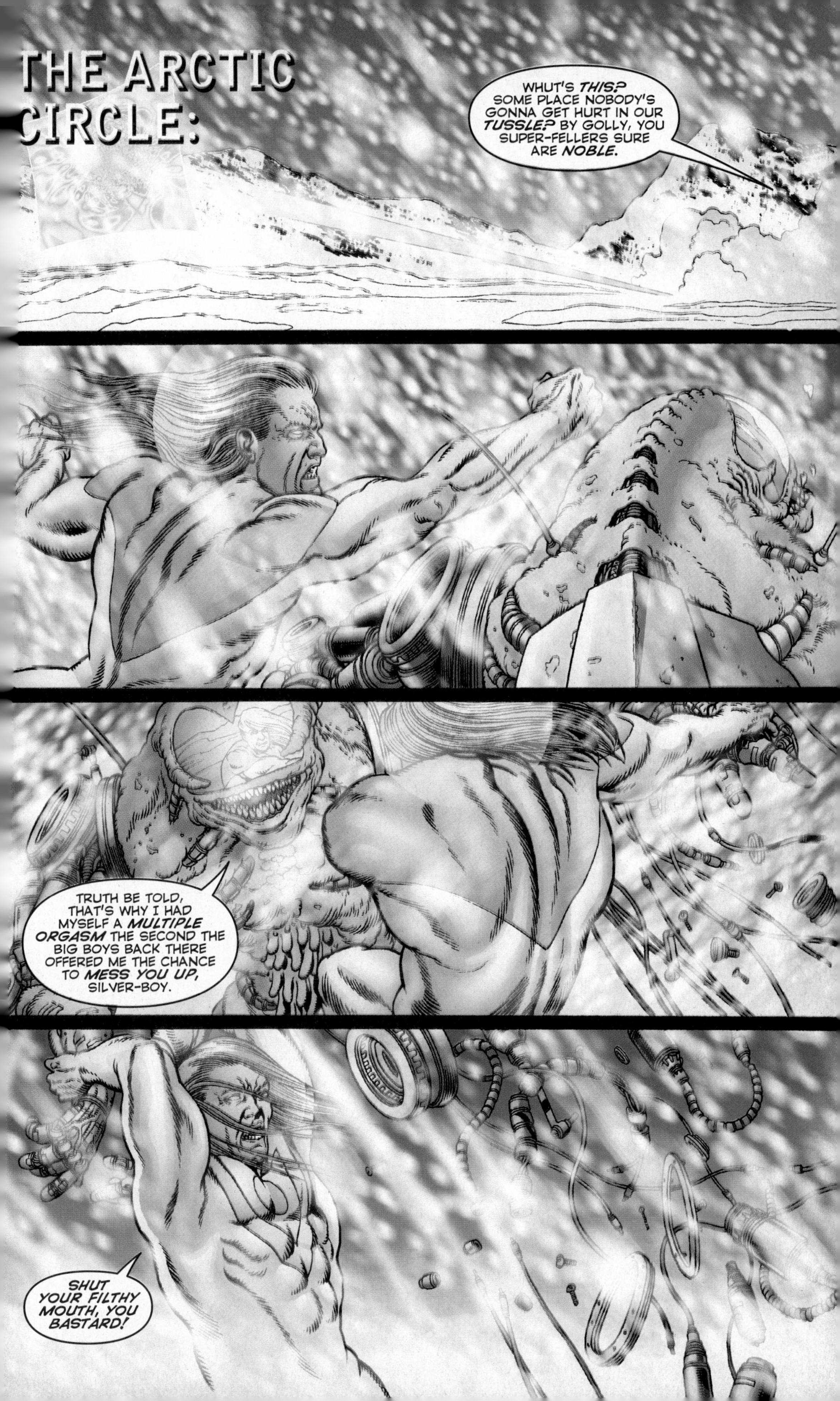
THE ARCTIC CIRCLE:
WHUT'S THIS? SOME PLACE NOBODY'S GONNA GET HURT IN OUR TUSSLE? BY GOLLY, YOU SUPER-FELLERS SURE ARE NOBLE.
TRUTH BE TOLD, THAT'S WHY I HAD MYSELF A MULTIPLE ORGASM THE SECOND THE BIG BOYS BACK THERE OFFERED ME THE CHANCE TO MESS YOU UP, SILVER-BOY.
SHUT YOUR FILTHY MOUTH, YOU BASTARD!

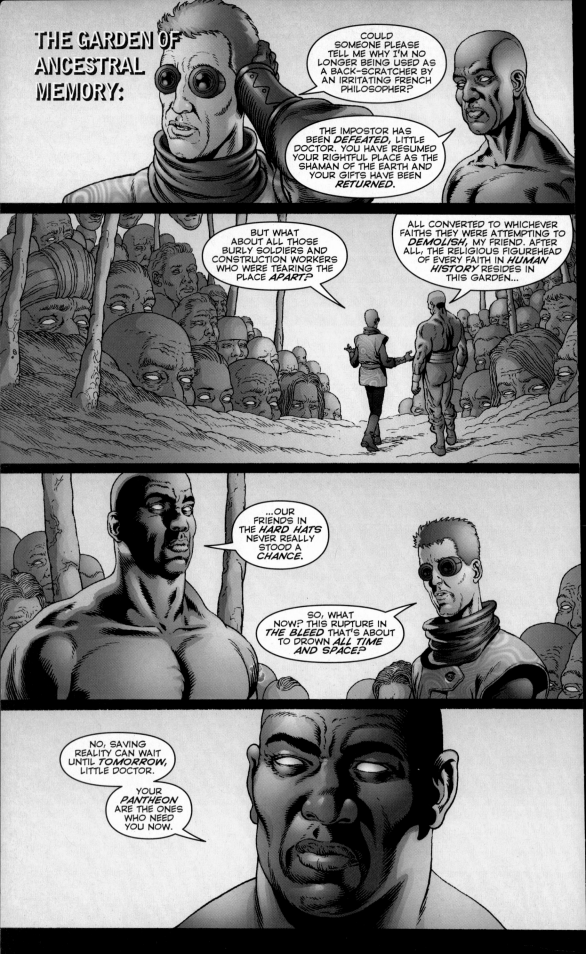

THE GARDEN OF ANCESTRAL MEMORY:

COULD SOMEONE PLEASE TELL ME WHY I'M NO LONGER BEING USED AS A BACK-SCRATCHER BY AN IRRITATING FRENCH PHILOSOPHER?

THE IMPOSTOR HAS BEEN *DEFEATED*, LITTLE DOCTOR. YOU HAVE RESUMED YOUR RIGHTFUL PLACE AS THE SHAMAN OF THE EARTH AND YOUR GIFTS HAVE BEEN *RETURNED*.

BUT WHAT ABOUT ALL THOSE BURLY SOLDIERS AND CONSTRUCTION WORKERS WHO WERE TEARING THE PLACE *APART*?

ALL CONVERTED TO WHICHEVER FAITHS THEY WERE ATTEMPTING TO *DEMOLISH*, MY FRIEND. AFTER ALL, THE RELIGIOUS FIGUREHEAD OF EVERY FAITH IN *HUMAN HISTORY* RESIDES IN THIS GARDEN...

...OUR FRIENDS IN THE *HARD HATS* NEVER REALLY STOOD A *CHANCE*.

SO, WHAT NOW? THIS RUPTURE IN *THE BLEED* THAT'S ABOUT TO DROWN *ALL TIME AND SPACE?*

NO, SAVING REALITY CAN WAIT UNTIL *TOMORROW*, LITTLE DOCTOR.

YOUR *PANTHEON* ARE THE ONES WHO NEED YOU NOW.

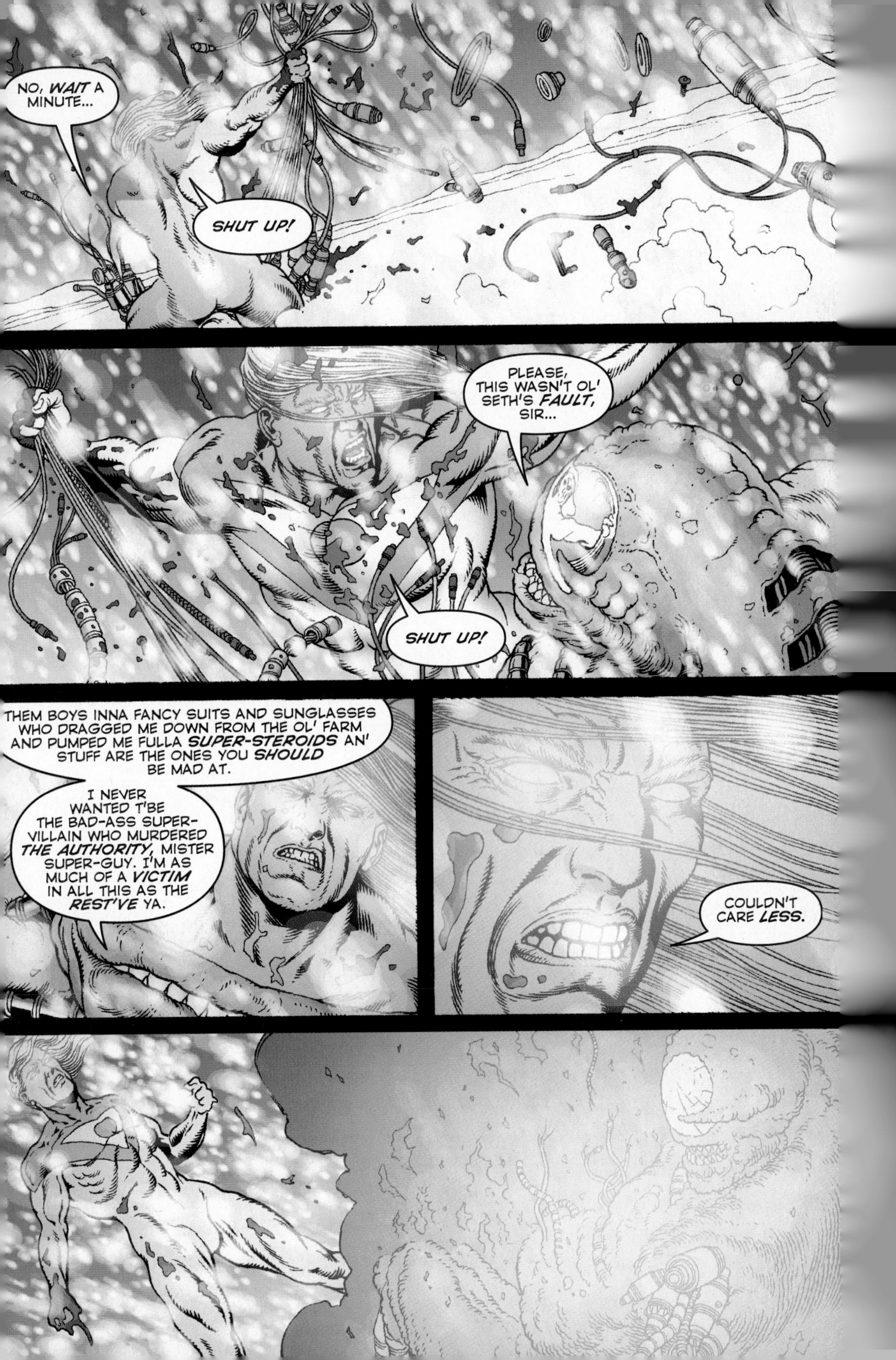
NO, WAIT A MINUTE...
SHUT UP!
PLEASE, THIS WASN'T OL' SETH'S FAULT, SIR...
SHUT UP!
THEM BOYS INNA FANCY SUITS AND SUNGLASSES WHO DRAGGED ME DOWN FROM THE OL' FARM AND PUMPED ME FULLA SUPER-STEROIDS AN' STUFF ARE THE ONES YOU SHOULD BE MAD AT.
I NEVER WANTED T'BE THE BAD-ASS SUPER-VILLAIN WHO MURDERED THE AUTHORITY, MISTER SUPER-GUY. I'M AS MUCH OF A VICTIM IN ALL THIS AS THE REST'VE YA.
COULDN'T CARE LESS.

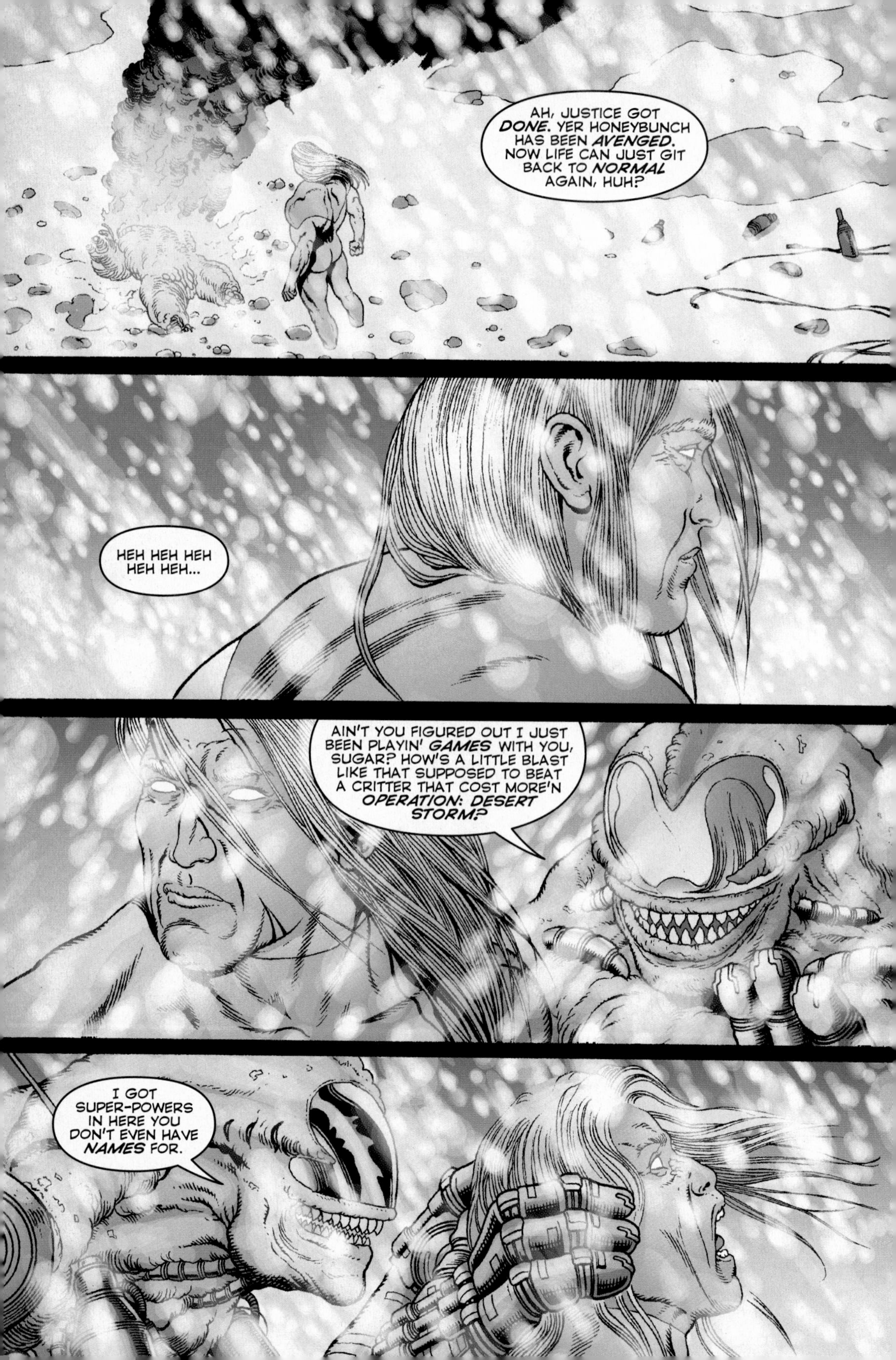

AH, JUSTICE GOT DONE. YER HONEYBUNCH HAS BEEN AVENGED. NOW LIFE CAN JUST GIT BACK TO NORMAL AGAIN, HUH?
HEH HEH HEH HEH HEH...
AIN'T YOU FIGURED OUT I JUST BEEN PLAYIN' GAMES WITH YOU, SUGAR? HOW'S A LITTLE BLAST LIKE THAT SUPPOSED TO BEAT A CRITTER THAT COST MORE'N OPERATION: DESERT STORM?
I GOT SUPER-POWERS IN HERE YOU DON'T EVEN HAVE NAMES FOR.

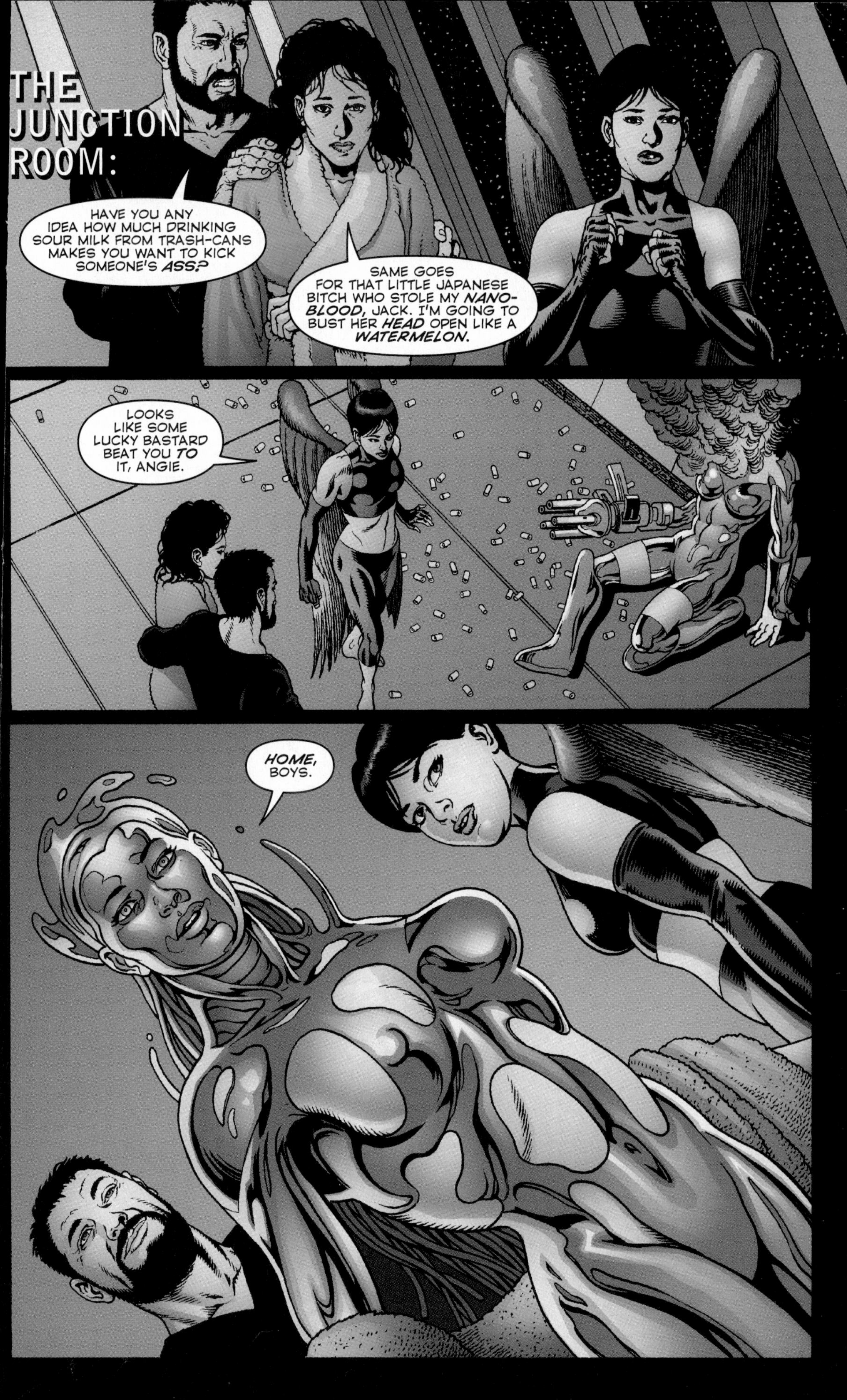
THE JUNCTION ROOM:
HAVE YOU ANY IDEA HOW MUCH DRINKING SOUR MILK FROM TRASH-CANS MAKES YOU WANT TO KICK SOMEONE'S ASS?
SAME GOES FOR THAT LITTLE JAPANESE BITCH WHO STOLE MY NANO-BLOOD, JACK. I'M GOING TO BUST HER HEAD OPEN LIKE A WATERMELON.
LOOKS LIKE SOME LUCKY BASTARD BEAT YOU TO IT, ANGIE.
HOME, BOYS.

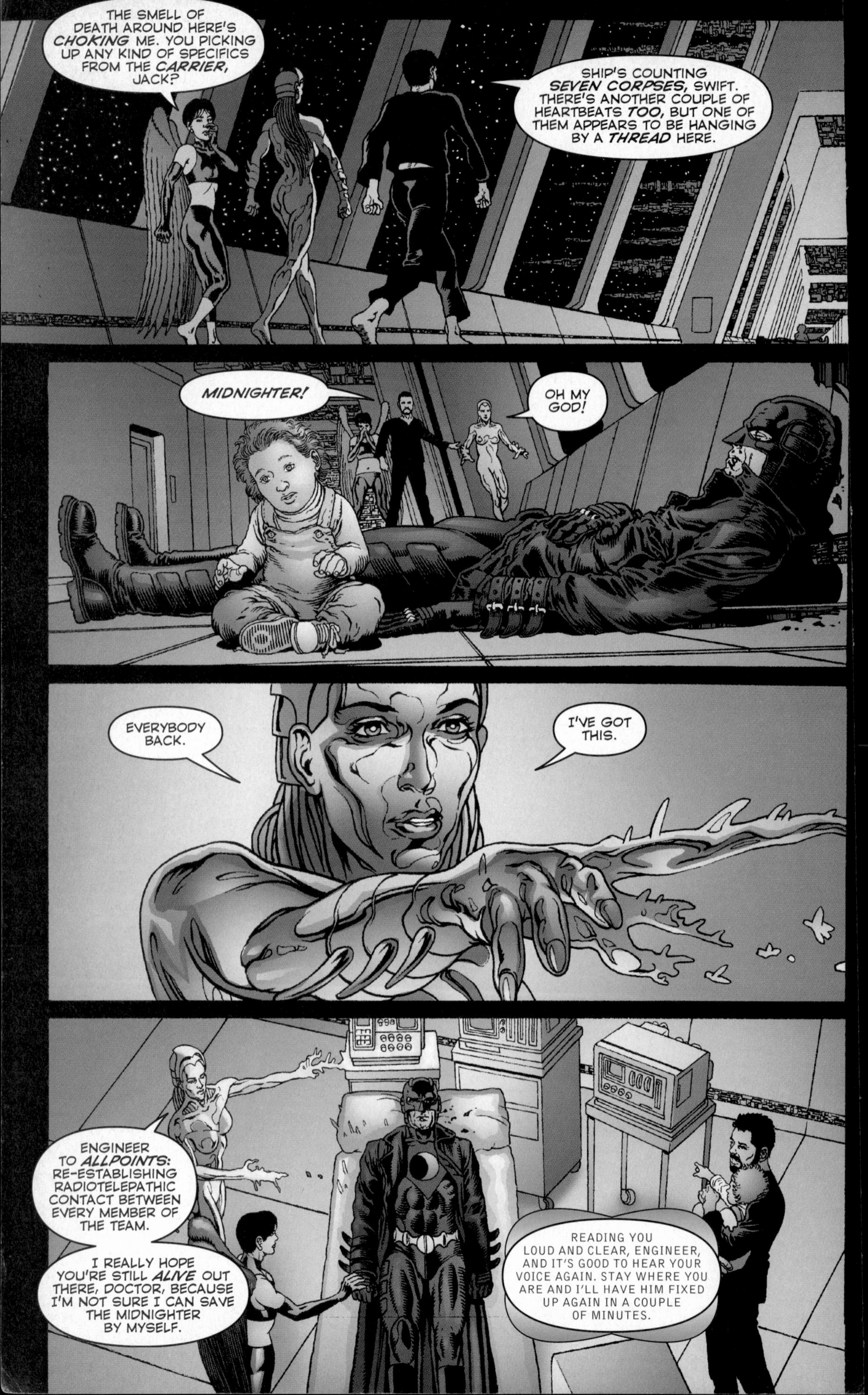
THE SMELL OF DEATH AROUND HERE'S *CHOKING* ME. YOU PICKING UP ANY KIND OF SPECIFICS FROM THE *CARRIER,* JACK?
SHIP'S COUNTING *SEVEN CORPSES,* SWIFT. THERE'S ANOTHER COUPLE OF HEARTBEATS *TOO,* BUT ONE OF THEM APPEARS TO BE HANGING BY A *THREAD* HERE.
MIDNIGHTER!
OH MY *GOD!*
EVERYBODY BACK.
I'VE GOT THIS.
ENGINEER TO *ALLPOINTS:* RE-ESTABLISHING RADIOTELEPATHIC CONTACT BETWEEN EVERY MEMBER OF THE TEAM.
I REALLY HOPE YOU'RE STILL *ALIVE* OUT THERE, DOCTOR, BECAUSE I'M NOT SURE I CAN SAVE THE MIDNIGHTER BY MYSELF.
READING YOU LOUD AND CLEAR, ENGINEER, AND IT'S GOOD TO HEAR YOUR VOICE AGAIN. STAY WHERE YOU ARE AND I'LL HAVE HIM FIXED UP AGAIN IN A COUPLE OF MINUTES.

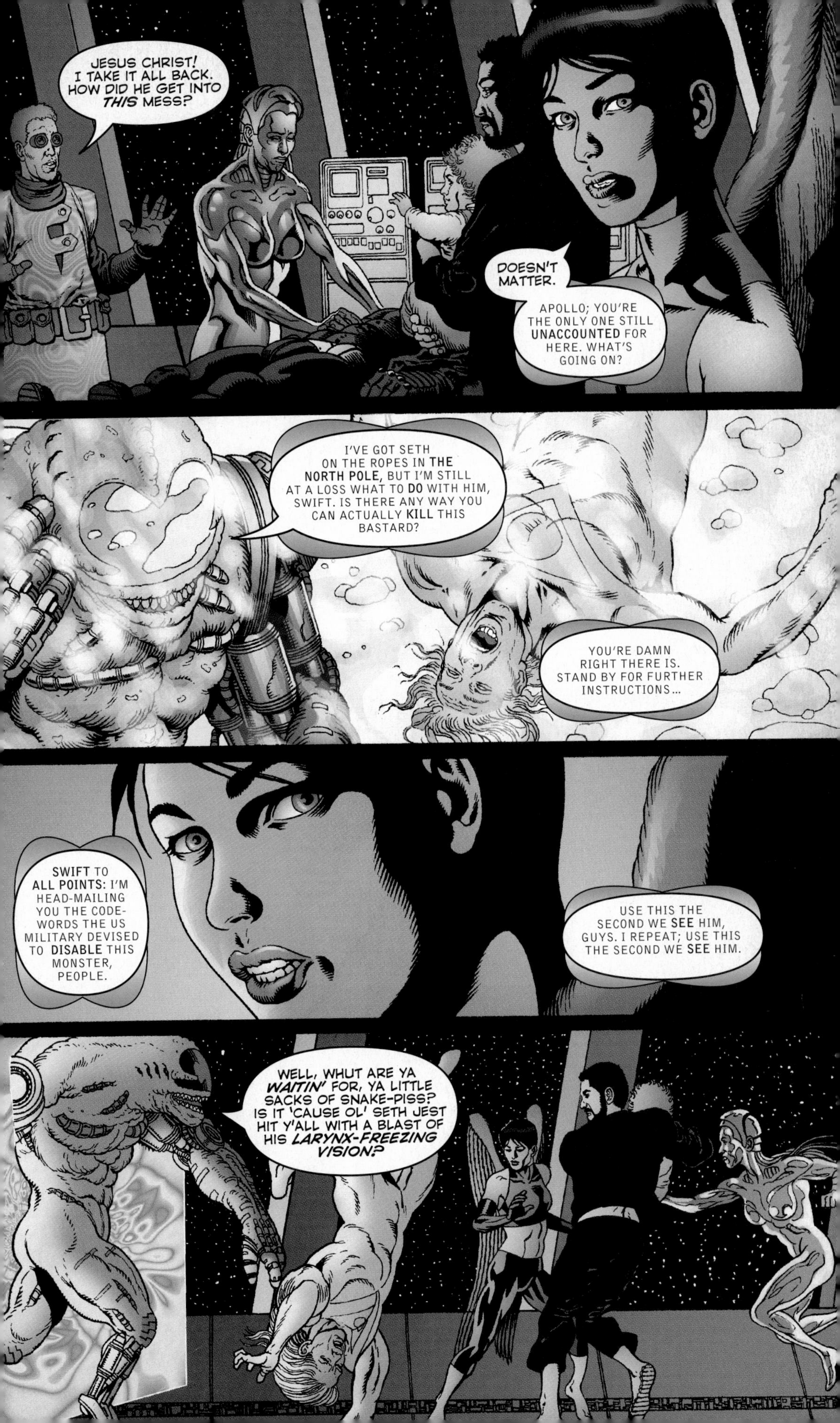

JESUS CHRIST! I TAKE IT ALL BACK. HOW DID HE GET INTO THIS MESS?
DOESN'T MATTER.
APOLLO; YOU'RE THE ONLY ONE STILL UNACCOUNTED FOR HERE. WHAT'S GOING ON?
I'VE GOT SETH ON THE ROPES IN THE NORTH POLE, BUT I'M STILL AT A LOSS WHAT TO DO WITH HIM, SWIFT. IS THERE ANY WAY YOU CAN ACTUALLY KILL THIS BASTARD?
YOU'RE DAMN RIGHT THERE IS. STAND BY FOR FURTHER INSTRUCTIONS...
SWIFT TO ALL POINTS: I'M HEAD-MAILING YOU THE CODE-WORDS THE US MILITARY DEVISED TO DISABLE THIS MONSTER, PEOPLE.
USE THIS THE SECOND WE SEE HIM, GUYS. I REPEAT; USE THIS THE SECOND WE SEE HIM.
WELL, WHUT ARE YA WAITIN' FOR, YA LITTLE SACKS OF SNAKE-PISS? IS IT 'CAUSE OL' SETH JEST HIT Y'ALL WITH A BLAST OF HIS LARYNX-FREEZING VISION?

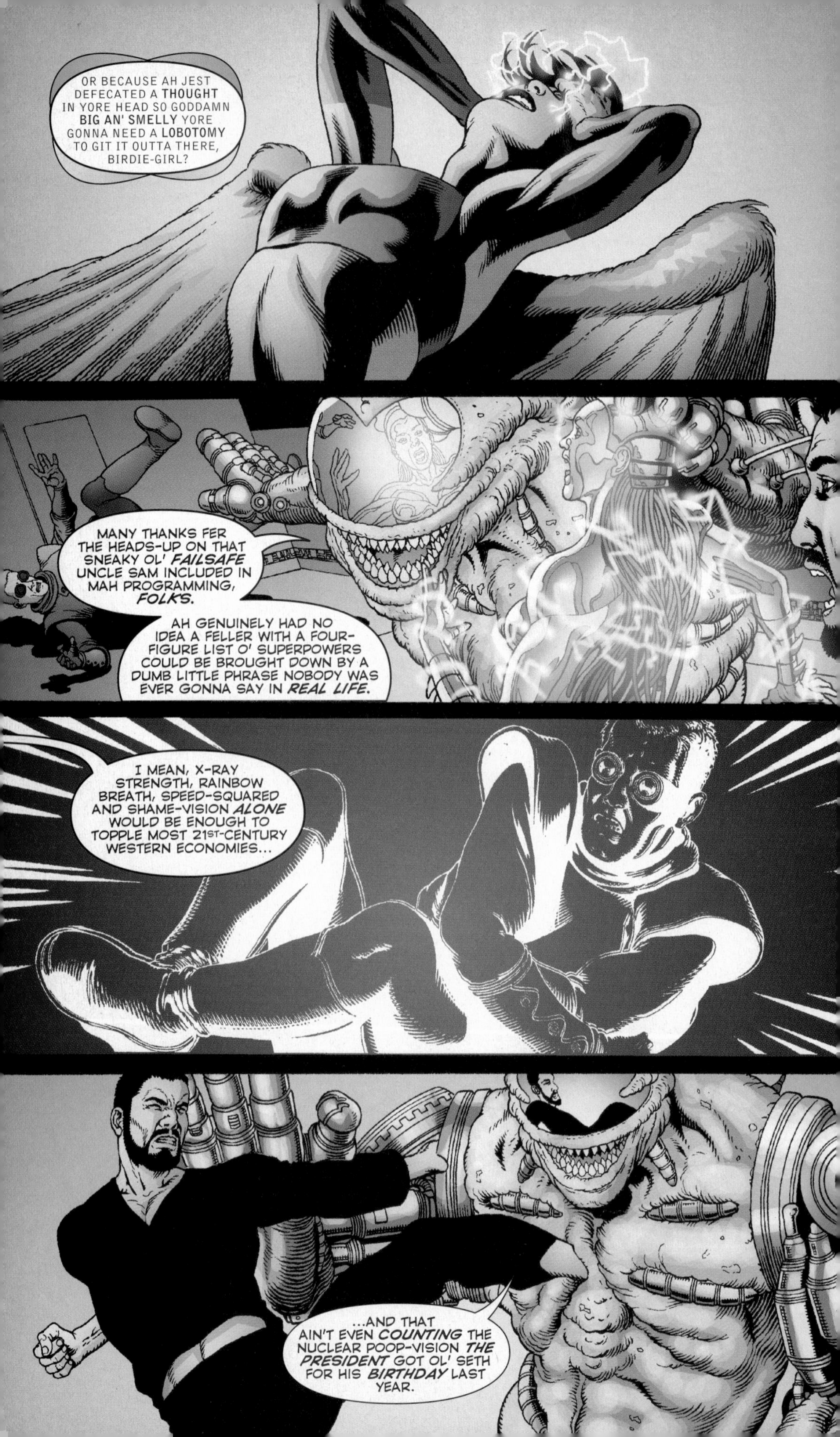
OR BECAUSE AH JEST DEFECATED A THOUGHT IN YORE HEAD SO GODDAMN BIG AN' SMELLY YORE GONNA NEED A LOBOTOMY TO GIT IT OUTTA THERE, BIRDIE-GIRL?
MANY THANKS FER THE HEADS-UP ON THAT SNEAKY OL' FAILSAFE UNCLE SAM INCLUDED IN MAH PROGRAMMING, FOLKS.
AH GENUINELY HAD NO IDEA A FELLER WITH A FOUR-FIGURE LIST O' SUPERPOWERS COULD BE BROUGHT DOWN BY A DUMB LITTLE PHRASE NOBODY WAS EVER GONNA SAY IN REAL LIFE.
I MEAN, X-RAY STRENGTH, RAINBOW BREATH, SPEED-SQUARED AND SHAME-VISION ALONE WOULD BE ENOUGH TO TOPPLE MOST 21ST-CENTURY WESTERN ECONOMIES...
...AND THAT AIN'T EVEN COUNTING THE NUCLEAR POOP-VISION THE PRESIDENT GOT OL' SETH FOR HIS BIRTHDAY LAST YEAR.

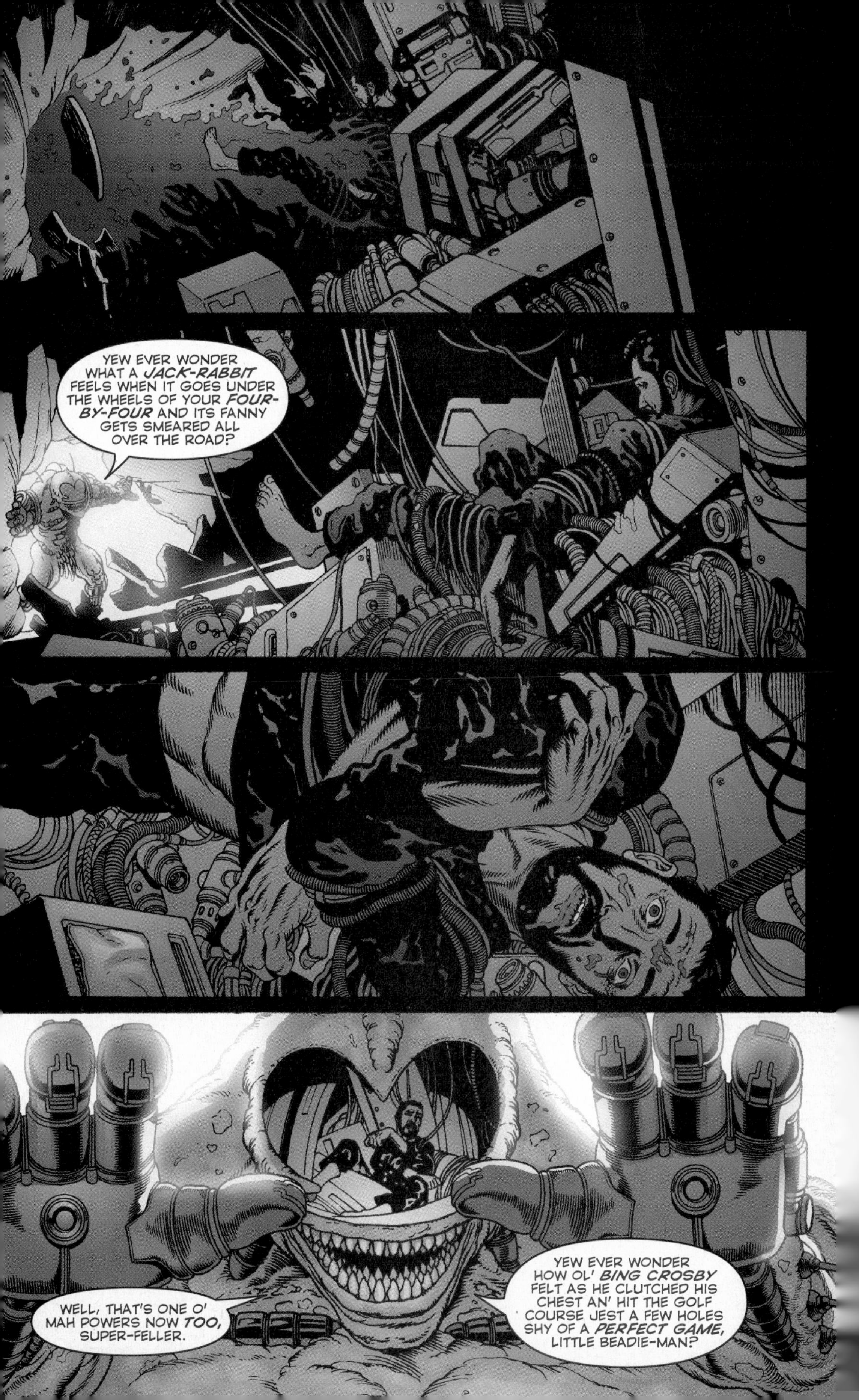
YEW EVER WONDER WHAT A *JACK-RABBIT* FEELS WHEN IT GOES UNDER THE WHEELS OF YOUR *FOUR-BY-FOUR* AND ITS FANNY GETS SMEARED ALL OVER THE ROAD?
WELL, THAT'S ONE O' MAH POWERS NOW *TOO*, SUPER-FELLER.
YEW EVER WONDER HOW OL' *BING CROSBY* FELT AS HE CLUTCHED HIS CHEST AN' HIT THE GOLF COURSE JEST A FEW HOLES SHY OF A *PERFECT GAME*, LITTLE BEADIE-MAN?

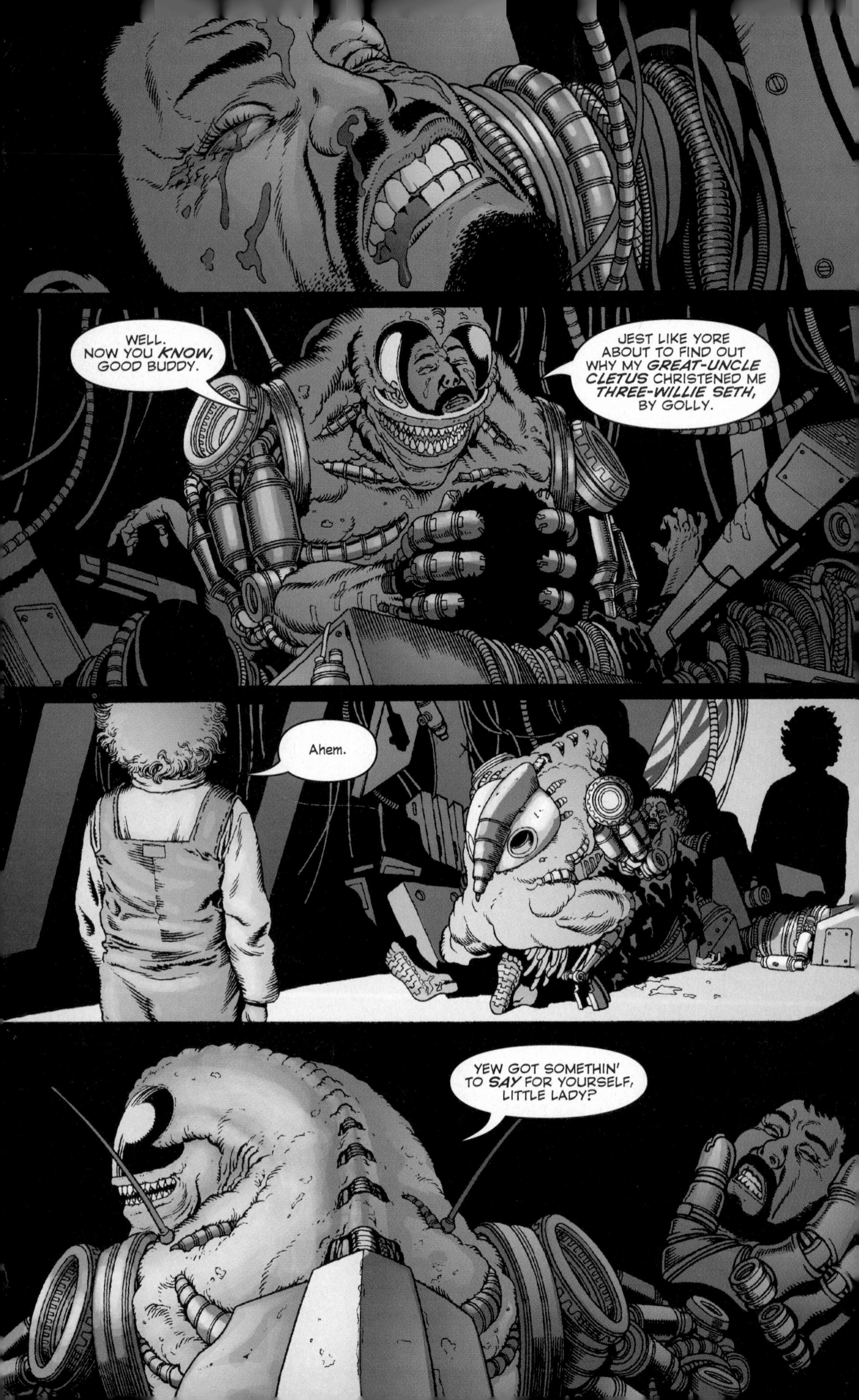
WELL. NOW YOU KNOW, GOOD BUDDY.
JEST LIKE YORE ABOUT TO FIND OUT WHY MY GREAT-UNCLE CLETUS CHRISTENED ME THREE-WILLIE SETH, BY GOLLY.
Ahem.
YEW GOT SOMETHIN' TO SAY FOR YOURSELF, LITTLE LADY?

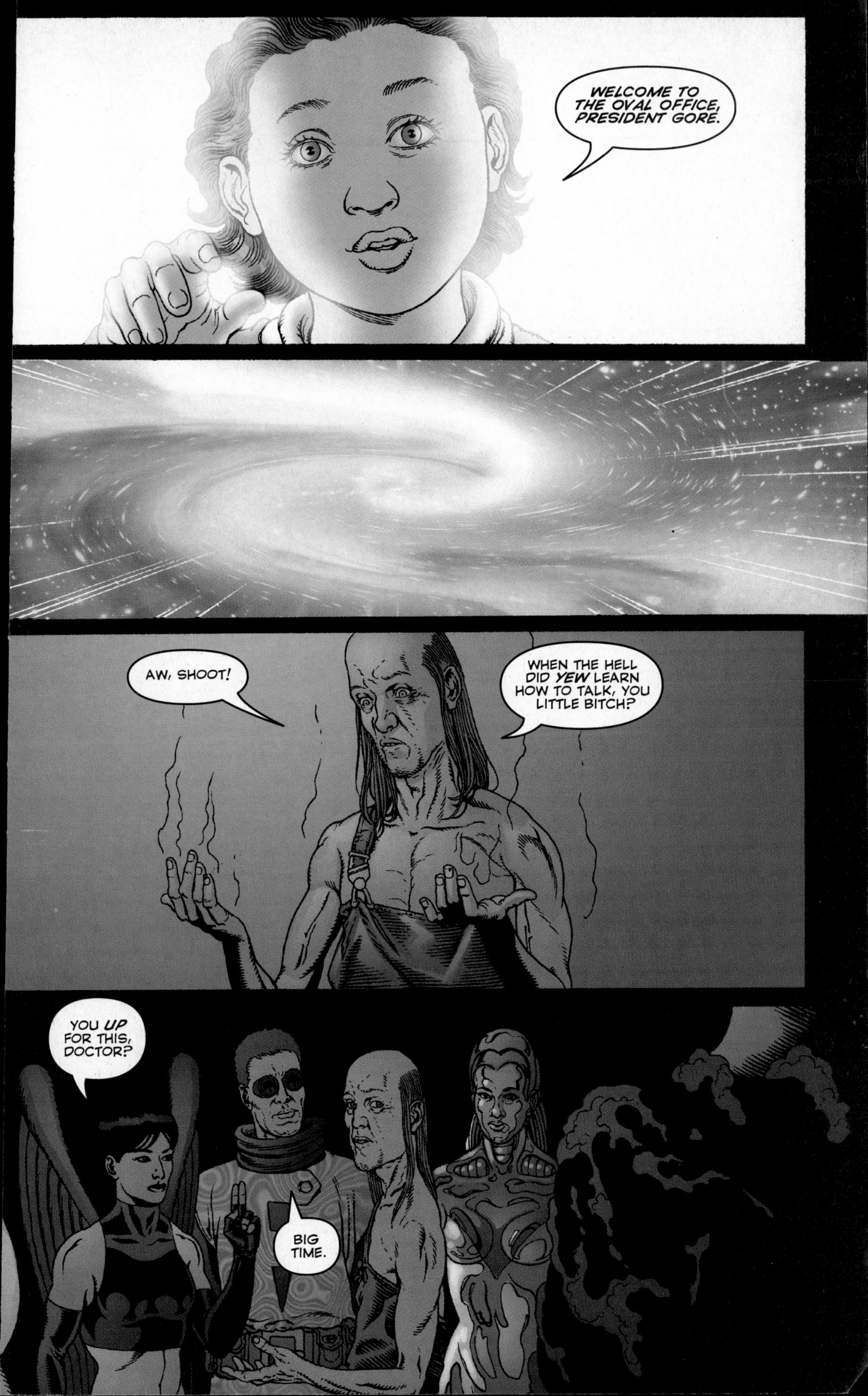
WELCOME TO THE OVAL OFFICE, PRESIDENT GORE.
AW, SHOOT!
WHEN THE HELL DID YEW LEARN HOW TO TALK, YOU LITTLE BITCH?
YOU UP FOR THIS, DOCTOR?
BIG TIME.

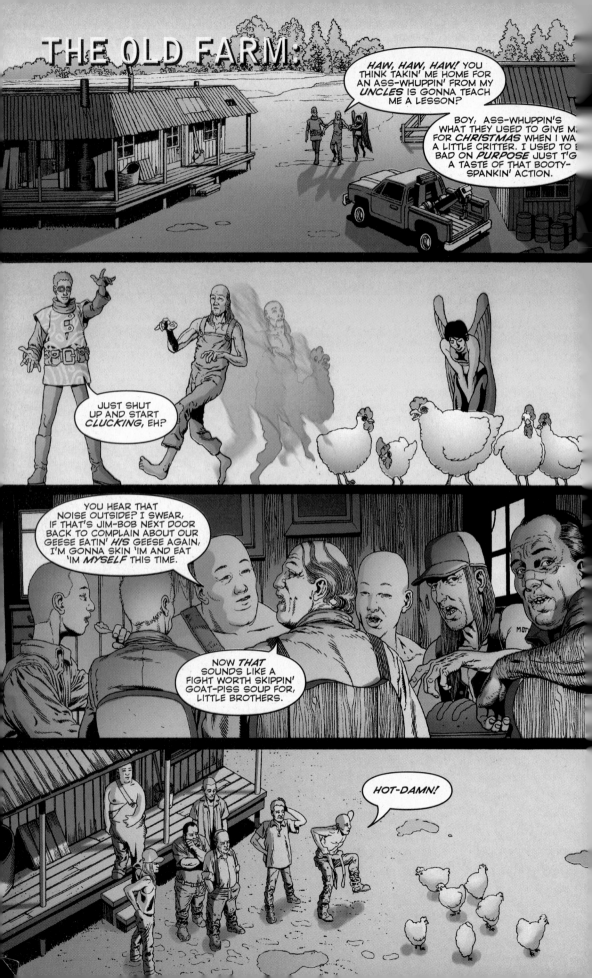

THE OLD FARM:

HAW, HAW, HAW! YOU THINK TAKIN' ME HOME FOR AN ASS-WHUPPIN' FROM MY *UNCLES* IS GONNA TEACH ME A LESSON?

BOY, ASS-WHUPPIN'S WHAT THEY USED TO GIVE M[E] FOR *CHRISTMAS* WHEN I WA[S] A LITTLE CRITTER. I USED TO [BE] BAD ON *PURPOSE* JUST T'G[ET] A TASTE OF THAT BOOTY-SPANKIN' ACTION.

JUST SHUT UP AND START *CLUCKING*, EH?

YOU HEAR THAT NOISE OUTSIDE? I SWEAR, IF THAT'S JIM-BOB NEXT DOOR BACK TO COMPLAIN ABOUT OUR GEESE EATIN' *HIS* GEESE AGAIN, I'M GONNA SKIN 'IM AND EAT 'IM *MYSELF* THIS TIME.

NOW *THAT* SOUNDS LIKE A FIGHT WORTH SKIPPIN' GOAT-PISS SOUP FOR, LITTLE BROTHERS.

HOT-DAMN!

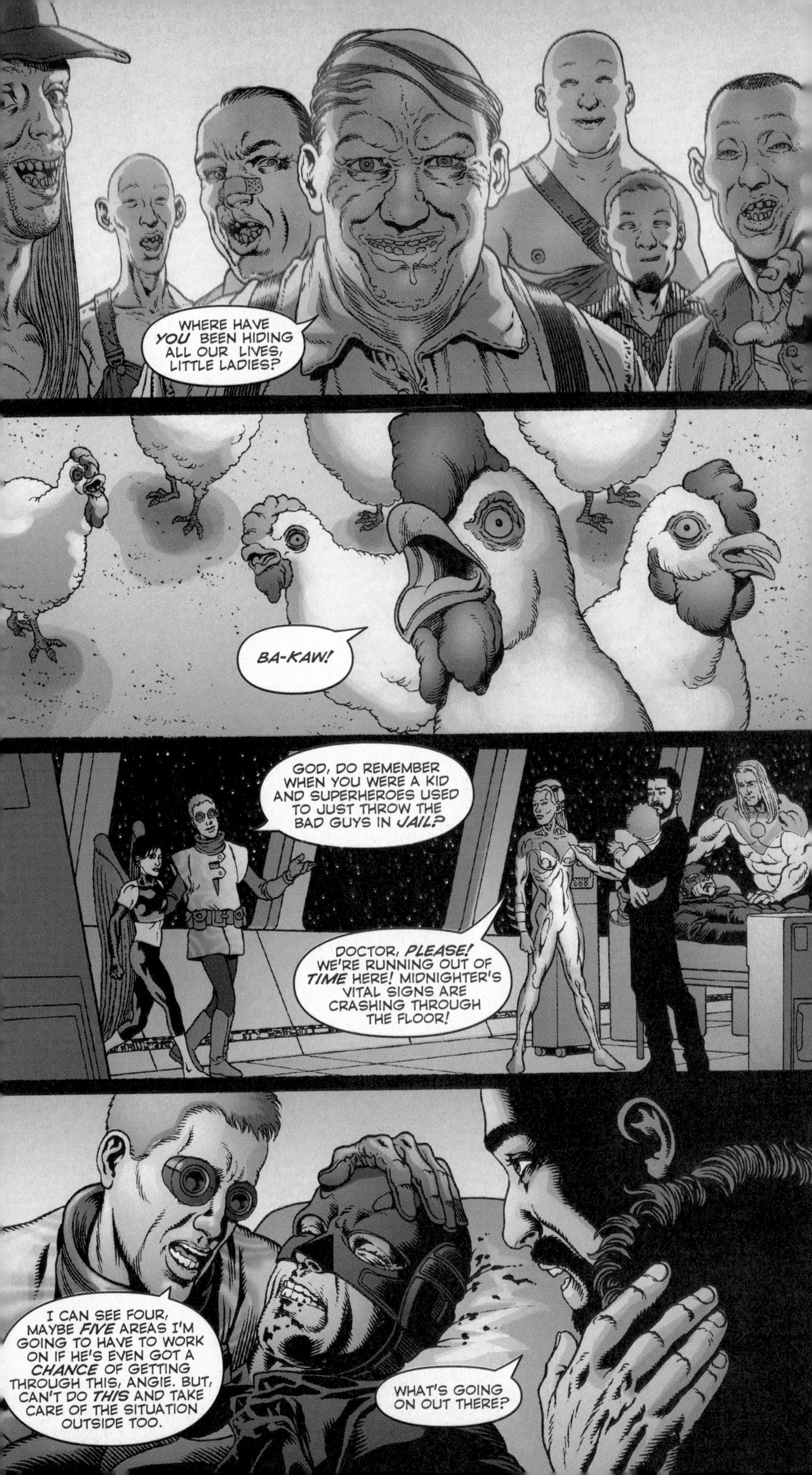
WHERE HAVE YOU BEEN HIDING ALL OUR LIVES, LITTLE LADIES?
BA-KAW!
GOD, DO REMEMBER WHEN YOU WERE A KID AND SUPERHEROES USED TO JUST THROW THE BAD GUYS IN JAIL?
DOCTOR, PLEASE! WE'RE RUNNING OUT OF TIME HERE! MIDNIGHTER'S VITAL SIGNS ARE CRASHING THROUGH THE FLOOR!
I CAN SEE FOUR, MAYBE FIVE AREAS I'M GOING TO HAVE TO WORK ON IF HE'S EVEN GOT A CHANCE OF GETTING THROUGH THIS, ANGIE. BUT, CAN'T DO THIS AND TAKE CARE OF THE SITUATION OUTSIDE TOO.
WHAT'S GOING ON OUT THERE?

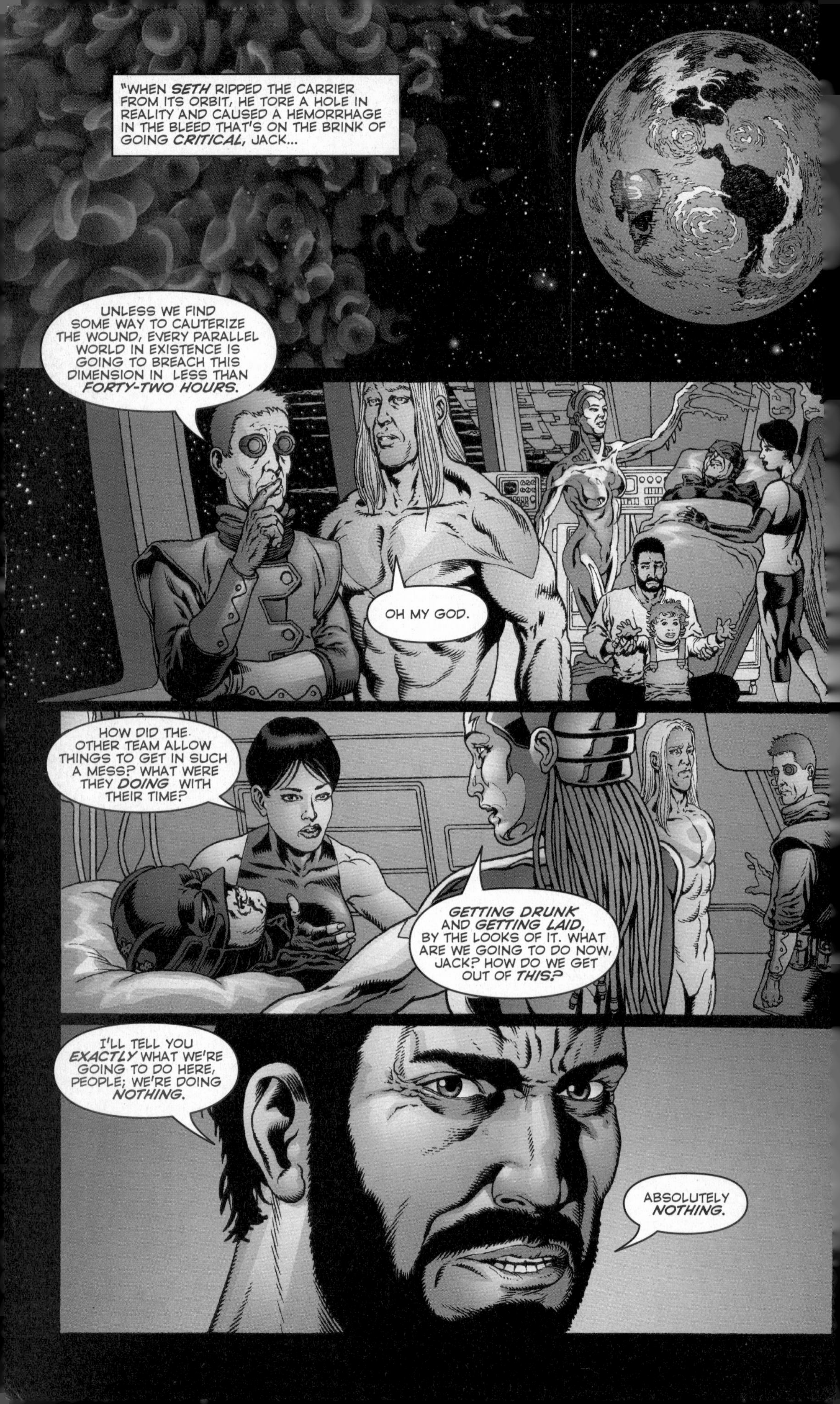
"WHEN SETH RIPPED THE CARRIER FROM ITS ORBIT, HE TORE A HOLE IN REALITY AND CAUSED A HEMORRHAGE IN THE BLEED THAT'S ON THE BRINK OF GOING CRITICAL, JACK...
UNLESS WE FIND SOME WAY TO CAUTERIZE THE WOUND, EVERY PARALLEL WORLD IN EXISTENCE IS GOING TO BREACH THIS DIMENSION IN LESS THAN FORTY-TWO HOURS.
OH MY GOD.
HOW DID THE OTHER TEAM ALLOW THINGS TO GET IN SUCH A MESS? WHAT WERE THEY DOING WITH THEIR TIME?
GETTING DRUNK AND GETTING LAID, BY THE LOOKS OF IT. WHAT ARE WE GOING TO DO NOW, JACK? HOW DO WE GET OUT OF THIS?
I'LL TELL YOU EXACTLY WHAT WE'RE GOING TO DO HERE, PEOPLE; WE'RE DOING NOTHING.
ABSOLUTELY NOTHING.

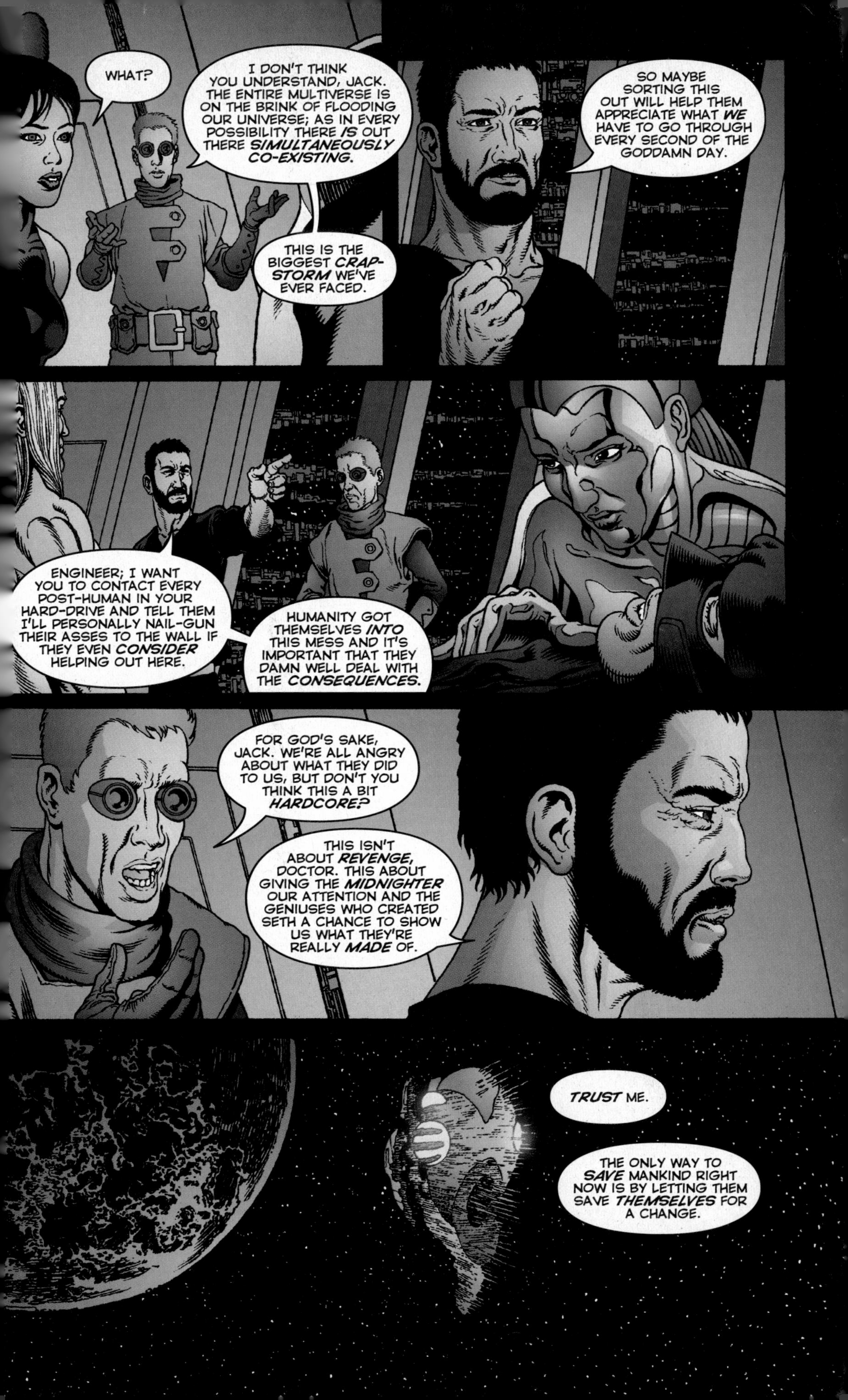
WHAT?
I DON'T THINK YOU UNDERSTAND, JACK. THE ENTIRE MULTIVERSE IS ON THE BRINK OF FLOODING OUR UNIVERSE; AS IN EVERY POSSIBILITY THERE IS OUT THERE SIMULTANEOUSLY CO-EXISTING.
THIS IS THE BIGGEST CRAP-STORM WE'VE EVER FACED.
SO MAYBE SORTING THIS OUT WILL HELP THEM APPRECIATE WHAT WE HAVE TO GO THROUGH EVERY SECOND OF THE GODDAMN DAY.
ENGINEER; I WANT YOU TO CONTACT EVERY POST-HUMAN IN YOUR HARD-DRIVE AND TELL THEM I'LL PERSONALLY NAIL-GUN THEIR ASSES TO THE WALL IF THEY EVEN CONSIDER HELPING OUT HERE.
HUMANITY GOT THEMSELVES INTO THIS MESS AND IT'S IMPORTANT THAT THEY DAMN WELL DEAL WITH THE CONSEQUENCES.
FOR GOD'S SAKE, JACK. WE'RE ALL ANGRY ABOUT WHAT THEY DID TO US, BUT DON'T YOU THINK THIS A BIT HARDCORE?
THIS ISN'T ABOUT REVENGE, DOCTOR. THIS ABOUT GIVING THE MIDNIGHTER OUR ATTENTION AND THE GENIUSES WHO CREATED SETH A CHANCE TO SHOW US WHAT THEY'RE REALLY MADE OF.
TRUST ME.
THE ONLY WAY TO SAVE MANKIND RIGHT NOW IS BY LETTING THEM SAVE THEMSELVES FOR A CHANGE.

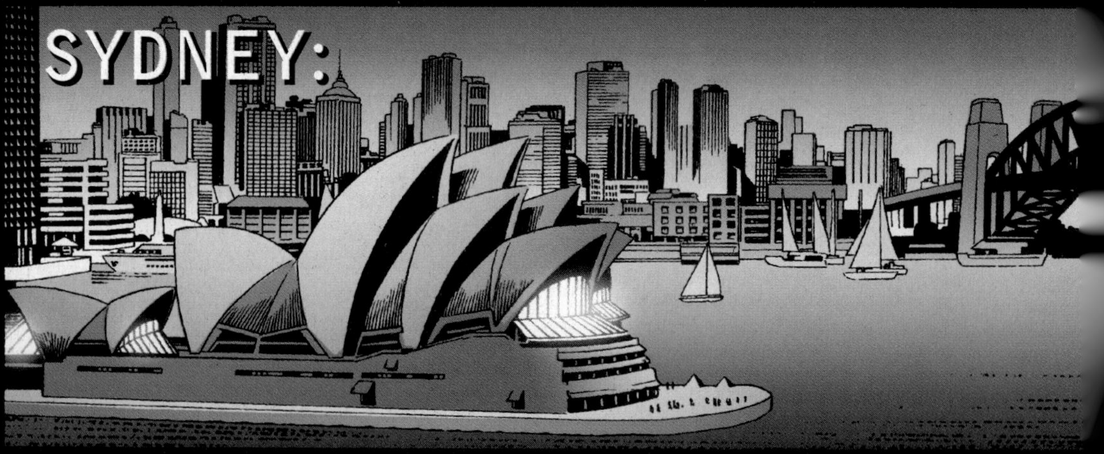
SYDNEY:

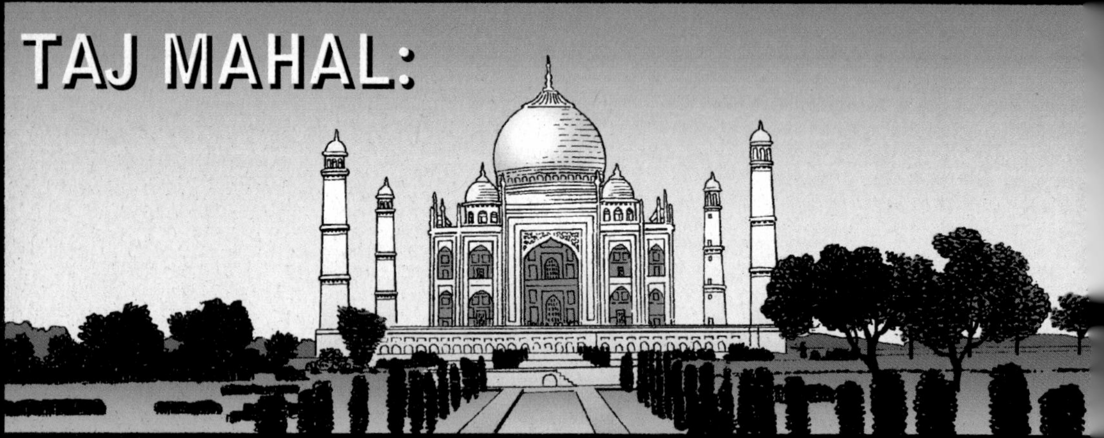
TAJ MAHAL:

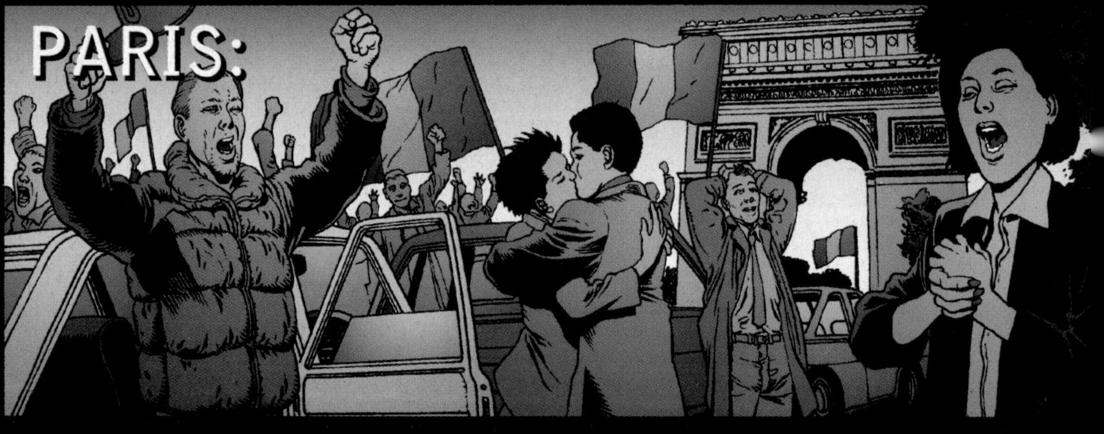
PARIS:

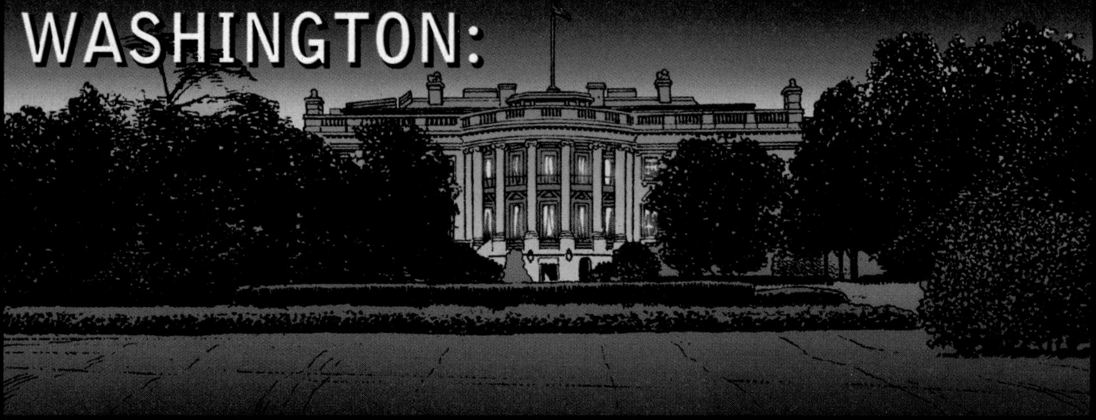
WASHINGTON:

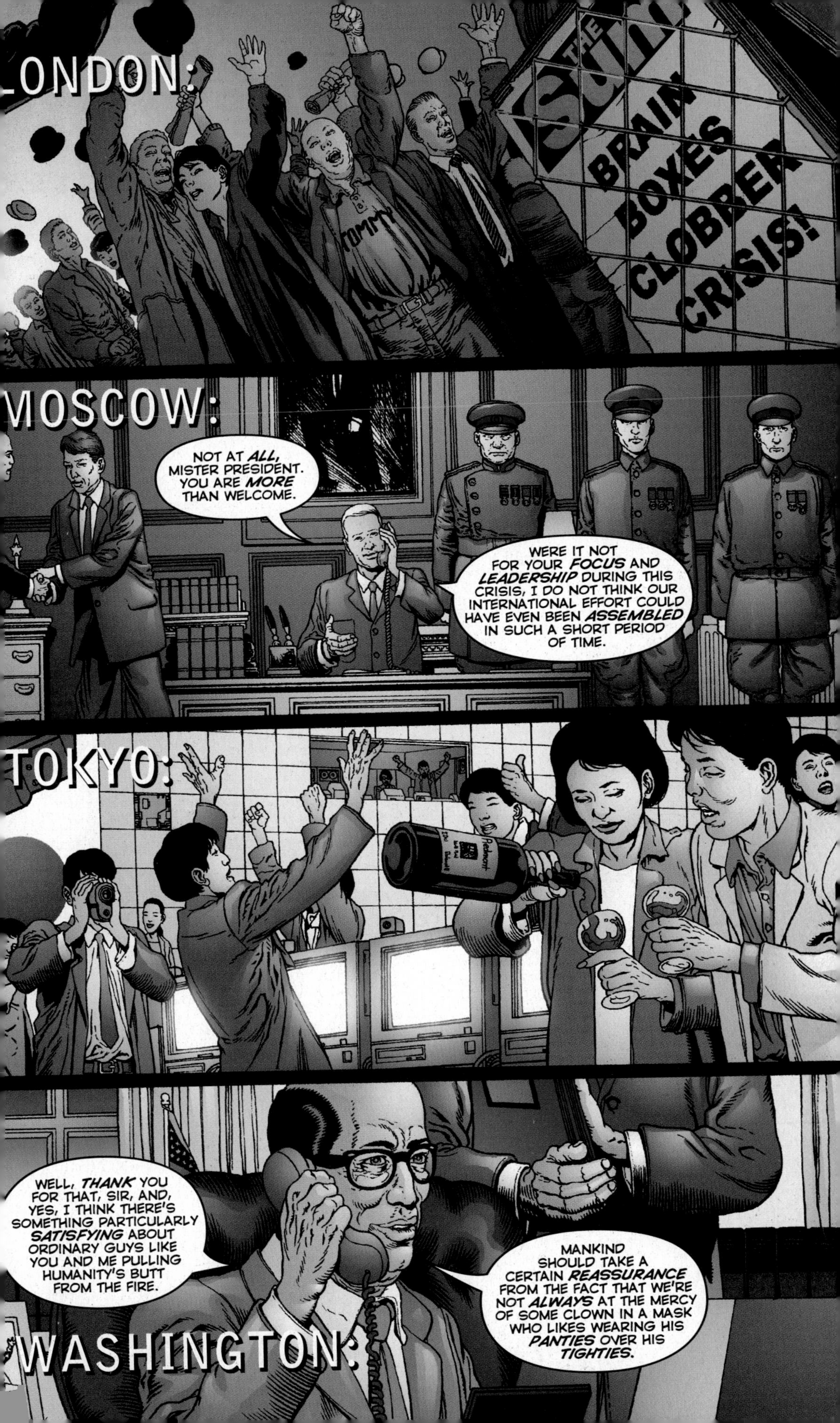
LONDON:
THE SUN
BRAIN BOXES CLOBBER CRISIS!
TOMMY
MOSCOW:
NOT AT ALL, MISTER PRESIDENT. YOU ARE MORE THAN WELCOME.
WERE IT NOT FOR YOUR FOCUS AND LEADERSHIP DURING THIS CRISIS, I DO NOT THINK OUR INTERNATIONAL EFFORT COULD HAVE EVEN BEEN ASSEMBLED IN SUCH A SHORT PERIOD OF TIME.
TOKYO:
WASHINGTON:
WELL, THANK YOU FOR THAT, SIR, AND, YES, I THINK THERE'S SOMETHING PARTICULARLY SATISFYING ABOUT ORDINARY GUYS LIKE YOU AND ME PULLING HUMANITY'S BUTT FROM THE FIRE.
MANKIND SHOULD TAKE A CERTAIN REASSURANCE FROM THE FACT THAT WE'RE NOT ALWAYS AT THE MERCY OF SOME CLOWN IN A MASK WHO LIKES WEARING HIS PANTIES OVER HIS TIGHTIES.

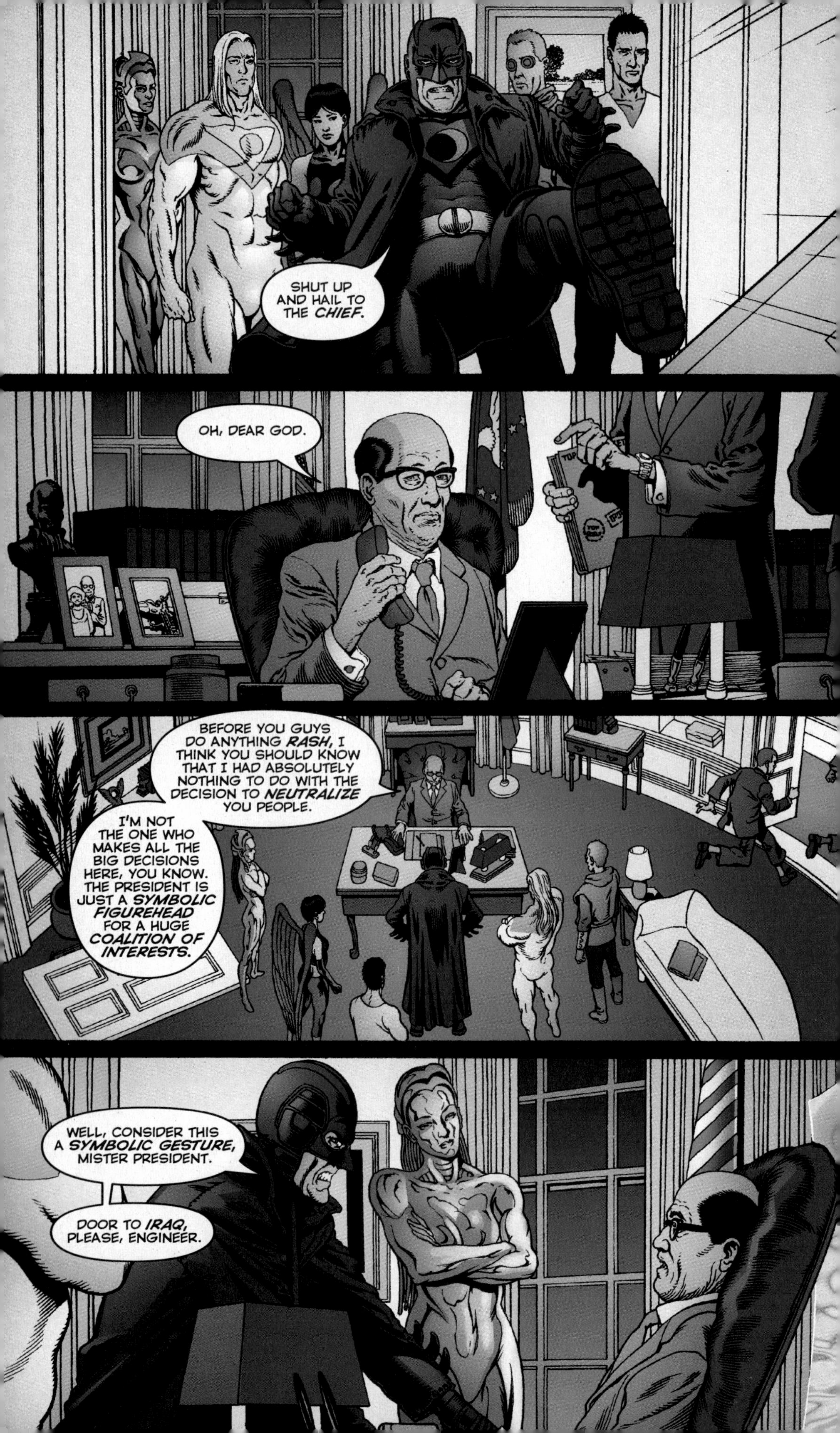
SHUT UP AND HAIL TO THE *CHIEF*.
OH, DEAR GOD.
BEFORE YOU GUYS DO ANYTHING *RASH*, I THINK YOU SHOULD KNOW THAT I HAD ABSOLUTELY NOTHING TO DO WITH THE DECISION TO *NEUTRALIZE* YOU PEOPLE.
I'M NOT THE ONE WHO MAKES ALL THE BIG DECISIONS HERE, YOU KNOW. THE PRESIDENT IS JUST A *SYMBOLIC FIGUREHEAD* FOR A HUGE *COALITION OF INTERESTS*.
WELL, CONSIDER THIS A *SYMBOLIC GESTURE*, MISTER PRESIDENT.
DOOR TO *IRAQ*, PLEASE, ENGINEER.

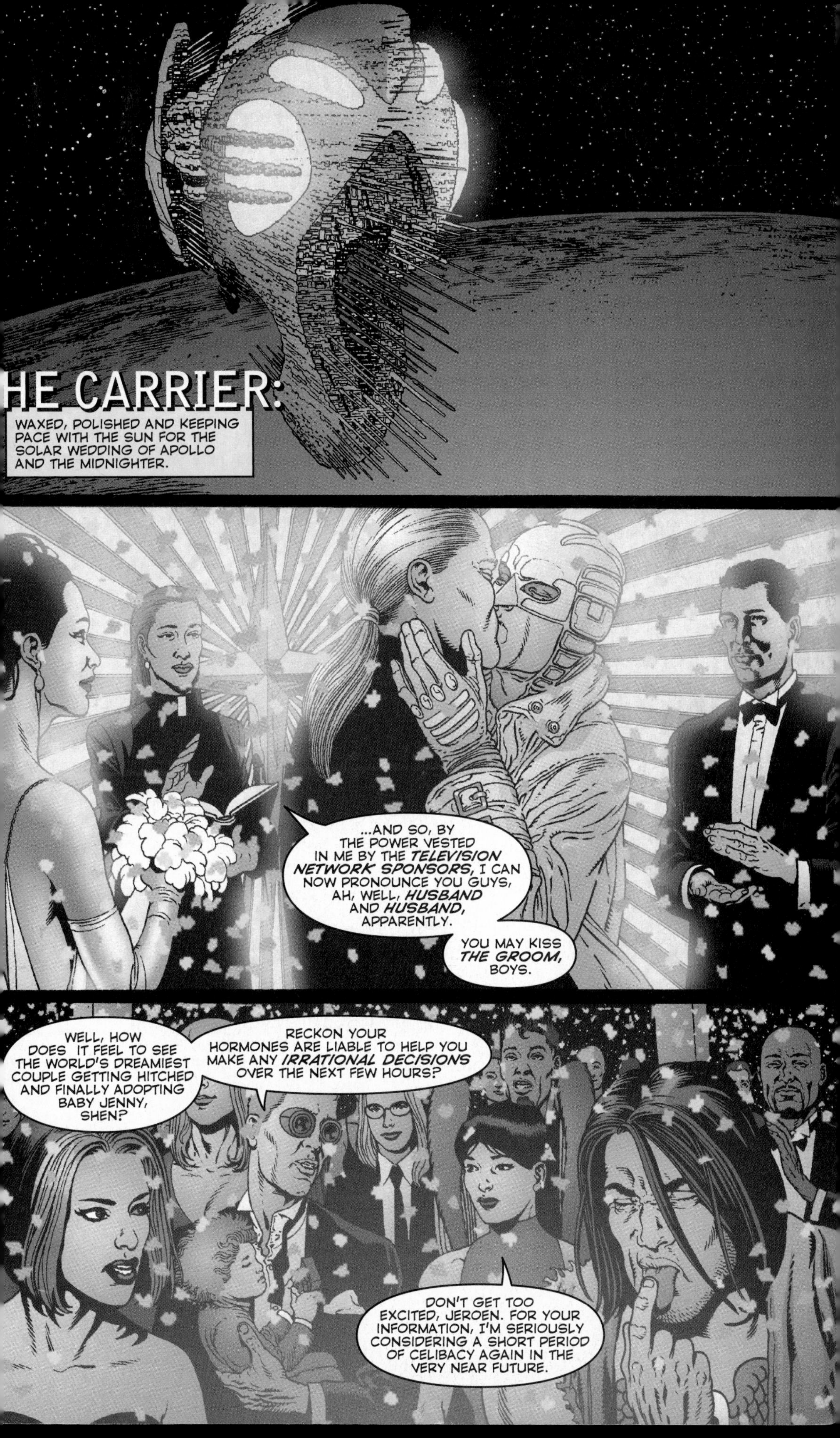
HE CARRIER:
WAXED, POLISHED AND KEEPING PACE WITH THE SUN FOR THE SOLAR WEDDING OF APOLLO AND THE MIDNIGHTER.
...AND SO, BY THE POWER VESTED IN ME BY THE TELEVISION NETWORK SPONSORS, I CAN NOW PRONOUNCE YOU GUYS, AH, WELL, HUSBAND AND HUSBAND, APPARENTLY.
YOU MAY KISS THE GROOM, BOYS.
WELL, HOW DOES IT FEEL TO SEE THE WORLD'S DREAMIEST COUPLE GETTING HITCHED AND FINALLY ADOPTING BABY JENNY, SHEN?
RECKON YOUR HORMONES ARE LIABLE TO HELP YOU MAKE ANY IRRATIONAL DECISIONS OVER THE NEXT FEW HOURS?
DON'T GET TOO EXCITED, JEROEN. FOR YOUR INFORMATION, I'M SERIOUSLY CONSIDERING A SHORT PERIOD OF CELIBACY AGAIN IN THE VERY NEAR FUTURE.

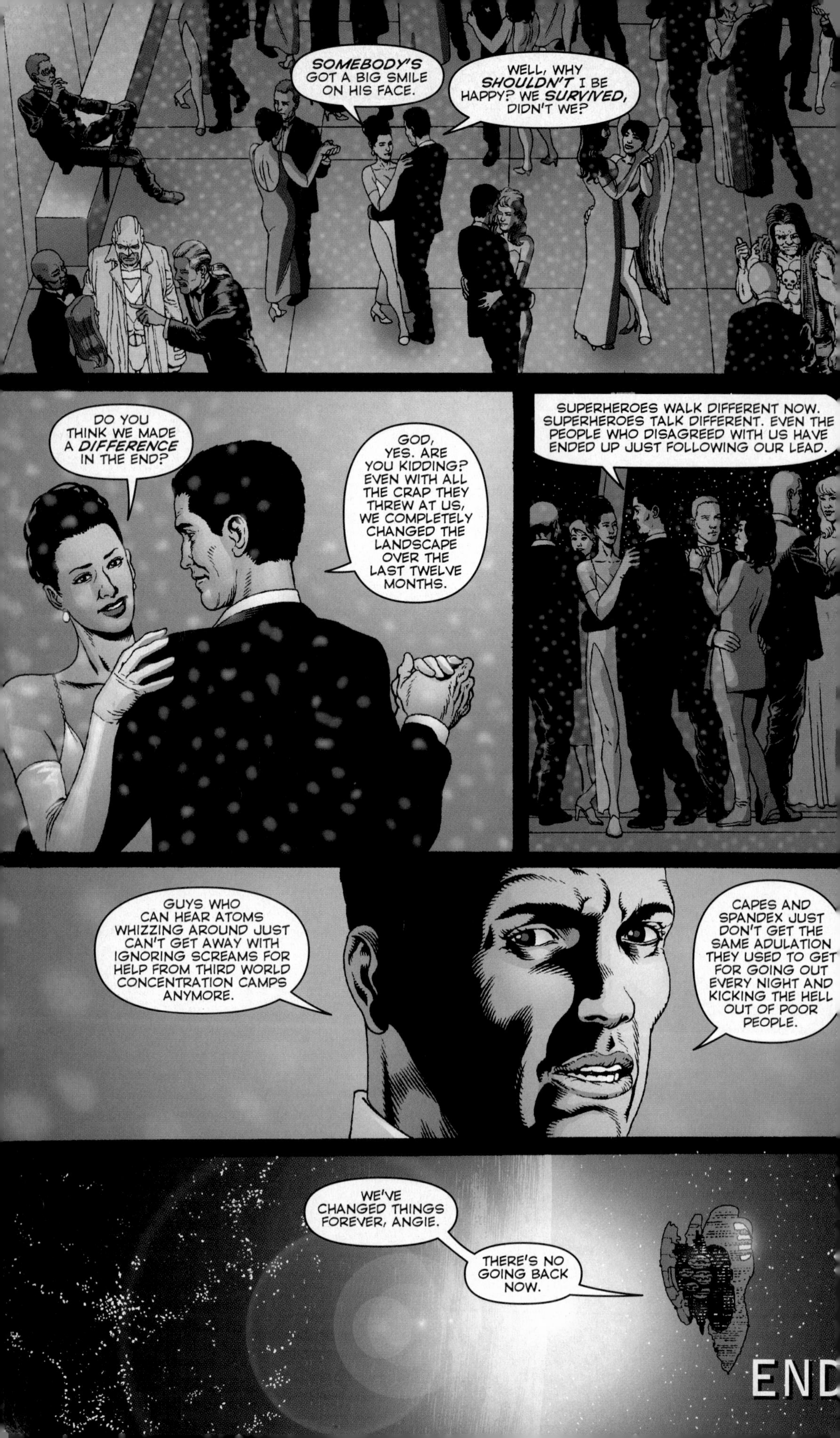
SOMEBODY'S GOT A BIG SMILE ON HIS FACE.
WELL, WHY SHOULDN'T I BE HAPPY? WE SURVIVED, DIDN'T WE?
DO YOU THINK WE MADE A DIFFERENCE IN THE END?
GOD, YES. ARE YOU KIDDING? EVEN WITH ALL THE CRAP THEY THREW AT US, WE COMPLETELY CHANGED THE LANDSCAPE OVER THE LAST TWELVE MONTHS.
SUPERHEROES WALK DIFFERENT NOW. SUPERHEROES TALK DIFFERENT. EVEN THE PEOPLE WHO DISAGREED WITH US HAVE ENDED UP JUST FOLLOWING OUR LEAD.
GUYS WHO CAN HEAR ATOMS WHIZZING AROUND JUST CAN'T GET AWAY WITH IGNORING SCREAMS FOR HELP FROM THIRD WORLD CONCENTRATION CAMPS ANYMORE.
CAPES AND SPANDEX JUST DON'T GET THE SAME ADULATION THEY USED TO GET FOR GOING OUT EVERY NIGHT AND KICKING THE HELL OUT OF POOR PEOPLE.
WE'VE CHANGED THINGS FOREVER, ANGIE.
THERE'S NO GOING BACK NOW.
END

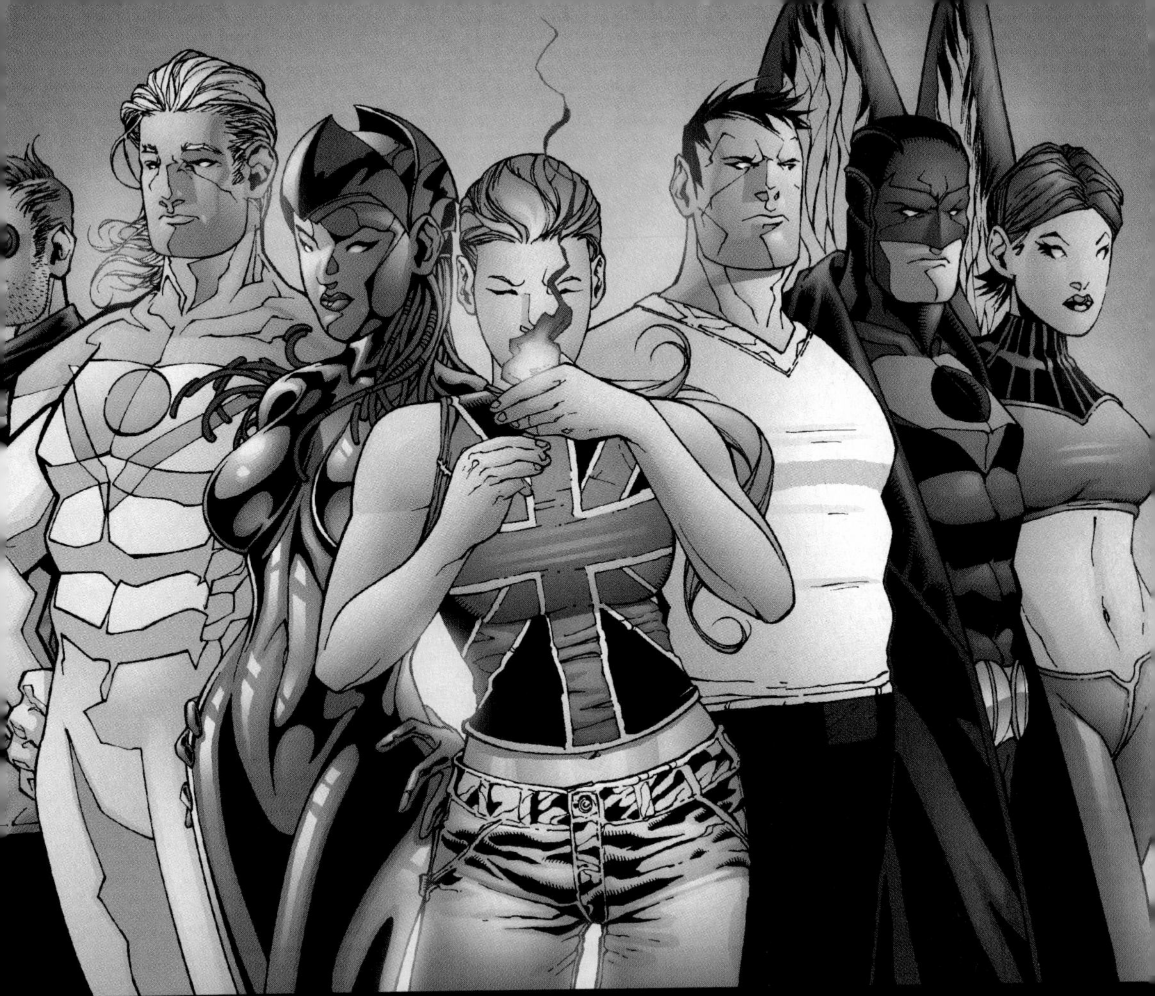

COVER GALLERY

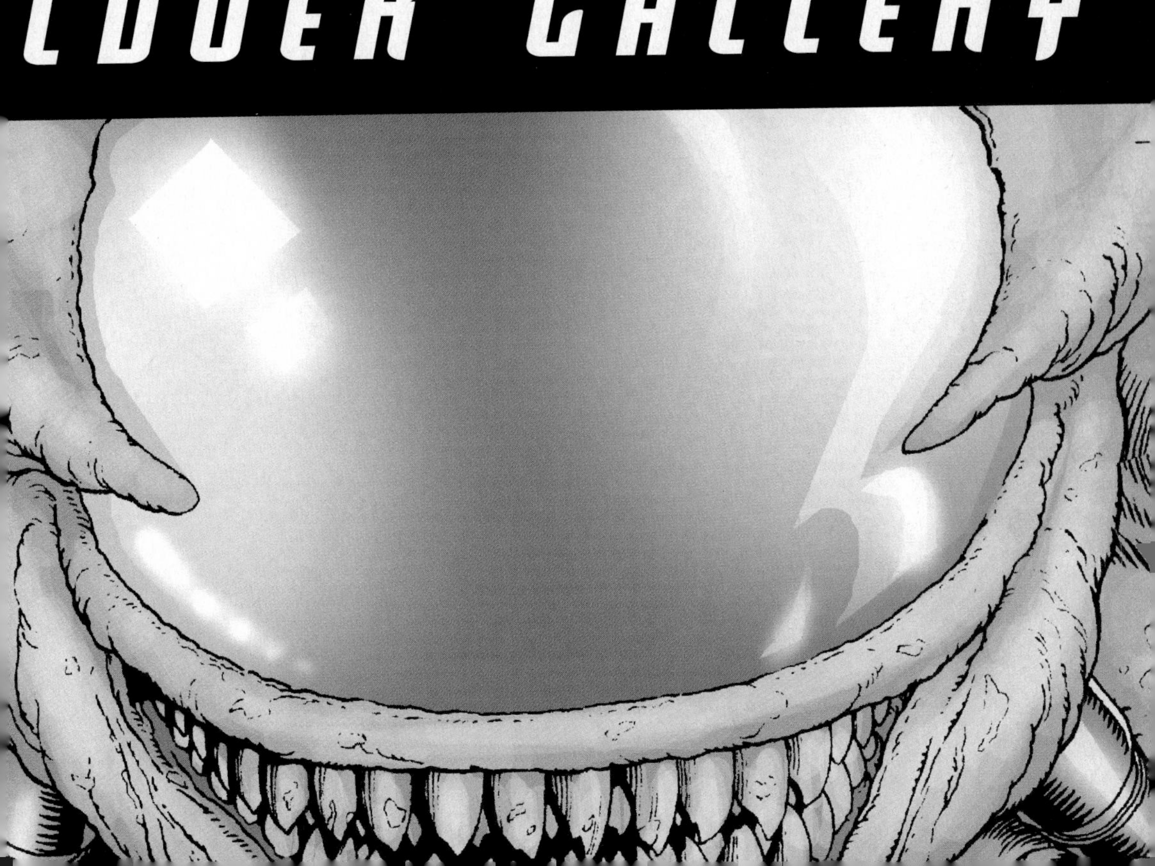

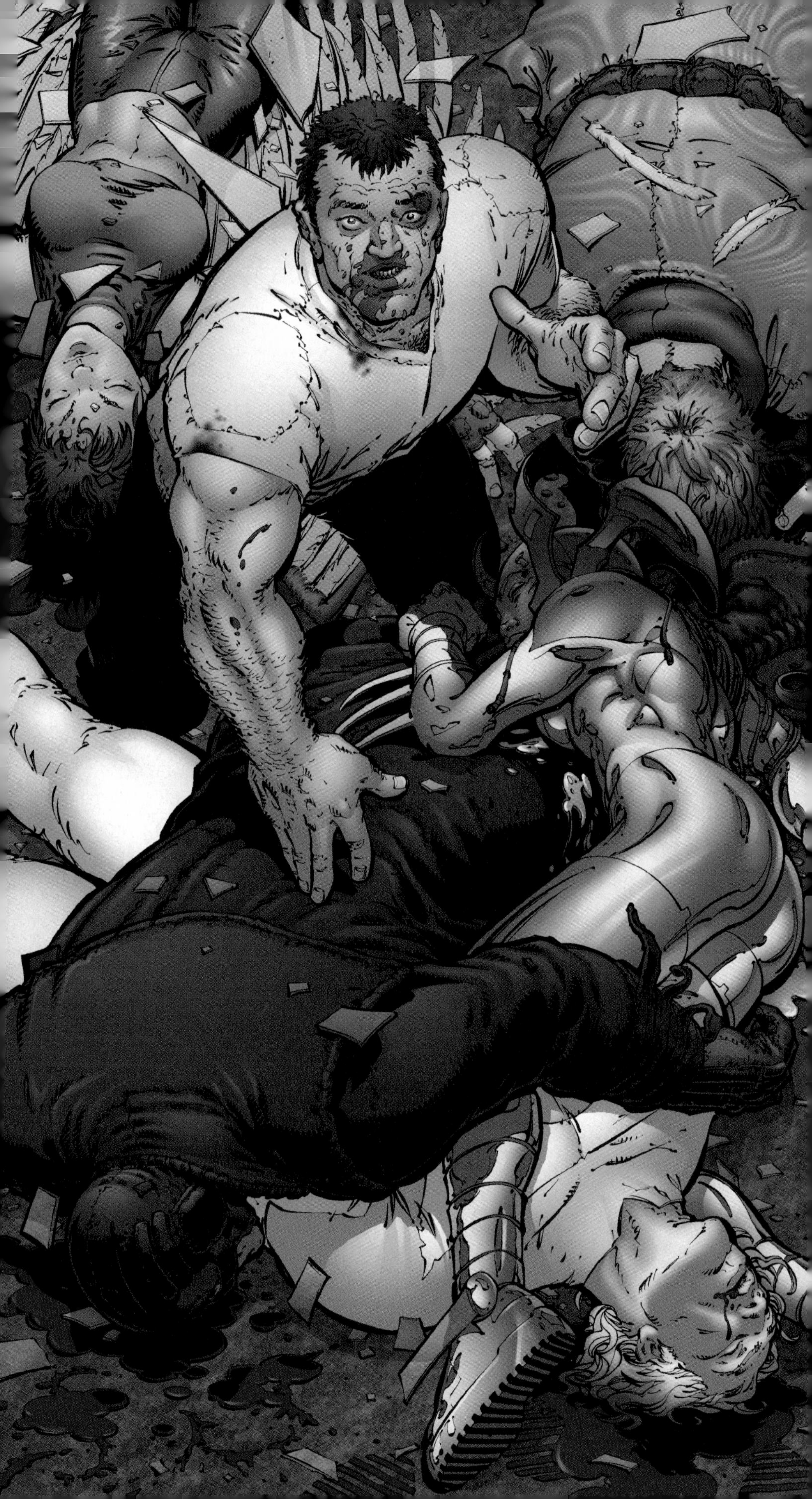

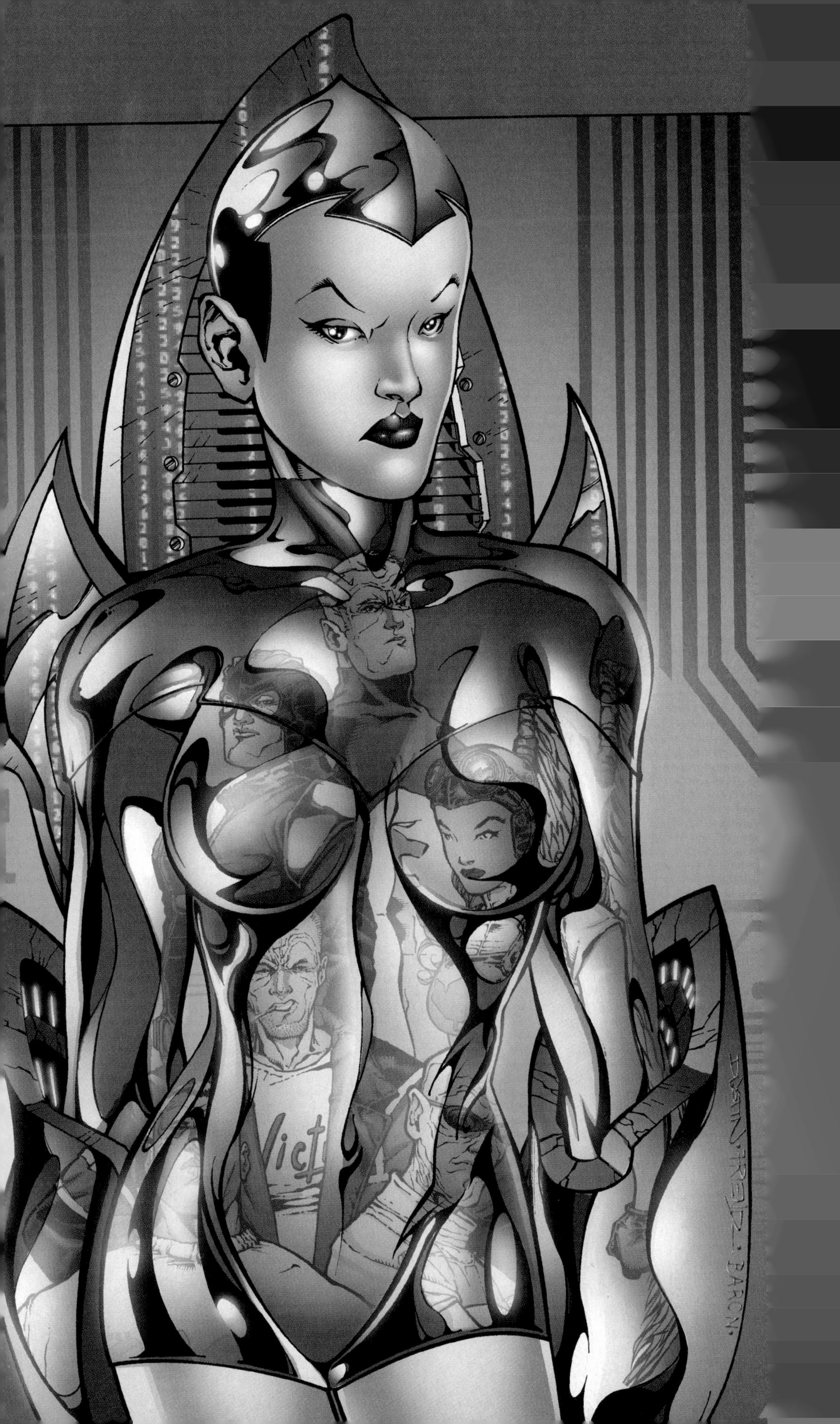

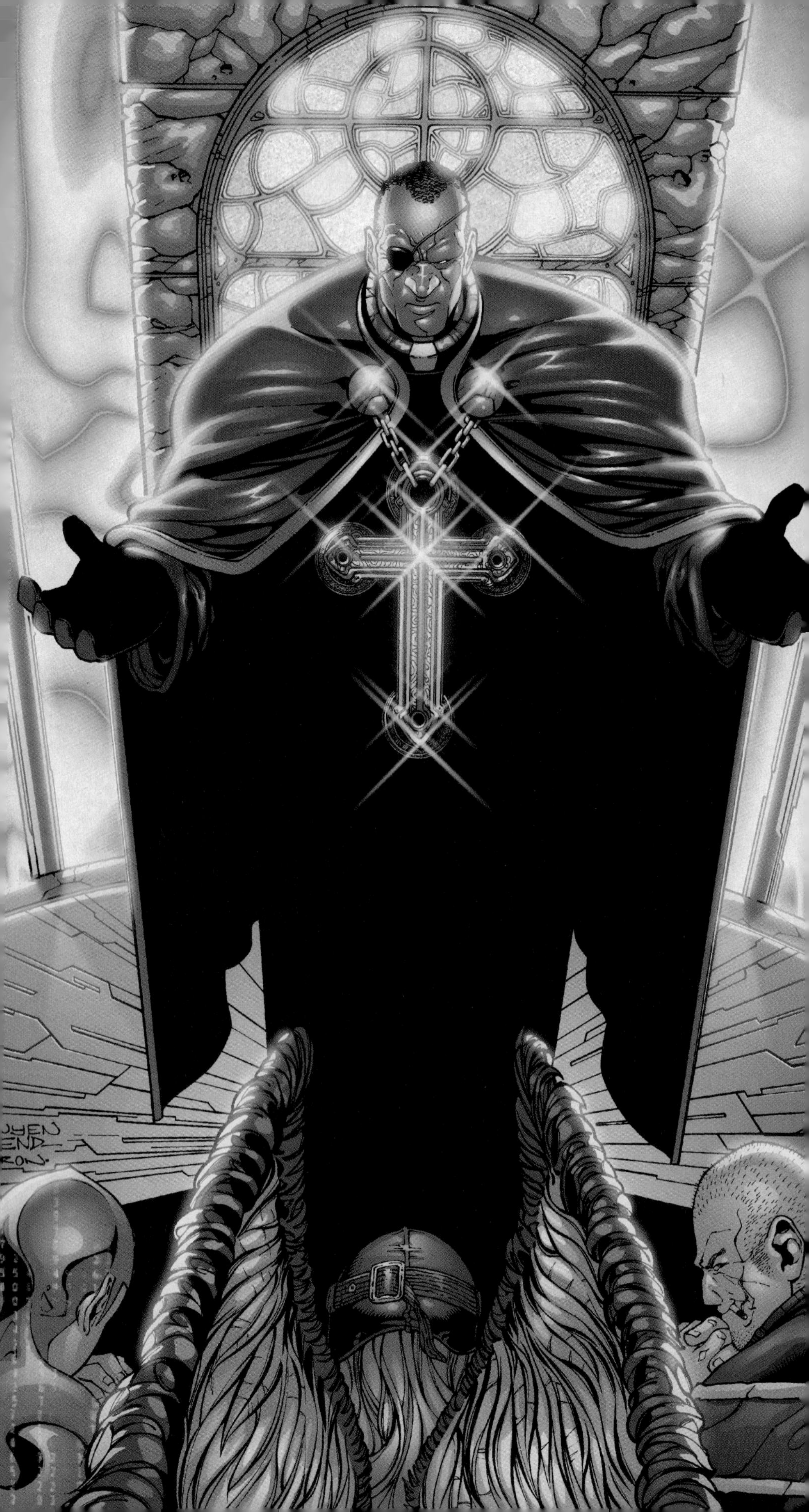

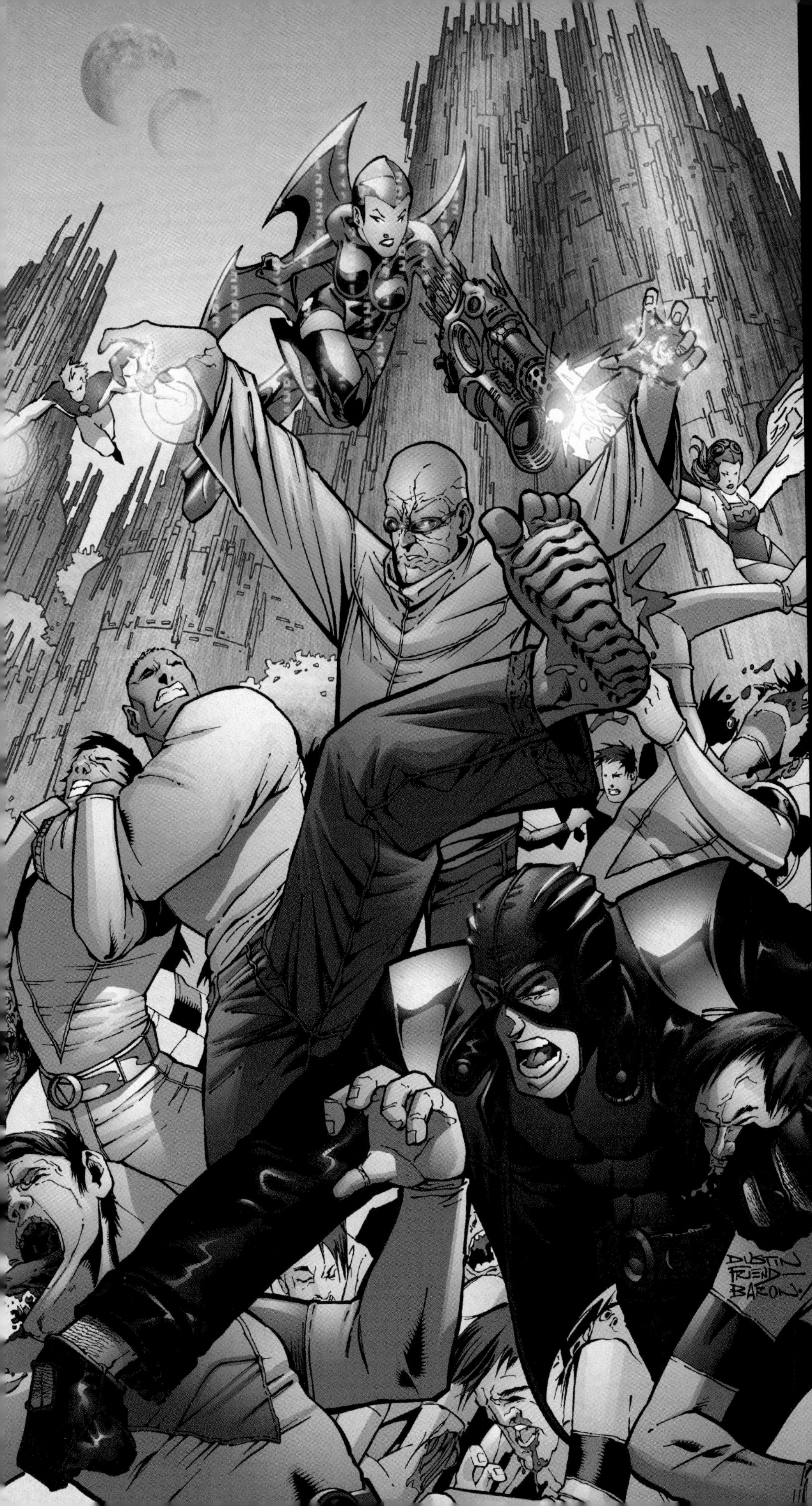
DUSTIN
FRIEND
BARON

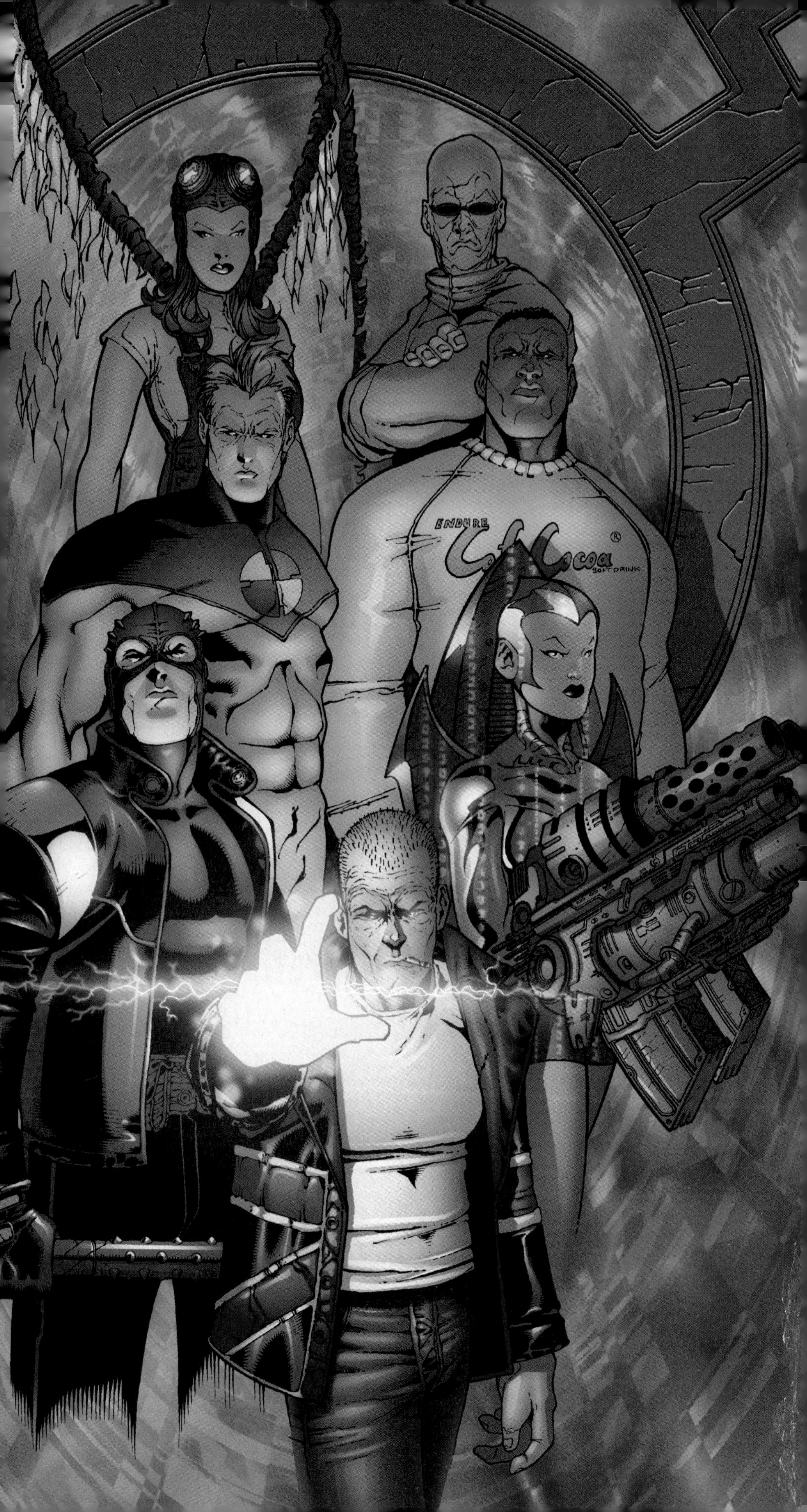
ENDURE
SOFT DRINK

Art by Arthur Adams and Tim Townsend   Color by David Baron

Art by Arthur Adams and Tim Townsend   Color by David Baron   THE AUTHORITY #28

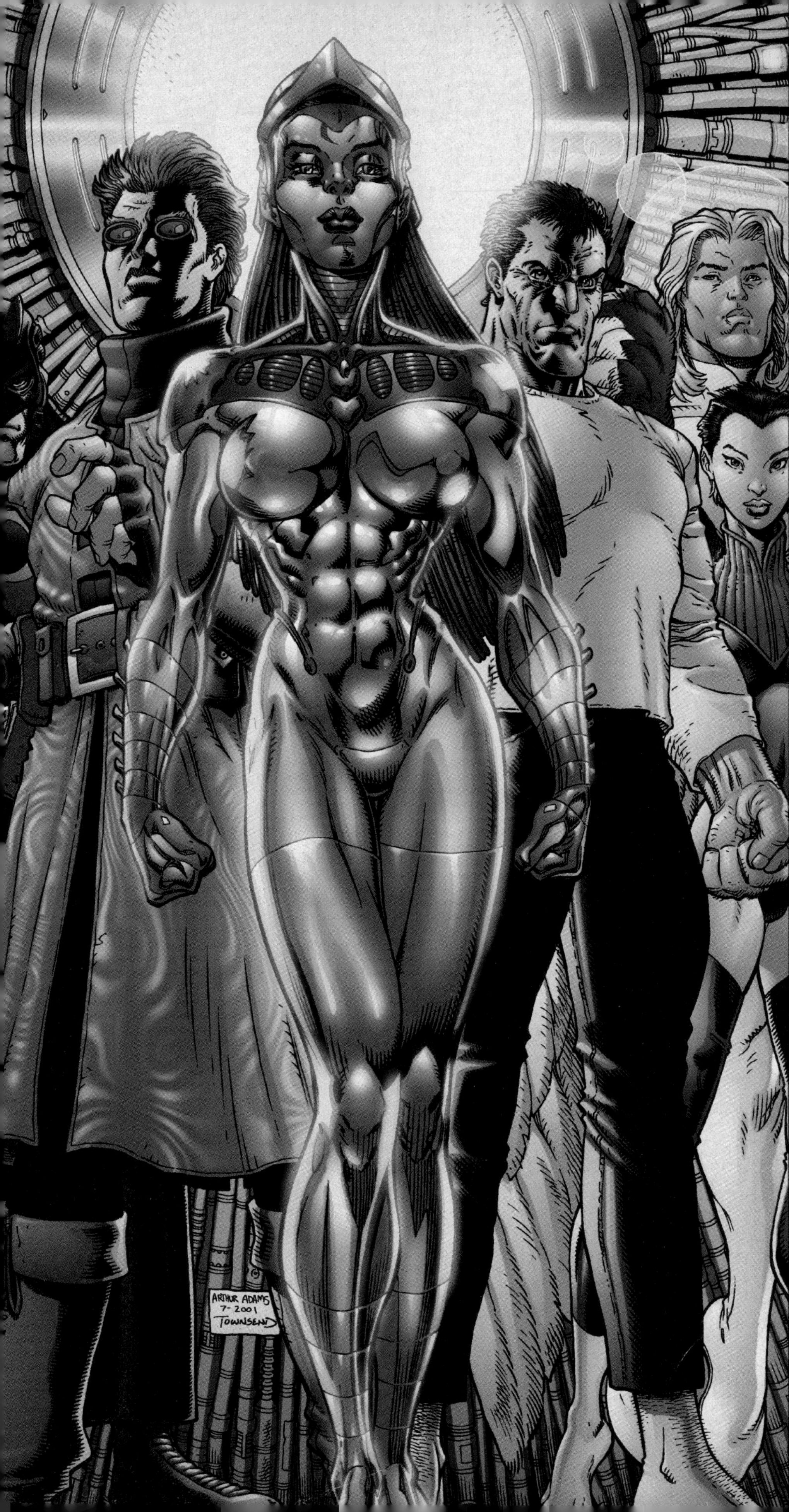
ARTHUR ADAMS
7-2001
TOWNSEND

Art by Arthur Adams and Tim Townsend   Color by David Baron   THE AUTHORITY #29

To find more collected editions and monthly comic books from WildStorm and DC Comics, call 1-888-comic book for the nearest comics shop or go to your local book store.

Visit us at www.dccomics.com

WS0011